# Flying Ahead of the Airplane

NAWAL K. TANEJA

ASHGATE

Published by
Ashgate Publishing Limited
Gower House
Croft Road
Aldershot
Hampshire GU11 3HR
England

Ashgate Publishing Company
Suite 420
101 Cherry Street
Burlington, VT 05401-4405
USA

www.ashgate.com

**British Library Cataloguing in Publication Data**
Taneja, Nawal K.
  Flying ahead of the airplane
  1. Airlines - Management 2. Strategic planning
  I. Title
  387.7'068

**Library of Congress Cataloging-in-Publication Data**
Taneja, Nawal K.
 Flying ahead of the airplane / by Nawal K. Taneja.
    p. cm.
 Includes index.
  ISBN 978-0-7546-7579-2 (hardcover) 1. Airlines--Management. 2. Aeronautics, Commercial--Management. I. Title.

 HE9780.T363 2008
 387.7068--dc22

2008029386

ISBN: 978 0 7546 7579 2

Mixed Sources
Product group from well-managed forests and other controlled sources
www.fsc.org Cert no. SGS-COC-2482
© 1996 Forest Stewardship Council
FSC

Printed and bound in Great Britain by
TJ International Ltd, Padstow, Cornwall.

# Contents

# List of Figures

# List of Abbreviations

| | |
|---|---|
| ASEAN | Association of Southeast Asian Nations |
| ASM | Available Seat Miles |
| ATC | Air Traffic Control |
| ATM | Air Traffic Management |
| BPO | Business Process Outsourcing |
| BRIC | Brazil, Russia, India, and China |
| CASM | Cost per Available Seat Mile |
| CRM | Customer Relationship Management |
| GenX | Generation X (born between 1965 and 1979) |
| GenY | Generation Y (born between 1980 and 1997) |
| LCC | Low Cost Carrier |
| NASCAR | National Association for Stock Car Auto Racing |
| O&D | Origin and Destination |
| PRASM | Passenger Revenue per Available Seat Mile |
| RASM | Revenue per Available Seat Mile |
| RPM | Revenue Passenger Miles |
| SARS | Severe Acute Respiratory Syndrome |
| TPG | Texas Pacific Group |
| UNICEF | United Nations Children's Fund |
| VLJ | Very Light Jet |
| 3XX | The 300 Series of Airbus Aircraft, including the 300, 310, 318, 319, 320, 321, 330, 340, 350, and 380 |
| 7YY | The 700 Series of Boeing Aircraft, including the 717, 727, 737, 747, 757, 767, 777, and 787 |

# Preface

## Why So Many Forewords?

While change itself is not new to the global airline industry, at this time it is the rate and the scope of change that is unprecedented. Not only are the economics of the industry changing, but also the very nature of competition, the impacts of emerging disruptive technologies, and consumer demographics, lifestyles, and expectations. Does the dramatically and fundamentally changing marketplace represent a decline for airlines and related businesses or an opportunity? There is no clear answer. For example, while most airlines are suffering financially, the two major aircraft manufacturers have huge orders for new aircraft. Within the airline industry, some analysts foresee a recasting of players, a redistribution of capacity, and an emergence of new business models. Within the area of new business models, options being discussed include: mergers and acquisitions; more integrated strategic alliances; organic growth; multi-brands; virtual airlines, and on-demand possibilities.

Given the variability in opinion regarding the probable direction of the global airline industry, some practitioners expressed the desire to compare perspectives and outlooks. This recommendation, combined with the encouragement of airline practitioners to write this series of books, lead to an initiative. Airline CEOs, each based in a different part of the world, were asked if they would like to contribute a foreword that would be published as part of a set. This resulting collection provides added value for global readers (who are also practitioners) through the different perspectives of these knowledgeable and insightful people on how they see the airline world changing. These forewords by global airline CEOs will hopefully provide different perspectives from those presented in this book. It is this diversity of views that will add unique value for practitioners (within, for example, airlines, related businesses, labor leadership, government policy makers, and financiers), all of whom are struggling to grasp the implications of the potential "step-phase changes" that face them.

## Why So Many Case Studies From Other Businesses?

One often hears about the insularity of the airline industry. There are airline executives, government policy makers, and academics who have considered the airline industry to be different from other businesses. Some have gone so far as to say that it is unique. What makes the industry unique is not the existence of any one of a dozen or so individual characteristics (for example, product perishability, industry economics, government regulations, power of different players in the value chain, and the nature of competition), but rather the combination and simultaneous existence of all these fundamental characteristics in the airline business. A few executives acknowledge that airlines can indeed gain some valuable insights from best global business practices. Given that only a few airlines have managed to develop revered brands, practitioners again suggested to me the value of a collection of insights from brands representing different businesses based in different parts of the world. Hopefully, Chapter 7 fulfills this goal by providing 20 examples from a broad array of industries and businesses based in different parts of the world. These case studies provide insights into the successful strategies that have created respected brands, as well as the strategies and tactics that should be avoided. Maintaining the success of a revered brand also requires strategy and attention that will not jeopardize the brand's reputation and foundation (as appears to be the challenge at Starbucks, as this book goes to the press).

Together, the forewords and the deliberate collection of the case studies provide an array of perspectives and strategies that aim to broaden the viewpoint of each reader. In a world that is globalizing, having an appreciation for global perspectives is essential to be competitive and successful.

# Foreword

Professor Israel (Izzy) Borovich
*Chairman of the board*
*EL AL Israel Airlines*

Let us start by presenting two quotes that, in my opinion, tell the story of the aviation industry, a relatively young industry. The first one by Winston Churchill (1874–1965). "The farther backward you can look, the farther forward you are likely to see." The second one is by Charles Darwin, British naturalist and author (1809–1882). "It is not the strongest of the species that survive, nor the most intelligent, but the one most responsive to change." The first quote relates to the fact that we fail to understand the reshaping of the industry that took place during the last few decades. It means that learning from history can help management to determine the right direction. The effect of the low cost phenomenon on the structure of the industry was ignored in the beginning and by the time the legacy airlines realized their contribution to the new shape of the industry it was too late. As a result a large number of airlines departed the domestic routes and increased their share in international long-haul markets. Looking backward into history, as Winston Churchill said, would tell us in advance the new direction. When changes take place, it is necessary to adapt as quickly as possible to these changes as said by Charles Darwin.

The aviation industry, like many other industries, is continually going through changes. Therefore, airlines must adapt continually to these changes. A new trend that is taking place presently is the formation of mega companies via mergers and acquisitions. Looking into the future, based on past experience, shows us that the number of large carriers will be reduced significantly. I believe that the structure of the alliances is also due to change. Originally, the alliance objective was to set up a "virtual airline" that provides the customers with possible seamless journey worldwide. However, lately the alliances are joined by many airlines where their networks are overlapped by other members of the same alliance. As a result, often, large carriers in the same alliance that overlap the small carriers increase their profitability while small carriers, in many cases, end up with a loss. Therefore, it is clear that the next big change in the aviation industry will be the formation of mega companies, which in many cases will be from different alliances. This process might force the alliances to change their business model.

When trying to predict the future of the aviation industry, it is necessary to explore the effect of information technology on the industry as well as learn from the history of the relationship between aviation and information technology. In the seventies, airlines that developed computer reservation systems used these systems as competitive tools to put, in some cases, other airlines out of business. The use of owned-online systems and a technology-empowered public may force the industry to go through even more changes. On the one hand, the industry is reforming the relationships with travel agents by trying to favor more direct sell. This process is transforming the power from the travel agents to the online marketing systems. On the other hand, given that at present the number of online marketing systems is very small, it means that the aviation industry is putting the power in the hands of few.

Another reason for the reshaping of the industry is the process of the worldwide privatization, which has left only few large carriers still owned and controlled by governments. This situation exists in specific regions of the world where these airlines are also protected by their governments as for rights to airport slots. Hopefully, this situation will end soon and the aviation industry will become a truly competitive industry. In any case, governments should stay out of this game.

No question, the industry is still in the process of maturity. This book by Professor Nawal Taneja deals with the issues mentioned in this foreword and therefore can be used as a tool to help managements guide their airlines in this stormy environment. Chapters 2 and 3 describe in detail the environment in which airlines operate and help to understand it more clearly. Chapter 4 ("Are Airline Managements Prepared?") tells us what managements need to do to prepare for the future. Learning from experience and from other industries is considered to be a good practice by great and successful management. The many cases presented in Chapter 7 light up many ideas that can be adapted by airline managements. As Professor Taneja illustrates in Figure 1.2, information technology has and will continue to influence all aspects of the business: internally and externally; employees and customers; and, of course, marketing. The book describes in detail and wisely how managements can navigate to adapt their companies to the future.

In summary, the two most important points that airline managements should acknowledge are to learn from history (as there is so much information there), and once the direction and actions are determined, to act fast. Adapt to change. There is no time to wait. This book should always be available to management, so that it can be used as a handbook on an ongoing basis.

Tel Aviv, Israel
August 2008

# Foreword

Russell Chew
*President and Chief Operating Officer*
*JetBlue Airways*

Every five years, an unanticipated major event has threatened the stability of the U.S. airline industry. In the nineties, we were not prepared for the emerging congestion from our rapid growth. In 2001, we could not have predicted the terrorist events of September 11. In the last year, many airlines were unprepared for and have already succumbed to the combination of higher oil prices, the credit crunch, and slowing economic growth. But these new unanticipated challenges are now being largely driven by the emerging global economy. Not long ago, the global influence of the United States virtually dictated the cost of a barrel of oil. We painfully learned earlier this year that we're not nearly as relevant anymore, and that this declining relevance extends directly to the U.S. airline industry.

With jet fuel at more than 40% of direct operating costs, U.S. airlines must reduce domestic capacity to raise yield. This further depresses the core demand for both domestic and international air travel services, which will ultimately make it even more difficult for U.S. carriers to compete with their international counterparts. Globalization is now imposing a faster pace of required change just to survive, let alone thrive. Once again, the U.S. airline industry is finding itself unprepared for it. For the first time in our proud history, the global leadership and dominance of the U.S. airline industry is in jeopardy.

In the years ahead, globalization will also impact the very infrastructure that the U.S. airlines depend on for basic service delivery – the system of airports and airways that comprise the U.S. air traffic control system. The U.S. is in a global technology race with Europe and Asia to modernize the crowded system of airports and airspace around the world. Before long, the health of U.S. airline balance sheets will feel even more pressure from the excessive operating and environmental costs related to an inefficient U.S. system. If airlines choose to ignore this, we will again find ourselves handicapped against our global competitors in competing for gates, slots, and routes within a system of rapidly growing congestion at key international airports and trade routes.

However, with such challenging changes to our competitive operating environment, U.S. airlines can succeed if we can learn to quickly recognize, adapt, and take advantage of the opportunities that come from such dramatic change. In *Flying Ahead of the Airplane*, Nawal Taneja challenges today's leaders of the U.S. airline industry to be prepared for the rapidly changing paradigms in our customer segments, and focus on the most basic element of all business success -- the customer. Fueled by a new generation of travelers who are more demanding and discriminating of their travel experience, conventional web storefronts are being transformed into more integrated sales interactions that generate important ancillary up-sell revenue. The GDS models that exist today will need to evolve with these trends as customers demand more seamless ways to customize their travel experience.

Using many non-airline examples, Nawal explains how companies have recently recognized and taken advantage of changing customer demographics. One theme clearly emerges – that airline leaders must build more agile organizations that better understand and can more quickly respond to new technologies that differentiate their brand through customer choice. Traditional marketing departments must learn to incorporate the emerging power and influence of social networking, which also puts more pressure on airline operations to consistently deliver on marketing promises. Perhaps most important, many examples in this book make it clear that healthy labor-management relationships are required to succeed.

Just to survive, the U.S. airlines are now distracted with resizing their capacity through consolidations, retiring aging fleets, and shoring up their balance sheets. But in the era of globalization, survival will not be enough. Readers of this book will clearly understand why success will only be achieved when airlines that look beyond our own industry to better understand the emerging customer and consistently deliver to their expectations. Finally, applying these principles will also strengthen the ability of any airline to thrive no matter what unexpected challenge inevitably appears in the years ahead.

New York, USA
September 2008

# Foreword

Tim Clark
*President*
*Emirates Airline*

The closing years of the twentieth century witnessed an indisputable acceleration of global wealth creation driven by a combination of complex forces which were both unknown and unprecedented in history. The speed of this metamorphosis, coupled to the step change in consumer aspirations and behaviour, has altered the global demand dynamic forever: companies must recognise and react to this commercial imperative or fail. A mere adjustment or realignment of business models will not suffice as clearly a new DNA is emerging on a global scale. It is around this that the business model and building block architecture of the twenty first century company must be defined and shaped.

The airline industry can be no exception to the paradigm shift towards globalism, and the broad spectrum of product offerings, from low cost to long haul network carriers, must accommodate and harness this unrelenting migration of globality. To ignore it would be folly and those companies that do will perish.

Global brand strength, extensive and robust networks, seamless hub connectivity, quality customer service products and the unfettered embracement of technology will characterise the successful network carriers of the early twenty first century. Emirates will be one of these operating from its hub in Dubai, one of the fastest growing cities in the world.

Mr. Taneja's book successfully navigates the reader through the emerging complexities of airline management in modern times. It is a compelling read.

Dubai, UAE
September 2008

# Foreword

Dr. Andres Conesa
*Chairman and Chief Executive Officer*
*AeroMexico*

Every industry around the world needs to permanently adapt itself to the fast, and sometimes dramatic, changes in the setting in which they are inserted. Changes stemming from demographic, technological, political and economic trends all embedded in an increasingly global economy.

Because of its intrinsic global nature, Commercial Aviation is particularly affected by these changing conditions. In the recent past, several events have forced companies in the industry to redesign their flight charts in order to land into profitability and, in extreme cases, in order to survive. The response to global events like 9/11, the SARS epidemic in Asia, lower labor mobility associated to migration concerns and the recent surge in oil prices, demonstrate that Darwin's "survival of the fittest" is a prevalent condition in this fascinating industry.

What can we expect in the near future and how will it shape the industry? Obviously we do not have full certainty. However, Nawal K. Taneja's book provides us with an extraordinary monolith in which we can stand on to reach a better view of the horizon as an initial step for insightful thinking. It is possible that many of the airlines will not have tail-wind for the near future, but those companies able to understand that "globality," as referred in the book, is a trend and defining force in today's world rather than a term, will increase its odds to land successfully.

The need for transportation is a constant in any country or society as evidenced by humankind's history. In our modern society, the correlation among economic growth and air traffic is particularly well documented. Within developing countries, air travel is an important growth factor as it generates spillover effects through connectivity, not just within a given country but with the rest of the world. Air connectivity is indeed an essential component of the globalization process as it facilitates the movement of people, goods, technology and ideas all over the world, helping to allocate resources where they yield the highest productivity.

In a scenario where the world economy evolves through a path of continued growth and considering long-term convergence in living standards, it is expected that developing countries will experience higher growth rates than high-income countries. Thus, in nations like China, India, Brazil, Russia and Mexico, an increasingly mid-class population is gradually enjoying the benefits of these higher living standards, including the access to air transportation.

Unfortunately, recent trends in fuel prices seem to pose a threat to the otherwise attractive future for the aviation industry. Despite the industry's continuous efforts towards increased productivity, historically high oil prices are forcing airlines to reverse the downward trend in ticket prices and naturally reducing the rate of growth of passenger demand. We are witnessing the interplay of two economic forces impacting commercial aviation in opposite ways: increasing purchasing power as a result of economic growth across the globe and unprecedented high fuel prices. In this environment, the question becomes: will air travel continue to grow and add passengers from a broader base?; or, on the contrary, will air travel become a "luxury product" with only few consumers able to afford it?

Whatever the scenario, air transportation companies will have to compete under new *globality* conditions, and not all air carriers are prepared for that. We are seeing increasingly merging trends in the industry. Are these mergers preparing the ground for a globalized competition? Or, are the mergers the response to the current conditions prevailing? I do believe they are part of both. The next question is if size and scale will be the dominant marker in terms of evolution. Definitely they will be important markers but not the only ones. The airlines' strategy must include also levers like flexibility, technology innovation, continuous cost controls, and client focusing. Moreover, airlines should keep in mind that investment on marketing research would become a critical success factor. In addition, companies would need a well-calibrated radar to anticipate emerging trends and navigate through changes and convert this into opportunities.

We mankind consider ourselves as capable of transforming our environment rather than adapting to it. Nonetheless, generally, industries must fit to the environment while gradually contributing to re-shape it, and the aviation industry is not the exception. How to successfully fit is the core question, and I am sure you will find Nawal K. Taneja's book as a valuable source of insight when you think about the future of the airline industry.

Mexico City, Mexico
August 2008

# Foreword

Geoff Dixon
*Chief Executive Officer*
*Qantas Airways*

This is an important and timely work.

As Nawal Taneja demonstrates, aviation lags behind other industries in achieving the full benefits of globalisation, including strong brands, global scale, and global sourcing of capital, inputs and customers.

But things are changing, and quickly. Right now the global aviation industry faces, not a shock or a blip – not even a crisis – but a permanent transformation. The driver of this transformation will be globalisation, accelerated by permanently high fuel price. And the result will be a new aviation world order.

This new order will see a few, very large and extremely efficient global airlines with a portfolio of interests and brands. These players will have enormous power in marketing, in fuel buying and hedging, in aircraft purchasing, and in reach. There will still be niche airlines with specialist offerings – whether for business or leisure travellers – but these will need to be run very skillfully, and any weakness will lead to a quick demise. And there will also remain those powerful, government-backed airlines, particularly from the oil rich states. These governments will continue to use aviation services as instruments of national economic development.

As outgoing CEO, I believe the potential of Qantas in this new world order is very strong.

Since 2003, Qantas has taken billions out of its legacy cost base. This has given the Group a strong balance sheet: it has enabled a 35 billion dollar capital expenditure program for new aircraft which should give Qantas one of the world's more fuel efficient fleets over the next decade. And we have heavily invested in Qantas international and domestic product and service – an investment that has consistently placed Qantas in the top-five of premium airlines worldwide.

Qantas has also gone down the path of segmenting all areas of our business, in order to maximise each one's operating efficiency and growth potential on a global basis.

Most important of all, the Group has two exceptional brands in Qantas and Jetstar. Qantas is still the only legacy airline to have introduced a successful low cost carrier into markets alongside its premium brand, and grown both businesses. In a rapidly changing environment, these two brands deliver the flexibility to meet the needs of a wide range of customers while better aligning costs, revenues and product offerings in individual markets.

Qantas has the potential to be a serious player in the new order that will unfold over the next five to twenty years. But there's a great deal of work to be done. Taneja challenges all airline leaders to get out of yesterday's mindset and set about preparing for – and creating – the new aviation world order of tomorrow.

Sydney, Australia
August 2008

# Foreword

Mark Dunkerley
*President and Chief Executive Officer*
*Hawaiian Airlines*

Confronted by crisis, participants in our industry tend to focus intently on short term survival. A look in the rearview mirror, however, reminds us that the crisis of the day is not a one-off period of intense drama but in fact just the latest in the long list of successive crises that have afflicted our industry since air transport began eight decades ago.

There are clear economic reasons why the transport of passengers and cargo by air will always be given to volatility but they lie beyond the scope of my comments here. Because of this volatility, the challenge facing airline managements is not just one of choosing the right business model, but also of making sure that they create and maintain enough flexibility to deal with the next crisis that lies around the corner.

Creating and maintaining flexibility is tough when two of your three major costs elements (labor and aircraft) are fixed over the short term and the third (fuel) is largely beyond your control. These realities of our business mean that the way managers manage the areas that they do control makes all of the difference between those airlines that succeed and those that fail.

Success is dependent on three core principles. First, it is vital that, despite the problems of the day, the company remains focused on a long term strategy. There is a natural gravitational force that draws a manager's focus to the problem of the day and the more severe the problem, the stronger that force. However, having a long term strategy and making sure that all decisions made in the short term bring the long term strategy closer to fulfillment is the only path to improvement.

Second, always seek to increase the amount of flexibility you enjoy as you never know when you are going to need it. Achieving the first dicta of staying focused on the long term in the face of a volatile environment may require frequent changes in course and having the ability to change direction is essential.

Third, always be resolute in seeking improvements to your cost effectiveness. In a business which sees perpetual change, the only constant has been that, all other things being equal, the airline which is most cost effective wins. With rivals operating the same sorts of aircraft that consume the same sort of fuel flying between the same cities, information technology has become the deciding factor in this competition and the continuous pursuit of emerging solutions a requirement for survival.

Living by such rules – or 'Flying Ahead of the Airplane,' as Nawal describes in the following pages – requires a corporate culture that is open to change and in which employees feel that they are stakeholders in the business. It seems an obvious point, but fostering such a corporate culture is no easy task – yet all the more important – in times when the industry news and consequences to employees are unremittingly bad.

At Hawaiian, we have tried to put all of this into practice. We have a long term strategy which we share with stakeholders inside and outside the company and against which we assess all significant short term decisions. We try to maximize management flexibility with decisions such as our fleet plan, which will allow us over the next decade to grow, hold steady or shrink the overall size of our fleet according to the economic circumstances we face. We have 'modularized' many of our activities and moved several of them to third parties in order to focus on a narrower core of the business and to give us flexibility to make changes as conditions warrant. We have pursued a broad range of initiatives that save costs and seek to improve the 'value for money' characteristics of our service. And none of this would be possible without the unique and positive culture that we enjoy at Hawaiian Airlines.

Honolulu, USA
August, 2008

# Foreword

Gary Kelly
*Chairman, President, and Chief Executive Officer*
*Southwest Airlines*

This is an extraordinary time for the airline industry. Customers are seeing things they have not seen in the past: capacity cuts, a flurry of fees that keep adding up, and record energy prices. At Southwest, we have great challenges and great opportunities ahead of us; however, all airlines and the Employees that run them must be resilient and face change head on, because the public needs us to persevere. Airlines must implement the necessary changes to adjust to this very difficult environment. We do not know what the future holds, but uncertainty and change are certain. This book provokes thought leadership by providing a variety of possible landscapes of the future, and whichever one holds true, the industry as a whole must adapt and move forward.

Currently, we face the dual threat of a recessing economy and skyrocketing fuel costs. Satisfying Customers has never been more important than it is today. The decisions we make as an airline will impact how Americans travel in the future. Southwest is well versed in change and in leading the industry as an innovator with warrior spirit. We are committed to continuing our legacy of Customer Service, which will never change.

Throughout, Southwest has managed to remain profitable with lots of liquidity; very modest levels of debt; and low operating costs; but our financial results would have been dramatically worse were we not prepared with an industry leading fuel hedge. Still, our operating costs are up 33 percent in just five year's time, faster than any other five year period in our history, simply because energy prices have quintupled. Our hedges do not make us immune; they only buy us time to adapt, to revolutionize, to implement innovative technology, and to face increasing competition.

There is much work to do to address the known challenges facing all airlines, and much of that work is well underway.

To combat escalating fuel costs, we must continue to innovate, improve efficiency, reduce consumption, and, by doing so, reduce emissions.

The People of Southwest Airlines have helped carry the American flying public to the greatest heights in history. Our future is in maintaining that focus and dedicating ourselves to embracing the opportunities of the future and continuing our legacy of giving America the Freedom to Fly.

Dallas, USA
September 2008

# Foreword

Dr. Temel Kotil
*Chief Executive Officer*
*Turkish Airlines*

Harshly intensifying competition, incessant surge of oil prices and severely increasing operational costs pose major challenges to airlines heaped by political fluctuations, emerging forms of business models and, of course, globalization. All these determinants tilt industry leaders towards restructuring their stance as the playground for business shrinks for carriers. Many of these challenging trends are discussed in detail in this book by Nawal Taneja.

Abundance of oil reserves in particular regions of the world put relevant airlines into an advantageous status destructing the platform of natural competition among carriers. Airlines lacking such resources have no choice other than putting strict cost control and audit measures or retuning customer service level and quality to sustain profitability.

Recent regulations and market trends in the aviation industry lead carriers to join alliances to shelter themselves against global turmoil and polarizing competition. Carriers opting to join such alliances pin themselves among the spectrum of full autonomy on one end versus tighter integration with more business and cost reduction opportunities on the other.

Changing consumer behavior in terms of selecting pointtopoint travel options to avoid congested airports force airline companies to diversify their flight alternatives as well as introducing secondary hubs.

Regarding these developments in the sector, Turkish Airlines hesitates to name such trends as 'threats.' With its passionate and dynamic organization, Turkish adopted the vision to expand the pie and create new playgrounds on the basis of value creation not only for the industry and shareholders but also for its customers.

Rather than reflecting the additional cost burden to fares or cutting from the quality of service offered, Turkish prefers to offset the gap by attracting more transit and premium business class passengers. Turkish Airlines strives to take advantage of Istanbul's distinct and highly convenient geographical location as a hub.

With the intention of exercising lowcostfull service operation, combined with the aspiration of forming a second hub in Ankara, Turkish has launched its Anadolu Jet (sub-) brand for its price-sensitive domestic market. Although bundling lowcost operation with full service is tough at the first glance, Turkish overcomes this by introducing new stations for the lower end where there definitely is a promising market that exists, facilitated by Turkey's high-population dynamics that are in need of direct pointtopoint travel.

However, Turkish's passion to thrive does not solely cover the domestic market which is no longer an undercompeted backyard considering it contributes only a quarter to the entire revenue. In this context, Turkish moves an important portion of domestic flights from its main hub, Atatürk airport, to free up slots for more international flights.

Turkish, highly motivated with Star Alliance participation, is projected to carry 2% of the world's whole passenger traffic in five years. On its 75th year, Turkish is growing, more efficient, adding new aircraft to its fleet, establishing joint ventures and whollyowned subsidiaries as well as seeking consolidation opportunities. So, why Turkish should be challenged with so-called 'threats' rather than being pleased for the opportunities created? The thought-provoking ideas presented in this book, "Flying Ahead of the Airplane," could enable an airline's management to convert a challenge to an opportunity.

Istanbul, Turkey
August 2008

# Foreword

Pham Ngoc Minh
*President and Chief Executive Officer*
*Vietnam Airlines*

"Not the strongest nor the most intelligent, but the most responsive to change will survive". This is truly the point quoted by Nawal Taneja in his several books.

Working in the airline industry for nearly 30 years and being in the executive board for more than half of that time, I understand the importance of foreseeing the changes and the trends of the industry and I also understand the needs of "management innovations" and "innovation within management," because each airline itself is so sophisticated that we cannot apply old standard strategic levers in managements.

As a matter of fact that businesses now go beyond boundaries, the industry becomes more vulnerable due to global changes, either political, technological, even environmental. Facing the unprecedented, changing dynamics, airline managements are forced to adapt to new business model, or at least adjust their current ones systematically in order to be more competitive and profitable. I believe there is no perfect model for all of us as we are now running in different environments with different cultures and different people. However the underlying principle is in-depth integration of strategy and branding, as discussed in the introductory chapter of this book.

For Vietnam Airlines' successes, as the national airline, we feel it is both obligatory and advantageous to be part of this national effort. And we have been, among others, for and always in the front line. The nation's traditional characteristics are featured in the airline's product and services. Programs such as road show, cultural festivals, etc. organized or sponsored by the airline have left so much in the memory of the people in many parts of the world. This smooth, successful execution from strategy into branding has in fact secured us competitive advantages against others, especially when customers become more and more perceptive and discerned about the brand values and how you are differentiated from the rest. Affirming the distinctive brand values then helped us obtain customers and make them stay with us.

Over the last decades, Vietnam Airlines has transformed itself into an airline equipped with the youngest, state-of-the-art fleet in the region. Along with that, a comprehensive technology transfer campaign has been carried out to meet the new operation requirements. Though we did not radically reorganize the whole system to match with the new Western technology standards; we let each sector in the system to adjust to cope with new realities.

With more than 83 million inhabitants and the economy enjoying a growth rate that is one of the highest in the region, Vietnam has been becoming a potential air transport market. Besides, we advantageously benefit from the booming of air travel in the region which is forecast a grow rate at 10–15% annually and Vietnam's domestic air travel market also to increase by 20%. These serve as solid foundations for Vietnam Airlines to materialize its plan to expand into a sustainable group with the airline as its core business and to build up our airline into one of the top three leading airlines in the region.

In the year 2008, at least two new airlines have been set up and five new foreign players have launched their flights to Vietnam. In pursuit of the goal to become the top conventional airline in the region and dominate the regional market including Indochina, the South of China and to the northern part of South East Asia, Vietnam Airlines has been maintaining the power of a network carrier and defending the market from the penetration of other competitors with the unique weapon for each market thanks to the careful study about the competitors and a strong customer base.

The forthcoming time will not be an easy period for businesses and the airline is not an exception. The fuel cost has risen from 28% of the total cost last year to more than 44% now. In addition, substantial rise on government levies and duties, airport and air traffic charges, and costs also pose another pressure to us. Competition escalation stemming from continuing open sky tendency and the booming of LCCs can be counted in the airlines managers' list of challenges. The outbreak of epidemic diseases now becomes one of the most serious threats to inbound tourism. Another challenge worth noted is a gap between infrastructure and strong tourism demand which includes a serious shortage of acceptable hotel rooms, congested airports and an inconsistency in service quality levels and professionalism.

But, "flying ahead" of these challenges, we found opportunity to reorganize the airline, to adjust our flying network and frequency, even to optimize our fleet and, most important, is the chance to improve our competitiveness and to meet demanding needs of our customers in a rapidly changing commercial aviation environment as recommended in this book. It is essential for the airline executives who want to "fly ahead the airplane".

Hanoi, Vietnam
August 2008

# Foreword

Captain David Barioni Neto
*Chief Executive Officer*
*TAM Airlines*

How can an executive manage a business in which the executive has very little control over most of the variables that affect the operation? In the case of an airline, how can it become profitable when around 40 percent of its costs are represented by a commodity whose price increases more than 40 percent in a few months? Writing from within the eye of the storm, when oil was frighteningly getting close to US$150 a barrel, Nawal Taneja provides the global airline industry with a realistic and current view of the challenges that airline executives are facing.

Many of the topics discussed by Mr. Taneja in *Flying Ahead of the Airplane* are present in our deliberations and discussions at TAM. As the Brazilian market leader, both on domestic and international routes, our airline has traveled through the industry's crisis supported by three strategic pillars: Excellence in Services; Technical-Operational Excellence; and Excellence in Management. And the focus of our third pillar, Excellence in Management, is exactly one of the points emphasized by Nawal Taneja in his new book, in which he discusses different contexts and scenarios with impact on the airline industry throughout the world.

The emerging marketplace for airlines is being shaped by globalizing economies, geopolitics, the so-called "social media," and disruptive technologies, in the areas of both information and aircraft. These forces are fundamentally changing the relationship between customers and businesses, requiring not only greater management innovations, but also more innovation in the management of the companies that intend to win the game, says the author. This point supports, once again, our third pillar, Excellence in Management.

Let me give two examples of the areas in Management that we are focusing on at TAM. The first relates to the area of branding that is critical for an airline like TAM that is going through extraordinary growth in domestic and international markets. Based on an in-depth study on branding, the essence of our branding philosophy is: "Passion for Flying and Serving." This motto not only encourages us to pursue excellence demanded by our customers, but it also differentiates us from our competitors.

Second, since we serve different segments of the marketplace, we are fine-tuning our pricing policies that not only meet the needs of a broad spectrum of our customers, but that also do not jeopardize the airline industry's already narrow profit margins. This is an enormous challenge in any business; in our business it can be life threatening, given the network and product-perishable nature of the airline business and the existence of cut-throat competition at all levels. We handle this issue by adopting, among other tools, a model of *fare bundles* that enables us to meet the needs of a wide array of customers, both on the ground and on board of our aircraft. In both areas, branding and pricing policies, we integrate across our three pillars to not only have a strong link between brand and strategy but also to ensure the successful execution of our strategy across all functions such as marketing and operations.

The title chosen by Nawal Taneja, *Flying Ahead of the Airplane*, could seem to be just a catchy line for someone like me, a pilot and manager of airlines for over 30 years. But it is much more than that. It can help airline managements to develop insight from foresight relating to the combination of powerful and complex forces to realign our business models.

São Paulo, Brazil
August 2008

# Foreword

Fernando Pinto
*Chief Executive Officer*
*TAP Portugal*

My father was an airline pilot and flight Instructor for almost 40 years. He flew from the 5 seater, 80 mph "Junkers F-13" to the giant Mach .86 Boeing 747. His most difficult experience in training pilots was to adapt them to the new speeds of the jet age. Approaching the crowded New York area in bad weather at 350 kts asked for much more developed "planning skills" from the pilots in order to allow them to be prepared for the multitude of situations they could face and act fast. They had to be trained to know what could be the possible "next steps" in their flight and be ready to adapt the plane to those situations. In summary, he used to say that the good pilots were the ones that were always flying "ahead of the airplane". What I could never imagine was that I would have to apply the same discipline years later when "flying an airline" and having to "adapt it to the changing market place".

When I arrived in TAP with a team of professionals in the year 2000, we found the perfect example of a good airline not adapted to the constant changes of the market. First, it was clear that it needed **focus** on its strategy. We decided to concentrate our energy in the African and Brazilian routes which made a lot of sense both in historical links and geographical terms. Second, since a good network understanding is absolutely necessary we went deep into analysing the possible traffic links between these two focal points and several European capitals. What came out was a comprehensive feeding system that boosted the passenger numbers to a growth of more than 30% almost immediately. I have to admit that fundamental to that quick reaction was a good dose of unconventional thinking. Whilst most airlines tended to concentrate in one or maximum two hubs in foreign countries, we decided to surprise the market, progressing at a fast pace to a total of 8 destinations in Brazil (instead of the typical two: Rio and São Paulo). Due to the better feeding we were also able to multiply twofold the frequency of African routes served. But, despite all that strategic success, we knew that without hard and difficult decisions we would never make the turn-around of that airline. We had to reduce costs deeply and the workforce had to participate with a 10% staff reduction. Since we could not give any chances to work stoppages (which would have killed the airline), we had to "sell our survival plan" to the unions, employees and the public in general, through constant internal meetings and lectures and updating briefings to the media. That allowed for good support and motivation to go through those hard times and also provided the airline with additional strength to jump ahead on another hard decision; TAP integrated a lossmaking regional carrier called Portugalia and made it viable by reducing its headcount by almost 50%. The resulting synergies allowed for a further increase in our market reach, completing the necessary breadth and depth of the network.

By reading this book I was fascinated with the way it is presented. It really shows how to fly ahead of the airplane in simple ways i.e. by looking at what the landscape looks like and adapting to it by taking the correct directions: focus, unconventional thinking, hard decisions and systems optimization are key subjects presented which were also fundamental in my "real life" experience. It will, for sure, help the airline industry overcome today's and future crisis.

Lisbon, Portugal
August 2008

# Foreword

Steve Ridgway
*Chief Executive*
*Virgin Atlantic Airways*

Air Transport is a fascinating business, but certainly not one for those looking for a quiet life. It is a roller-coaster industry that, overall, has managed to destroy more capital since its inception than it has created. It is subject to so many external influences, not least from governments and regulators, that normal business principles often do not apply. At the time of writing we are passing through another major crisis, this time caused by sky-high oil prices and an economic downturn, which has already seen the demise of several airlines and will undoubtedly see the failure of many more. Who would have guessed that just a few years after the catastrophe of 9/11 we would be facing a crisis that looks like being even more damaging to the airline industry?

It is times like this that brings out the fact that not all airlines are the same. A small number of well-run, profitable, successful carriers stand out from the crowd. Among them is certainly Virgin Atlantic. Although a relatively young airline, Virgin Atlantic has expanded rapidly to be one of the leading long-haul carriers in the world. Our reputation for customer service and innovation stands comparison with any other airline. We have overcome enormous hurdles, not all strictly above board, to become a voice that is listened to in the industry and beyond. And we did all this while having fun, and sharing that sense of fun and even mischief with our customers.

To have survived and prospered in the environment we have faced has, of course, required a serious business plan and high quality managers and staff. We have all this in abundance. The proof can be seen in the fact that Virgin Atlantic was far better positioned than the majority of airlines to face the current economic downturn, having reduced its expansion plans and inaugurated cost cutting initiatives well in advance. But one cannot discuss the success of Virgin Atlantic without mentioning one other key component: the power of the brand.

The Virgin brand, applied to numerous companies in many sectors, is a global phenomenon. Nowhere, however, is its power and importance illustrated better than with Virgin Atlantic, the iconic company in the Virgin Group. As Professor Taneja points out, so many airlines regard branding as little more than a new aircraft paint scheme and cabin crew uniform. There is so much more to it than that, and only a handful of carriers have come anywhere near to mastering the concept. It is no accident that those who have are among the most successful airlines in the world.

At Virgin Atlantic, like all the Virgin companies, the brand permeates everything. It is the company culture which is readily visible to, and appreciated by, our customers. As Noel Capon commented in his book *The Marketing Mavens*, Virgin is above all "a brand of customer service and customer experience." It was this culture that gave us the confidence to take on a so-called national airline champion, and win against all the odds. It is a confidence that has led us repeatedly to challenge the apparently unchallengeable, to shake up the marketplace time and again with innovative initiatives that eventually became industry standards. Copying a new product is relatively easy, of course. It is far more difficult to replicate the "magic touches" that Virgin Atlantic staff apply every day. That is the power of the brand.

We live in interesting times. The airline industry is going through a transformation and will look very different in a few years time. I have no doubt that Virgin Atlantic will be a survivor and will go on to make an even greater contribution to the industry. But whatever ownership structures emerge, the brand values of the company will still be there. In his concluding chapter Professor Taneja poses the question "What makes your airline unique?" Some carriers might find the question difficult to answer. Not Virgin Atlantic.

London, UK
September 2008

# Foreword

Girma Wake
*Chief Executive Officer*
*Ethiopian Airlines*

Beyond the current turbulence, which was categorized as "a perfect storm" by IATA CEO Mr. Giovanni Bisignani at the last AGM, the long term view of the airline industry is bright. When we cross the rough weather caused by the negative impacts of the three F's (fuel, food, and financial crisis) and baring the normal economic cycle, the future is promising.

The increasingly flattening borderless world is stimulating mobility of people and their products across regions and this creates an opportunity to increase passenger and cargo traffic to airlines. Relatively higher rate of growth in the GDP of the developing and emerging countries are creating a new middle-class society with a high propensity to fly. New trade lanes among the BRIC's are opening new and huge opportunities in the airline industry, especially for airlines based in the region.

Yet, as we all know, the airline industry is not efficient both from a management and from an industry structure point-of-view. It is with this inefficiency that Professor Nawal Taneja is challenging us and we need to embark on a seemingly tough and long journey towards change which is a life saver for some traditional network carriers.

However, equally important is addressing the structure inefficiency in the airline industry. All airlines know that there is excess capacity in the industry and they feel the negative impacts of unhealthy competition among themselves but very little is being done to trim capacity to match market demand. Competition is the mother of efficiency as it creates value for the customer. While I think this is beyond dispute, too much competition can also destroy value as overly ambitious cost-cutting can compromise initially basic customer services, and later gradually may inadvertently compromise safety.

Under-investment in aviation infrastructure is another perennial problem in the industry. Airports and navigational services in developing countries in Africa, South America, and parts of Asia are a nightmare to airline management. Restrictions to markets through the age old bilateral air services agreements are another bottleneck for industry players. As if these are not enough, environmental regulators are also wrongly focusing their attention to the airline industry while the reality is that the airline industry is among the least polluters.

If we analyze the airline industry using Michael Porter's market forces model, it is apparently visible that the industry is inherently sick. Major suppliers are either monopolies or duopolies and they flex their monopolistic powers on the airlines. There are only two suppliers of large jet aircraft in the world. There are only one or two caterers, aircraft fuel providers, and ground handlers in most of the airports in the world. Airports keep increasing their charges at will and beyond the control of the airlines. Customers have too much purchasing power. In the last decade, the world has been awash with easily accessible capital which has softened entry barriers to new entrants in the industry. To make things worse, there is too much competition among existing players. Hence, I believe the airline industry needs fundamental restructuring for sustainable long term economic viability.

In our part of the world, it is even worse than what is narrated above where every little country in Africa aspires to have a flag carrier. Usually, establishing a flag carrier is seen as national pride rather than economic necessity. We know that the fact that the airline industry is a highly capital intensive business and the fixed cost component is relatively high. This makes critical minimum volume of production a necessary condition for profitability, as the fixed cost needs to be spread among higher volume of operation so that the unit cost could be lowered. This leads to economies of scale and scope advantage which boils down to size. In order to achieve this much needed economies of scale and scope advantage, a group of small countries need to collaborate and for a regional airline which will be economically sustainable and can serve the public in the region. But that is not happening in our continent. I think we can learn a lot from Group TACA in the Caribbean.

This book has both an inside-out and outside-in outlook to the airline industry. It is challenging the very core principles of traditional airline management. It is a call for action and a paradigm shift for airline management. While I have a great appreciation for this book and the author which reveals fundamental management challenges in the industry, I also believe that we need to give equal focus to the structural inefficiencies of the industry and treat the inherent sickness of the airline industry which in most cases goes beyond the executive management of airlines.

Addis Ababa, Ethiopia
September 2008

# Acknowledgements

I would like to express my appreciation for all those who contributed in various ways, especially my research assistant, Angela Taneja, an analyst of best global business practices, and Dr. Dietmar Kirchner (formerly with Lufthansa and now a Senior Aviation Consultant) for discussions on challenges and opportunities facing the global airline industry.

The second group of individuals that I would like to recognize include, at: ABN AMRO—Andrew Lobbenberg; Accenture—Guido Haarmann; Aer Lingus—Dermot Mannion; AeroMexico—Nicolás Rhoads; Air Berlin—Wolfgang Kurth; Air Canada—Charles McKee; Airline Monitor—Edmund Greenslet; Airline Intelligence Systems—Stephen Johnston and Roy Miller; Air Transport World—Sandra Arnoult and Geoffrey Thomas; All Nippon Airways—Masashi Izumi; Amadeus—Stephane Druet and Paul Heighway; American Airlines—Scott Nason; American Express—Barry Herstein; @aquila—Brendan Hickman and David Palmieri; Austrian Airlines—Walter Reimann; Boeing—Fariba Alamdari; Bombardier Aerospace—Chuck Evans, Trung Ngo and Jim Dailly; Cape Air/Nantucket Airlines—Dave Bush; Centre of Asia Pacific Aviation—Peter Harbison, Kapil Kaul, and Binit Somaia; Continental Airlines—John Slater; Delta Airlines—Chul Lee; Forrester Research—Henry Harteveldt; Expedia—Greg Schulze; General Electric Finance Aviation Services—Bill Carpenter; Hawaiian Airlines—Richard Peterson; IATA—Paul Clark and Kan Hou; Jet Airways—Wolfgang Prock-Schauer; jetBlue—Rick Zeni; Kahn Consulting—Robert Kahn; Kingfisher Airlines—Vikram Malhotra and Vijay Mallya; Lippincott—Simon Glynn; LSG Sky Chefs—João Monteiro; Lufthansa Airlines—Nico Buchholz, Martina Groenegres, and Christoph Klingenberg; Mesa Airlines—Paul Skellon; OgilvyOne Worldwide—Michelle

Bottomley; Outrigger Hotels and Resorts—Robert Solomon; Petroccione Group—Lucio Petroccione; Southwest Airlines—John Jamotta and Pete McGlade; Royal Jordanian—Hussein Dabbas and Guido Ruther; Teradata—Stephen Brobst and Peeter Kivestu; TAP Air Portugal—Luís Monteiro and Fernando Pinto; TNS—Tom Costley; Turkish Airlines—Temel Kotil, Candan Karlitekin; Unisys—Ron Khulman; Virgin Atlantic—Barry Humphreys; Y Partnership—Peter Yesawich. In addition, there are Don Garvett (ex Alaska Air Group) and Jim Hunt (ex Air Canada).

Third, there are a number of authors whose work and ideas have been referenced numerous times in this book. They include Allen Adamson, Chris Anderson, David Apgar, Rick Barrera, Patrick Barwise (with Seán Meehan), Rohit Bhargava, Robert Bloom, Mike Brewster (with Frederick Dalzell), Barbara Bund, James Canton, Noel Capon, Taylor Clark, Rita Clifton (with John Simmons), Ian Cocoran, Steve Cone, Scott Davies (with Michael Dunn), Des Dearlove, Chris Denove (with James Power), Paula Dumas, Dianne Durkin, David Evans (with Richard Schmalensee), Sydney Finkelstein (with Charles Harvey and Thomas Lawton), Thomas Friedman, Guy Garcia, Michael George (with Stephen Wilson), James Gilmore (with B. Joseph Pine II), Gary Hamel (with Bill Breen), Steve Hamm, Mary Hatch (with Majken Schultz), Tom Hayes, Lisa Johnson, John Kador, Mira Kamdar, Kirk Kazanjian, Lois Kelly, Parag Khanna, Barbara Kiviat, Duane Knapp, V. Kumar, Charlene Li (with Josh Bernoff), Ben McConnell (with Jackie Huba), John Mariotti, Rita McGrawth (with Ian MacMillan), Robyn Meredith, Joseph Michelli, Sramana Mitra, Greg Niemann, Geoffrey Precourt, Russ Prince (with Lewis Schiff), Frederick Reichheld, Ron Rental (with Joe Zellnik), Martin Roll, David Rothkoph, Libby Sartain (with Mark Schumann), Bernd Schmitt, Robert Shapiro, Denise Shiffman, Michael Silverstein (with Neil Fiske), Harold Sirkin (with James Hemerling and Arindam Bhattacharya), Raj Sisodia (with Jag Sheth and David Wolfe), Adrian Slywotzky, Jonathan Tisch, Jack Uldrich, Dave Ulrich (with Norm Smallwood), David Vise, Larry Weber, James Wetherbe, and Fareed Zakaria.

Fourth, there are a number of other people who provided significant help: at the Ohio State University— Gary Doernhoefer, Josh Friedman, Robyn Litvay, and Jim Oppermann; and at the

Ashgate Publishing Company (Guy Loft—Commissioning Editor, Nikki Dines—Editorial Manager, Bob Rowinski—Jacket Designer, and Luigi Fort—Senior Marketing Executive).

Finally, I would also like to thank my family for their support and patience.

# Chapter 1

# Introduction

*Flying Ahead of the Airplane* is a fifth book in a series written for, and at the encouragement of, practitioners in the global airline industry.[1] According to Thomas Friedman, the world is flattening due to such factors as convergence of technology, rise of emerging markets, proliferation of knowledge, and the increase in the capability to collaborate all over the world.[2] Sirkin and his colleagues at the Boston Consulting Group describe the world as "globality" (a new and different term for globalization), meaning "competing with everyone from everywhere for everything."[3]

Take, for example, two fast-developing markets, China and India. Not only are they becoming integral components of the global supply chain, but the size of their middle classes is growing substantially to create huge markets for consumption and materialism, developed internally and externally. This "flattening" of the world and "globality" are enabling companies to enter the marketplace with heroically new business models. For example, Li & Fung, a Hong Kong-based company is producing more than $8 billion in garments and other products without owning a single factory.[4] In the case of airlines, clear examples would be Ryanair and Jet Airways. Ryanair flies within Europe with ultra low fares, relying significantly on ancillary revenue. Jet Airways flies within India, and has operations that now cover the world, including flights to the US across both the North Atlantic and the Pacific.

Unfortunately, while other businesses are focusing on opportunities brought about by the "flattening" of the world and "globality" (where a wide array of producers are using unconventional business models to produce and market to existing and new consumers), most traditional airlines (conventional as well as the established low cost, low fare) seem to be preoccupied with their conventional on-going challenges. Even when dealing with challenges, mostly operational and tactical, the approaches used are incremental, as opposed to strategic.

Regrettably, some of the expected tidal forces, and even worse, the potential impact of their confluence (the potential "perfect storm"), can no longer be addressed incrementally. Here are a few examples of game-changing forces that could have an enormous impact on airlines:

- rising expectations of passengers relating to transparency, experience, innovation, interaction, and customization based partly on their changing lifestyles and partly on the availability of some of these product/service attributes from other industries;

- emergence of technology that, on the one hand, is raising the expectations of passengers, (for example, mobile devices, wireless communications, self-service systems, sophisticated search engines, and social networking), and, on the other hand, could raise the planning capability of progressive airlines (reduced cycle times, dynamic revenue management systems, integrated planning systems, and mass customization);

- emergence of some airlines with new business models, relating, for example, to their financing, products, or their operations (for instance, those based in the Gulf region of the Middle East);

- emergence of not only higher prices for fuel, but also much greater volatility;

- concern for climate change increasing to a level that governments take actions that impact costs and operations.

If the airline industry is expected to face these unprecedented, changing dynamics, the strategic levers that airline managements have used in the past to deal with the changing environment seem

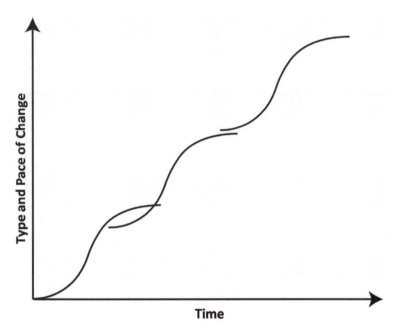

**Figure 1.1    Step-phase changes**

to be rapidly becoming ineffective, if used in the conventional form. For example, there is a limit to how much labor costs can be further reduced or productivity improved using the conventional methods. Unfortunately, given that the profit margins of most airlines have been inadequate historically to meet their costs of capital, how are these incremental changes going to help airlines deal with the emerging forces from the "flattening" world and "globality?" In the new world, management innovations might be enough just to stay in the game. To win the game or choose the game to win will require more innovation in management.

The aforementioned examples of game-changing forces and the incremental and operational initiatives taken by many airlines lead to three clear recommendations. First, executives in the airline industry and related businesses should not continue to believe that the future will be a continuation of the past, plus or minus small deviations. The game-changing forces, along with other trends discussed in the next chapter, will most likely produce "step-phase changes," illustrated in a broad brush-form in Figure 1.1. While a number of senior executives, obviously, have the foresight of potential "step-phase changes," they are struggling for insight into how to conceive new business models while simultaneously optimizing their current business models.

An example of a company that leveraged its foresight of and insight into "step-phase changes" would be IBM. It was that leverage that changed a declining manufacturing business into a services business, in fact into an e-business, a term that was certainly popularized by IBM, if not coined by them. Similarly, Nokia is an example of a company that has propelled its brand to be in the top half dozen global businesses by understanding the rising customer expectations and changing customer behavior by virtually living in its customers' shoes. In the airline business, examples of leveraging "step-phase changes" would include Emirates (with the matriculated execution of its global expansion, capitalizing on its geographic location, ultra long-range aircraft, and the economic development of the region), Ryanair, with its business model of charging ultra low fares and making profit through ancillary revenue, and Virgin, with the unique business model of expanding its powerful brand globally and "creating" its very own strategic alliance that spans Europe, Africa, Australia, and the US.

If the need to prepare for the "step-phase changes" in the upcoming business environment is the first recommendation, then the second recommendation is that airlines must align their organizations, internally and externally, to revitalize their business models by integrating innovation and managing risk. It is interesting to note that one of Thomas Friedman's world "flatteners" (number 3) relates to the application for all internal departments to become "interoperable," enabling work to flow smoothly and effectively.[5] Likewise, Harold Sirkin's recommendation in "globality" is that incumbent businesses need "to organize for collaborative arrangements, partnerships, and acquisitions with challengers."[6]

Now, look at the typical building blocks within airline organizations, shown in Figure 1.2. Think, for a moment, how integrated the airline business is in the creation of its product, and the associated irony. Regardless of whether you start with the brand or strategy (interchanging the top two blocks in Figure 1.2), there is need for integration. To begin with, in the

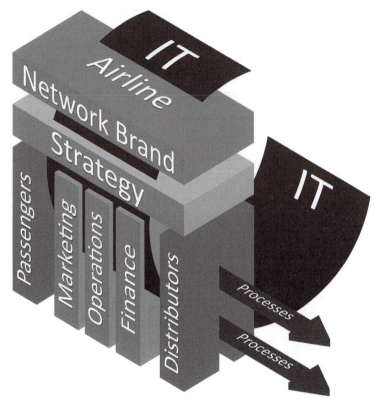

**Figure 1.2    Misalignment within airline organizations**

airline business, network and brand are inextricably linked. However, at many airlines both brand and strategy seem to be missing. Look next at the two outside blocks. Customers are unhappy, at least in the US, and, as for distributors, many airlines are trying to distance themselves and go direct, as much as possible. Again, such a situation is ironical, given that in many regions, and for some segments, distributors can add lot of value (either brick-and-mortar, or online, or both types). While the airlines are working with the three pillars shown in the bottom row of Figure 1.2, most airlines are too often functioning in an isolated manner, and technology is dead on arrival. It is ironical that, whereas technology should be the dynamic linkage between these building blocks, instead, too often, it is a constraint for integrating strategies and breaking silos to introduce innovation. It is this lack of integration that has lead to, for example, (a) inconsistent customer experience (over time, during different phases of the trip, or within an alliance), and (b) the ineffectiveness of action to achieve consistent and across the board product profitability.

Moving to the third recommendation, if, as Sirkin says in "globality," this means that everyone is competing from everywhere for everything, then the role of branding becomes even more important than ever before. At the beginning of 2008, in order to travel between Mumbai and San Francisco, a passenger had a choice of selecting a US airline, a European airline, or an Asian airline. In June 2008, a passenger could fly on an Indian airline, and in October 2008, on an airline based in the Gulf region of the Middle East. On top of that, as mentioned earlier, passengers are getting more demanding and more discerning. Let us also not forget that consumers from the developing economies are also rapidly beginning to care about differentiation and brand values. Consequently, the branding function, with the exception of a few airlines, has been initially done poorly, and must now be addressed much more seriously with a commitment from the top management and the involvement of all.

The aforementioned three recommendations reflect the general framework of this book. Noted futurists are envisioning a world that is radically different from the past, not just from the viewpoint of consumers and suppliers, but also from the viewpoint of societies in general. The emerging world, described by such words as "flattening" and "globality," will bring both challenges and opportunities. In the case of airlines, those who are willing to adjust and adapt in line with the "step-phase changes" will finally earn sustainable margins that exceed their cost of capital. In the category of others, some will fail, some merge, some shrink, some will become more dependent on their governments, and some will become simply irrelevant.

Chapter 2 identifies some key trends that could change the way the airline business is conducted. Examples of these trends include "demanding" consumers worldwide, the emergence of "killer" competitors, and the emergence of "disruptive" technologies that are making customers "smart" and "demanding" on the one hand, and competitors increasingly powerful on the other hand. It is important to recognize that while each trend discussed is sufficiently significant by itself, it is the confluence of trends that leads to the potential emergence of "step-phase changes." Such a confluence will be a challenge for most airlines, but an opportunity for few.

Chapter 3 focuses on the need to think through some thought-provoking scenarios—stories of futures relating to the global airline industry. There are two parts of these scenarios. First, a scenario can relate to the economic and business-related developments outside the airline industry, but have an impact within the airline industry, such as the developments in the Gulf region of the Middle East. The second part relates to the potential aviation-related developments within the aviation industry, such as the development of ultra long-range aircraft and the proliferation of the liberalization movement.

To deal with the challenges and opportunities resulting from the trends and scenarios discussed in Chapters 2 and 3, Chapter 4 deals with the need to transition from traditional management, based on functions, to integrative management, based on the creation of innovation and value, by integrating the end-to-end process. If the conventional business models, management thinking, and business-strategy levers are inadequate to deal with the future trends and scenarios, then how do we close the gap between the airline management practices/systems that we have and integrative airline management practices/systems that we need? This chapter sheds light on this question.

Since this book deals with emerging trends and one major emerging trend relates to social technology, Chapter 5 deals with the growth of the social networking phenomena. The social Web has evolved from people using search engines, to using blogs, to collaboration among users at various levels. Where is this phenomenon going, and what does it mean for airlines? This chapter provides a brief overview of the Web evolution and its implications for businesses, including airlines. The second part of the chapter provides a brief introduction to online communities, some examples of businesses that have used the power of communities to their own advantage, and a glimpse into how airlines can transform themselves by proactively riding the social technology wave.

The social networking phenomenon discussed in Chapter 5 is now becoming integrated into the broader marketing function.

As a result, Chapter 6 begins with some observations on how the world of marketing has evolved from one in which the suppliers were in the driver's seat to one in which customers now sit in the driver's seat. Think seriously about the recommendation from A.G. Lafley, the Chairman and CEO of Procter & Gamble: "Make consumers and customers the boss, not the CEO or the management team."[7] Within the much larger sphere of marketing, this chapter focuses on just two areas that have significant impact on the global airline industry: branding and passenger loyalty. If the airline business has become a commodity, as many writers believe, then effective branding can help to differentiate services, enable the successful airlines to receive a premium for their services, and build sustainable loyalty.

The power of branding is substantiated in Chapter 7 where the reader is taken on a worldwide tour of an extremely broad array of 20 businesses that have developed successful brands: from Starbucks in the US, to BMW in Europe, to the Park Hotels in India, to Banyan Tree Hotels and Resorts in Singapore, to Samsung in Korea, to Shiseido in Japan, and to Cemex in Mexico. This chapter synthesizes not only insights from this extremely broad array of businesses based around the world, but also provides one or two key takeaways for airlines. Airlines may want to keep in mind that the same customers of these global brands may also shop for and buy airline services.

The final chapter deals with a question that was summarized from the comments of some readers of the draft contents of the first seven chapters. "OK, I understand some of the trends and scenarios presented as well as the need to transition from traditional management to integrative management. Also, while I do not agree with the relevancy of all the case studies presented since the airline business operates in a different framework, I do see that it is possible to improve in a number of areas. My question is, "Where do I start?" In response to this question, Chapter 8 (entitled, *Preparing for Tomorrow*), recommends that the starting point should be the process to align the airline organization to enable the selection of the right network, market segments, and the branded offers to customers. The key ingredient of such an alignment is technology that must be deployed as an enabler as well as a differentiator, and not a constraint, to identify and execute enlightened and aligned strategies.

A few airline managements are clearly on the right track, by focusing on both the opportunities and challenges of a customer-driven perspective, optimizing the complexity-simplicity tradeoffs, trying to execute relentlessly current strategies while adapting to manage proactively for the future. This book is about developing insight from foresight, and developing a roadmap for integrating the customer and airline needs through an alignment of the blocks shown in Figure 1.2. It is also about strategizing only what management can control, and then controlling what management promises to deliver. Airline managements willing to fly ahead the airplane will have a much better view of the upcoming landscape and ability to flight-plan their course dynamically to their desired destinations.

The main audience of this book continues to be senior-level practitioners of different generations of airlines worldwide as well as related businesses. As with the earlier books, the approach is still not some "intellectual theorizing," but rather its intent is to provide impartial, candid, and pragmatic analyses based on *what is happening in the actual marketplace in and outside the global airline industry.*

## Notes

1 The first, *Driving Airline Business Strategies through Emerging Technology* showed that in the rapidly evolving airline industry, emerging technologies could indeed play an increasingly critical role in the delivery of real and perceived customer value. The second, *Airline Survival Kit: Breaking Out of the Zero Profit Game*, wrestled with the precipitous decline in the profitability of the industry and discussed some strategies for dealing with the heavy burden of excessive complexity incorporated within the operations of legacy airlines. Having realized that the industry and the environment were experiencing step changes, the third, *Simpli-Flying: Optimizing the Airline Business Model*, drilled deeper into the discussion on restructuring of markets and the critical need for strategies to adjust to the new aviation realities. The central theme of the fourth, *FASTEN YOUR SEATBELT: The Passenger is Flying the Plane* was that core customers—not airline management—are beginning to seize control of the direction of the industry.

2    Friedman, Thomas L., *The World is Flat: A Brief History of the Twenty-First Century* (New York: Farrar, Straus and Giroux, 2005), front jacket.

3    Sirkin, Harold L., Hemerling, James W. and Arindam K. Bhattacharya, *GLOBALITY: Competing with Everyone from Everywhere for Everything* (NY: Business Plus, Grand Central Publishing, 2008).

4    Fung, Victor K., Fung, William K. and Yoram (Jerry) Wind, *Competing in a Flat World: Building Enterprises for a Borderless World* (Upper Saddle River, NJ: Wharton School Publishing, 2008), front jacket.

5    Friedman, Thomas L,. *The World is Flat: A Brief History of the Twenty-First Century* (New York: Farrar, Straus and Giroux, 2005), p. 73.

6    Sirkin, Harold L., Hemerling, James W. and Arindam K. Bhattacharya, *GLOBALITY: Competing with Everyone from Everywhere for Everything* (NY: Business Plus, Grand Central Publishing, 2008), p. 195.

7    Lafley, A.G. and Ram Charan, *The Game-Changer: How You Can Drive Profit Growth with Innovation* (NY: Crown Business, 2008), from jacket cover.

# Chapter 2

# Monitoring Über Trends

There are a number of global über trends that will not only affect businesses but also the way people live and work. Being cognizant of these trends will help businesses, and in our case airlines, to shape their futures.[1] While there are numerous key trends described by futurists that will have a significant impact on societies and businesses in general[2] (ranging from biology to computers, to communications technology), this chapter will touch upon trends in just four areas:

- accelerating globalization;

- changing consumer demographics, lifestyles, expectations, incomes;

- increasing levels and types of competition;

- emerging disruptive technology.

Before reading these trends readers should keep in mind two important considerations. First, many trends in each area discussed have counter trends. In the area of globalization, for example, while information technology and global travel are converging consumer desires and lifestyles, there is also a counter trend that is creating a desire for local regional products, based, presumably, on the emotional aspects of trust. Similarly, the counter trend to convergence is specialization, and the counter trend to complexity is simplicity. The counter trend for the growing middle class in the developing economies is the declining middle class in the Western economies due to stronger competition from the new competitors based in the developing economies. Consequently, scenario planning (discussed in the next chapter) should consider both trends and counter trends.

Second, while each of the trends discussed is powerful in itself, their confluence would have a game-changing impact on most businesses. Take, for example, the emergence of disruptive technology, convergence of products and services, and the movement toward social networking. The ramification of such a confluence of forces could produce enormous challenges as well as opportunities, leading to the potential emergence of some thought-provoking scenarios (discussed in the next chapter).

## Accelerating Globalization

Although the globalization process (integration and free flow of trade among nations) has been underway for some time, the pace began to increase substantially with the availability of CNN worldwide, the decision of the former Soviet Union, China, India, and the former Eastern Europe to move toward market economies, and the availability of the Internet/Web. Now, the impact of globalization is evident in almost every sector of global economies. Developing markets in the world are now reporting some of the world's eye-catching statistics. For example, consider the following announcements:[3]

- The largest investment fund is in Abu Dhabi.

- The largest publicly traded company is located in Beijing.

- The largest refinery is being built in India.

- The world's tallest building is currently in Taipei, and will soon be in Dubai.

The combined population of China and India is approaching 2.5 billion, about one-third of the total world's population. Moreover, not only are the economies of both countries growing at well above the world average, they are also transforming themselves into market economies and as such becoming much more integral components of the global economy. China is proving to be strong in manufacturing while India is gaining strength in services.

Some see the twenty-first century as the Asian century.[4] This idea is strengthened by reports that China now exports *in a single day* more than it did *during the entire year* of 1978, when China began opening its economy, an explosive growth that has the potential to make China a global power and reshape its population.[5] The segment of the Chinese population achieving middle-class purchasing power could easily exceed 100 million, a number higher than the population of any country in Europe.[6]

One business analyst estimates that whereas in 2005 there were 100 million Chinese able to afford nonessential goods, this number is expected to double by 2010, creating a market comparable in size to the one in the US or Europe, although admittedly at lower income levels.[7] However, one cannot assume that the developing market in China is simply for lower-priced merchandise. Again according to experts, in the past decade, China has become the third-largest luxury goods market in the world after Japan and the US, with the Chinese spending about 2 billion dollars per year. Amazingly, but by 2015, according to Ernst & Young, China will pass the US and show expenditures on luxury goods as much as Japan, that represents nearly one-third of the global market. Since the Chinese population is so large, even a small percentage increase in the middle class creates a market as large as an increase in a number of European countries.[8]

Compared to India, described below, China is positioning itself very well to race with the US and the EU for one of the top three positions. The Chinese leaders are well focused on the key strategies needed to win the race (physical, telecommunication, and financial infrastructure, population educated with the right skills, and incentives to attract global investors). Just imagine what China could be like if it were successful in copying the developments that made Hong Kong a globally powerful city. China is becoming a much more innovative economy and a capitalist society. And once it resolves its issues, such as those relating to Taiwan, piracy, ecology, open society, and energy independence, it will be ready to emerge as a superpower.

In terms of India, businesses in India are proving their capability to produce and deliver high-quality goods and services at incredibly low prices, from US$50 airline seats between Delhi and Mumbai, to very clear phone service at less than three cents a minute, to US$3,000 cars, to major heart surgery performed by high-quality surgeons at a tiny proportion of what it would cost in the US. Once branded, such next-generation, price-service options (coupled with the availability of relevant management skills) would produce a competitive disadvantage for numerous multinational businesses.[9] Given that services make up more than two-thirds of every advanced economy, this trend could have a substantial impact. [10]

What stimulated the growth in the economies of China and India are not just government reforms, but also the common usage of the Internet, facilitated by user-friendly browsers, websites and e-mail. Anyone with a computer and access to the Internet could be connected globally, so that certain type of high quality work could be done around the clock, around the year, and around the globe. The Indian wages for professional workers may be between 20 and 30 percent of their counterparts in the West and Japan. Add to this advantage that India is graduating a very high number of students, especially in technology, engineering, and business. So, it is no wonder that the economy of India is moving at a rate three times the level of the West given the three advantages—highly educated work force, low wages, and the availability of the Internet/Web.

The source of employees can be explained in two ways. Not only are the workers in India willing to work at lower wages than their counterparts in the West, but more and more they are becoming trained to fill not just blue-collar positions but also white-collar positions, including those requiring specialized knowledge. While many are still answering 800-number customer service calls, many are now writing software for business on Wall Street and designing products for auto manufacturers in Detroit. The specialized white-collar jobs, many of which were performed by Westerners can now be performed by the locally educated people. India (along with China) now produce more college graduates than the US and Europe combined.[11]

The changing dynamics of the Indian economy is well illustrated by many business analysts. One shows the following example. Let us assume that 1 million college graduates in India (out of a population of more than 1 billion) end up obtaining reasonable jobs, for example, as engineers writing computer codes or working in the business process outsourcing (BPO) sector. These jobs would stimulate many other parts of the economy, from the opening up of restaurants to the sale of mini scooters. According to Meredith, the author of *The Elephant and the Dragon*, there were less than 200,000 cars sold in 1991 (when reform began) but reached a level of 1.1 million in 2006, and is expected to top 2 million by 2010.[12]

As for the impact of this trend on the airline industry in India, for decades, domestic markets in India were served by Indian Airlines, a state-owned carrier that came into being in the early 1950s. Service was limited and fares were high for a large segment of the local population to travel. Four decades later when the Indian Government allowed private airlines to enter the domestic marketplace, a number of airlines began service, for example, Jet Airways, Air Deccan, and Kingfisher Airlines. These carriers were able to overtake Indian Airlines relatively quickly with respect to network, schedules, prices, and customer service. In some markets, the higher productivity of new airlines enabled them to offer fares that were comparable to the fares charged by trains for their first-class ticket. Traffic increased enormously. The availability of new low-fare air transportation services in India is having enormous impact on the population, enabling a very high percent of first time air travelers. India's Kingfisher group of businesses launched Kingfisher Airlines in 2005—an airline branding itself on luxury and pleasure and focusing on the young business traveler. "Fly the good times" is the company's motto, with reclining seats, individual entertainment consoles, and gourmet meals. An estimated 100 million new middle-class Indians will become potential air travelers by 2010.[13] The experience of the telecom industry was similar.[14]

The fact that half of India's population is under the age of 25 and the middle class is growing at a phenomenal rate, substantiates the forecast of an enormous market for a wide array of products and services. Some business writers report that India has a middle class the size of which approaches the entire population of the US. This is not to refute that there are 800 million people in India who live on less than $2 per day. And while from some

perspectives the future looks good, there are also challenges—
"from combating terrorism, poverty, and disease to protecting the
environment and creating jobs."[15] Parag Khanna, author of *The
Second World*, also recognizes these challenges in India, especially
the country's desperate need for infrastructure development—
"the link between trade and development that China exemplifies
is almost absent in India." This fact alone is holding India back,
while China forges ahead with its skyscrapers and roadways. One
only needs to spend a day in Mumbai and one in Shanghai. The
differences in the economic development are enormous and self
evident. Khanna remarks that "India is big but not yet important."
Consequently, while India has the potential to become a leader,
it is extremely far behind other countries, especially China, in
achieving this status.[16]

Another aspect of globalization is that multinational
corporations are quickly learning to globalize their products,
West-based businesses producing products to meet the needs
of consumers in the East and East-based businesses producing
products to meet the needs of consumers in the West. One example
is McDonalds, which has more than half of its restaurants outside
of the US. Specifically, McDonalds has created specialties to adapt
to the local market, for example, the McCalabresa garlic sausage
patty in Brazil, the Shogun burger (a pork bun with cabbage and
teriyaki sauce) in Hong Kong, and the McKofta meatball sandwich
in Pakistan.[17] Then, there are young well-educated entrepreneurs
from developing markets who are not only just as comfortable
conducting business in their own countries as in the developed
countries, but also transporting the market trends from one
market to another, whether it is the Starbucks in China or the
Indian "chai" in the US. Similarly, the attitudes and aspirations
of the young people in developing markets are significantly
different than those of previous generations. They are beginning
to resemble those in Europe and the US.

Developing markets are playing a vital role in the globalization
process to develop products at lower costs and at a greater pace.
Motorola, for example, has an R&D center in Bangalore that
produces about 40 percent of the software in its new phones
while the hardware is assembled and partly designed in China.[18]
According to Robert Shapiro, author of *Futurecast*, by 2020, most

of the items that Americans, Asians, and Europeans consume will be not only from China, but also from Bangladesh, Brazil, Ghana, Indonesia, Malaysia, Mexico, Poland, Romania, and Tunisia. Shapiro goes on to cite examples that are occurring today, thus leading to shape this trend: [19]

- Companies that are already producing in Ghana include Pioneer Foods' StarKist tuna, Kaiser, Alcoa aluminum, and Coca-Cola.

- Companies that are already producing in Romania include Daewoo, DaimlerChrysler, Renault in terms of cars, Hewlett-Packard and IBM in terms of computer components, along with Qualcomm and Vodafone in terms of electronics, as well as Coca-Cola, Colgate, and Procter & Gamble.

While most of the characteristics of globalization have presented the positive side, one must now look at some negative aspects. Let us start with an enormously important aspect of globalization, the concern for climate change and environmental threats. First, it is no longer an issue concerning the developed region as climate change threatens the fundamental aspects of water and food production to meet the growing needs of developing regions in Africa, Asia, and Latin America. There could, in fact, be a major conflict between the nations that are using the energy and those that need to protect the environment for their much more basic needs. Take, for example, the case of the US that did not sign the Kyoto Protocol implemented in 1997 to address climate change by assigning targeted "greenhouse gas" emission limitations. One analyst estimates that while the US accounts for 5 percent of the global population, it contributes to 25 percent of the global greenhouse emissions.[20]

Although the climate change problem will affect societies, businesses, and individual lifestyles, its impact could be devastating on the air transportation industry, given the relatively high visibility of this industry. In October 2006, the UK Government initiated an independent review (that became known as the Stern Review) to look into the economic impact of climate change and the costs of stabilizing the detrimental environmental impact. It is interesting to note that according to the Stern research, while the transport sector (as a whole) contributed 14 percent of the total $CO_2$ emissions, the contribution of the aviation industry was only 1.7 percent of the total $CO_2$ emissions in the year 2000.[21] The issue appears to be that it is the projected growth of the global aviation industry that concerns the environmentalists. For example, while the contribution of the aviation industry may only be less than 2 percent of the total $CO_2$ emissions, it could grow to 5 percent by 2050. This concern could easily lead to financial taxes, limitations placed on operations, and further emission trading schemes. Such actions, likely to be taken based on emotions rather than facts, could cripple the airline industry. Examples of emotions include thinking of air travel as a luxury for the privileged, basing the growth of air travel on the growth of low-cost carriers since 1990, and seeing advertisements by the oil companies, more than by airlines, on the oil companies' green initiatives.

It is, however, interesting to note that while climate change represents a challenge and a threat, it also represents an opportunity. The "Clean Tech" industry is booming. As James Canton, a renowned global futurist, says, "Leave it to business to figure out a new way to monetize pollution and environmental disaster." [22] For its part, the aviation industry is making significant progress. Relative emissions per seat-kilometer (fuel efficiency of aircraft) have improved by 70 percent in the past 40 years and the next generation aircraft promise another 20 percent improvement. Governments can help much more through improvements in the air traffic management (ATM) system.[23] However, the industry must become proactive in demonstrating and communicating its actions. How far can a 2-mile runway take a passenger compared to a 2-mile road? One could argue that a full, high-density aircraft would need less primary energy per passenger on a 500-mile trip than a relatively modern high-speed train. How much does the aviation industry contribute to the economic growth of nations compared to other industries? The fast growth of the middle class with lifestyles formerly experienced by the "Western" middle classes also means that consumption standards of energy, water, food, and other raw materials are coming closer to the levels of the "Western" economies.

Next, look at the concern that globalization may produce on the "have" segment and the "have not" segment. While the middle classes are increasing in developing markets, major issues remain relating to poverty, disease, and the poor quality of life in many parts of Africa, Asia, and Latin America. How will poverty be reduced, let alone eliminated, given that financial aid is neither enough, nor the right strategy? One solution might be to provide the right infrastructure (running water, housing, health care, transportation system, and so forth). Especially in Africa (but, unfortunately, not limited to it), there are many examples of "poor governance," where unscrupulous groups exploit countries into poverty and famine. Then there are issues relating to religious extremists and terrorism. Canton, the author of *The Extreme Future*, sums up these concerns eloquently by listing them into "Five Wars of Globalization: terrorism, crime, drug trafficking, counterfeiting, and poverty."[24] In the developed countries there is a tendency for a "split" of the middle class. Those adaptable to the effects of globalization earn higher incomes than before, while those "victims" of outsourcing or technology-based rationalization may drop out of the middle class. To some extent, the US real-estate crisis has been triggered by that effect.

Finally, some companies are now pursuing a new avenue in terms of corporate social responsibility within the context of globalization. Instead of leaving the issues to activists, companies are actually getting involved in the causes, even working with campaigners whom the companies had originally once fought. Examples cited in *The Economist* include Limited Brands, which prints millions of catalogues for its Victoria's Secret division, now works together with ForestEthics in terms of alternatives for sourcing paper, whereas earlier the group was demonstrating against the company. Marriott International has formed an alliance with Conservation International and the Brazilian state of Amazonas in an effort to protect a large region of the Amazon rainforest. Specifically, this project will allow guests staying at Marriott's hotels to help offset the greenhouse gas emissions associated with their hotel stays. It has been reported that companies are eager to follow this new way of dealing with corporate social responsibility in terms of forming partnerships with environmental groups as a means of avoiding being the source of attack or being accused of not walking the talk in terms of making efforts to become "greener."[25] In the airline industry, Sir Richard Branson of the Virgin Group is committing billions of dollars to explore the development of alternative fuels. Lufthansa cooperates with an organization myclimate where passengers can donate funds supporting climate protection projects to reduce greenhouse gas emissions.[26]

For airlines these effects are expected to result in a geographical shift of the typical economy class passenger from developed to developing markets. Second, it also means a significant growth in the development of value-focused airlines (discussed in the next chapter). Third, it means a potential increase in the price of fuel. Finally, it could mean an increase in the regulations relating to the environment.

## Changing Consumer Demographics, Lifestyles, and Expectations

The combination of Generation X (born between 1965 and 1979) and Generation Y (born between 1980 and 1997) is known as the "Connected Generation," given its embracement of technology (mobile phones, message texting, and social online communities) to become connected. Given that the Boomer generation in the US has begun to retire, it is the Connected Generation that is expected to have a major influence in the marketplace by reshaping it.[27] In the travel industry some hotels (for example, Starwood's new line of hotels, called Aloft), are now catering to the connected generation.[28] According to the Y Partnership, this generation wants casual food available anytime, free Internet, and self-service systems. This generation is powerful not just because its members are connected (through the Internet, information, and social technologies) but also because they are proactive. Moreover, this generation appears to be more interested in loose connections that reflect common interests and lifestyles than the conventional, structured social and professional networks such as clubs and associations.[29]

The connected generation is interested in:

- customized products and services that reflect their interest and lifestyles;

- experiences, resulting, for example, from not just innovation but also interaction with suppliers as well as with like-minded people through online communities;

- branded products and services that promote their lifestyles. Starbucks, for example, was one of the first to install wireless networks in their stores to enable customers not only to enjoy a customized cup of coffee but also to catch-up on their e-mail or to do office work.

Another key consumer group that is emerging is what has been referred to as the "Karma Queen." Specifically, these women tend to be in their forties or fifties. "These are women who have lived long enough to know who they are, what they want, and what they believe in." These women tend to spend a lot on services such as spa treatments rather than the traditional big-ticket items such as a big house, an expensive car, or jewelry. They focus on health and wellness, including natural and organic foods and clothes made primarily of natural fibers. They are interested in supporting companies who, in turn, support the environment and social issues. The sphere of influence of a Karma Queen is very large and a Karma Queen can be very influential. For example, their purchases for their households as well as for gifts can expose consumers to goods and services they were not aware of previously. Also, Karma Queens have helped contribute to the rise of yoga and Pilates. More than 20 million people in North America alone now do yoga, and approximately 80 percent of fitness/health services arenas include yoga classes.[30] Think about appealing to special segments such as these for travel-related products and services.

A Karma Queen is interested in:

- handmade, natural, organic and environmentally friendly products and services;

- mind-body-spirit approach;

- emotional fulfillment.

A third area of demographic change is the increase in the purchasing power of different ethnic groups within countries in the US and Europe. The growth of the Hispanic, Asian, and Central/Eastern European segments in the US is one example. This demographic trend warrants a much greater change in the business strategy than placing ads in magazines targeted at different ethnic groups since the purchasing behavior differs significantly among different ethnic groups. Here are two examples. The online shopping and purchasing behavior is substantially different for different segments, warranting, for example, specialized content to make emotional connections.[31] Second, the economically better-off ethnic segments tend to impact purchasing behavior in the native lands. For example, a financially well-off person of Indian background in the US could easily purchase airline tickets for her relatives in India for travel to the US. In Europe, people with a "migration background" generate a lot of travel once they have reached a certain level of income. Finally, a third area of demographic and cultural change is the greater entry of women in the workforce in Asian countries (such as India) and their ability to become more independent.[32]

The well-off Indians are changing their lifestyles and purchasing luxury goods and services, exemplified by the increase in sales of luxury cars, patronage at high-end hotels, and designer saris. According to India's National Council of Applied Economic Research, 53,000 households in India had annual earnings of one crore (10 million) rupees, or about US$250,000, in 2005, a number that was expected to grow to 140,000 households by 2010. The next tranche, households earning 5–10 million rupees (US$125,000 to US$250,000), will jump to 250,000 households by the end of the decade. "The most striking thing about luxury establishments in India—whether a hotel, a restaurant, a boutique, or a posh office or home—is the amplitude of the service. There is someone to open the door of your car, to open the door of the building, to offer to fetch you something to drink—a cup of tea, a chilled soda, fresh coconut juice—and to offer something to eat. There is someone who can be sent out to pick up anything you might need."[33] The story is not only similar in China but even more eye opening.

There is another trend related to lifestyles, trading down in some areas to trade up in other areas. A significant and growing segment of the market in the US and Europe is experiencing the phenomenon of trading down to trade up. This segment is willing, even eager, to pay less for certain products and services so as to be able to pay a premium price for other products and services that they value. For example, a couple on vacation may be willing to buy the lowest-priced seat on a discount airline and then use the money saved to stay at a higher-priced hotel. This trend is clearly visible in observing the quality of cars parked outside the airport terminal of low-cost airlines and the parking lots of discount stores such as Aldi and Wal-Mart.

Some business analysts refer to people, who are "trading up" for real and for emotional reasons, as "New Luxury." Examples of products and services include the lower end of the line cars manufactured by Mercedes, premium economy seats introduced initially by Virgin Atlantic, Starbucks beverages, and Bath and Body Works offerings. Silverstein and Fiske, authors of *Trading Up: Why Consumers Want New Luxury Goods—and How Companies Create Them*, refer to a class of products as "Masstige" goods, short for "mass prestige." Specifically, products in this category occupy a "sweet spot" in the market "between mass and class," commanding a premium over conventional products, but priced well below super-premium or "Old Luxury" goods. Another description of this trend uses the words "cheap chic."

Silverstein and Fiske note that this trading-up phenomenon is both prevalent in the US as well as worldwide for the following reasons:

- The social structure is changing in Europe in ways similar to those in the US, such as women have increased their influence and roles in the economy in terms of having greater influence on purchase decisions than in earlier times. There are many more unmarried people, and when people do marry, they tend to marry later in their lives, delay having children, and have fewer children when they finally do have them. Therefore the average household size is decreasing, and many women continue to work after marriage and after having children, thus increasing the number of dual-income households.

- The nature of the European consumer has also changed in that they have a greater amount of education than before. More Europeans are traveling to international destinations, and, just like Americans, Europeans feel the stresses and pressures of complex, fast-paced lives, feeling anxious and pressed for time.

- Japan is also an important market for the trading-up activity with two key distinctive consumer segments. First, a group of approximately 5 million young working women who live at home with their parents, have most of their income available for discretionary purposes. Known as "parasite singles," these young women spend up to 10 percent of their annual salary on fashion items, and are the largest-spending segment of Japanese society. Second, the other group is Japanese seniors, who account for the largest-single group of the population. As this consumer group approaches retirement, its members tend to spend more liberally on quality goods that provide emotional engagement.[34]

Back in the US, business analysts have found another interesting customer segment that is proving to be extremely powerful in both its purchasing power and its word-of-mouth marketing (see Chapter 6 for more on this topic). Analysts, Prince and Schiff, refer to this group as the "Middle-Class Millionaires." This group, which represents approximately 7.6 percent of households in the United States (8.4 million households)[35] has a unique set of qualities, one being its unusual juxtaposition between the typical millionaires and the typical middle class, thus the group's name. For example, while this group is classified as millionaires (net worth of approximately US$1 million–US$10 million),[36] unlike traditional millionaires, the members of this group do work, and thus have been called "the working rich." While the members of this group have achieved success financially, they cannot afford to cease working all together. However, most of them do not hold traditional jobs, but rather tend to be entrepreneurs, and have earned their millions rather than inherited it. Specifically, the top three areas in which this group is involved and has made their income include entrepreneurship, real estate, and technology. More than 80 percent of Middle-Class Millionaires either own their own business or are part of professional partnerships. Their presence can be found across the US; however, they do tend to congregate on both of the coasts. Finally, they tend to fall within the Baby Boomer age bracket, but some members of this group are also younger.

One of the most interesting attributes of this group is their ability to, and their inclination to, network. Specifically, they view networking as "a way for you to connect with people you can turn to for information." They are natural "apostles" for products and services that they utilize, and these endorsements and recommendations eventually trickle down to the rest of the population, thus having a great influence on consumption patterns in the US. It is both interesting and important, however, to note that studies show that the extremely wealthy, unlike the Middle-Class Millionaires, do not have much of an influence on the rest of the population, partially because they do not tend to share information about their purchases and services. The Middle-Class Millionaires are great influencers, though, and therefore are a key group to target, especially by the airlines.

Specifically, their approach and attitude is: "that most problems are solved with a mix of creative thinking, the right people, and an open wallet." They have the means to get things done, both in terms of networking and financially, more efficiently. For example, members of this group have set up a health care advocacy company, which is neither a health care provider nor an insurance company, but rather is a corporation which offers memberships in which holders have access to a trained staff who in essence manage the members' health. This staff, which includes nurses and social workers, monitors members' diets, prescriptions, settles insurance issues, and even accompanies members to medical appointments if they wish. If a member has an emergency while traveling in another city, the staff works to get the member into a specialist rather than the member sitting in an emergency room all day or night. The staff is there to look out for the members, almost like a financial advisor but for health issues rather than finances. They are in direct alignment with the approach and attitude mentioned above in that creative thinking, the right people, and an open wallet can get things done.

This trend of influence by this group will not only continue, but greatly expand, as it has been reported that the number of millionaire families in the US will increase by approximately half over the next ten years. Thus, it is imperative to tap into this influential group now, as their influence on spending habits will only continue to increase in the future.[37]

Like the Middle-Class Millionaires in the United States, researchers have been studying an equally interesting segment of the population, although this group is far more global. Business analysts are referring to this group as the "Superclass." This group, which comprises only a mere 6,000 members of the world's population, is distinguished by the element of power. Specifically, this group's power in terms of international influence is what distinguishes them, more than simply financial means. This power is a result of fortune, talent, work, or a mix of the three elements, and it crosses borders, influencing millions or even billions of other individuals. The members of this group obtain this power through several channels—"they employ people or move markets or launch invasions or inflame passions or alter deeply held beliefs." This group includes political leaders, military leaders, religious leaders, social leaders (artists, academics, and scientists), as well as business and finance leaders, which is the single largest group within the Superclass group. Analysts also note that the Superclass can include what they refer to as "shadow elites—terrorist leaders and criminal masterminds." Specific examples of the Superclass quoted include the President of the United States, the Pope, and Osama bin Laden.

One of the most interesting attributes and distinguishing features of this group is their connectivity, thus linking their individual groups of power. These connections occur for a myriad of reasons, from the individuals attending the same prestigious universities to serving on boards to business deals. Thus, as global as the members are physically, they are actually a rather tight-knit community due to these many connections. In essence, these connections further strengthen the power and influence of the members of this elite group.[38]

For airlines, these trends mean an exposure to a very diverse group of customers with all sorts of priorities, expectations, behaviors, and service-to-price preferences. For example, it appears that the Russian tourists are challenging the top positions of Germans in many resort areas around the Mediterranean and the Persian Gulf. Some airlines, exemplified by those based in the UAE area are working closely with their aviation/tourism sectors to integrate their operations within the supply chain.

## Increasing Levels and Types of Competition

While most businesses recognize that competition will increase in the coming years, it is the nature of competition that could be most challenging for existing businesses, including airlines. But, if one is to draw some conclusions contained in Thomas Friedman's *The World is Flat*, there could also be opportunities for businesses to compete in the new developing market environment. Here are just two examples of companies taking advantage of competing in the "flattening" world, one in India (Wipro) and one in China (Li & Fung). These companies are examples of companies re-writing the rules of global competition and demonstrating how to compete in a "flattening" world. While companies such as Wipro and Li & Fung are forcing other businesses to become more competitive, ultimately they are also providing an advantage to consumers worldwide.

These are examples of companies designed for the era of globalization. The key value proposition of both companies is similar. Decades ago, the business model of large companies was based around vertical integration. As Hamm suggests in his book, *Bangalore Tiger*, think about Standard Oil whose business units included divisions that extracted the oil, then transported it to petrol stations that sold the oil. Now, in the "flattening" world the idea is for businesses to stick to their core business and outsource all non-core functions. Dell would be a good example of a computer company that neither manufactured computers nor even components of computers. Dell simply focused on managing customers, suppliers, distribution, and the brand.[39] The development of these virtual companies is a major trend, exemplified most clearly by Li and Fung, that produce more than US$8 billion in garments and other goods for the world's top brands and retailers, without owning a single factory.[40]

*Wipro*[41]

Wipro is one of the largest information technologies outsourcing company based in India. In 2006, Wipro had a market value that exceeded Electronic Data Systems, a US company that practically invented and subsequently dominated the outsourcing business relating to information technology. Although not the largest (Infosys is reported to be larger), Wipro's explosive growth can be attributed to world-class business processes, customer and employee focus, and corporate vision for long-term strategy.[42] Companies such as Infosys and Wipro are changing the rules of the game for traditional Western companies such as the US-based IBM and the France-based Capgemini. Traditional companies must implement major structural changes to remain competitive in these areas. Just opening up low-cost divisions in India may help in the short term but not necessarily in the long term. Consider the 2005 average net profit margin reported by Bernstein Research (in Steve Hamm's book) for the top six Indian technology services companies compared with the top six Western technology services companies, 21.7 percent versus 4.3 percent, respectively.[43]

While it is true that in the early years the competitive advantage of the Indian companies may have been the lower staff costs, year by year, the cost difference may be declining as some of the staff begin to work closer to their clients to facilitate the integration of technologies. Also, the Indian companies are expanding their services to more complex businesses such as legal, financial, and medical. What makes Wipro more competitive than its Western counterparts? According to Hamm, to begin with, "Wipro is like Wal-Mart. It's everywhere, offers a wide selection, and charges low prices." Next, Wipro works with a different business model, perform work where talent is located, and strive relentlessly to achieve operational efficiency while maintaining quality.[44]

The opportunities for companies like Wipro are enormous given the virtualization of companies' trend. While it started with the standard outsourcing of technology-related functions, it broadened into the operation of call centers, then into handling the back-office activities in other businesses such as accounting, travel and entertainment, mortgage related for real-estate transactions, and into the medical field. In the later area, Wipro has on staff a team of radiologists who can read X-rays of patients in hospitals in Western countries.[45]

So, what are the critical success factors for Wipro. Steve Hamm, the author of *Bangalore Tiger*, summarizes it as, "Wipro matters the same way as Wal-Mart matters. Wal-Mart has transformed the retail business for consumers. It is everywhere, with a wide selection of merchandize and low prices."[46]

## Li & Fung

Li & Fung, founded in 1906 in Guangzhou, the PRC, is a multinational group of companies engaged in three core businesses, export sourcing, distribution, and retailing. Now a Hong Kong-based company, it has a staff of over 26,000 working in more than 40 countries and a revenue base of US$14 billion in 2007.[47] A sentence written above is worth repeating, Li and Fung "produces more than US$8 billion in garments and other goods for the world's top brands and retailers—without owning a single factory." [48] So, what is the secret to their success?[49]

- Build enterprises for a borderless world since geography may be less relevant in the future.

- Focus on supply chain from the viewpoint of both costs and opportunities and re-design the business around the optimal supply chain.

- Try to become a "network orchestrator," exemplified by Li & Fung "orchestrating" a global network of more than 8,000 suppliers through 70 sourcing offices in more than 40 countries.

- Use technology creatively.

The really unique element of Li & Fung's strategy is that the company takes care of *all* aspects of the supply chain, eliminating the need for its customers (retailers and brands) to focus on their ultimate customers. In its website, Li & Fung provide an excellent diagram that shows that if one starts with the ultimate customer, they take care of product design, product development, raw material sourcing, factory sourcing, manufacturing control, shipping consolidation, custom clearance, local forwarding consolidation, wholesaler, and retailer.[50] In the "flattening world," it is truly a total consumer sourcing company.

The question is not whether competition will increase in the global airline industry, but rather, in what form will it come. From the conventional point of view, proliferation of the liberalization movement will bring airlines in the marketplace with different business models. In some regions, it could be high speed trains. In other regions, it could be format invaders with a totally different way of conducting business.

## Emerging Disruptive Technology

It has already been mentioned that technology has been a powerful stimulant for globalization. However, it is disruptive technology in almost every field (computers, information, telecommunications, materials, medicine, and so forth) that is having enormous impact on the way people live and work, as well as the way businesses organize and conduct their operations. Consider, for example, how the convergence of technology relating to mobility is impacting the way people live and conduct their business. The mobile telephone can now also have a camera, a global positioning system, e-mail capability, a Web browser, and access to high speed wireless data services. Will the next generation iPhone feature a body thermometer and a leveling device? Two extremely powerful technologies, the personal computer and the Internet, have gone mobile. It is this enormous capability, built into a single mobile unit that is making consumers informed, empowered, and demanding. Airlines need to develop serious strategies to capitalize on the power of mobility as it relates to their products and services.

As for the power of technology, one only needs to look at the operations of Li & Fung, briefly described above. And, again, it is not just the introduction of disruptive technology in individual fields, but rather the confluence of disruptive technology and its broad adoption that will enable visionary companies to redefine the rules of competition in their industries. Changes in business, resulting from the use of disruptive technology, may come in the form of huge reductions in unit costs, dramatic improvement in time to market, substantial improvement in profit margins, or a radical improvement in customer service, or some combination of all four. Readers interested in enablers of technology should read Jack Uldrich's book on *Jump the Curve*.[51] And it is these disruptive technologies that will be deployed by visionary business leaders to develop innovative models and processes to create new value in the marketplace.[52]

As for the role of technology in the airline industry, consider for a moment, what consumers want:

- Control, not only the ability to design the product by having choices and transparency relating to price and service options, but also to be able to make changes.

- Personalization and simplicity relating to the process of change, for example, when an agent has to recalculate fares, compute penalties, and re-book passenger (in situations when delays and cancellations occur).

- Reliability, timeliness, and speed of information, at any time, at any place, and through any mode of communication (a call center, a kiosk, a website, and so forth).

- Ability to check-in and board through various identification systems, a frequent flyer number, a passport number, a driving license number, a national ID number, an RFID based smart card, and then once a passenger is identified, the system can retrieve all the information to process an individual passenger.

- Recognition and rewards that are relevant, based on customer value, current and future.

- Comprehensive information while on the move, given, as mentioned above, that a mobile phone now virtually has the capability of a small computer, and can be equipped with a GPS sensor, a sophisticated compass, and a computational software package.

- Pro-activeness on the part of the airline, for example, information that the passenger's baggage is not on the aircraft, and what action the airline is planning to take.

- Not have customer relationship management used by an airline in reverse to mistreat because he/she is not a frequent traveler with the particular airline.

Some business analysts say that we are entering into an "experience economy." Others say, we are entering into an "innovation economy." In either case, emerging disruptive technology can, and, indeed, will transform the passenger experience through much greater innovation? There are a number of ways relating to the airline business. First, new technology can help us to look at the process from the beginning of the trip to the end of the trip, starting with search and book, through change, check and board, in flight, transit, retrieval of baggage, update and reward, and promotional initiatives. Although, customer value is, and should play a role, but all passengers need to be treated with some dignity. Doesn't everyone who buys a ticket deserve to be treated properly, or only frequent flyers, who, in some cases may be less profitable?

Second, technology can provide the support, assuming that integrated processes are in place, to enable an airline to offer *à la carte* type of services giving airlines the ability to breakdown their products and services, on the one hand, and link value-adding services based on customer value, on the other hand. Third, technology can provide the capability for interaction and customization between an airline and its passengers in as real time as possible. The key requirements, as discussed in Chapters 4 and 8, are (a) for leadership to layout strategic requirements for technology, and (b) require an alignment between an airline's business strategy and its technology strategy. Emerging technology can provide not only high performance and reliability but also the flexibility for an airline to change its business model to meet the changing needs of its customers.

## Takeaways

- The world is becoming much more globalized as a result of major forces such as the shift of the former Soviet Union and China toward market economies and the explosive growth and acceptance of the Internet and the Web. The increase in globalization—the availability of almost anything, anywhere, at anytime—is making it more and more difficult for businesses, including airlines, to compete. In our case, airlines now need to re-think their strategies—form, structure, and implementation (outsourcing, integrated alliances, and so forth).

- Consumer demographics, lifestyles, expectations and incomes are undergoing a discontinuous change. The middle class segments in emerging markets such as China and India are expanding at a phenomenal rate. Greater percentages of populations are becoming more educated, more technologically savvy, and more brand conscious. The aging population in some regions (the West and Japan) and the younger population in other regions (India and the Gulf States of the Middle East) will have a significant impact on purchasing abilities and behavior.

- China is already a low-cost, high-quality producer. It is innovating faster than India and is investing more strategically to become a global power. All businesses, including airlines, need to understand that China will shape the world.

- Competition will increase as a result of businesses with very different models. In the airline industry examples already include Emirates and Ryanair. And, that is just a beginning. Outside the airline industry examples include Wipro and Li & Fung.

- Disruptive technology is emerging and converging, and it will empower both buyers and sellers around the globe.

This chapter has provided only a glimpse of a few global *über* trends that have the potential to re-shape the global marketplace, exemplified by the shift in the global economies, the power of the consumer, on-demand supply chains, and virtual production. Most of these aspects are part of the globalization process which is expected to be driven by innovation, and expected to improve the life of people in emerging markets as well as really step up competition in the developed markets. Then there is technology, especially the development of the mobile phone that is in an "always-on" multi-purpose personal assistant form. Such a technology could produce substantial reduction in costs and improvements in customer service. On the other hand, airlines who do not capitalize on emerging technology could face customers who are well informed, powerful, and demanding. Some of these trends are translated into a few scenarios in the next chapter.

## Notes

1   Hiemstra, Glen, *Turning the Future into Revenue: What Businesses and Individuals Need to Know to Shape Their Futures* (Hoboken, NJ: John Wiley, 2006).

2   See, for example, Canton, James, *The Extreme Future: The Top Trends That Will Reshape the World for the Next 5, 10, and 20 Years* (NY: Dutton, Penguin Group, 2006).

3   Zakaria, Fareed, "The Rise of the Rest," *Newsweek*, May 12, 2008, pp. 20–29.

4   Kamdar, Mira, *Planet India: How the Fastest-Growing Democracy Is Transforming America and the World* (NY: Scribner, 2007), pp. 7–8.

5   Meredith, Robyn, *The Elephant and the Dragon: The Rise of India and China and What it Means for All of Us* (NY: W.W. Norton, 2007), p. 16.

6   Meredith, Robyn, *The Elephant and the Dragon: The Rise of India and China and What it Means for All of Us* (NY: W.W. Norton, 2007), p. 37.

7   Meredith, Robyn, *The Elephant and the Dragon: The Rise of India and China and What it Means for All of Us* (NY: W.W. Norton, 2007), pp. 60–61.

8   Meredith, Robyn, *The Elephant and the Dragon: The Rise of India and China and What it Means for All of Us* (NY: W.W. Norton, 2007), p. 70.

9   Engardio, Pete (ed., BusinessWeek), *CHINDIA: How China and India Are Revolutionizing Global Business* (NY: McGraw-Hill, 2007), p. 17.

10 Shapiro, Robert J., *Futurecast How Superpowers, Populations, and Globalization Will Change the Way You Live and Work* (NY: St Martin's Press, 2008), p. 12.

11 Meredith, Robyn, *The Elephant and the Dragon: The Rise of India and China and What it Means for All of Us* (NY: W.W. Norton, 2007), p. 13.

12 Meredith, Robyn, *The Elephant and the Dragon: The Rise of India and China and What it Means for All of Us* (NY: W.W. Norton, 2007), pp. 88–9.

13 Kamdar, Mira, *Planet India: How the Fastest-Growing Democracy is Transforming America and the World* (NY: Scribner, 2007), p. 122.

14 Meredith, Robyn, *The Elephant and the Dragon: The Rise of India and China and What it Means for All of Us* (NY: W.W. Norton, 2007), pp. 55–6.

15 Kamdar, Mira, *Planet India: How the Fastest-Growing Democracy is Transforming America and the World* (NY: Scribner, 2007), front jacket.

16 Khanna, Parag, *The Second World* (NY: Random House, 2008), pp. 275–7.

17 Shapiro, Robert J., *Futurecast How Superpowers, Populations, and Globalization Will Change the Way You Live and Work* (NY: St Martin's Press, 2008), p. 89.

18 Engardio, Pete (ed., *BusinessWeek*), *CHINDIA: How China and India Are Revolutionizing Global Business* (NY: McGraw-Hill, 2007), pp. 15, 22–3.

19 Shapiro, Robert J., *Futurecast How Superpowers, Populations, and Globalization Will Change the Way You Live and Work* (NY: St Martin's Press, 2008), p. 8.

20 Price, Lauri and Mott MacDonald, "Aviation Policy in the shadow of climate change," *Airfinance Annual*, 2007/2008, p. 32.

21 Price, Lauri, "Aviation Policy in the shadow of climate change," *Airfinance Annual*, 2007/2008, p. 32.

22 Canton, James, *The Extreme Future: The Top Trends That Will Reshape the World for the Next 5, 10, and 20 Years* (NY: Dutton, Penguin Group, 2006), pp. 161 and 173.

23 Price, Lauri, "Aviation Policy in the shadow of climate change," *Airfinance Annual*, 2007/2008, p. 34.

24 Canton, James, *The Extreme Future: The Top Trends That Will Reshape the World for the Next 5, 10, and 20 Years* (NY: Dutton, Penguin Group, 2006), pp. 200–201.

25 "Strange Bedfellows: Activists and companies can move from confrontation to co-operation," *The Economist*, May 24th–30th 2008, p. 89.

26 For more on Lufthansa's green initiatives, see: http://www.lufthansa.com/online/portal/lh/us (Quicklink: Climate care contribution).

27  Johnson, Lisa, *Mind Your X's and Y's: Satisfying the 10 Cravings of a New Generation of Consumers* (NY: Free Press, 2006), p. 4.
28  Van Dyk, Deirdre, "The Generation Y Hotel," *Time Magazine*, 23 June 2008, p. Global 1–5.
29  Johnson, Lisa, *Mind Your X's and Y's: Satisfying the 10 Cravings of a New Generation of Consumers* (NY: Free Press, 2006), p. 61.
30  Rental, Ron with Joe Zellnik, *Karma Queens, Geek Gods, Innerpreneurs: Meet the 9 Consumer Types Shaping Today's Marketplace* (NY: McGraw-Hill, 2007), pp. 17–18, 20, 24.
31  Garcia, Guy, *The NEW Mainstream: How the Multicultural Consumer Is Transforming American Business* (NY: HarperCollins, 2004), pp. 91, 217–18.
32  Kamdar, Mira, *Planet India: How the Fastest-Growing Democracy Is Transforming America and the World* (NY: Scribner, 2007), p.114.
33  Kamdar, Mira, *Planet India: How the Fastest-Growing Democracy Is Transforming America and the World* (NY: Scribner, 2007), pp. 125–6.
34  Silverstein, Michael J. and Neil Fiske, *Trading Up: Why Consumers Want New Luxury Goods—and How Companies Create Them* (NY: Penguin Group, 2005), pp. 5, 246–7, 251.
35  Prince, Russ Alan and Lewis Schiff, *The Middle-Class Millionaire: The Rise of the New Rich and How They Are Changing America* (NY: Currency, Doubleday, 2008), p. 8.
36  Prince, Russ Alan and Lewis Schiff, *The Middle-Class Millionaire: The Rise of the New Rich and How They Are Changing America* (NY: Currency, Doubleday, 2008), p. 3.
37  Prince, Russ Alan and Lewis Schiff, *The Middle-Class Millionaire: The Rise of the New Rich and How They Are Changing America* (NY: Currency, Doubleday, 2008).
38  Rothkopf, David, *Superclass: The Global Power Elite and the World They are Making* (NY: Farrar, Straus, and Giroux, 2008).
39  Hamm, Steve, *Bangalore Tiger: How Indian Tech Upstart Wipro Is Rewriting the Rules of Global Competition* (NY: McGraw-Hill, 2007), pp. 18-19.
40  Fung, Victor F., Fung, William K. and Yoram (Jerry) Wind, *Competing in a Flat World: Building Enterprises for a Borderless World* (Upper Saddle River, NJ: Wharton School Publishing, Pearson Education, 2008), front jacket.
41  Most of the insights on Wipro are synthesized from the excellent research conducted by Steve Hamm and reported in his book, *Bangalore Tiger: How Indian Tech Upstart Wipro Is Rewriting the Rules of Global Competition* (NY: McGraw-Hill, 2007).
42  Hamm, Steve, *Bangalore Tiger: How Indian Tech Upstart Wipro Is Rewriting the Rules of Global Competition* (NY: McGraw-Hill, 2007), the jacket, pp. 1, 5,6.
43  Hamm, Steve, *Bangalore Tiger: How Indian Tech Upstart Wipro Is Rewriting the Rules of Global Competition* (NY: McGraw-Hill, 2007), p. 9.

44  Hamm, Steve, *Bangalore Tiger: How Indian Tech Upstart Wipro Is Rewriting the Rules of Global Competition* (NY: McGraw-Hill, 2007), p. 17.

45  Hamm, Steve, *Bangalore Tiger: How Indian Tech Upstart Wipro Is Rewriting the Rules of Global Competition* (NY: McGraw-Hill, 2007), p. 20.

46  Hamm, Steve, *Bangalore Tiger: How Indian Tech Upstart Wipro Is Rewriting the Rules of Global Competition* (NY: McGraw-Hill, 2007), p. 17.

47  For more on Li & Fung, see: www.lifunggroup.com/front.html

48  Fung, Victor F., Fung, William K. and Yoram (Jerry) Wind, *Competing in a Flat World: Building Enterprises for a Borderless World* (Upper Saddle River, NJ: Wharton School Publishing, Pearson Education, 2008), front jacket.

49  Fung, Victor F., Fung, William K. and Yoram (Jerry) Wind, *Competing in a Flat World: Building Enterprises for a Borderless World* (Upper Saddle River, NJ: Wharton School Publishing, Pearson Education, 2008), preface.

50  For complete service chain, see: www.lifung.com/eng/business/service_chain.php

51  Uldrich, Jack, *Jump the Curve: 50 Essential Strategies to Help Your Company Stay Ahead of Emerging Technologies* (Avon, MA: Platinum Press, 2008). Chapter 3 describes seven enablers: The Law Firm of Moore, Dickerson, and Metcalfe; A Growing Flock of Mavens; A Better Code; The Open-Source Movement; Money Makes the World Go Round; The Competitive Spirit; and Mind Wide Open.

52  Hoque, Faisal and Terry A. Kirkpatrick, *Sustained Innovation: Converging Business and Technology to Achieve Enduring Performance* (Stamford, CT: BTM Press, 2007).

# Chapter 3

# Game Changing:
# Potential Airline Scenarios

How many airline executives in 1993 could have imagined that the environment in 2005 would be like the following?

- Some passengers would be asked to come to the airport as much as three hours before the departure time.

- Every passenger going through an airport in the USA would be required to take off shoes and a jacket, not be able to carry a small bottle of drinking water, display every bottle with liquid in a see through plastic bag and to ensure that each such bottle did not contain more than 3 ounces (including toothpastes), and send laptop computers through the screening machines in separate rubber containers.

- See a significant percentage of the traveling public become its own travel agent to search for schedules/fares and make reservations using the Internet.

- Observe the phenomenal growth of low-cost carriers in Europe.

- Have an airline based in Europe charge fares practically close to zero, but earn its profit through ancillary revenues.

- See the Swiss Federal Government let its powerful brand-named, global, flag carrier (Swissair) go bankrupt.

- See almost half of the US major airlines file for bankruptcy court protection.

- Have an event, like SARS, that would result in having powerful airlines such as Singapore and Cathay Pacific ground almost half of their capacity in a very short period of time.

While hard to envision, all of these unforeseen situations did become a reality in 10-plus years. Dealing with the outcomes of these situations has been, and continues to be, particularly painful, especially for two stakeholders, the non-executive airline workers, whose wages and benefits declined significantly, and the traveling public, that now faces an enormous increase in the hassles related to air travel. In light of the recent past experience, exploring a few potential stories of futures (commonly referred to as scenario planning) should help airline management make better decisions during a time when the marketplace may go through, as mentioned in the Introduction, "step-phase changes."

The purpose of this chapter is not to lay out a step-by-step method for scenario planning and executing different strategies.[1] Rather, the purpose is, first, to describe three possible futures that could take place during the next ten, or so, years, and, second, to show their relevance within the global airline industry in the form of five specific scenarios. These scenarios raise the obvious question: Are most airline managements prepared to face the challenges and take advantage of opportunities created by such scenarios?

## Scenario-related Assumptions

- Blue Skies—nothing serious will happen.

- Frequent Thunderstorms—growing discrepancies will unload in eruptive events.

- Sun and Rain—discrepancies will cause adoption problems, that are somewhat manageable.

Clearly the assumptions relating to the Blue Skies future and the Frequent Storms future represent the two extremes while the Sun and Rain is in the middle. The section below lays out some of these assumptions. In the case of Blue Skies, the assumptions are divided into two categories, those from outside the aviation industry, and those from within the aviation industry. For the next future, Frequent Storms, the assumptions listed come only from outside the aviation industry. The premise is that nothing changes from the current situation. Similarly, the Sun and Rain future does not contain many specific assumptions related to the aviation industry. Some of those listed under the Blue Skies would apply to the case of Sun and Rain.

*Blue Skies*

*From outside the aviation industry*

- With globalization in full swing, all economies of the world became connected, offering opportunities for the smart and busy. The living standards of individuals and societies of inferior capabilities do not become threatened. As the broad middle classes develop in the leading "new" economies, the old middle classes in the former first world lose sufficiently in size and influence, but this situation does not cause any serious problems. The trade balance between major countries (such as between the US and China) or the Chinese foreign currency reserve of US dollars do not reach levels that lead to economic and or political tensions, not an unreasonable assumption if China begins to use more of its production for domestic consumption than international export. The price of oil follows the rate of inflation from the level at the beginning of 2008. The development in the summer of 2008 turns out to be an abnormality.

- The climate change challenge does not lead to drastic changes in consumer patterns. A new, viable, renewable fuel source is discovered and implemented, reducing dependence on the Middle East and reducing gas emissions. The remaining major countries join the Kyoto protocol, an action that, in turn, triggers massive campaigns in those countries to raise the energy efficiency of their industries. In the US, cars begin to consume 5 percent less gas, private households consume 3 percent less heating energy, and the industry's consumption remains flat despite considerable growth.

- The ongoing technological evolution continues to link hundreds of millions with voice and data exchange, leading to positive results such as the globalization of knowledge work without negative consequences such as "eTerror." Technology continues to shape the lifestyles of people and the way businesses produce and market their products and services, along the lines suggested in the previous chapter.

- The economic growth continues in large countries like Brazil, Russia, India, and China (BRICs) and some of their smaller neighbors. China continues to adapt its political system to the new socio-economic realities, resolves its relatively minor issues such as conflicts with neighbours, while India manages to reach a peace treaty over Kashmir with Pakistan. A growing demand for energy, water, and other resources from those "BRIC" countries is satisfied without a conflict resulting from competition for and price of resources, such as the price of oil. Also, the new resource-saving techniques developed in Europe and the US are quickly transferred to the evolving markets.

- After far-reaching reforms of the labor markets in France, Italy, and Germany the economy of EU recovers to healthy growth rates. The UK finally does end up joining the Euro zone. While major currencies may experience small deviations, they remain stable, such as the US dollar, the European Euro, and the Japanese Yen.

- The slowdown in the US in the 2007/8 period, driven by, among other events, the weak real-estate market, does not become long or deep, and does not spread to other regions. The new administration in the US is not only successful in withdrawing from Iraq using a framework that protects the integrity of the country, but is also able to work with other countries to maintain relative peace in the region. The "new" Middle East creates a reasonably strong boom in the whole area with the UAE, especially Dubai, becoming one of the top regions in the world, despite the complexity within the region.

- The founders of Mercosur (Chile, Argentina, Uruguay, and Brazil) agree on a common currency, the New Peso, and are joined by a number of other countries in the region (Paraguay, Bolivia, Peru, and Ecuador).

- There is some improvement in the "left-behind" situation in most African countries as the "Good Governance" code helps to establish more and more efficient, non-tribal administrations throughout the continent.

*From within the aviation industry*

- Governments ease up on ownership and control rules, enabling trans-border mergers, acquisitions, and partnerships. This aspect of liberalization allows airlines such as British Airways and American Airlines to buy each other, and Emirates to buy airlines based in other regions such as British Midland in the UK, Shanghai Airlines in China, Virgin Blue in Australia, JetBlue in the US, and LAN in Chile.

- A "Single Sky" agreement is implemented for one integrated Air Traffic Control system in Europe, and Eurocontrol takes over the entire airspace between the Atlantic Ocean and Russia. In the US, the FAA does implement the Next Generation Air Transportation System ("Next-Gen"), with satellite-based navigation technology for guiding airplanes and managing the Air Traffic Control (ATC) system.

- All ICAO member states accept "Free Flight," formerly called FANS (Future Air Navigation System). Above Flight Level 200, all flights are allowed to follow the minimum time track.

- The airline industry obtains another 15 percent in fuel savings from the next generation of narrow-body aircraft from the new technology coming from airframe and engine manufacturers. For example, Bombardier is able to develop its C-series aircraft (100–130 seats) that not only has US continental and limited transatlantic range, but it is able to achieve at least a 5 percent reduction in costs from the scaled-down technology used in advanced wide-body aircraft such as the Boeing 787 and the Airbus 350s.

- Airport expansions together with the new navigation systems help to further reduce congestions at major airports such as New York, London, Tokyo, Sydney, and Los Angeles. The Government of India facilitates the timely development of sufficient airports throughout India. The Government of China opens up its airspace to keep up with the expected growth in the commercial aviation industry.

- New technology-based airport screening systems allow passengers to be checked much more efficiently and with some dignity. Airlines reduce the check-in deadlines to 1990 levels again.

- The free trade mentality brings along a wave of "Open Sky" treaties. The agreement between the US and EU implemented in two stages, beginning in 2008, is joined by Mercosur in Latin America, the ASEAN in Asia, and subsequently by Russia, China, the rest of Asia, and finally by Africa.

- The Chinese Government facilitates the development of commercial aviation by not just opening up the use of its airspace (as mentioned above), but also by allowing its airlines to buy their own fleet instead of allocating which airline gets how many airplanes of which types. Suppose, further, that "internal domestic" markets are opened up, such as "to and from Hong Kong."

*Frequent Thunderstorms*

- The gap between winners and losers of globalization widens, as some countries and some regions profit more than others. Also, different individual abilities to cope with the new challenges create wider gaps even within the population of a given area. Tensions within and between societies grow, resulting in non-violent conflicts (strikes, embargoes, and so forth) as well as all sorts of conflicts (riots, guerrilla-type wars, terrorism, and so forth).

- The changing climate creates weather phenomena not known before, especially impacting the populations of poorer countries. Governments impose high taxes on the airline industry and in some areas restrict operations.

- The fast-growing metropolitan areas attract millions of migrant workers who in some places live in very poor housing conditions. Health and hygienic conditions cause ideal incubators for all sorts of diseases.

- Fast-growing economies create an enormous appetite for all kinds of natural resources, energy, food and clean water being among the most important. In ten years China, for example, grows to a level that its population alone needs most of the oil produced in the world. China is able to get a large quantity of oil it needs, having invested heavily in oil-producing countries (such as in Africa and having helped them out economically), and locking up huge amounts of money in oil future contracts. However, such a situation not only raises the price of oil to unprecedented levels but also leads to serious political tensions among nations. Alternatively, fast-growing economies go through phases of over-heating and cooling, causing periodic financial crisis through an unbalance in the demand and supply in real-estate markets. Some of the manufacturing activity moves back to the US due to the increase in the price of energy and foreign exchange rates. The enormous population will not only raise social demand but the gap between the rich and the poor could lead to significant problems. The enormous population could also raise problems related to the environment and public health.

• The US goes through a strong recession sparked by a collapse of the US real-estate market. Many households lose their retirement reserves, resulting in a rapid decline in consumer spending. Banks become very reluctant in granting mortgages on homes. With the strong dependency of the US economy on consumer spending, stock prices of retailers, auto companies, and airlines take a nose dive, creating a massive withdrawal of funds from private investment companies.

• The outbreak of a recession in the US causes an enormous devaluation of the US dollar. This event affects all the suppliers of US-bound consumer goods around the world and subsequently creates a devaluation of the Euro, Yen, and Chinese RMB. So, soon after the collapse of the US real-estate market, a worldwide and deep recession brings growth rates to an immediate stop.

• After a few relatively quiet years a wave of terror strikes the US again—in the lobby of a major hotel in a major city, at a major US seaport, in a major shopping mall, and in the airspace surrounding a major airport. The subsequent safety measures issued by the US Government bring public life almost to a standstill. The effects on the stock markets around the world are almost disastrous. The US economy, in particular, takes a nose dive, with other parts of the world following, albeit to a somewhat lesser extent.

• After a recovery period of about a year, a series of terrorist power boat attacks are launched on some of the largest oil jetties in the Gulf area. Additionally, a super tanker is attacked and set on fire in the Strait of Hormuz, bringing all shipping traffic to a halt. Within minutes the oil price skyrockets to US$300 a barrel and only drops slightly to US$295 after one blast is extinguished the next day.

- After a rapid withdrawal of US and allied troops from Iraq, the civil war intensifies to all-out chaos. After a few months, a UN conference accepts a peace plan, which *de facto* results in splitting the country in different parts. The instability spreads to other parts in the region, including some effects in the otherwise stable Gulf region.

- The news of SARS-like symptoms in a major country like China or India impacts many parts of the world. As the virus is unknown and all available medicines show no effect, to prevent a further extension of the pandemic disease, the UN issues a complete "stay-where-you-are" circular, endorsed by all member states.

*Sun and Rain*

The assumptions relating to the Sun and Rain scenario would be some combination of the assumptions hypothesized in the two previous stories, Blue Skies and Frequent Thunderstorms. Let us take two assumptions from each side.

- The US and EU do end up agreeing on a truly open skies environment between the two continents. All airports are open, including London's Heathrow. The US lifts its conditions on foreign ownership of its airlines. Not only are transatlantic mergers allowed (say between British Airways and American Airlines), but antitrust immunity is provided immediately. Europe also liberalizes its ownership rules, enabling an airline like Emirates to buy at least British Midland, if not British Airways, enabling Emirates to now have access to major transatlantic markets. Assume also that government rules ease up to enable members of a strategic alliance to agree to establish a multinational corporation that would establish one set of governance for all members. Not only will it purchase standardized aircraft, but it would decide which member flies which route with which aircraft and sell seats at what fare. All members simply operate within the framework of a wet lease to the multinational company using pilots from the pool operated by the multinational.

Governments also agree to a common set of maintenance standards such that maintenance performed by one member is accepted by all members. The multinational develops a very powerful brand with multiple sub-brands that are totally harmonized by the multinational among the members.

- A serious real-estate crisis (as a result of many who had joined the "Gold Rush" with mortgages put on their houses) in China causes a decline not only on its stock market, but also has an impact on stock exchanges in other global financial centers, particularly in the shares of export-oriented companies. Or suppose, although unlikely, that there is a change in the political party, and that real power change not only reverses strategies but also the processes. Such a change could have significant negative impact on the Chinese currency and, in turn, on other major global currencies. Suppose further, although not very likely, that whereas if the traditionally communist group may not have just challenged the "progressive" open market politics, the new group in power promotes a "Back to the Roots" movement. To gain momentum, the new group could call for nationalization of the banks, infrastructure industries, and airlines, place heavy import duties on foreign consumer products, and a heavy "luxury tax" on international air tickets. Now suppose, in order to limit the fallout of the "Chinese Typhoon", a number of key countries impose protectionist measures against imports from China, which then extends to other low-cost exporters. This situation leads to a "Cold Trade War" between the former First World and the "Boom Countries."

- It takes almost three years for the new scene to stabilize. However, just as the economies begin to recover after three years of the crisis in China, another war breaks out in the Gulf (this time, perhaps, over the Iranian nuclear program). Again, such an event leads to high fuel prices, collapses stock markets, and proves especially hard for some airlines, for example, through a closure for months of airspace over the Gulf.

- On the positive side, China's economic power and the "progressive" people in power in the Party stay in place or are replaced by hand-picked people with similar views and policies. This is a reasonable assumption in light of the resiliency of the Chinese, in light of the past experience of China dealing with crisis such as the financial one in the late 1980s, followed by the incidents in Tiananmen Square, and much later SARS. Moreover, not only are the economic or the political strategies and processes of China not affected, but also three cities in China achieve true global status as financial and business centers, in order, Shanghai, Beijing, and Hong Kong.

The aforementioned assumptions, perhaps dramatized, could come into play, individually or in some combination. Let us not get bogged down into a discussion of the plausibility of any one or more of these assumptions. Rather, it is more valuable for senior airline management to ask if they are prepared to handle the potential scenarios that could result from such assumptions. Examining such scenarios might prove to be helpful in preparing for the future, not by eliminating risk, but by being better prepared to manage it proactively.

## Five Airline-related Scenarios

The following scenarios are based on examples of the trends discussed in the previous chapter[2] as well as a few of the aforementioned assumptions. The forces behind some trends are much more powerful than others. However, if there was a convergence, even among the less powerful trends, the result could be game changing for many businesses, especially airlines. As one business analyst articulated, "In meteorology the build-up of tensions unloads in thunderstorms, in geology we call it earthquakes, in history it is wars, and so forth." While the material presented in this chapter is not forecasts of future events, it does lay out, hopefully, some thought-provoking scenarios, or stories of futures, that encompass "customer" and "business model" risks[3] as well as opportunities and challenges facing the global airline industry in the next ten or so years.[4]

*New Generation Airlines in Intercontinental Markets*

It would be unreasonable to think that the current and past low-cost, low-fare airlines will stay with their old business model, characterized by leisure travel segment, point-to-point markets, a single distribution channel, no interlining, and so forth. Even the most conservative of them all (and the grandfather of all), Southwest is beginning to change its business model. In fact, the business model of a number of low-fare airlines has already been evolving for some time, and now includes various aspects, such as:

- generating ancillary revenue through the sale of in-flight products and services, deploying the inside and outside of the aircraft to advertise, and selling some travel-related products such as phone cards and travel insurance;

- expanding the customer base to include some higher yield domestic and international business passengers;

- making major acquisitions to turn into global hybrid airlines (for example, Air Berlin attempting to integrate LTU's long-range network);

- operating in medium-haul markets (up to five and six hours in flight time);

- multiple fleet types (for example, Virgin Blue adding the Brazilian E-jets to its fleet of Boeing 737s and expecting to add Boeing 777–300s to fly between Australia and the US West Coast);

- two-class cabin service;

- in-seat entertainment systems;

- multiple distribution channels (for example, to attract corporate customers);

- interlining with other airlines and travel partners;

- implementing valuable loyalty programs;

- advanced seat assignments, airport lounges, early boarding privileges.

Consequently, low-cost airlines have already proven that they are capable of transforming their model in three broad areas—adding some full service amenities, generating ancillary revenue, and operating in relatively long-haul markets. Up until now, the legacy airlines had assumed that the operations of low-cost, low-fare airlines could not be extended to long-haul intercontinental markets for a variety of reasons:

- Most long-haul, intercontinental routes require wide-body aircraft with higher operating costs and limitations on frequency due to their size. Limitations on frequency can also be the result, in some cases, of provisions incorporated in the bilateral agreements.

- The costs of service are higher in intercontinental markets since passengers demand many more amenities and services, such as more food, in-flight entertainment, more bathroom facilities, and more flight attendants, much more than bare-bone services in short and even medium-haul markets. Costs would also be higher due to longer turnaround times and extra crew costs due to the nature of long-haul intercontinental flights.

- Most long-haul intercontinental routes require much larger catchment areas and, very likely, interline agreements (again not only raising the costs but also complexity of operations). Local markets may be sufficient in only a handful of very high density markets such as between New York and London.

- Even in cases where the local market may be sufficient in size, frequency would be limited without feeder traffic. Consider the case of Oasis Hong Kong while it was still in business. This airline provided one flight between Hong Kong and London Gatwick in competition with the multiple flights offered by the two primary carriers, British Airways and Cathay Pacific. Leaving aside these two primary carriers with access to enormous catchment areas, there were additional carriers offering point-to-point services, such as Virgin Atlantic, Air New Zealand, and Qantas. It was easy for just the two incumbent carriers alone to offer a small percentage of their capacity on each flight to match the fares of the new entrant and make up the difference on the remaining capacity through sophisticated yield-management systems.

- Fluctuations in the value of foreign currencies can have a significant impact in one or the other direction.

- Fuel represents a higher percentage of the costs of low-cost airlines.

Conventional thinking has also been supported by the demise of a number of new entrants in intercontinental markets—Eos, Maxjet, Oasis Hong Kong, and Silverjets. While three of these airlines are not reasonable comparisons, since they were all-business service providers, Oasis Hong Kong is a valid case. However, even in that case, it can be argued that the airline had a relatively poor business model, relating, for example, to the cabin configuration. First, the carrier could have put more seats in total and second, the carrier should not have put as many seats in its "business class" cabin. Also, it operated the largest aircraft possible, and it chose to enter a market dominated by two strong incumbents.

Let us assume in this scenario that the new generation, low-fare airlines do become successful in long-haul intercontinental markets, particularly if they change their focus from low cost to great value. Based on the initial direction of the strategy of carriers such as AirAsia X, Jetstar, Tiger Airways, Virgin Blue, and Air Berlin it appears that these carriers are pushing the envelope of their business model. These carriers are developing new business models that overcome many of the limitations contained in the business models of the carriers that failed or the abovementioned constraints listed by the conventional airlines. Consider, the progress of just three carriers—Jetstar, AirAsia X, and Air Berlin:

- Jetstar began as a separate, low fare, and profitable brand of Qantas operating an extensive domestic and trans-Tasman network in Australia (operating with Airbus 320s).

- It then expanded its services in long-haul markets using the Airbus 330-200s, presumably for a way for Qantas to expand beyond its home market and grow in the Asia-Pacific region, not to mention to be able to compete with the low labor cost entrants, such as AirAsia X and Tiger Airways. Subsequently, it appears to be setting itself up to compete with Virgin Blue in the trans-Pacific markets. Initially, Jetstar started international operations from secondary airports to insulate Qantas from its higher fare levels.

- Next, Qantas established Jetstar Asia based in Singapore, and acquired a financial interest in the Hanoi-based Pacific Airline in Vietnam to become that country's low-fare airline. Qantas will undoubtedly use its purchasing power to acquire the latest technology aircraft, and put it in service with Jetstar. This is an enormous advantage for a low-cost, low-fares airline in a tight credit environment. It is reported that the first 15 Boeing 787s are planned for Jetstar to replace the Airbus 330-200s.[5]

- AirAsia X, a new Malaysian long-haul budget airline, is an offshoot of AirAsia, Asia's largest low-cost carrier. AirAsia X began its operations between Kuala Lumpur, Malaysia and the Gold Coast of Australia using Airbus 330-300 aircraft. The airline is owned by AirAsia and in part by Sir Richard Branson's Virgin Group.

- AirAsia X has the potential to become a major global player for a number of reasons. It is owned by financially strong entities—AirAsia and the Virgin Group. In addition it is reported that AirAsia has established a joint venture with Vietnam Shipbuilding Industry Group (a very large state owned corporation in Vietnam) to set up a budget airline based on the AirAsia business model.[6] In light of the relationship with the Virgin Group, at the very least,

AirAsia X could code share with Virgin Blue, based in Australia, and possibly even buy Virgin Blue. Besides flying to major destinations in Europe and China, it could also be a major player within Asia in light of the ASEAN countries' potential decision to implement "capital city" liberalization that would eliminate restrictions on passenger services among the capital cities of member states.

- Air Berlin began as a charter airline in 1978 and began to operate scheduled services in Europe in 2002. In 2006, it acquired dba (formerly, Deutsche BA) to have access to domestic markets as well as feed for its international operations. In 2007, it acquired LTU, a large charter airline, enabling Air Berlin to go after both business and leisure segments. Air Berlin also owns 49 percent of the Swiss-based airline, Belair, that, in turn, is a subsidiary of the tour operator Hotelplan.[7] Let us assume that Air Berlin does become a major global player (a) through other acquisitions, (b) by expanding its partnerships along the lines of the one with the China-based Hainan Airlines, (c) by getting its cost structure in line with such players as AirAsia X, (d) by becoming a dominant player at Düsseldorf, (e) by managing the complexity of its fleet, operations, and multi-segment traffic base, by aligning its brand structure, and (f) having sufficient funds throughout that development.

This scenario assumes that value-focused airlines (AirAsia X, Air Berlin, Jetstar, Shanghai Airlines, Tiger Airways, V Australia, and so forth) do succeed in intercontinental markets and provide substantial competition for existing legacy carriers by depressing yield. The impact could be enormous if a number of other existing airlines (such as easyJet, Ryanair, Spring Airlines, Westjet, and Southwest) that are currently known as low-cost airlines also became value-focused airlines through changes in their current business model. Assume further, that not only these value-focused airlines are successful in their own regional and or intercontinental markets, but they, in fact, become successful in establishing a strategic alliance that can carry value-conscious passengers globally, virtually from anyplace to anyplace. Go even further and assume that the downturn in the economy in one region, such as the US is followed by downturns in other parts of the world, resulting in the diversion of a very high percentage of traffic from the major legacy players. Are most legacy carriers prepared for such a scenario? A few are thinking about it and capitalizing on the trend, exemplified by the initiatives of Qantas to establish Jetstar and Aer Lingus itself to become a value-focused airline.

## A Global Virtual Airline

Suppose a private equity firm becomes successful in acquiring a number of global airlines and putting together its own alliance in a much more integrated manner where each component is literally told to simply, "crew the plane, fuel it, fly it, and maintain it." Leave all other management decisions to the holding company — "which brand flies where, how reservations are made, how revenue management is performed, and how the product is distributed." Admittedly so far, such initiatives have been unsuccessful. Consider, for example, when Airline Partners Australia, funded by the private equity firm TPG (Texas Pacific Group) and the Macquarie Bank, were unsuccessful in taking Qantas private.[8] TPG, who had already made an investment in Ryanair in the 1990s, was also reported to be interested in acquiring Alitalia and Iberia.

Many airline executives and government policy makers are most likely to throw out such a scenario on the grounds of existing government rules relating to ownership and control rules, government ownership of airlines, and opposition of unions, not to mention strong egos of existing management. But, suppose a powerful and global private equity group (with really powerful and influential people behind it and with impeccable timing and resources) was successful in acquiring control of a number of airlines based in different parts of the world. Such a group could truly integrate the operations of all its acquisitions, unlike anything that has been achieved or even dreamt about by even the most forward thinking strategic alliances. It is such a group that not only would achieve high efficiencies through the purchase of common aircraft and the operation of a single platform IT system (used for scheduling, reservations, departure control, inventory, revenue management, call centers and so forth). Second, the group could also move up the vertical integration ladder by acquiring strategic business entities such as brick-and-mortar or online travel agencies. Finally, such a group would be in a position to develop a truly global brand, and deliver globally and consistently on a sought-out value proposition. Are current airline managements prepared to even accept the plausibility of such a competitor, let alone compete with it?

Such a scenario is very plausible given the achievements that Lan has already made in its own region. Not only has Lan expanded its own brand by owning airlines within the region but it has been able to integrate the route authority of its various members and optimize, not only on aircraft but also on crew utilization. One can envision Lan Peru flying into Los Angeles from Lima, with a Peruvian crew and the aircraft flying back from Los Angles to Santiago with a Chilean crew. Now, expand the scenario by adding other origin and destination points.

*Gulf Region of the Middle East Becomes an Aviation Powerhouse*

The Gulf region of the Middle East is becoming a potential powerhouse within the global aviation industry. Consider, for a moment, the confluence of the following forces:

- just about a perfect geographic location;

- high traffic growth;

- sufficient aircraft and airport capacity;

- availability of large amounts of capital investment;

- integrated management of aviation/tourism supply chain;

- robust expansion;

- drive to create an alternative to oil production.

Consider just the first point. About 5 billion people live within 8 hours of flight time and more than about 6 billion, within 16 hours from the UAE. Given that today's ultra long-haul aircraft have the capability to fly more than 16 hours nonstop, it means that a carrier based in the UAE can take a passenger from virtually any point in the world to any other point with one stop.

The Middle East region is quite misunderstood by the average person in the West, particularly within the US. It is not a homogeneous region in which one can lump together the economic, political, and cultural attributes of different states. To begin with, there are different parts of the Middle East, ranging from North Africa, to the Levant area, to the Gulf area. Then there are major differences in states such as Lebanon and Dubai or even within the Gulf area between Saudi Arabia and the UAE, or even within the UAE, between Dubai and Abu Dhabi. But it is the transformation of the UAE that has been spectacular. This transformation has not been random, but rather, it has been planned. In the past five years the transformation has gone from government-controlled monopolies to businesses that are deregulated, privatized, and exposed to competition as well as the establishment of a business environment that attracts global brand-named businesses. Not only is the petrochemical sector growing in light of growing demands from the likes of China (and to a lesser extent India), but the previously desert area is even developing a manufacturing base. As three business analysts sum it up, "the region—once an end consumer in the world market—has begun to transform itself into a supplier."[9]

While the above statements are a fact, a number of analysts question the degree to which the UAE-based carriers can succeed relying on sixth freedom traffic. It is true that until a few years ago, and to some extent it still is true, the volume of O&D passenger traffic was limited. However, due to the enormous growth of the region (particularly Dubai), not only has the O&D traffic been growing at spectacular rates, but the forecasts are even more spectacular in light of the planned development of the region—the man-made Palms (Deira, Jebel Ali, and Jumeirah), the Dubai Waterfront, the 300 man-made islands in the shape of the World, Dubailand, not to mention shopping malls, residential developments, museums, sporting events (the Dubai World Cup,

Dubai Rugby, Dubai Desert Classic), and a hotel that incorporates one of the largest indoor ski resorts.

The area is not just being developed to attract high end tourists; it is also being developed as a global business center to compete with cities such as New York, London, and Hong Kong. A few statistics are emerging to support the explosive growth of O&D traffic. At the beginning of 2008, the capacity offered by Emirates at Dubai International Airport was about one half of the total capacity. Consequently, a significant portion of the capacity offered by other airlines must be there to transport the O&D passengers.

While four major carriers are developing global networks in the greater UAE region (Emirates, Etihad, Gulf, and Qatar), the growth to date and the expected growth of Emirates has been phenomenal. Beginning with just two aircraft in 1985 (an Airbus 300B4 and a Boeing 737-200), the airline had about 155 wide-body aircraft (the Airbus 330s and 340s and Boeing 777s) at the beginning of 2008, flying to more than 100 destinations in more than 60 countries. Think of not just the number of these aircraft, but the capacity of these aircraft, and think of not just the number of passengers carried, but the number of passenger kilometers flown. Within the next four years, Emirates is expected to take delivery of another 100 wide-body aircraft, more than half of which are expected to be the Airbus 380-800s. Again, focus not just on the total number of airplanes in the fleet in four years (that may be less than half of the world number 1 and 2 carriers), but rather of the capacity of Emirates' expected fleet. Next, look at the breadth and depth of Emirates network and the rate at which it is growing. Consider its weekly service between Dubai and the UK alone at the beginning of 2008:

- Heathrow      35
- Gatwick       21
- Manchester    14
- Birmingham    14
- Glasgow        7
- Newcastle      7

With such a large, high-capacity fleet, the airport capacity to match it, a relatively low-cost structure compared to other global network carriers, and service standards that have taken the flying experience to new heights, the Gulf region of the Middle East is becoming an aviation powerhouse. It is a plausible scenario. The development of major aviation hubs in the Gulf region (along with those in Asia) have the potential of diminishing the role of European hubs, particularly those that are highly congested. Why connect through Heathrow with potential delays (not to mention burning extra fuel) when one could connect through Dubai with fewer chances of delays? If this scenario was not alarming enough, imagine if Emirates was able to acquire airlines based in strategic locations to enable it to have access to global traffic, as mentioned above, in the UK, in India, in China, in Australia, in Latin America, and in the US. Some airlines could go into denial phase and self destruct.

*A Format Invader from Within the Industry*

Format invaders are businesses that enter the marketplace with radically different business models. These new business models could be based on radically new business models, different ways collaborating, using disruptive technologies, using different ways of segmenting the market, or some combination of these areas to develop new ways of doing business (see Figure 3.1). Format invasion is not restricted to particular businesses or companies. Shelton, Hansson, and Hodson of Booz Allen Hamilton provide plenty of examples of the enormous difference in shareholder return for new-format invaders, and old-fashioned incumbents. In the auto industry, it is General Motors and Ford versus Toyota and Nissan. In the steel industry, it is Bethlehem versus Nucor. In personal computers, it is Compaq versus Dell. In consumers electronic, it is Circuit City versus Best Buy. In airlines, it is American versus Southwest. In home improvement, it is Lowe's versus Home Depot. In retail financial investment services, it is Paine Weber versus Charles Schwab.[10] Even though the explanations of incumbents usually include excessive labor costs (especially relating to high pensions) and costs of maintaining and operating systems, the real explanation according to these and

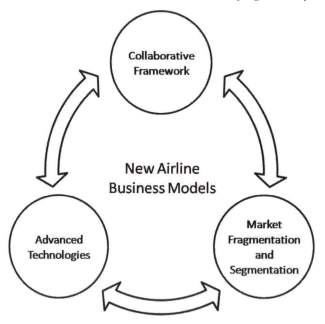

**Figure 3.1 Frameworks for new airline business models**

other business analysts, is that format invaders find new ways of doing things. Whether it is Zara in the fashion apparel business or Ryanair in the airline business, the new way of doing business could be the result of a different way of customer segmentation, manufacturing, providing service, or using technology. The end result could be in areas where revenue might be improved, costs might be decreased, quality could be improved, customer service could be improved, or some combination. The changes are substantial, not incremental.

Think about the Polaroid Corporation that was a winner in the 1970s with its brand promise of instant pictures, something that no other company could offer at the time. However, Polaroid got beaten at its own game, not by another conventional competitor *per se*, but rather by an innovation, digital photography.[11] Instant film was the "brainchild" of Edwin Land, Polaroid's founder. Land (inventor of the "Land" camera) originally started working on the notion of instant film in the early 1940s, but after a 60-plus year run, the film will soon no longer be available for consumers to purchase as Polaroid exits the instant film business. The company already stopped producing instant cameras more than a year ago. While Polaroid survived a potential takeover in the late 1980s, the occurrence left the company burdened with debt. The company filed for bankruptcy protection in 2001. Polaroid is now owned by Petters Group Worldwide which sells computer monitors, digital cameras, and flat-panel TV sets under the Polaroid brand name.[12] The Massachusetts-based brand that became famous around the world has now abandoned its core technology and competency due to an industry invader.

How about airlines? There are plenty of areas where format invaders could enter the market place. There are companies looking at using very light jets (VLJ) for short-haul transportation in the form of on-demand air taxis. The FAA in the US has already certified two models (the Eclipse 500 and the Cessna Mustang), and at least three more will be coming up for certification in the next couple of years (the Embraer Phenom 100, the Adam Aircraft A-700, and the Honda Jet).[13] Key advantages of these aircraft include a price between US$1–3 million, a capability to operate from hundreds of uncongested satellite airports throughout the US and Europe, and fares comparable to the full fares offered by traditional airlines in their unrestricted economy-class categories.

Let us also not forget about the firms specializing in the fractional ownership of business jets who may be exploring the use of their resources to offer customized service to passengers and improve the utilization of their aircraft and crews with the advanced use of the Internet and innovative pricing policies. Similarly, a format invader could come in with a business model that makes use of the private general aviation aircraft, again capitalizing on the use of the Internet and flexible and customized pricing policies.

What if a successful courier service provider, such as FedEx, decided to buy a passenger airline and operate it in a modified form of its package business? Here is a company that is able to operate worldwide within the current bilateral system, charge prices that do not vary by the minute, utilize capacity reasonably well without knowing the demand precisely, and, most importantly, provide an enormously high on-time performance, while working at the same congested airports, within the same antiquated ATC system, and within the same volatility of weather condition. "That is lunacy just to think about it," is likely to be the response from legacy carriers. The two businesses are as different as day and night. (At first, Fred Smith's concept of FedEx was also considered to be a lunacy by the conventional cargo carriers.) But, what if the CEO of the courier service company gave the marching order to his or her troops, "Don't give me the obstacles, just find ways of making it viable and profitable?" What if the CEO said "Let us do it in two phases?" First, "we take over the baggage business of a passenger airline. They carry the passengers and they outsource the baggage to us."

Legacy carriers are likely to have similar denials for other potential format invaders. In the case of air taxis using very light jets, the response is likely to be something like this. Their costs would be very high because of very low utilization of aircraft and the necessity to use two pilots in the cockpit. One should not underestimate the viability of such an initiative in light of emerging Internet-based technology for making reservations and pricing policies, and the ability to reach a critical mass quickly. The later development is certainly plausible if the security-related hassles become worse at major airports. The impact on traditional carriers would be minimal in terms of traffic diversion but huge in terms of revenue diversion. Another format invader could come from the area of experts in mobile computing (for example, Apple®, Blackberry®, and Google®). They have the right customers (well-educated "road warriors"), the right devices, the right computing capabilities, and the guts. They also know how to make use of third party hardware networks.

## A Reduction in the Aviation Activity

Recall a number of negative events included in some of the above assumptions in some scenarios. For example, a wave of terror strikes the US, serious problems emerge after the US withdrawal from Iraq, an unknown disease breaks out and the UN orders people to stay at their original location during the incubation period, and a terrorist activity follows in the Middle East. All such events could have an enormous negative and immediate impact on the global airline industry. Depending on which event and the combination of more than one event could lead to a substantial reduction in aviation activity, and an equally substantial increase in the price of travel. Problems could become really serious if the two major aircraft manufacturers were to deliver the high capacity aircraft at the same time as travel takes a nose dive. Besides the inability of airlines (and leasing companies) to take delivery of new capacity, the price of new airplanes drops substantially with an increase in the number of "White Tails" parked.

One can imagine a broad spectrum of related initiatives. For example, with some of the successful low-cost companies being in trouble, former regionals like FlyBe in Europe or Air Midwest in the US, use the opportunity of inexpensive, used airplanes, and enter the market with innovative business concepts and costs well below the traditional LCCs. Recall the scenario of a war in the region involving Iran. Again, such an event could mean high fuel prices, collapsing of stock markets, and, especially hard for some airlines, a closing of airspace over the Gulf for months. Some Gulf-based carriers may have to move their home bases to different locations to try to keep the connecting traffic. What if these carriers had to postpone all the new wide-body aircraft on order, and find subleases for their new fleets? While the smaller planes could be used by the new low-cost, long-range carriers, the larger wide-bodies, with their substantially different interiors, may not find other users and may need to be put in storage.

## Takeaways

- In light of the global über trends mentioned in the previous chapter, one could envision a few thought-provoking scenarios.

- These scenarios are neither comprehensive nor meant to be forecasts. They are simply some possibilities to consider. The question is not related to the probability of their occurrence; rather, it is more to do with questioning if managements are prepared to deal with the expected changes in the marketplace, and will the past strategic levers ensure future success? Assuming that the answer is no, then it is time for managements to seriously review the potential changes, regroup, and refocus on the development and, much more importantly, the effective implementation of viable levers, strategies, and processes.

## Notes

1   A good reference on Scenario Planning is a book by Bill Ralston and Ian Wilson *The Scenario Planning Handbook: Developing Strategies in Uncertain Times* (Mason, OH: Thomson South-Western, 2006).

2   For a comprehensive list of trends and their potential outcomes, readers are referred to the excellent work of James Canton in his book, *The Extreme Future: The Top Trends That Will Reshape the World for the Next 5, 10, and 20 Years* (NY: Dutton, Penguin Group, 2006).

3   Customer risk relates to customers shifting their buying behavior as a result of broad spectrum of factors such as availability of different price-product options and enormous amounts of information. "Business model" risk could be the result of a change in technology or a totally new competitor. See Slywotzky, Adrian J. with Karl Weber *UPSIDE: The 7 Strategies for Turning Big Threats Into Growth Breakthroughs* (NY: Crown Publishing Group, 2007), p. 53.

4   As some insightful contributors in *The Economist* asked who would have considered that banks could face competition from supermarket chains, exemplified by the strategies of Tesco in England and Seven-Eleven in Japan to competing with them in financial services. Think also, point out *The Economist* contributors, how much new competition a British retailer like Marks & Spencer faces competing now globally with clothing chains like Zara from Spain, The Gap from the USA, Uniqlo from Japan, and Hennes from Sweden. Clifton Rita, Simmons, John, and others from *The Economist BRANDS AND BRANDING* (Princeton, NJ: Bloomberg Press, 2003), p. 174.

5   Flottau, Jens, "Qantas Leap: Can Australia's biggest carrier jump from a springboard of regional growth into success in Asia?" *Aviation Week & Space Technology*, February 2008, p. 44.

6   Thomas, Geoffrey, "High Yield: Boom times for Australasian airlines," *Australian Aviation*, October 2007, p. 25.

7   "Air Berlin: Expanding into a global hybrid," *Aviation Strategy*, November 2007, p. 16.

8   Flottau, Jens, "Qantas Leap: Can Australia's biggest carrier jump from a springboard of regional growth into success in Asia?" *Aviation Week & Space Technology*, February 2008, p. 46.

9   Saddi, Joe, Sabbagh, Karim, and Richard Shediac, "OASIS ECONOMIES: Surrounded by tension, the nations of the Middle East are building their own kind of sustainable prosperity,"*strategy + business*, Booz Allen Hamilton Inc., Issue 50, Spring 2008, p. 46.

10 Shelton, Bernard, Hansson Thomas, and Nicolas Hodson, "Format Invasions: Surviving Business's Least Understood Competitive Upheavals," *strategy + strategy*, Booz Allen Hamilton, issue 40, pp. 46, 9.

11 Barrera, Rick, *Over Promise and Over Deliver: The Secrets of Unshakable Customer Loyalty* (NY: Portfolio, Penguin Group, 2005), pp. 139–41.

12 Bray, Hiawatha, "Polaroid Shutting 2 Mass. Facilities, Laying Off 150 As Company Exits Film Business," *Boston Globe* (boston.com), February 8, 2008, and "Instant Consternation End of Polaroid Film Leaves Many in Lurch," February 27, 2008.

13 "Faster, Smaller, Cheaper," *ascend: A Magazine for Airline Executives*, 2008 Issue No. 8, p. 91.

# Chapter 4

# Are Airline Managements Prepared?

The last two chapters discussed key global forces and potential scenarios that could affect the global airline industry, individually or in combination. This chapter raises the question as to whether some airline managements are prepared adequately to face the challenges and/or capitalize on emerging opportunities. Consider the comment of a relatively young, mid-level executive at an airline about the proposed strategy offered by the airline's CEO. "We cannot survive with the fuel at its current price (at the time, US$120). We must hasten the merger initiative and seek out a good partner before we are pre-empted by one of our competitors." The young executive wonders what senior management would come up with in the way of an innovative strategy when the price of oil climbs to US$150 a barrel, and a number of other forces combine to create a perfect storm. The young executive wants to know why the top brass is not trying to answer strategic and tactical questions such as the following:

- Can our current business model cope with the potential internal and external threats? If not, should we revitalize the existing business model, or do we need a new one based on some innovation?

- Do our passengers and employees perceive our airline as a sought-after brand? If not, how do we develop a viable brand instead of just making undeliverable promises? And, do we have enough patience from our shareholders and the time to do this?

- Is our marketing up-to-date with the new trends in customer interaction? If not, shouldn't we quickly bring in someone from outside of the airline industry, regardless of whether he or she has any airline experience?

- Does our IT provide the necessary flexibility and analytical capability to be able to battle with "category killer" competitors? It is ironic that while our airline is inundated with data, many of our senior executives appear to be flying blind.

The young executive touches a wide array of subjects, some at the strategic level and some at the tactical level. The changing dynamics of the global airline industry (competition, regulatory policies, new technologies, shifting demographics, and so forth) represent both challenges as well as opportunities. However, while a number of senior executives have the foresight of potential "step changes," they are still struggling for insight into how to conceive new business models while optimizing the current model. This dilemma of having to run two business models simultaneously is proving to be extremely challenging. Depending on how successful an airline is in resolving this dilemma will determine whether the airline is able to stay in the game, win the game, change the rules of the game, or choose the game to win.

This chapter tries to address some of these issues, namely, how to conceive new business models while optimizing the current model. This chapter begins with a review of the past strategy levers to deal with historical changes in the marketplace to determine if they still have sufficient pulling power left to deal with the volatility of the emerging marketplace. Knowing which levers have run out of steam and which ones still have varying degrees of pulling power will help in the identification of areas and depth of change. Then, based on some best practices, both within the global airline industry and other businesses, the chapter touches on three specific areas of change to optimize the current business model, namely, the need to align airline organizations, optimize on the complexity-simplicity dimension, and implement analytically based decisions.[1] The chapter ends with a few comments on the other part of the dilemma, the need to conceive new business models to deal with the future.

## Reviewing Past and Current Strategy Levers

Historically airlines have dealt with business cycles using a number of strategy levers to reduce costs, increase revenue, and improve operations. These levers, overlapping in some cases, have included:

- refinancing

- cost reducing

- mergers and acquisitions

- productivity improvements

- outsourcing and selling assets.

At the beginning airlines owned their fleet, some financed through banks. Other assets were also almost always owned — ground equipment, spare parts, hangars, and so forth. Next came leasing. Then different versions of lease financing were created to improve balance sheets such as through sale-and-lease back initiatives. Next, some carriers began to finance their growth through alliances instead of expanding their own operations, a strategy that not only provided asset-free growth (sharing of fleet as well as airport facilities such as gates) but also enabled entry into global markets. Other carriers increased debt through the use of the merger lever, and, of course, a number of poorly run but government-owned airlines have and, in some cases, continue to rely on their owners for refinancing. Now, for most airlines, the refinancing lever appears to have declining effectiveness, in its traditional usage, given the limited availability of debt for many airlines. However, there is still plenty of pulling power if airlines are willing to restructure the governance of their alliances. One example would be the establishment of a multinational company that would be allowed to "control" the activities of its partners.

Such a strategy would enable an airline to compete effectively with the global virtual airline scenario listed in the previous chapter.

The cost reduction lever was initially deployed to reduce labor costs by making commitments related to job security and introducing two-tier pay scales (lower wages for new employees relative to more senior employees). Later, labor costs were reduced significantly through the use of bankruptcy provisions (especially by challenging the old and costly pension schemes). Aircraft costs were reduced through such measures as the postponement of the purchase of new aircraft, the deployment of standardized single-aisle aircraft, and the extraction of concessions from aircraft manufacturers and leasing companies using the provisions of bankruptcy laws. The cost reduction lever for legacy carriers also has limited value in future (at least in the areas relating to labor and aircraft costs) if airlines are not willing to change their thinking. A typical mode of operation is to continue to operate in the same way, and to try to find more efficient ways of doing the same thing, rather than trying to do something different. Once again, there is plenty of pulling power in the cost lever if airlines are willing to work seriously in the collaborative mode with partners, not just distributors as shown in Figure 1.2, but also other airlines, vendors, and so forth.

Although many airlines have given mergers and acquisitions as one rationale for reducing costs, some analysts have questioned the use of such initiatives to reduce costs. One can examine such cases as USAirways and America West, before and after the merger. One major reason for their lack of success relates to the fact that merger decisions did not thoroughly address the integration of organizational cultures. Next, alliances were quoted as a rationale for cost reductions. Again, history shows that while some cost benefits have been achieved, they have been limited by the poor quality of implementation and integration, at least from the viewpoint of cost reductions. However, compared to the previous two levers, this lever has the most potential pulling power (for both cost reductions and revenue improvements) if, and only if, the implementation and integration processes can be improved in a step form, with focus on culture and brand.

The productivity improvement lever has been used by a number of legacy airlines, in some cases, by copying the concepts implemented by low-cost airlines in areas relating to optimization of fleet utilization, staff productivity, and check-in processes. More recent examples of productivity improvement include "de-peaking" of operations at major hubs, moving lower yield traffic to secondary hubs, consolidation of call centers, and introduction of Internet-based self-service systems and processes. As with previously discussed levers, this lever has declining effectiveness left due to the limitations of the degree of flexibility in its current operational context. Consider, for example, an airline that operates multiple hubs some of which compete with each other, so, the airline faces competition not just from competitors, but also within its own operations. Similarly, in alliances some airlines are much more aggressive competitors than they are partners.

The last example of strategy levers is related to outsourcing and the sale of assets. Examples of areas where functions have been outsourced by airlines include heavy maintenance and information technology. Further leverage of this lever is limited in its current mode of operation due mostly to objections of labor. However, under different organizational structures and governance, at the expense of being repetitive, this lever still has a lot of pulling power. Just think of the organizational structure of Li & Fung's business model described in Chapter 2.

While the implementation of the aforementioned levers in the past 15–20 years did provide airlines with various amounts of benefits, additional benefits from these levers are limited in their current form. The airline industry has pushed the potential benefits to a maximum without changing the organizational structure, for example, within the context of alliances. Further wage reductions, for instance, seem to be doubtful as some legacy carriers are beginning to pay less than some low-cost carriers. Now, only regional airlines in developed regions and other airlines based in developing regions seem to have a labor cost advantage.

The last two chapters described some examples of new challenges that airlines are likely to face in the coming years including more demanding passengers and more formidable competitors, just to name two. These challenges, as well as new opportunities, call for a review of ways to extract more pulling power out of existing levers, and to complement them with additional, effective levers to facilitate adaptation to the expected volatility.

## Optimizing the Current Business Model

*Align the Airline Organizational Structure*

The first chapter presented some observations and impact of the lack of alignment in various functions within a typical airline organization. This section provides specific examples of three areas of alignment within an airline organization that would provide enormous benefits in terms of a step increase in productivity through integration.

First, at a typical airline, optimization is performed at the functional level. For example, the crew-scheduling group acquires a more sophisticated way of scheduling crews that saves crew costs. However, the new crew-scheduling system may increase delays for customers, leading to a defection of a significant percentage of premium-paying passengers. Similarly, the finance department may implement an increase in the fee for making changes to reservations. Again, some premium-paying passengers may defect. What is required instead is an optimization on a systems basis or a balanced approach—balancing revenue, costs, reliability, passenger service, growth, competitive advantage, and so forth. This requirement means changing the ways costs, revenue, and customer service are managed. Such an organizational change may lead to the elimination of functional budgets, require much greater focus on overall profitability, and, of course, the optimization should be continuous in as real time as possible.

The second area relating to the alignment of airline organizational structures should aim to increase flexibility with respect to resources, aircraft, crews, facilities to deal with a broad spectrum of future scenarios. This requirement would enable an airline to expand or contract the network, for instance, by being able to move assets at a short notice. Flexibility also means the availability of capability to optimize profitability not only on a continuous basis, but also right up until the day of execution. From a technology point of view, the flexibility requirement calls for information, such as passenger demand in terms of bookings and fares, in real time as well as technology capability that enables timely (compressed cycle time) redesign of a product, exemplified by the following:

- introduction of a new class of service;

- use of a new distribution channel;

- introduction of an additional bucket in revenue management;

- introduction of code-shared flights with a new partner;

- improvement in the integrity of revenue (by eliminating revenue leakage, for example).

Lack of flexibility in current airline organizations is the result of misalignment in many areas of an airline's organization. However, the major cause is that most functions within an airline use IT systems based on different platforms. A common IT platform (such as jetEngine™ O/S developed by Airline Intelligence Systems Inc.) would offer a much higher planning capability as illustrated by the following situations.

- It would facilitate optimizations on a systems basis (mentioned above). The impact of a strategic initiative in one area would be seen in all other areas before the initiative is implemented. Moreover, the compression in cycle times would allow management to evaluate different versions of an initiative in almost real time. For example, an airline could evaluate very quickly (and on a systems basis) the impact of a decision to enable a passenger to re-book for a charge. Suppose an airline does not charge for re-booking, and this feature attracts a lot of business passengers who need to change their plans often. Initiating a re-booking charge may generate money but may also cause some business passengers to defect and choose a competitor who has better schedules.

- It would improve the dynamic packaging capability, especially the functionality relating to the up-sell component. For example, the capability to simply add-on features or products is not sufficient. There must be a capability to "create" an up-sell structure for an airline's basic fare (such as, the nesting type of structures for sub-packages).

There are many other opportunities relating to dynamic packaging mentioned in the second bullet. It would be helpful to keep the customer on your website instead of simply transferring the customer to the website of a partner (hotel, car rental, and so forth). It is not convenient for the customer to visit many websites let alone use the credit card multiple times to pay for different components of the package. This requirement calls for agreements to be in place with partners not only on an airline's ability to make reservations for partners' products through its own reservation system, but also having in place sales agreements with the partners. Consequently, Web design, branding, and maintenance would require input from many departments for an overall alignment. The objective is (1) to make it easier for the customer to make a purchase, (2) to make the customer feel that she has purchased a "customized" product, and (3) generate additional revenue for the airline.

The third area of alignment relates to an airline's schedule, the heart of its business. Assuming the rationality of this statement, it should be reasonable to assume that the scheduling function (process and systems) should be the most important value driver within an airline organization. In this framework, it would appear that all key planning functions relating to the schedule should be combined—the scheduling of aircraft, crews, maintenance, ground facilities, manpower, and the decision on operational metrics such as block times. The objective should be to optimize the profit-generating capabilities (the schedule) of an airline by creating the lowest total costs, the highest revenue, and the most cost-effective reliability.

In light of its centrality, the combined scheduling function should report directly to the President. The combination of the key planning functions relating to the schedule will lead to a balanced design where input from all the groups can be factored in at earlier stages of schedule planning, leading to a much more effective level of integration. It is this lack of integration that has lead some airlines to acquire the wrong fleet, expand or contract the network in inconsistent directions, join the less effective alliance partnerships, and introduce either a wrong product and/or one introduced at a poor time. Also, airlines often lost precious time to recover in cases of sudden market or operational disruptions.

In such a framework of schedule planning, groups responsible for network and marketing would not be part of the scheduling planning group even though they provide vital input to the scheduling group (markets served, frequency, time of day for departures and arrivals, and so forth). These two groups would focus, instead, on the identification and exploration, on a continuous basis, of future scenarios of the type discussed in the last chapter that create value or lead to changes in the marketplace. Examples include the entrance of totally new competitors (conventional, Gulf-based airlines, for example, or unconventional airlines, such as air taxis using very light jets), or different types of internal and external risks and opportunities. Consider, for a moment, the potential implications of the trends in social technology discussed in the next chapter.

An example of another area of corporate alignment is the creation of a framework that allows optimization on a systems or balanced basis versus divisional or functional basis. Take, for example, the case when an airline decides to optimize a function based on one criterion only. The marching order from the CEO of one airline might be to reduce costs per available seat mile (CASM) to, say 10 cents, or for a different airline to increase passenger revenue per available seat mile (PRASM) to, say 11 cents, or for a third airline to improve operational performance (on-time departures) by getting down to 14 minutes of the published arrival times. Such optimizations based on the performance of an individual criterion have been the cause of many problems at a number of global airlines. In one case the dramatic reduction in CASM lead to a dramatic reduction in customer service and the loss of a substantial percentage of the premium fare-paying segment. In another case, the pressure to achieve the number one status in terms of on-time performance raised costs to unacceptable levels from the perspective of costs and benefits. In a third case, the pressure to increase PRASM lead to an increase in distribution costs and costs of customer service, both totally out of line with the increase in PRASM.

If an airline is serious about improving its cost structure, productivity and passenger experience, the key is to align the airline organization internally and externally. The type of alignment discussed can only be achieved with the commitment of the leadership from the very top. This requirement is necessary because, from a strategic point of view, there must be alignment between the brand and business strategy, between business strategy and technology strategy, and, even more importantly, between corporate capability and technology strategy. At the functional level, there must be alignment between business processes and customer interfaces and behavior. In the final analysis, an aligned airline organizational structure along the lines discussed will lead to flexibility through compressed cycle times for developing and introducing products as well as implementing competitive moves and timings to make faster and smarter decisions.

*Optimize the Complexity-Simplicity Dimensions*

In recent years, a lot of discussion in the airline industry has centered on reducing complexity to save costs. While at first this concept appears to have a tremendous appeal, there are other considerations.

- An airline's business is quite complex to begin with, particularly for airlines with global networks, serving a wide array of customers, and working with an equally broad spectrum of competitors, alliance partners, suppliers, distributors, and government agencies. In addition, there are major uncertainties relating to, for example, the price of oil, climate change, terrorism, and animal diseases. These uncertainties call for flexibility that, in turn, leads to complexity. At a much more tactical level, consider, for instance, the complexity relating to revenue integrity. Legacy airlines obviously feel the need to reduce revenue leakage. While booking and paying for a ticket online is a straight-forward transaction with little room for revenue leakage, selling through agents and offering special fares and premium fares that do not require immediate payment represent another story. Then there are airlines who must find different ways for accepting payments for reservations made in second- and third-tier markets in developing regions. This situation is particularly important in remote, emerging markets where people still want to deal with "people" and not the Internet or even kiosks. In some cases, people do not even want to deal with call centers. They really want to communicate with people from whom they are buying a ticket. Dealing with such strategic and tactical situations adds complexity.

- The travel process itself is extremely complex. There are multiple customer touch points, some initiated by or under the control of a customer and some initiated by or under the control of an airline. There is a need to adapt to continuously changing technology, such as wireless and the Internet. Adapting legacy systems to accommodate to the contemporary needs of airlines and their customers has added to the complexity. Furthermore, while all airlines have a broad spectrum of IT systems (in some cases, the best of the breed) for individual functions, the disparate IT systems produce feasible solutions, not optimal solutions.

- According to the trends discussed in Chapter 2, there are segments of customers who want for product features such as the availability of price-service options, customization and personalization, transparency relating to fares and operations, customer control, product differentiation, and self-service. While some see airline pricing becoming less complex, others see it becoming much more complex. Just think about pricing policies in the context of un-bundling (*à la carte* pricing) and then re-bundling, capability to show comparison prices on the Web, monitoring and adapting to the input from travel search engines (for example, Kayak and Sidestep), and online marketing such as "blogvertising," "podvertising" and "chatroomvertising."

- Airlines initially developed their own websites with the clear advantage of lower distribution costs and with focus on their own product with respect to the basic aspect, namely reliable information relating to the availability of the product and selling their own inventory. Now they are beginning to look at other aspects, such as real-time information, differentiation based on experience, branding, and loyalty, all important for the sale of upscale products such as premium travel.

Consequently, a certain amount of complexity is to be expected, depending on the current and future network and customer base of an airline. There is nothing inherently wrong with complexity if it adds value for the targeted customer base and the targeted customer base is willing to pay for such complexity. While the goal normally is to reduce complexity, it could be that it is the added complexity that might give a full-service airline a competitive edge over a low-cost, low-fare airline that is working with less complex systems that are likely to be less capable of providing an integrated and customized product/service with respect to, for example, the choice of the use of distribution channel.

While the use of a relatively simple website certainly reduces distribution costs and may bring the airline closer to a customer, it is also necessary to consider the sale of upscale products and the provision of a better shopping experience through customization and personalization to increase loyalty. With the average revenue per seat going down, the interest in ancillary revenue is increasing significantly to increase the revenue per flight, for example, through dynamic packaging. Then, there are airlines that are relying heavily on connecting traffic that can perhaps come more easily through traditional channels in certain regions.

On the other hand, companies such as ALDI, Dell, Toyota, Wal-Mart and Southwest Airlines have been successful due in part to that each was able to manage the complexity factor within its own business. Specifically, they have avoided the trap of "uncontrolled proliferation" that is a common downfall in business today. A common myth is that adding products and services will instantly boost sales, but there is a real cost to this increase in complexity if not managed. The effects of technology and globalization have increased the number of choices, and therefore further increased the complexity issue. Experience has shown that complexity is one of the largest detrimental factors to profits. Specifically, Michael George and Stephen Wilson, authors of *Conquering Complexity in Your Business*, state that "portfolio and process complexity is often a larger drag on profits and growth than any other single factor in a business." They note that complexity has been called "the silent killer," and the best remedy is prevention. [2] According to George and Wilson, there are three key rules of complexity:

1. Eliminate complexity that customers will not pay for
   *Example: Southwest Airlines*—The carrier recognized that its customer segment would not pay for any of the typical costs of complexity that are usually a part of the airline business. Specifically, it only operates one type of aircraft, the Boeing 737. Thus, unlike other airlines, it saves on costs such as supporting and maintaining training for mechanics and pilots for several lines of aircrafts, multiple FAA certifications, and scheduling.

2. Exploit the complexity customers will pay for
   *Example: Capital One*—The credit card company recognized that the credit card business had little to no complexity, as there was just one offering at a fixed percentage rate regardless of the consumer's credit. Thus, Capital One saw an opportunity for a differentiated offering, and actually added complexity by offering more options than its competitors. However, they were able to do so as they kept the cost of complexity low due to smart investments in information technology, product design, and testing. While Capital One's competitors caught on to this strategy, it took them almost five years to do so.

3. Minimize the costs of the complexity you offer

*Example: Toyota*—Early on, the car manufacturer implemented the complexity reduction strategy of standardization in order to eliminate waste in the company's internal products and processes. It conducted this strategy through the entire cycle—from product development to sales. This strategy allowed Toyota the ability to focus on external needs— producing variants to meet customer needs. Toyota has been careful not to eliminate complexity at the expense of the customer's desire for quality and variety. Toyota's complexity and associated cost have been far less than that of Ford or General Motors. In addition, Toyota's shares have held steady, while those of Ford and GM have lost significant value.

As mentioned above and in Chapter 6, complexity can also have an impact on branding. It can dilute and even erode the brand. Specifically, an unmanaged proliferation of products and services causes confusion in the mind of the customer. It challenges the brand drivers discussed in Chapter 6, especially the consistency driver, as to how can a company manage the consistency of its brands over such a great many offerings? As John Mariotti, author of *The Complexity Crisis*, notes that even the greatest brands can struggle with the challenge of complexity. He sites the example of Hilton Hotels which, like so many hotel chains these days, has multiple unrelated offerings under its umbrella—Hampton Inn, Embassy Suites, even the Waldorf-Astoria. Consumers may be unaware that these offerings are part of the Hilton brand, and as Mariotti states, the hidden connection with Hilton does little good and may actually dilute the brand, with the exception of the Waldorf-Astoria. Even so, consumers may be unaware of the Waldorf-Astoria's ties to the Hilton brand. His point being that the brand has an identity and image that is connected with it, and the thinner it gets as it is spread due to complexity, the less meaning the brand has, especially in the eyes of the consumer. He summarizes this problem in stating, "When complexity strikes, it can damage or kill a brand."[3]

In the final analysis, the issue is not whether or not complexity is needed, but what is the least amount needed to profit from the selected business model. And a certain amount of complexity is needed if an airline is to move away from a culture of selling volume at any price to practicing the true art and science of pricing and marketing.

*Implement Analytically Driven Strategies*

Airlines have lots of information available to them. What is missing is the ability to exploit it for competitive advantage. The traditional areas of competitive advantage are eroding rapidly. Products and services are similar. Innovation is becoming increasingly difficult and expensive and non-sustainable for long. Now, with the relaxation of regulatory control (for example, the recent EU-US agreement), another area of competitive advantage is evaporating. This situation is leading to a conclusion that it is not just information, but information-driven and analytically based strategies that will differentiate the winners from the losers. Consequently, and perhaps, the most important lever to deal with the expected "step-phase changes" is the development and implementation of analytically based strategies.[4] Specifically, systems are needed to:

- monitor what is happening as it is happening;

- understand not just what happened, but why it happened;

- anticipate what could happen.

Technology is becoming available to quantify, in virtually real time, how profitable a flight or a new market is individually and in the context of a portfolio, how a customer segmentation strategy is working, how a loyalty program is working, how customer experience is changing (positively or negatively), or how an airline is doing with high margin passengers. It is possible to measure the costs and benefits of self-service systems and processes, profitability of products marketed through alliance partnerships, and the costs and benefits of Web crawlers. Moreover, technology is even available to make sense of unstructured data. For example, it is now possible to have a system that reads all the e-mails from passengers, find key threads, and present the results in actionable forms.

Systems are also available to present the information in a "visual" format so that it is easily understood and prioritized for actions. For example, what would be the impact of a late inbound flight? There will be a color-coded "visualization" of the impacts on aircraft, crews, passengers, facilities, manpower, and so forth. When disruptions occur, as they often do in the airline industry, management needs not only all kinds of information (on passengers, aircraft, crews, and baggage), but also it needs that information in real time and all at one place. Unfortunately, there are airlines that have neither the capability of real-time information nor information that is integrated due to the existence of numerous islands of data, not to mention the lack of analytics.

Even more important, while an entire airline would need actionable information, the front line needs high performance access to the integrated and real time data more than the back office since the front line operational staff make decisions that may be small and tactical but they impact passengers directly. Consequently, most of the current systems result in poor decisions and poor actions in situations that really make a difference— decisions involving re-accommodation of passengers, swapping of aircraft and crews, cancellation of flights, and so forth. Even the back office has used the information in the passive mode— for generating bookkeeping types of reports on key performance indicators, history of sales, inventory, cash flows, and so forth, instead of executing strategy in real time relating to proactive event management.

Monitoring what is happening, as it is happening, is one phase of the analytically based strategies. Understanding why something happened is a second component. This understanding requires not only integrated data from the entire company but also the capability to drill down to the lowest granular level. Why is the yield lower for reservations coming through the Web? Why did some passengers defect? Why is there a difference in maintenance for similar airplanes operating in the same market? Why is a passenger booking the very lowest air fare yet making hotel and car rental reservations in much higher categories? Here are two more examples of the need to data mine in the data bank.

Direct distribution capability is a concern of some airlines that are based in regions where customers' access to the Internet is limited. However, one must treat this statement with caution. Just because only a small percentage of the general public has access to the Internet, a much higher percentage of the population that flies may have access to the Internet. Think of a developing country that may have only a third of its population that has access to the Internet. But, 80 percent of people who travel may have access to the Internet and the number may be 95 percent frequent flyers based in that country.

The second example relates to the use of the Web for direct distribution. Some airline executives question whether they are simply trading off the money saved through the use of the Web for simply offering more discounts for having passengers book through the Web? So, is the problem related to distribution strategy or Web functionality? Again, there is a need to drill down in the costs information relating to distribution. What are the *total costs* of direct distribution?

- Costs of dedicated Web customer e-mail/telephone support?

- Costs of website content management (including developing dynamic packaging)?

- Costs of functionality management (support/upgrade of booking engines for fare quotes in foreign currencies, contents offered in native languages, local payment considerations, including taxes)?

- Costs of third party Web support (requiring the use of specific Web devices that are not supported in house, for example, in wireless areas)?

- Potential costs of concerns about the privacy/security issues relating to online information (transmission as well as in airline databases)?

- Potential costs of the Internet making the airline business even more of a commodity business?

- Costs associated with differentiating the services of an airline for customers coming in via the Internet channel?

- Costs of less sophisticated pricing systems, as fares have to be understood by customers and not just by well-trained agents?

Anticipating what can happen is the third component of analytically based decisions. Business surprises can be minimized. If an airline can know the likelihood of misconnects before that happens, it should also be able to predict situations where a customer will defect before the defection takes place, assuming that the airline has "business intelligence." Business intelligence, in turn, comes from data and the analytics to enable the airline to translate the data into actions. Consequently, why develop tight connections through congested airports? Why schedule a regional jet aircraft with limited payload capacity in a market where the majority of passengers will be making connections to international flights and will have heavy bags? Why add insult to injury by actually charging a passenger excess baggage fees for bags that will most likely be off-loaded due to payload restrictions? Why place passengers who are at the point of defection in such situations?

Take the case of understanding why the conversion rate (look to booking ratio) is low. It requires knowledge of the quality of the search engine relating to the presentation of comprehensive content, and the ease to make search. Second, how much transparency is being delivered. Third, how easy is it for "lookers" to find information, make a booking, and process the transaction based on individual needs. For example, some passengers may not want to use their credit cards to pay online. Are there other ways to make that payment? Online credit-card security is becoming a serious issue in some developing regions. Is there the right type and amount of offline communications that will persuade potential customers to go online?

Technology is now emerging that can help airlines with predictive analyses. For example, technology can provide access to passenger preference models that can be used to optimize revenue. Historically, the objective was simply to forecast demand in each fare bucket with the further objective to keep in inventory a certain number of seats available for premium fare passengers who might be looking for reservations much closer to the flight date. Now the objective can be not only to try to "estimate" the demand curve, but also to find an optimal point on the demand curve. Consequently, information technology can now enable an executive to quantitatively analyze and predict the desirability of any flight. How much more would a passenger pay if the flight was nonstop, or for an aisle seat, or for a flight on a mainline jet versus a regional aircraft, and what if the flight was nonstop in a thin market, but on a regional aircraft? For real competitive advantage, it is the airline that can set fares knowing the demand much more comprehensively—for example, establishing a different price based on the value and the loyalty of the customer. Yet, unlike many other industries, it is difficult to quantify passenger reaction before rolling out a new fare or a marketing campaign or promotion.

## Conceiving, Evaluating, and Implementing New Business Models

Depending on the breadth, depth, speed, and the degree of confluences of the forces discussed will determine the degree of revitalization of the current airline business models. Think about the Apple Company for a minute. Apple not only transformed the company, but to some extent also transformed the entire music industry. Likewise, Whole Foods entered the food business and turned itself into a supermarket empire.[5] Breakthrough strategies like these require foresight to develop insight as well as the leadership to think and implement bold ideas. In the case of airlines, it is not that some senior management are incapable of thinking bold strategies. Some are simply not willing to discard the accepted day-to-day management and think in a counterintuitive or upside down way. Some are just not willing to take the risk because of the ambiguity related to the emerging marketplace. Some are not convinced that in this industry it is possible to separate yourself from competitors to a degree to create your own market space.

In spite of this reluctance, managements may be forced to turn traditional airline business practices upside down and conceive new business models to compete successfully in the "flattening" world. Such an initiative implies leaving behind conventional thinking and making counterintuitive decisions. It implies acting boldly instead of incrementally. It implies benchmarking less within the airline industry and much more outside the airline industry. Examine the 20 case studies provided in Chapter 7 to see how other leaders transformed their companies, Apple, Cemex, Nokia, and Samsung, for example. It means listening to not only employees but also customers and other members within the value chain. It means moving the innovation concept from buzzword to become core competency, not just for one time, but on a continuous basis. This initiative requires a pragmatic, disciplined, and systematic approach that includes (a) the creation of an appropriate cultural environment, and (b) the minimization of risk. The key would be to integrate innovation and airline business strategy to create new value in the upcoming marketplace.

There are examples of a few airlines that have been, and are, on such a track. Lufthansa is one good example of an airline that (a) has not always stuck to conventional wisdom, and (b) tried to develop some foresight based on continuous and serious analyses of changes in the marketplace. Consider the following initiatives taken by Lufthansa management going back to the 1980s:

- It operated a special Lufthansa feeder train from Düsseldorf/ Cologne to Frankfurt, later replaced by "blocked seats" on regular high speed trains into Frankfurt.

- It operated almost 3 dozen aircraft in Condor's charter network during the weekends, where, presumably, yields were higher than the scheduled network.

- It was one of the earliest recognizer of the potential opportunities in China: established Jade Cargo, a Lufthansa

Cargo/Chinese joint venture out of Shenzen; in conjunction with the start of China operations, established a German Center together with a Kempinski Hotel, a business center, and a beer garten in Beijing; established a Lufthansa Technik/ Air China joint venture for the overhaul of large aircraft.

- It started a "classic" low-cost subsidiary (GermanWings) that operates as a true low-cost operator (different staff, a different hub, no frequent flyer program integration, and so forth)

- It was the first operator of in-flight broadband Internet access (Connexion by Boeing, now replaced by a new consortium).

- It successfully integrated (at arm's length) the operations of Swiss (similar to the experience of Air France and KLM).

- It established a joint venture between Lufthansa Cargo and DHL for a Boeing 777F operation out of Leipzig (DHL's new European hub).

- It acquired shares in jetBlue, partially to develop "hybrid" connecting traffic at JFK in New York.

All of the above initiatives are not exclusive to Lufthansa. For example, a number of network airlines, in the US and in Europe, started low-cost subsidiaries. Almost all did not survive. Lufthansa has been an exception, due, in part to a more disciplined approach. Now, some other network airlines are developing their own "branded" low-cost subsidiaries using a disciplined approach. Examples include Singapore's Tiger and Qantas' Jetstar.

**Takeaways**

- The strategy levers used in the past to deal with the changing environment are no longer sufficient, in their current form, to deal with even the current environment airlines must optimize their current business models by

(1) improving dramatically the alignment in their organizational structures, (2) managing complexity, and (3) developing and implementing analytically based strategies. Technology, often viewed as a constraint, must be viewed as an enabler, as a differentiator, and possibly even a driver of future airline business strategy.

- To deal with the expected "step-phase changes" in the airline marketplace, airlines must conceive new business models. They must do this by (1) benchmarking less within the airline industry and much more outside the airline industry, and (2) moving the innovation concept from buzzword to become core airline competency.

## Notes

1   For a more thorough description of strategies to manage through business cycles, the reader is referred to a book by Peter Navarro, *The Well-Timed Strategy: Managing the Business Cycle for Competitive Advantage* (Upper Saddle River, NJ: Wharton School Publishing, 2006).

2   George, Michael, L. and Stephen A. Wilson, *Conquering Complexity in Your Business: How Wal-Mart, Toyota, and Other Top Companies Are Breaking Through the Ceiling on Profits and Growth* (NY: McGraw-Hill, 2004).

3   Mariotti, John, *The Complexity Crisis: Why Too Many Products, Markets, and Customers Are Crippling Your Company — And What To Do About It* (Avon, MA: Platinum Press, 2008) pp. 7, 13, 39–40.

4   A good reference for developing the capability to compete on analytics is a book by Thomas H. Davenport and Jeanne G. Harris, *Competing on Analytics: The New Science of Winning* (Boston, MA: Harvard Business School Press, 2007).

5   Schmitt, Bernd, H., *Big Think Strategy: How to Leverage Bold Ideas and Leave Small Thinking Behind* (Boston, MA: Harvard Business School Press, 2007), front jacket.

# Chapter 5

# Social Networking Phenomena

Based on the developments in the past few years it appears that the world could be transformed by the explosion of the social networking phenomena. The social Web started with people using search engines, followed by blogs, and then collaboration among users. With the evolution, companies must now adjust the way they conduct business to appropriately and effectively address customers in this new arena. Some businesses are viewing this (the force of customers) as a threat while others are viewing it as an opportunity. This chapter begins with a brief overview of the Web evolution and its implications for businesses, including airlines. The second part of the chapter provides a brief introduction to social networks, some examples of businesses that have used the power of online communities to their own advantage, and a glimpse into how airlines can transform themselves by proactively riding the social technology wave.

## Web Evolution

*Web Phases*

Sramana Mitra, a strategy consultant in Silicon Valley, provides definitions of different phases of the Web in terms of what she refers to as "the 4 C's" — *Commerce, Community, Content,* and *Context:*[1]

- Web 1.0[2] — *Commerce* had been the driving force that produced companies such as Amazon, eBAY, and Netflix.

- Web 2.0 — *Community* then became the greatest force, producing social networking websites such as Facebook, LinkedIn, MySpace, Wikipedia, and YouTube.

- Web 3.0—*Content* and *Context* will be the next focus, in addition to the original C's of commerce and community. It will be about personalization and vertical search.

To put the Web 3.0 framework in perspective, the content of the first part of this chapter is divided into four sections—Mitra's ratings of a few online travel industry sites (to show the use of her framework within the aviation community), a section on personalization, a section on digital and mobile concierges, followed by a section on Web branding.

In her evaluation of online travel sites, Mitra notes that the "context" element is poor on these sites, because while the sites let one choose between flights, hotels, car rentals, cruises, vacation packages, maps, hotel and destination reviews, trip planning, and so forth, they, for the most part, have not honed in on the more complex contexts such as student travel, luxury travel, adventure travel, romantic travel, etcetera. However, Mitra does indicate that the offerings on these sites in terms of "content" are quite good. She calls for a "vertical search" that allows users to "search by context." For example, a student may wish to search for hostels for other backpackers like this particular student, as well as other travelers to be around within a given location. She also thinks that the "personalization" element is "sub-par" in most of these sites, indicating a true opportunity for the online travel industry. Following are three specific examples of online travel sites rated by Mitra using her criteria:[3]

- Expedia

  — good contextual offerings such as Adventure, Romance, Beach, Family, Luxury, Golf & Spa themes; however, other contextual offerings such as Student Travel should be considered

  — good in terms of content, especially the ability to narrow choices down by amenities, although Mitra notes that the range of amenities and hotel classes covered could be a great deal more comprehensive

- — vertical search needs some work—Mitra thinks that it does not deliver what it promises

- — offers very little "true" personalization

- Orbitz

  - — good contextual offerings such as Family, Beach, Luxury, Golf, Gay/Lesbian, Racing, Romance, Sports, etcetera, as well as good contextual navigation for students; however, other contextual offerings could be enhanced such as Business Travel

  - — good content, although Mitra suggests that adding a "local secrets" content would enhance the site

  - — vertical search abilities are good and are "user friendly"

  - — in terms of personalization, Mitra notes that Orbitz is the first and only travel site with a team of experts that monitors nationwide travel conditions for passengers, offering "real-time" information to travelers

- Travelocity

  - — context is still limited to the conventional business and pleasure segments

  - — content is good—the site is "rich" in terms of content

  - — vertical search needs to be enhanced

  - — personalization—is basic (allows users to receive low-fare alerts, share pictures, etcetera)—this element is a definite source of opportunity

*Personalization*

Personalization plays an important role in Mitra's conceptualization of Web 3.0. Amadeus agrees with the idea that passengers want personalized service and adds further that the right technology can deliver "an engaging, human-centric interface with customers," responding to passengers' individual travel needs. Specifically, Amadeus identifies four areas of technology relating to the "human-centric focus."[4]

1. detailed personal passenger information held digitally (making access comparatively fast and easy) to enable the delivery of personalized service, for example, simple check-in and security processes and procedures

2. integrated information systems so that information combined from different sources becomes available at different touch points and through multiple channels

3. real-time information delivered to individuals based on need and location—for example, contacting a passenger via her mobile device if her luggage is going to be delayed to avoid her from waiting for an hour searching for her bags at the carousel

4. increased customer interaction through social computing to provide passengers with visual information—for example, simulations from gaming/virtual reality technologies that can enable passengers to experience certain aspects of the travel process or some cultural aspects of a passenger's destination

Another advantage of personalization is the ability of a business to capture ultra small segments of the customer base. As most retailers know, one downside to retail business is that there is not enough physical space to carry everything for everyone, whether it is CDs, DVDs, or movies offered in a theater. In a sense, the world of retail represents a world of scarcity. However, the new online business world changes that scenario drastically.

Specifically, online distribution represents a world of abundance. In the traditional "brick-and-mortar" retail world where shelf space is at a premium, stores tend to carry generally the "hit" items to maximize profits on the items sold. The cost of carrying inventory in the online world is so much less, that businesses can afford to expand their offerings exponentially, enabling them to include the "non-hit" or "niche" items as well.

This shift in focus between the "hit-driven" culture verses all offerings (a way of capitalizing on the personalization) represents the long-tail theory, as described by author Chris Anderson in his book, *The Long Tail*. Specifically, according to Anderson, the left-hand side of the (distribution) curve represents the "hit-driven" culture that companies focus upon in terms of capturing sales. However, he argues, that if one focuses upon the right-hand side, one will notice that the line is not quite at zero, and that demand actually exists in this area. While individual sales in these areas are small, they can add up, resulting in a significant amount of business. Anderson concludes that as fast as a company adds inventory, those products find an audience, even if it is just a handful of people every month, somewhere in the world, and this is the long tail. The long tail represents incredible potential opportunities for businesses and therefore companies can leverage this strategy.

One example of the long-tail effect is the business model of Blockbuster verses Netflix. Historically, Blockbuster has reported that approximately 90 percent of the movies they rent in their stores are classified as "new" releases. However, Netflix' online service only rents about 30 percent "new" releases, while the other 70 percent of rentals represents what they refer to as "back catalog." This difference can be attributed to Netflix's strategy of creating demand for content. Netflix is able to implement this strategy through recommendations and ratings. Recommendations are very powerful, according to Anderson, because "recommendations have all the demand-generation power of advertising, but at virtually no cost." Furthermore, recommendations based upon knowledge of a customer's likes and dislikes as well as other customers' opinions are a far more personalized form of advertising than a generic billboard. Netflix's business model is quite unique because, in an industry where advertising and marketing often represent approximately one half of the cost of a "hit" film, the company "levels the playing field" by offering essentially free advertising through its recommendation system to all movies, including small films that would otherwise not be able to afford it.[5] In the airline industry, this concept could be explored to capture small segments of the demand that could be transported to the hub in non-conventional ways. Lufthansa experimented with such a system when it introduced personal jet service for first class passengers coming from small communities to make connections on Lufthansa's long-haul flights.

*Digital Concierges*

Passengers are interested in (a) a single point of contact, with choice, and (b) control over their decisions. Integrated technology systems and information can provide a single point of contact (a telephone, an agent in a call center or behind the check-in counter). Choice can be provided through mobile systems, a mobile phone or the Web, or the Web using a mobile phone. And control can be provided through self-service systems and customer-service programs. With respect to self-service systems as a way to provide control to customer, businesses must exercise great care. On the one hand, self-service customer-service programs would appear to be an efficient way to conduct business and to yield a cost savings in terms of reduced labor wages. On the other hand, a debate has also started as to whether customers view them as a way for a business to push work onto the customer. The key, of course, is for businesses to learn about when to serve a customer and when to let the customer serve herself.

Following are some examples of self-service technologies as noted by Barbara Kiviat in her article in *Time Magazine*:

- British Retailer Tesco has opened up dozens of its Fresh & Easy grocery stores in the US where all lanes are self-checkout (see Chapter 7 for more on Tesco).

- Also in Britain, NCR is trying out machines that let customers not only buy merchandise on their own, but also return it.

- In Malaysia, IBM has outfitted a chain of sushi restaurants with ordering screens linked directly to the kitchen.

- In the US, the Heritage Valley Health System in Pennsylvania will soon join the ranks of hospitals using check-in kiosks for emergency room visits—patients simply touch the image of the human body where it hurts.

- Alaska Airlines is finishing building its "Airport of the Future" in Seattle, where there are no ticket counters—only islands of self-check-in kiosks.[6]

There is no question that in some cases customers want to do the work—if it means that customers can be more in control of their experience, such as in the travel industry. Specifically, according to an article in the March 2008 issue of *Air Transport World*, a recent IATA survey indicated that "passengers not only expect but demand more opportunities to take control of their travel experience." In addition to e-tickets, Internet check-in, and self-service kiosks, passengers are becoming increasingly dependent on their mobile devices—PDAs, mobile phones and laptops. Airlines are realizing that high-speed broadband will be the next "must have." This technology is being discussed to be implemented as an in-flight feature in 2009. The article also includes examples of the latest technology being implemented by some international carriers:

- Swedish carrier, SAS, has introduced a biometric system in which passengers can "register" their fingerprint when checking their luggage.

- Air France has implemented a pilot program in which a small card, called a "smartboarding personal card," contains biometric information that will allow the entire passenger processing system to be improved. Capturing the passenger's finger prints at check-in will allow a passenger to insert the card at other check points such as at the gate as a positive match is made based on the passenger's biometrics.

SAS recognizes that implementing the latest technology is one way to maintain their drive of providing "smooth and easy" flying. Air France recognizes that passengers are seeking more autonomy, and if the carrier is able to provide this autonomy, "it creates a loyalty to the brand."[7]

Michelle Bottomley of Ogilvy illustrated many opportunities for airlines to provide relevant value-added information to the passenger while utilizing self-service kiosks:

- Add relevant "nuggets" of information at the bottom of airline travel receipts such as top restaurants in the passenger's destination city. Ideas could come from field employees. Continental Airlines did this when field employees suggested restaurants to go to in Hong Kong.

- Offer renewals for airline club memberships at appropriate times during travel instead of sending it to a traveler's home mail with all the other bills, etcetera. For example, if a passenger is standing at a kiosk at the airport and finds out that her flight is going to be delayed, an airline could pop up a message right there and then to (a) offer a free visit to the club due to the inconvenience of the delayed flight in hopes that the traveler will be enticed to join the club, or (b) offer a reminder of membership renewal at a pertinent time—when the value of the membership is fresh in the mind of the passenger.

Bottomley goes further and stresses that the digital age is such an opportunity to connect with your customers. How are you going to reach them? Not by getting them to your website. It is by pushing your content out to them, that is, pushing your content out of your website to where the consumers are.[8] American Airlines has done just that—they have brought their airline travel content out to where the users are—to the social network site, Facebook, which has more than 67 million active users. American Airlines was the first major airline to have such an offering on the site. Specifically, American's offering on the Facebook site is called "Travel Bag," and has two facets. First, there is an arena for users to share travel experiences with friends in their network.

Second, there is a link to American's website so users may learn about the carrier's destinations, check fares, make reservations, etcetera, all through the user's own unique profile page. American understands that travelers like to share their stories, offer tips and comments on where to eat, go, shop, and generally let friends know what they are up to, and the carrier has provided the arena for them to do so. American has also successfully brought its content out to its users and captured a whole new potential market of consumers by doing so. American's Managing Director of Interactive Marketing states, "If you read or see something during a Facebook session that inspires you to travel, the start of your trip is just a click away, at AA.com."[9]

The importance of the digital age stressed by Michelle Bottomley of Ogilvy is also articulated well by Peter Yesawich, of the Y Partnership, who illustrates the evolution of the pursuit of reaching consumers through technology during his presentation at an international airline conference. Specifically, he states:

- the first screen was the television;

- the second screen was the computer screen;

- the third screen is the mobile phone/the mobile device.

These represent the evolution of the struggle for dominance by companies in terms of getting consumers' attention.[10]

Numerous companies have, or are in the process of, implementing programs utilizing mobile devices in order to enhance their customer's experience through personalization. The following are examples that cross a variety of industries:

- An article in *Inc. Magazine* notes that in 2006, Mobo Systems launched a pilot program with a number of local restaurant franchises in New York City, enabling a customer to place an order from a set menu of options by text message. The company would charge the buyer's credit card, including a 10 percent transaction fee from the restaurant. When the customer reaches the store, she can skip the line and pick up her order. A restaurant can simply sign up online. The company was even considering working with sports venues that could use the system to enable fans to order food and other concession items from their seats.[11]

- As per Paul Springer, the Cadbury "TXT'n'WIN" contest was one of the first to use mobile phones as an advertising channel. Specifically, during 2001, confectionery sales in the UK were flat compared to previous years, and therefore they were looking for new ways of revitalizing its market presence, at a time when the mobile phone market was taking off. Research indicated that the biggest spenders on confectionery products were female adults, who tended to buy for themselves and their family, and were also heavy users of mobile phones. Triangle Communications created a way of making the consumption of chocolate relevant to mobile phones by devising a contest in which all customers had to do was text the serial number from the bar's wrapper to a Cadbury free-phone hotline to see if they had won a prize. The contest was successful in making Cadbury more relevant by realigning its confectionery range with the activities of the younger consumer segment. Specifically, the digital medium enabled customer involvement, a direct advertising channel, real-time information, and convenience and ease for customer response.[12]

- Airlines are currently testing a program that would allow PDA users to wirelessly check their flight's standby list, eliminating the need to talk to a ticket counter agent.

*Web Branding*

The aforementioned evolution of the Web and the availability of advanced technologies are not sufficient unless an airline has an appealing brand (see the discussion in the next chapter) that is embedded in the airline's website. If a consumer has already had a personalized experience in other businesses, or even within an airline outside of its website, then the consumer will expect the same persona of the airline on its website. Consistency, as elaborated in the next chapter, is important across all customer service touch points, and that includes the company's website. However, in some cases, the website may be the first experience a passenger has with an airline, and, therefore, it is imperative to consider all aspects and attributes of the airline's website's design, especially the passenger's first impression of the airline brand, its homepage. How will a passenger (looking at a website of an airline) "see" the airline and the brand(s) it represents?

The "About Us" tab could contain, besides history and facts, some information on the airline's brand(s) to provide a passenger with some idea of "personalization." Specifically, this section is the perfect place to illustrate the personality of the brand (see Chapter 6 for more on this topic)—an opportunity to connect with the potential or current customer and really bring the brand to life, rather than just being another faceless company in the sea of options available to the consumer. For example, the Dyson vacuum brand has used its website's "About Us" section to feature the inventor of the product, James Dyson, himself, sharing all of his trials and tribulations, in terms of designs, patents, and so forth, that occurred in making his vision come to life. Furthermore, the "About Dyson" section also includes a subsection, called "What makes Dyson different," which highlights the five key attributes of the product, complete with pictures and the catchy slogan, "Only a Dyson delivers all five," thus clearly differentiating its offering from its competitors. As Rohit Bhargava states, the actual Dyson product, a bagless vacuum, was certainly a distinctive offering in itself, but Dyson found a "truly passionate following" through a series of advertisements in which Dyson himself talked about creating the perfect vacuum. The brand extended this strategy to the Web, thus aligning all elements of the brand.[13]

Disney is another excellent example of a company that has successfully transferred its brand to the Web. Specifically, the site is an excellent portrayal of the Disney environment. A visitor gets a good feel of the "Disney-esque artistry and lampoon-like tones" through Disney's homepage and the site navigational options.[14]

In terms of airlines, Southwest Airlines' website comes close in alignment with its brand. From the minute a user logs on and the homepage comes up, the characteristics of the brand are apparent. Specifically, the simple, straightforward, and fun image is conveyed on the Web, with "fun" pictures, large, bright-colored text, and simple categories to choose from the page, making it easy to navigate. The site even offers a direct link to the carrier's blog, "Nuts About Southwest," which sports an open bag of peanuts as its logo, that again, is in alignment with the brand's "fun" image. On the blog site, the airline reiterates its commitment to both its passengers and its employees, and encourages readers to "share that passion" by posting their own comments.[15]

Lufthansa Airline's website has two unique links that are in alignment with the Web 3.0 characteristics discussed earlier in this chapter, especially in terms of personalization and context. The first example on Lufthansa's homepage is a "quicklink" called "WeFlyHome." Within this link, Lufthansa addresses a specific customer segment—those living in US communities with "strong ties to their homeland." Specifically, the carrier is trying to reach out to this customer group by "bridging the gap by offering (them) exclusive fares from its 17 US gateways to bring them closer together." The airline offers specials to a myriad of "homelands"—from Croatia to Greece to the UAE, and adding even more countries in order to be able to offer the ability of this customer segment to visit family and friends. The second example on the carrier's homepage is another "quicklink" named "Student Discounts" which links potential passengers in this customer segment to the carrier's unique program, "GenerationFly—where students save big and travel far." Specifically, the website is set up so that a student's .edu school e-mail address is the "ticket" into the student travel site. In addition to special fares for those on a student budget, the carrier offers "GenFlyLounge," a social networking site established to:[16]

- network, meet and connect with other students who love to travel internationally;

- find out what other travelers such as yourself recommend, like or dislike about destinations;

- write share, read and rate travel tips and destinations.

Another aspect of branding on the Web to consider is the global factor, which is vital for global airlines. As Cocoran, a business writer, points out, the Web is a "global medium," and therefore will be visited by consumers across the world, not just those who live in the country where the company is headquartered. Consequently, airlines must address more effectively the issue of how cultural influences across countries shape the minds of visitors to an airline's website globally. Cocoran sites the Atlanta-based Coca-Cola as a good example of global website branding. Specifically, Coca-Cola has done an excellent job of being "glocal." It is truly a global company recognized literally all over the world, but it also successfully caters to individual localities as well. Its homepage provides access to up to 100 individual country-specific websites. Each of these country-specific sites is written in the country's language. However, it is not a literal translation of Coke's American website. Rather, Coke has developed "individually tailored Web propositions geared to each nation's cultural and idiosyncratic tastes."[17]

## Social Networks

### Community Websites

Here are brief descriptions of some of the more popular social technology websites. This list is certainly not meant to be all-inclusive, but rather a highlight of some key sites. The data for 2007 is available in Tom Hayes' book, *Jump Point*.[18]

- Facebook
    - originated from the paper "Facebooks" which contain pictures of incoming students;
    - links people through school, workplace, or residential region;
    - by 2007, had 28 million visitors per month.
- LinkedIn
    - a networking tool for business professionals which

allows users to seek jobs, seek candidates, and network across industries through the sites' system of "connections;"

— by 2007, had more than 3 million visitors per month.

- MySpace

  — similar to Facebook, a way to keep in touch with friends, share pictures, as well as blog;

  — by 2007, had more than 200 million accounts—If it were a country, it would rank fifth—above Russia and Japan.

- Wikipedia

  — an online encyclopedia written and edited by users;

  — a free service in which thousands of volunteers around the globe collaborate to create a constantly evolving encyclopedia;

  — as of 2007, the site included eight million articles in 253 languages.

- YouTube

  — a means of sharing video clips—users can upload, view, and share video clips;

  — by 2007, was sharing more than 100 million video clips per day.

Tom Hayes, author of *Jump Point*, views these larger and somewhat generic social communities as "starter" communities. He predicts that the social communities of the future will continue to evolve from these "prototypes" into communities that are more "passion-centric" and "theme-oriented" that will, in turn, be more "useful, manageable, and engaging" for users, according to Hayes. Some niche sites have already sprouted. Examples include eHow and ExpertVillage that appeal to "do-it-yourselfers," or Eons that is a social networking website for Baby Boomers over the age of 50. Global virtual communities are also popping up—sites such as Wealink in China which connects the local growing business community. According to Hayes, these niche sites will be the "true market spaces" of the future. Julie Wittes Schlack, vice president of innovation and research for *Communispace* concurs with this theory stating, "Big public communities may attract more eyeballs, but they may not be the answer for marketers who are looking for deep engagement with customers."[19]

In addition to such sites, Web 2.0 yielded another offering to users—a whole other virtual life, thus appropriately named, *Second Life*. Specifically, *Second Life* is a living, breathing site developed by Linden Lab where users are referred to as "Residents." Residents (of which there are two million)[20] are able to customize their surroundings and are able to interact with one another through "avatars," which represent the user's persona in the *Second Life* scenario. Specifically, *Second Life is* a sophisticated social network service in which users can explore, meet and socialize with other users, and participate in individual and group activities.[21]

The main idea behind *Second Life* is that users can be anyone they want to be, and can do anything they want to do. Unlike social networking sites, such as MySpace and YouTube that are for view and comment, *Second Life* is three-dimensional, creating an interactive experience.[22] *Second Life* appears to have business implications for companies. For example, *Second Life* can provide an opportunity for companies to be able to "test" new products and services, before entering them in the "real" marketplace. Clothiers can "sell" a "virtual" item of clothing in *Second Life*, thus providing a new outlet for advertising.[23] The Starwood Group has simulated one if its latest hotels in *Second Life*.[24] One can even test-drive a Pontiac in *Second Life*.[25] An airline could use this framework to enable a passenger to "test fly" its new business class seat in its ultra-long-haul markets. Denise Shiffman recognizes the potential of *Second Life* for companies in terms of marketing as companies are already launching and selling products, holding events, and having discussions with customers in this venue. She views it as a marketing vehicle to definitely watch in the future.[26]

*Business Opportunities*

The social Web is proving itself to be an effective channel through which users with a common interest can gather to share ideas and points of view. As stated in the introduction to this chapter, it started with people using search engines such as Google, Yahoo, and Ask. Next, came the blogs; online journals where people can express their thoughts and ideas on businesses, products, services, as well as images, and links to other webpages or sites. Then like-minded users began to collaborate. In light of this evolution of the social networking phenomena, businesses must adjust the way they conduct business in order to appropriately and effectively address consumers in this new arena.

According to Larry Weber, author of *Marketing to the Social Web*, the best way of marketing to consumers in this era of online communities is to participate in, as well as organize, and encourage the overall usage of social networks. The days of talking *at* the consumer are over. Companies must engage in dialogue *with* their consumers, and the social Web is the most effective way to do so. Specifically, Weber equates the strength of a company's brand with the quality of the company's dialogue with its consumers. "The stronger the dialogue, the stronger your brand; the weaker the dialogue, the weaker your brand." He cites Google as a good example of a brand that understands and promotes dialogue, through its features such as Google Talk, Google Groups, and Blogger. In fact, it is reported that Google is always developing new features, asking for feedback on its "beta" elements, and monitoring to see how people use Google. See Chapter 7 for more on Google. Weber goes on to say that to participate in this new world, businesses should provide relevant and engaging content on their websites and participate in relevant online discussions. He provides some examples of how businesses can get involved:

- If you are in the energy business, you should be participating in the energy blogosphere.

- If you are a pharmaceutical manufacturer, you should be participating in discussions about disease and its treatment.

- If you are a small fly rod maker, you should be participating in discussions about fly fishing.

Weber's advice is to "join the bandwagon" of marketing in the new social website world. Those businesses that wait may lose their customers to their competitors and they may "have to work three times as hard to get them back."[27]

According to Evans and Schmalensee, authors of *Catalyst Code: The Strategies Behind the World's Most Dynamic Companies*, MySpace was established in 2003 and was originally intended to be an arena for musicians to showcase their work and for fans to enjoy and discuss it. However, one of the founders, a musician himself, convinced his "Hollywood network" to join MySpace, and from there the social networking site exploded into what it is today. It has been reported that members of the MySpace community check their bulletin boards on the site as much as they check their e-mail.[28] These users are "shaping fashion, technology, and retail trends," which is very powerful considering that it has been reported that in mid-2006, MySpace was ranked second in the entire US Internet arena (with respect to total page views).[29]

Some companies have already recognized this power of the MySpace network, along with that of other similar social networking sites. For example, Victoria's Secret, a division of Limited Brands, has already involved itself with MySpace, where Victoria's Secret has connected with more than 200,000 "friends" via the site. Furthermore, Victoria's Secret has also created a profile on Facebook in order to reach out to other Facebook members and create relationships.[30]

Charlene Li and Josh Bernoff, authors of the book, *Groundswell*, point out some excellent examples of business opportunities having synthesized that in this social trend era, people use technologies to get the things they need from each other as opposed to from traditional businesses. According to these business analysts at Forrester Research, this trend started even before the appearance of sites such as MySpace and Facebook. The company eBay, for example, enabled people to buy from one another rather than a store. Given this different way for people to relate to companies, businesses must adapt swiftly to respond to this trend and take advantage of it. Airlines are no exception. The two key ingredients behind this movement are technology and people, the people being customers. Li and Bernoff identify, in their groundbreaking book, five areas that businesses can explore to choose their strategy. Besides a description of the five areas (listening, talking, energizing, supporting, and embracing), they also provide excellent examples that illustrate their five points.

First, the area of listening involves monitoring social networking sites in order to obtain consumer insights pertaining to the brand. For example, Mini USA, a division of BMW, used this technique in order to "hone in on the brand's competitive advantage" as it was facing increased competition in its segment. Through this technique, Mini management gained several key insights about its consumers including that they were very interested in community activities, especially joining local clubs, and that they enjoyed being a part of the "Mini culture" — bonding as members of this special group. Moreover, they learned that, at that time, Mini surpassed every other brand in terms of owners' likelihood to recommend the Mini to others. (See the discussion on loyalty in the next chapter.) These insights led Mini to revamp its strategy, and to market the car to owners rather than prospective buyers — the rationale being that the Mini owners would use word of mouth to promote the brand.

Second, the area of talking involves utilizing social technology (whether it be participating in blogs as well as other social networking sites, sharing video clips, or even creating a community) in order to spread messages about the brand. For example, HP incorporated blogging into its business strategy in an attempt to reach customer segments individually. Currently, HP has nearly 50 blogs to address all of its customer segments as well as different topics. Such a practice promotes awareness, discussion, and also a sense of trust as consumers have the chance to hear from executives.

Third, the area of energizing involves capitalizing on the word of mouth potential of "enthusiastic" customers. One example of an energizing technique involves the implementation of ratings and reviews, as has been done for example, by companies such as Amazon.com and Netflix. Another example of how this technique can be implemented in a company has been done by the Lego Group. Specifically, the Lego Group, which is headquartered in

Denmark and is the sixth largest toy manufacturer in the world, has another customer segment besides the traditional users, children—there is also the adult customer segment who view the Lego products as "creative building material." The Lego Group decided to create a program called "Lego Ambassadors" in an attempt to reach out to this adult consumer group. Specifically, Lego enthusiasts compete to be chosen for the 25 open spots. The Ambassadors are "paid" in Legos, which is a win-win strategy as it is both low cost for the company but extremely valued by the consumers. The goal of the program is for enthusiasts to become spokespeople and promote the brand.

The area of supporting involves establishing tools in order for customers to help other customers. This practice can result in a cost savings in terms of reducing customer service calls/support. For example, Dell has established a community forum (www. dellcommuity.com) in which individuals can post questions, such as what to do if one receives an error message during the installation or usage of certain systems/programs. A user can ask if somebody can help via a posting on the Web. Other users who may have experienced similar problems can write back and help the user asking the question.

Finally, the area of embracing involves working with consumers to design products, innovating with your customers. (For more on this topic, see the "Creativity and Innovation" section in the next chapter.) One example of a company who has used this strategy is Del Monte Foods. Specifically, the company identified a unique customer segment—pet owners who treat their pets like members of their own family. Del Monte refers to this segment as "Dogs are people, too." To embrace this customer segment, Del Monte established a community called "I love my dog/Dogs are people, too." Specifically, the company wanted to gain insights from this customer segment on what products to offer, how to package these products, and how to market these products. The company posted questions and mock-up packaging on the site in order to gain feedback and insights from its customers in creating products.[31]

Li and Bernoff's five examples provide more than enough ideas for airlines to use their concepts to learn to market to their passengers. There are dozens of questions where passenger insights are needed. How far should an airline go in its *à la carte* pricing strategy? Clearly, it works for Ryanair. Would it work for other, more traditional airlines? In fact, one could ask if passengers would prefer to have transportation provided virtually free and pay for taxes and fees as well as support services. Again, Ryanair is almost following such a strategy. Finally, if an airline is looking for word-of-mouth promotion, can the techniques described by Li and Bernoff, and used by other successful businesses, apply to airlines? Once again, Ryainair's strategy to virtually give away the seats has certainly raised the "buzz" bar and got passengers talking. There is, however, one serious caution with respect to "blogging." While online discussions and commentary are an informal source of consumer-generated opinions and experiences, they may not be representative of the majority of customers of a particular company, or in our case, an airline. "Blogging" currently appeals to specific segments of the population, which may or may not be a large portion of an airline's intended market segment or customer base. There may be other online tools/ resources that may be more effective. One example could be "sticky" websites that offer games or contests to keep potential customers at their websites and entice them to give information, including opinions.

Delta Airlines' website has an online link to user-interested information, such as a discussion of Seattle and its attractions as well as one on Shanghai (both complete with videos via YouTube). In addition, it lists the current month's boarding music and makes the music available as an iMix on iTunes. It offers articles covering topics such as Delta's current project of redesigning the Kiosk interface and experience, for which the airline had asked passengers for some feedback earlier in the project, and also information on Delta's new comprehensive recycling program. Delta Airlines' blog site includes a link called "Planeguage," which offers dialogue and video clips on subjects that are concerns to passengers, such as passengers who aggressively, and without warning, recline their seats into the lap of passengers seated in seats behind them. Such an incidence is illustrated through a video clip through YouTube. Delta's management ensures its passengers that they are being heard, and encourages and welcomes ideas from travelers for the future series of Planeguage videos.[32]

The days of only having to worry about reviews by experts (such as those at *Car and Driver* magazine rating the latest car or a restaurant critic at the local newspaper) are over—technology has made everyone a reviewer.[33] Many business writers have pointed out that companies must not only review blogs to keep current on customers' comments and concerns, but also companies must be prepared to respond appropriately. It has also been noted that if companies choose to set up blogs, the blogs must be relevant—inactive blogs are worse than not blogging at all. Tom Costley of TNS provided an illustrative example of the power of online communities in his presentation at an international airline conference. Specifically, Costley recounted the story of HSBC bank in the UK, who was planning on implementing a program that would start charging for their student accounts. Within a few days of the announcement of the plan, a campaign was organized through Facebook with 45,000 signatures petitioning the new fees, and by the end of the week, HSBC withdrew plans to do so.[34] Peter Yesawich of the Y Partnership provided another illustrative example of the power of online communities in his presentation during the same conference. Yesawich recounted the story of Spirit Airlines in which a disgruntled passenger posted a message about his bad experience with Spirit Airlines in terms of a delayed flight. An executive sent an internal e-mail that had negative remarks regarding this customer, and that e-mail, within minutes, was leaked out onto the Web, for all potential consumers to view.[35] The transparency and speed of social networking tools can also have positive results. For example, JetBlue, posted an apology on YouTube regarding the mistreatment of their passengers during inclement weather over a holiday weekend. In just a few days, JetBlue had reached 200,000 people at no cost, and the video clip was even reposted on various other blogs as well.[36] According to Rohit Bhargava, author of *Personality Not Included*, The Consumerist is one of the most popular blogs—it was founded as an arena for consumers to speak their mind on both positive and negative interactions with companies. Specifically, it has become "a champion for consumers everywhere who have had an experience they want to share with the world."[37]

Finally, business analysts point out that online communities can serve as "free" focus groups for businesses. Consequently, there is less of a need to organize traditional focus groups when a business can just jump online and see what its customers are saying about its products and services. For example, a community has been set up by frequent travelers (FlyerTalk.com) in which passengers can share their views on the subject on this site. The site offers a broad spectrum of information—everything from comments on the best food/dining in a given city to discussions on seat maps offered by airlines on their websites. The site even has a Town Hall, where one can volunteer to participate in the current FlyerTalk administration.[38] This site could be an excellent source of insight for airlines in terms of potential opportunities to enhance service offerings.

## Takeaways

- While the online social networks have not been powerhouses in terms of revenue generation, as originally hoped through advertising, they have had an enormous effect on the world socially.[39] As Johnson points out, these networked consumer communities are a potent force.

- The online community arena has connected consumers, causing a fundamental shift in the way businesses must connect with their customers. In the past, businesses "targeted" customers, whereas in the new environment, customers can initiate the relationship, learn about products, service, and businesses from their online social community, and evaluate the products for relevance and value. "It's a fundamental power shift," states Johnson.[40]

- The social networking communities are, and will be, a key consumer force, and therefore companies, including airlines, should stay in tune to them. Specifically, these communities could become the marketing department—it will be the social communities that will be determining what to offer in terms of products and services. On the other hand, there is one serious caution with respect to "blogging." While online discussions and commentary are an informal source of consumer-generated opinions and experiences, they may not be representative of the majority of customers of a particular airline. "Blogging" currently appeals to specific segments of the population, which may or may not be a large portion of an airline's intended market segment or customer base.

In essence, these communities could become "prosumers" — the combining of the roles of both producers and consumers, thus possibly replacing the traditional corporate marketing sector of organizations.

## Notes

1   For more on the evolution of the Web, see: www.sramanamitra.com
2   The phrase 1.0 is simply a designation in the computer world.
3   For more on online travel site analysis, see: www.sramanamitra.com
4   Amadeus, *Future Traveller Tribes 2020: Report for the Air Travel Industry*, Developed by the Henley Centre, HeadlightVision, in partnership with Amadeus (2007), pp. 12, 14–15, 17, 36.
5   Anderson, Chris, *The Long Tail: Why the Future of Business is Selling Less of More* (NY: Hyperion Press, 2006), pp. 17, 18, 20, 22, 109, 110.
6   Kiviat, Barbara, "10 Ideas That Are Changing The World" — "#2 The End of Customer Service," *Time Magazine*, March 24, 2008, p. 42.
7   Arnoult, Sandra, "When Self-Service is Better Service," *Air Transport World*, March 2008, pp. 48–9, 52.
8   Bottomley, Michelle, Ogilvy, Presentation at the OSU Conference in Portugal, November 2006.
9   "American Airlines Launches Exciting New Application Using Facebook Platform," *Air Transport News*, March 25, 2008.
10  Yesawich, Peter, Y Partnership, Presentation at the OSU Conference in Turkey, September 2007.
11  "Noah Glass has built a service that lets you order coffee or takeout food via text message" (as told to Max Chafkin), *Inc. Magazine*, September 2007, p. 40.
12  Springer, Paul, *Ads to Icons: How Advertising Succeeds in Multimedia Age* (London: Kogan Page, 2007), pp. 85–7.
13  Bhargava, Rohit, *Personality Not Included: Why Companies Lose Their Authenticity — And How Great Brands Get it* Back (NY: McGraw Hill, 2008), pp. 118–19 and corporate website, www.dyson.com
14  Cocoran, Ian, *The Art of Digital Branding* (NY: Allworth Press, 2007), pp. 53, 80, 88.

15  For more on Southwest and Southwest's blog, see: Southwest.com and blogsouthwest.com

16  For more on Lufthansa's international offerings for those visiting their homeland, see: http://www.lufthansa.com/online/portal/lh/us (Quicklink: WeFlyHome), and for more on Lufthansa's offerings for students, see: http://www.lufthansa.com/online/portal/lh/us (Quicklink: Student Discounts)

17  Cocoran, Ian, *The Art of Digital Branding* (NY: Allworth Press, 2007), pp. 95–8.

18  Hayes, Tom, *Jump Point: How Network Culture is Revolutionizing Business* (NY: McGraw-Hill, 2008).

19  Hayes, Tom, *Jump Point: How Network Culture is Revolutionizing Business* (NY: McGraw-Hill, 2008), pp. 53, 59–62, 203.

20  Hayes, Tom, *Jump Point: How Network Culture is Revolutionizing Business* (NY: McGraw-Hill, 2008), p. 53.

21  Teradata Magazine, Volume 7, Number 4, "Get a Second Life" by Lisa Campbell, pp. 52–3.

22  Shiffman, Denise *The Age of Engage: Reinventing Marketing for Today's Connected, Collaborative, and Hyperinteractive Culture* (Ladera Ranch, CA: Hunt Street Press, 2008), p. 180.

23  Teradata Magazine, Volume 7, Number 4, "Get a Second Life" by Lisa Campbell, pp. 52–3.

24  Hayes, Tom, *Jump Point: How Network Culture is Revolutionizing Business* (NY: McGraw-Hill, 2008), p. 203.

25  Li, Charlene and Josh Bernoff, *Groundswell: Winning in a World Transformed by Social Technologies* (Boston, MA: Harvard Business School Press, 2008), p. 23.

26  Shiffman, Denise, *The Age of Engage: Reinventing Marketing for Today's Connected, Collaborative, and Hyperinteractive Culture* (Ladera Ranch, CA: Hunt Street Press, 2008), pp. 180-81.

27  Weber, Larry, *Marketing to the Social Web: How Digital Customer Communities Build Your Business* (Hoboken, NJ: John Wiley, 2007), pp. 3–4, 13–14, 15, 32, 34.

28  Evans, David and Richard Schmalensee, *Catalyst Code: The Strategies Behind the World's Most Dynamic Companies* (Boston, MA: Harvard Business School Press, 2007), p. 50.

29  Evans, David and Richard Schmalensee, *Catalyst Code: The Strategies Behind the World's Most Dynamic Companies* (Boston, MA: Harvard Business School Press, 2007), p. 51.

30  Li, Charlene and Josh Bernoff, *Groundswell: Winning in a World Transformed by Social Technologies* (Boston, MA: Harvard Business School Press, 2008), pp. 23 and 65.

31  Li, Charlene and Josh Bernoff, *Groundswell: Winning in a World Transformed by Social Technologies* (Boston, MA: Harvard Business School Press, 2008), pp. 9–10, 17, 37, 68–9, 82, 89–93, 103, 108–10, 134, 145–6, 159, 179–82.

32  For more on Delta's blog, see: blog.delta.com
33  Li, Charlene and Josh Bernoff, *Groundswell: Winning in a World Transformed by Social Technologies* (Boston, MA: Harvard Business School Press, 2008), p. 28.
34  Costley, Tom, TNS, Presentation at the OSU Conference in Turkey, September 2007, p. 11.
35  Yesawich, Peter, Y Partnership, Presentation at the OSU Conference in Turkey, September 2007.
36  Shiffman, Denise, *The Age of Engage: Reinventing Marketing for Today's Connected, Collaborative, and Hyperinteractive Culture* (Ladera Ranch, CA: Hunt Street Press, 2008), p. 9.
37  Bhargava, Rohit, *Personality Not Included: Why Companies Lose Their Authenticity—And How Great Brands Get it Back* (NY: McGraw Hill, 2008), pp. 20–21.
38  For more on the frequent air traveler blog, see: flyertalk.com
39  "Online Social Networks Everywhere and Nowhere," *The Economist*, March 22–28, 2008, pp. 71–2.
40  Johnson, Lisa, *Mind Your X's and Y's: Satisfying the 10 Cravings of a New Generation of Consumers* (NY: Free Press, 2006), pp. 157–8.

# Chapter 6

# Building Airline Brands and Developing Loyalty

As with other trends discussed in Chapter 2, the function and practice of marketing are going through unprecedented change. This chapter begins with few observations on the changing role of marketing within the airline industry and other businesses. The chapter then moves on to a lengthy discussion on brands and branding. These are critical functions for businesses with such attributes as commodity products and services and thin margins. Given the linkage between brands and loyalty, the last part of the chapter touches on a few important aspects of managing loyalty.

## Changing Role of Marketing

From a near-term viewpoint the role of marketing for airlines (as a global business) is limited for two reasons.

- Airlines have a "regional" relevance whereas most other goods and services are ubiquitous. If you live in Amritsar, India, you can buy a Mercedes car or watch CNN news. Travel on Lufthansa or American Airlines, however, is not possible. They are irrelevant airlines in that city. With present airline ownership rules limitations and hub structures, airlines cannot become brands of non-local relevance, let alone global brands.

- Airlines have very little control over airports, even in their own countries, let alone in foreign countries. Given that they cannot operate this important component of the aviation business with their own staff, it is difficult to control the brand.

Despite these structural constraints, marketing in the airline industry is changing dramatically, and can benefit from some of the insights presented in this chapter. From a longer-term viewpoint, the benefits could be much larger in light of the following developments, both within and outside the airline industry:

- The roles of consumers are changing. They are more informed, proactive, and decisive with respect to their preferences, and this is exemplified by the consumer desire for more definitive range of price-service options.

- Competitors are becoming more and more ubiquitous and powerful—not only are there new powerful and well financed airlines, such as those based in the Middle East Gulf Region, but viable low-fare airlines are beginning to appear in intercontinental markets. We are also seeing low-cost airlines offering seat concepts and other in-flight products that are superior to those offered by conventional airlines.

- A large segment of travelers neither understands nor trusts airline pricing systems. These passengers comprehend that fares vary by class of service, by season, by the amount of competition, and even by other conditions, such as advance purchase, but it is the huge volume of different fares, the lack of transparency, and the dynamics relating to any changes that is puzzling. The spread of fares within one class (economy) of service also puzzles the traveling public.

- The role of technology is shifting from being a constraint to becoming an enabler, and in a few rare cases, even a driver of business strategies.

- A very large segment of the traveling population in major regions such as the US (and to a lesser extent in Europe) simply does not trust airlines to provide the level of service consistent with their expectations. In most hub airports, particularly "fortress hubs," the treatment of passengers appears disrespectful and degrading.

- Airline delays, at least in the US, have reached an unacceptable level, as evidenced by calls on the government to take action. Most travelers tend to blame the airlines for delays even when the causes relate to poor infrastructure, such as the lack of sufficient airport capacity and old technology-based air traffic control systems.

- Traditional mass marketing (as well as media) appears to be no longer viable, requiring airlines to find alternative ways to communicate with passengers.

- Mergers and alliance partnerships make it difficult to portray a particular brand image and attributes when different parts of the airline network and products are actually serviced and delivered by other carriers/vendors. In some cases, experienced travelers view code share agreements as simply sub-charters to regional carriers.

- The historical distribution system made it easier to customize a product or service to meet the needs of an individual traveler when there was a one-on-one relationship with a "human" travel agent. Now the focus is on the use of the Internet to make travel arrangements.

While the structural constraints remain in place, the evolution of marketing in the airline industry continues. Some aspects of this evolution contain negative potential opportunities and some contain positive opportunities. For example:

- According to many frequent flyers in intercontinental markets, many airlines ruin their own brand promise by code sharing with inferior airlines. This is the case for a number of European airlines with excellent brands who dilute their brand in this way, but less true for US airlines who tend to have a poorer brand in the first place.

- With the economy in a downturn, both in the US and, to a lesser extent, in Europe, people will become more concerned about price and costs. The final outcome will be that although growth in travel may decrease a little, low-fare airlines such as Ryanair and Southwest will do well. As the price of fuel increases (already at US$139 a barrel at the beginning of June 2008), and depending on the degree to which low-fare airlines pass on fuel price increase to their customers, the price gap between low-fare and conventional airlines is likely to increase.

• Low-fare airlines may also introduce new policies to change their cost and fare structure. It is reported that Ryanair is allowing more hand luggage and discouraging checked luggage, thus reducing the resources required at both check-in counters and in baggage claim areas.

While the aforementioned points relate specifically to the airline industry, it might be useful to review the points made by Denise Shiffman, author of *The Age of Engage* who summarizes the evolution of marketing for businesses in general in the following way:[1]

• Marketing 0.0—Marketing at "ground zero," with businesses marketing to the masses, using television as a main source of advertising. In comparison to the current era, competition was limited.

• Marketing 1.0—Although businesses evolved from marketing to the masses to marketing to specific segments, the textbook use of the "4 Ps" of marketing continued to dominate—product, price, place, and promotion.

• Marketing 2.0—In the current marketplace, leading businesses are learning to *engage* their targeted audiences—not talk *to* them or *at* them, but *with* them to drive their companies' growth agendas. This approach redefines the practice of marketing, capitalizing on the proliferation of social technology and networking.

This new world of marketing, while very complex even for visionary and leading businesses, represents both a challenge as well as an opportunity. From the viewpoint of challenge, airlines should realize that they are beginning to have far less control over passengers, due mostly to the fact that consumers now are able to search, converse, and collaborate. This new marketing environment can also present an opportunity for airlines to present offerings that not only satisfy, but even more importantly to anticipate the needs of their targeted segments. Moreover, there are now opportunities for even the smallest companies to attract new customers, due in part to the increasing use of the Internet and word-of-mouth.[1] Studies show, for example, that traditional advertising is on the decline, while word-of-mouth advertising is on the rise. While the restaurant industry is number one in terms of utilizing word-of-mouth advertising (more than eight out of ten people determine their new restaurant choices based on a referral), other industries such as the hotel industry, are also enjoying success from this form of advertising (more than six out of ten people for the hotel industry). According to the firm BIGresearch, word-of-mouth is currently the most influential media on purchasing decisions among all age groups. Given this evidence, the airline industry must find a way to capitalize on this extremely powerful channel. "How?" one might ask. McConnell and Huba point out a few strategies to achieve this goal:[2]

- Continuously gather customer feedback—understand what customers love by continuously gathering their input. For example, Build-A-Bear, the store where children can build their own personal stuffed animals, has a board made up of twenty kids ages 8–12 who review and vote upon new product ideas—99 percent of products in the store are the result of customer ideas. The new Fiat 500 was developed very closely with customers and "aficionados" discussing design idea. Now it is an extremely popular car in Europe.

- Make it a point to share knowledge freely—the more knowledge you share with the world, the more people will tell others about it. Share your content—let your customers have photos, stories, and statistics about your company so they can post it, write about it, and share it with other consumers.

- Expertly build word-of-mouth networks—build the buzz by allowing customers into a special program to try new products or meet the key faces of your company.

- Encourage communities of customers to meet and share— allow like-minded customers the chance to communicate and interact with one another. These communities allow current customers to sell your company, its products, and its services to other potential customers.

- Devise specialized, smaller offerings to get customers to bite—allow potential customers to try before buying.

- Focus on making the world, or an industry, better. Companies that strive for a higher purpose such as Virgin Atlantic and Whole Foods, tend to find that all stakeholders—employees, customers, suppliers—naturally act as cheerleaders for the company's success.

Consequently, it would appear that whereas before an important marketing practice was to connect with and build relationships with customers, now the practice extends to current and future customers. To repeat, given its importance, while, in the recent past, some components of the marketing practice have changed more than others, placing the customer at the heart of marketing has been, and will continue to be, a critical success factor. However, engaging with customers and capitalizing on the powerful channel—word-of-mouth—requires a new focus on branding and the management of loyalty, the subject of this chapter.

While branding is important in any industry, it is particularly vital in the airline industry. Consider for a minute the list of the top 100 global brands. There is not a single passenger airline in the top 100 global brands.[3] Relatively well-known airlines could argue with such lists and point out that such rankings have been based on brand equity and the market capitalizations of the global airlines tend to be relatively small. Other arguments cited include factors that although they are global in operations, airlines are not considered global businesses due to the existence of bilateral and multilateral agreements. These are valid explanations.

Despite the aforementioned limitations, a few airlines have developed reputable brands. Examples include, Lufthansa and Virgin Atlantic in Europe, and Singapore Airlines and Cathay Pacific in Asia. Kingfisher Airlines is an example of an emerging brand in India. The situation in the US, on the other hand is quite poor. Even when one sees an airline such as Southwest ranked as number one relative to other airlines operating within the US domestic markets, the customer satisfaction ranking of the US airline industry as a whole in the context of all businesses is very low. In a recent survey conducted by the University of Michigan, the airline industry within the US ranked close to the US Internal Revenue Service, which is just about at the bottom.[4] The quality of airline service has deteriorated to the point that in a recent survey, 42 percent of the respondents said that they would avoid traveling on an airline if they could get their business conducted in a different way.[5]

As to the question of brand-related loyalty, it is also deteriorating in the airline industry. Consider, again, the information available from a recent survey reported by Forrester Research. Less than one quarter of passengers said that they prefer to travel on a legacy airline. Almost one-third preferred a low-fare airline, and 44 percent had no preference. Consequently, almost three-quarters of the passengers surveyed either have no preference or would prefer a low-fare airline over a legacy airline.[6]

This chapter focuses only on these two components of the marketing practice—branding and loyalty. The first part provides some insights into the role and process of branding, with a focus on important brand drivers. The second part touches on some key issues relating to loyalty—key drivers of loyalty and the importance of implementing strategies to build loyalty of current and future customers that are profitable. The next chapter provides insights from the actual experience of 20 brands from around the world and some implications for airlines, recognizing that the airline industry operates within the structural constraints mentioned above.

## Brands and Branding Airlines

As with any business, unbranded airline products and services are simply commodities, providing airlines with little choice but to compete on price. And a generic airline brand promise or value proposition has no relevant meaning to discriminating passengers. According to a recent publication by Unisys, this is in fact, the sentiment by consumers regarding US carriers. However, this is not as much the case for Asian carriers. Specifically, studies show that, in contrast to both Europe and North America, only 19 percent (of Asians) chose an airline based on cost, while 30 percent made their decision based on service and amenities offered.[7] What's the difference among these groups? First, Unisys' paper points to the fact that the Asian culture has a deeply ingrained tradition of service and hospitality. Second, Unisys' paper notes that Asian carriers benefit from a rapidly growing consumer base, unlike the relatively mature markets in the US and Europe. Finally, since almost all of the Asian carriers excel in terms of service, carriers are subject to "peer pressure" in the market—if they do something like eliminate meal service, as the US carriers did, there would be strong repercussions.[8]

Airlines worldwide, but more so in the US, need to be distinctive and that requires in-depth knowledge about targeted passengers followed by specific value propositions. One example of a US carrier that has already embraced the idea of distinguishing itself is Continental Airlines. Specifically, Continental's recent advertisements highlight that the carrier is still offering complimentary meals at mealtimes, which is certainly no longer the case with most US carriers these days, even in first-class. Airlines in other parts of the world are way ahead. For example, Lufthansa has built separate terminals in Frankfurt and Munich for its first-class passengers traveling in intercontinental markets. These passengers are processed much more efficiently. Its flight attendants are also trained to meet, and in some cases, exceed the needs of its passengers.

Next, airline brands must fulfill the promises they make and do it consistently. An airline brand promise must not only describe what it will do for a targeted segment of passengers, but also show how it is different from competitors. Let us move to other businesses for a moment. For some, a car is not just a way to travel from A to B, and a BMW is not just a car. In the case of BMW, it is a brand promise of performance, engineering, styling, and status, and for some it is even a way of life. Similarly, Starbucks is not just a cup of coffee. It is an experience customized for an individual. There are some similar examples in the airline industry but they are rare. The following are a few examples of past airlines and current airlines with respect to branding:

- By the 1920s, Imperial Airways (now British Airways) produced a poster featuring "the dynamic and direct interactions taking place between people and technology." The poster then goes on, very creatively, to encourage people from all walks of life to "see the world anew."[9] This stimulated the demand for air travel in general and on British Airways in particular.

- Pan Am, despite its demise due to poor management decisions, can be described as a powerful brand in its day. "Even amongst populations unlikely to fly, it connoted a sense of glamour, freedom and global scope."[10]

- During the 1950s, the threat of nuclear weapons got some people to re-think the value of technology. SABENA (the national airline of Belgium) took advantage of this situation by promoting the value of technology in its world fair (Expo '58) through a creative poster. The center of this poster contained the Atomium ("a metal model with nine spheres representing a molecule with nine atoms") representing Sabena's home base. The intention was to encourage Americans to travel to Expo'58, and, hopefully, to select SABENA.[11]

- Virgin Atlantic would be a current example of an airline that conjures up unusual sentiments. It was the first airline (around 1999–2000) to combine two of its premium class seats to make a double bed in the cabin. In addition, Virgin offered an onboard bar (surrounded by bar stools) and a dedicated beauty treatment area for a shoulder and hand massage.[12]

- Lufthansa would be another example of an airline that has developed a respected brand for innovation relating to passenger care, exemplified by such initiatives as single-aisle airplanes configured with all business-class seats, arrangements with operators of corporate jets to transport connecting passengers traveling in premium cabins in intercontinental markets, and separate check-in terminals for premium class passengers.

- Kingfisher would be an example of a new airline that is building its airline brand by extending its umbrella brand that covers numerous areas such as beverages, fashion, and sports. Passengers rave about the "upbeat" service, both on the ground and in the cabin.

Unfortunately, there are not too many other airline examples of successful branding at the global level (except for Singapore Airlines and Cathay Pacific), although the emerging airlines based in the UAE region of the Middle East, particularly Emirates, could prove to be exceptions.

Before proceeding with a discussion of brand drivers, it might be helpful to clarify some semantics. Although the terms "brand" and "branding" tend to be used interchangeably, they are quite different. According to one expert, brand is the idea, branding is the transmission of that idea.[13] Similarly, if one assumes that advertising is a way of transmitting the idea, the terms advertising and branding are sometimes interchanged. Furthermore, there are examples of airlines who have related the branding process to the development of a logo or a symbol, instead of to the fact that a brand is supposed to create a set of perceptions from which passengers develop preference and, ultimately, loyalty. In the airline industry, it may be the way a carrier conducts its business or the experience it provides (hassle-free, caring, and so forth), rather than the network it flies. At the moment, most airlines are seen as just providers of transportation—and, in some cases, inconsistent and unreliable. In successful businesses (as seen in the next chapter), consumers expect and hold brands to be accountable for what they promise compared to what they actually deliver. Consequently, a brand is not just a company's advertising campaign. Loyalty-building brands, such as Starbucks and Federal Express, have been built around a promise, not just advertising, as in the case of many airlines. Airlines might be wise to be reminded that if you are a brand, you have significant control over distribution but if you are a commodity, you are controlled by distribution.

The key, of course, is how the communicated message is received. In the case of an airline, for example, do passengers simply view branding as new paint schemes and new livery with insignificant changes in service? Even worse, do employees view it the same way or, does the message communicate and deliver a lasting benefit?[14] Interestingly, it has been reported that more than 80 percent of companies believe that they deliver a superior customer experience, but in reality, studies show that only 8 percent of their customers agree.[15] This is a very powerful statement illustrating not only a disparity in perceptions and expectations, but also that there is great opportunity in the area of branding.

According to Duane Knapp, author of *The Brand Promise*, great brands are passionate about their customers—"genuine brands are determined to enhance their customers' lives."[16] Sartain and Schumann add by saying that brands, in fact, communicate the heart of an entire organization, not just product offerings and value propositions, but also relevant and compelling images. Think of the power of phrases such as GE's "Imagination at work" or "There are some things money can't buy, for everything else there's MasterCard."[17] Taglines can be very powerful and can be associated with a brand for decades, as long as the company follows through on the brand promise behind the tagline. One excellent example is Federal Express' "When It Absolutely, Positively Has to Be There Overnight." This slogan was developed in 1982, but it is still recognized today, and most importantly, FedEx still fulfills this promise today. Another example is De Beers' "A Diamond Is Forever." This tagline is extremely powerful—it has been in existence since 1948, yet it still conjures up feelings of romance, timelessness, and eternal love. Steve Cone, author of *Powerlines*, recognizes that a "grand slam occurs when your slogan or tagline is also your unique selling proposition, that is, those few words that precisely define your core brand promise."[18]

In the case of most airlines, brands tend to be commodities, and therefore substitutable. If brand loyalty does exist, it is usually due to the frequent flyer programs offered rather than due to "pure brand preference" defined by the elements described in this chapter.[19] A few airlines that have succeeded in developing strong brands have, first, differentiated themselves in terms of product features, pricing strategies, distribution channels, and so forth, second, communicated effectively the difference, and third, delivered consistently on the promise. If an airline were to develop such a brand, it could then charge a premium fare some passengers would be willing to pay for the brand. Moreover, the same passengers would try to seek out the brand and be loyal to the brand. For these passengers the brand would represent the entire organization and be embraced by employees at all levels. The next section, *Brand Drivers*, expands upon these characteristics, in an effort to illustrate what an airline needs to do to successfully distinguish itself among its competitors.

## Brand Drivers

*Distinctiveness*

In an industry that is becoming hypercompetitive, it is imperative for an airline to differentiate itself from all the others to survive. If an airline fails to do so, which is the case with most airlines, then its service becomes a mere commodity competing on price alone. A brand representing more than price commands higher prices and creates loyalty. Let us take an example. On 8 May, 2008, a passenger wishing to travel from JFK in New York to Mumbai in India in business class (outbound on 16 May and return on 23 May) found that the lowest fare was available on Air India which, in fact, offered nonstop service with the least elapsed time. All other competitors (one with nonstop service and the others with connections) had much higher fares. Air India also had connecting service priced even lower in fare than its nonstop service. One can only conclude that Air India's competitors felt they had a better brand, and could therefore charge a higher fare even for lower level of service, and longer travel times.

To develop and protect its brand, an airline must communicate and illustrate what it is that makes it different from its competitors. Is it the features unique only to its service offering? Is it the way that it conducts business? Is it the experience that it provides its passengers? An airline must clearly state what it is that distinguishes it from its competitors, and then must deliver on it to its passengers. This distinction must be so clear to passengers that they remember it on cue; meaning they directly associate this attribute with an airline's brand. For example, everyone associates FedEx and UPS with providing dependable and on-time delivery, while Southwest Airlines and Virgin Atlantic are personified as being fun and upbeat. Decide what it is that makes your offering unique, then focus on those attributes, both in terms of illustrating them to passengers and making sure they are priority one within the airline's organization. "Differentiation and the benefits of belonging that corporate branding brings are the root sources of brand value."[20] According to Bob Lachky, vice president of brand management at Anheuser-Busch, a brand defines "a unique or differentiated product or service that has an identifiable image or personality, brought to life through a powerful relationship with a customer."[21] That is only a bottle of beer. What would be an example within the airline industry?

It is, however, important to note that any distinctive characteristics offered must be beneficial to the consumer. Airlines must be careful in that they should not choose differential aspects that hold very little value to the consumer. Consider the following examples of companies that have used this driver to build their brand:

- Australian beverage brand Foster's differentiation practice is key to its success—"Focus on your core products, clearly differentiate them, and build great brands. Great brands bring many other benefits, such as pride and excitement in the business. And people do love brands."[22]

- Clothier Zara distinguishes itself in the retail arena with its unique take on fashion. It thinks of clothes as a perishable commodity.

- Charles Schwab distinguished his financial brokerage business when he first began with the "No advice" rule — Chuck's mantra — no advice, no conflict, no sales person will ever call was the main differentiator between Schwab and its full-service or 'full-commission' competitors.[23]

- In Germany, Lufthansa has developed separate terminals at Frankfurt and Munich Airports for first-class passengers.

- In India, Kingfisher Airlines offers the "Fly The Good Times" proposition to travelers.[24]

- Virgin Atlantic Airways is recognized for its concern for the customer, and JetBlue Airlines has become known for its expansive in-flight television service for passengers' entertainment.

The UK design agency Brand Environment expands on this need to distinguish oneself by offering something extra, but with respect to the airline industry. Marketing efforts within the airline industry have usually been about the network and operation more than the promise of the brand, perhaps because the product is intangible. However, with an increase in competition, the quality of the brand as it relates to the entire customer experience is becoming an important differentiator. Unfortunately, most airlines either do not have a recognized and respected brand or the one that they have contains generic promises that are simply copies of other brands.

*Relevance*

As many experts have pointed out, one of the keys to building a successful brand is to differentiate yourself, then ensure that this differentiation is meaningful or relevant to others. As with differentiation, if an airline offers a unique feature or special service that passengers do not value, then its brand will not be able to command a premium price. Based on the "sameness of brands," one can only conclude that many airlines appear to have overlooked the point as to what passengers really desire, making some airlines' offerings to be irrelevant. Even when an airline does come up with a good idea (for example, as mentioned above, JetBlue's in-flight entertainment system), the airline becomes complacent and does not recognize that the needs of the customer may change, requiring a change in the product or service to meet those needs. As one expert points out, sometimes a company becomes too attached to its products and services and needs to step back to examine its customers' perspective relating to relevancy.[25]

Procter & Gamble is a good example of an organization that needed to step back and consider if one of the company's new products was relevant to the needs of its customers. P&G originally thought of its Febreze brand as a product to remove odors from fabrics, such as the smell of cigarette smoke from clothes. But by asking, "Who is this relevant to?" the marketers found that the brand was meaningful to people who wanted to remove odors from a broad array of other places—from smelly gymnasium bags to the seats of cars. It is reported that after P&G changed the way it promoted Febreze—from odor remover to fabric refresher—the product achieved phenomenal growth when non-smokers in addition to smokers learned about how to make fabrics smell better.[26]

Kodak has also acknowledged the need to be relevant for its consumers. According to Paula Dumas, Kodak's director and vice president of marketing and development, Kodak understands the risk of being apathetic and of failing to keep a brand relevant. Specifically, her role is to redefine the Kodak brand, as the trend from traditional to digital has dramatically changed the industry. She notes, "a great brand can transcend technological change as long as its attributes are relevant."[27] Another expert suggests that the right question to ask is this: "Does the buyer still need or want it?"[28]

While this question is certainly applicable to products, it is also applicable to services, including airline services. Airlines need to make sure every aspect of their services are needed and wanted—from routes served, to in-flight services offered, to partnerships with others within the airline industry. Simon Glynn, Senior Partner of Lippincott provides a good illustration of relevancy to passengers in terms of the pitch of passenger seats.

Seat pitch is certainly important to passengers, however, the perceived value of this product feature can vary significantly. For example, if a passenger is sitting comfortably with a 38-inch seat pitch, any additional pitch adds little value until the level reached is conducive to comfortable sleep (say a 55-inch pitch). Similarly, once a passenger has a lie-flat bed in a horizontal position (say 75-inch pitch), additional space again has decreasing value.

The other part of the relevance question is the gap between the product offered by an airline and its competitors and the relevance of the product features to customers. Let us say that seat pitch is very important to passengers flying in ultra long-haul markets in comparison to the number of meals or the variety of wines served. It is important to compare the performance gap among competitors. A large negative gap on an attribute considered very important by passengers can be exceptionally detrimental (seat pitch on long-haul flights or on-time performance for short- and medium-haul flights, for example) whereas a large positive gap relating to less important product features (such as the well recognized name of an airline's chef or the extent of the types of wines served on board) may not add much value.

Virgin Atlantic Airways illustrates the value of such an analysis when it introduced the Premium Economy Product. This product remains relevant to its customers, and has been copied by other airlines. Its relevance is substantiated by the high margins achieved by airlines offering such a product. Virgin Atlantic has been successful with this offering because it is relevant to, and adds value for, a key group of passengers who would like, and can afford, an upgrade from economy class. Virgin Atlantic is successful because it recognizes that the industry has come a long way from the old days of just business versus leisure travel, and they are able to remain relevant through offering further segmentations that add value to the passenger. [29]

*Consistency*

Once an airline has differentiated itself with a unique and relevant product or service, it is imperative that it deliver the product or service in a consistent manner every single time. If a passenger has a positive experience with an airline's product or service, and, therefore, chooses that airline again, only to have a lesser experience in terms of quality or customer service, the passenger will leave one airline for a competitor, regardless of how fantastic the first experience had been. According to *The Economist*, in observing the habits of leading brands, writers state that to deliver on a company's promise calls for the company to take a stand and not waiver to gain short-term benefits. This is a key point in brand management for airlines. You have to stick to your promise, even if it hurts from a cost point-of-view in the short run.

There is a clear need for consistency and clarity within the organization to articulate the product benefit(s) unmistakably. An organization that embraces the value of consistency is FedEx. FedEx delivers packages overnight consistently, to the right location and undamaged. Its reputation for consistency can be gauged from the observation that few people would say, "let's UPS the package" or "Emery it" or "Airborne Express it." What one is more likely to hear is, "FedEx it." How has FedEx achieved that remarkable brand reputation? FedEx will not compromise in any area that would jeopardize the delivery of its promise to customers.[30] Charles Schwab recognizes the importance of remaining consistent from office to office by enforcing rigorous quality control and commonality of experience across its branches. Similarly, customers can count on the predictability of experience, not just among chain restaurants within one country, but also around the globe.[31] Starbucks is another example of a brand that understands the need and strives for consistency in its organization and in its entire way of conducting business in a world where the value propositions offered by businesses are unpredictable. Given the current unpredictability of events in an average person's daily life, many are looking for a "familiar and comfortable refuge," and find it with a cup of coffee from Starbucks.[32]

Consistency also refers to ensuring a consistent experience in each phase of the service or the building of a product, not just from location to location, visit to visit, or the final product. For example, to ensure customer satisfaction, Nokia has "taken the view that it cannot rely solely on suppliers to deliver the components that comprise the products, so it is buying up its suppliers in order to have control of the whole process."[33] This concept would also be transferable and true with respect to an airline flight. Consistency in the level of customer service received when booking the flight, when checking in, when boarding the flight, the in-flight service, the baggage handling, and so forth, are all components of the service where consistent performance will be noted. Furthermore, consistency in the airline arena needs to extend across all partners, whether it be partnerships with other airlines or other providers of travel-related services. Most importantly, consistency must continue over time. A new airline cannot just offer great service in the beginning, then let that service quality erode over time—it must maintain quality standards in the future to be successful.

A number of frequent flyers in the US provided the following comment of the consistency driver. "Most US airlines <u>do</u> provide consistent service; unfortunately, it is consistently bad." A group of passengers go further and say, "Many airline executives are still influenced by those days when a good landing was the only thing passengers expected, and most other aspects could be excused with the 'natural' and/or 'external' factors influencing the experience—the weather, the ATC, and so forth. If airlines had to reimburse a passenger if the passenger arrived late, if their bag was not delivered, if the movie screen did not work, if the seat did not recline, if a flight attendant was rude, if the seat pitch was less than a standard, if a check-in took more than five minutes, or if the business lounge was over-crowded, then executives would either think twice before making undeliverable promises, rework their processes, or put real pressure on airports and ATC." What about the top brand airlines diluting their brand reputation by sharing their codes with airlines, not just one layer below, but many layers below? Are the evaluations made on the basis of value added to the network or the brand? What happened to the brand perception of Mercedes when it acquired Chrysler?

*Authenticity*

In this chaotic world where consumers are overloaded and burdened with information, advertisements, and gimmicks, passengers crave honesty and straightforwardness. They identify with the values portrayed by brands, and look to brands as a promise that their needs will be met. Some experts, in fact, believe that "rendering authenticity" could easily become as important as "controlling costs" or "improving quality," and since passengers want offerings that are real, some experts maintain that the *management of the customer perception of authenticity* could become a new source of competitive advantage.[34]

There are a number of ways a business could substantiate authenticity. Some business analysts suggest, for example, that a business could talk about its brand history and stability, followed by the brand's value and relevance, and support the brand's value proposition through credible and trustworthy endorsements (for example, advertising a car in *Car and Driver* magazine).[35] Subway became successful in the area of authenticity by utilizing the testimony of an "ordinary" customer from Indiana, Jared, to promote its brand. The allure being not that he was a celebrity, but rather quite the opposite, he was a "real person who had an authentic story and people believed it."[36] Johnson & Johnson is another example of a company that has actually used the concept of authenticity to augment its product offerings. Specifically, the company understands that listening provides insight into what concerns customers, what customers would like, and what trends are evolving. Furthermore, in Johnson & Johnson's experience, when customers feel that a company is listening, customers begin to develop a trust in their brand. More importantly is the realization that the more customers trust a brand, the more they are likely to tell the business about what they want.[37] Airlines need to build this type of credibility with passengers in terms of truly following through on promises, such as those related to timely arrivals and departures, as well as the quality of customer service throughout a passenger's travel experience. Compare the authenticity aspects discussed above with the experience of the following passenger. "The airline constantly puts me on flights with 35–40 minute connections at its major, congested airport hub. Even if the airplane were to arrive on time, it has taken 7 minutes for the jet bridge agent to show up and open the door, another 11 minutes for the last passenger on the Boeing 757 to deplane, and then I have been given the wrong information on the connecting gate. Then, to add insult to injury, the boarding agent for the connecting flight informed the passengers that the flight has been closed even though the plane was still there, and the jet bridge was still attached."

*Transparency*

As with authenticity, consumers are looking for what is real — they just want the plain truth. However, Rohit Bhargava, author of *Personality Not Included*, cautions one to not confuse transparency and authenticity. Specifically, he states that transparency involves being open about what the company is doing, while authenticity takes transparency a step further in terms of evaluating whether what the company is doing is right or wrong.[38] Here is how such a concept could apply in the airline industry. An example of transparency could be that an airline tells its passengers that its on-time performance as measured by the US Government is 80 percent. However, this particular flight has a track record of being late 40 percent of the time. Would such a communication represent authenticity even though it represents transparency?

In the times of Enron and MCI in the US, consumers are skeptical and businesses need to be transparent, meaning totally up front with good and bad news. Customers want realistic communications from genuinely transparent sources.[39] Specifically, according to *The Economist*, customers expect a brand to deliver on its promises, and the company behind the brand to respect them and be transparent with them.[40] Once companies are willing to go with full disclosure, be accountable, and take responsibility for their decisions, customers will be able to see transparency. Customers, at that point, may even be more willing to be "forgiving" when things go wrong. Some analysts go further and say that not only are morality and responsibility "in," but also now businesses are expected to report their environmental performance in addition to their financial performance.[41] Smart businesses understand that consumers want to know what is going on behind the products and services that they are supporting, and Whole Foods is one of these businesses. Specifically, Whole Foods CEO, President, Chairman, and Co-founder John Mackey believes in sharing information with both employees and customers, going so far as to invite customers to visit the farms where Whole Foods chickens are raised. [42]

The transparency brand driver is especially important in the airline business. For example, airlines must be upfront with what services are really associated with a particular fare. Passengers do not want to be "surprised" when they go to make a change— restrictions, fees and so forth must be clearly stated in an open manner. Passengers are surprised when they learn that hotel accommodations or endorsements of tickets to competitors are not allowed with certain fares even when situations occur in which passengers had no role or control. Some airlines may cancel their flight for reasons known only to the airlines. They should tell a passenger that she will not be re-accommodated on competitors because of the fare purchased by the passenger. It should be clear to a passenger prior to ticketing if re-accommodation on a competing airline is or is not possible in the event of a flight cancellation when that is a function of the fare charged. According to one business researcher, "airline fares have become increasingly convoluted and arbitrary."[43] It is reported that Air Canada has just rolled out a program, called *On My Way*, in which a passenger can take out insurance against costs incurred when an airline experiences irregular operations.[44]

Airlines must also be upfront about their frequent flyer loyalty programs. Specifically, airlines need to be much more transparent about their award inventory in terms of the number of seats actually available for frequent flyer travel, as well as disclosing in plain language the rules of the rewards program. It creates a bad feeling when a passenger is told that seats are not available at the standard number of redemption miles, but yet are available at double the miles. Passengers feel that they have been taken advantage of, thus detracting from future loyalty to the airline, and, in essence, reversing the whole idea behind the loyalty program in the first place. Redemption of frequent flyer miles is bad enough for travel within the US, but for overseas travel, it is truly awful. Again, it is emotionally detrimental when airlines state they have no free seats available on a particular flight, but if the passenger is willing to pay two or three times the number of miles, then, all of the sudden, a seat becomes available.

Similarly, some airlines are now stating that you can get a "free" seat easier by paying part in miles and part in cash.

These practices not only go against the whole idea of being loyal in order to earn a "free" flight, but also erode future customer loyalty as customers distrust towards airlines increases due to these practices. However, one airline stands out from the rest in terms of its loyalty program. Southwest Airlines' frequent flyer program appeals to consumers because it is straight forward and contains no frills, which is in alignment with its whole organization's way of conducting business. Specifically, Southwest keeps its loyalty system really simple by utilizing a credit system rather than calculating rewards based upon miles traveled. The redemption policy is also straight forward. If a seat is available for sale then it is available to a frequent flyer for free travel. Period.

*Experience*

In today's crowded global marketplace, one way to distinguish yourself is by offering your passengers an experience in conjunction with your product or service. Products and services by themselves are not enough. Consumers also want positive experiences and personalization, hopefully through engagement. Some customers simply want a positive experience each time they purchase a product or service. Others may want a longer-term relationship with the company. A passenger on Southwest Airlines may simply want on-time performance and a courteous flight attendant. A frequent flyer on American Airlines may want personal recognition at each and every touch point, and special recognition during irregular operations or seat availability when flights are heavy. Then, of course, there may be a few customers who may be looking for an experience that "enriches their lives." One senior executive from the hotel industry goes as far as to say that customers are seeking experiences that are "unique, memorable, delightful, comfortable, and deeply rewarding."[45] Another business writer provides a different example—the iPod. When a person is talking about her iPod, the customer may not be just talking about the physical music playing unit itself, but also about related components such as the iTunes Music Store, the iTunes system, and the iPod software. Consequently, the iPod "experience" encompasses the entire system.[46]

Whereas some businesses (such as Apple mentioned above) are beginning to incorporate the experience aspect into their products and services, other businesses have been started with that concept right in the business plan. Starbucks changed a common activity, the consumption of a cup of coffee, into a lifestyle-changing experience, brought about by providing a special atmosphere and highly customized drinks. It is amazing to see how much of a premium people are willing to pay for a basic commodity that is wrapped around experience (one element of the evolving marketing practice) and customer engagement (another element of the evolving marketing practice).

The airline business is ripe for enhancing the value of the service offering by improving the passenger experience. Many passengers feel that airlines *have* provided an experience, but a negative one, especially in the US! One often hears comments such as, "I need to attend this meeting," or "I would like to vacation at this location, but unfortunately, I need to travel on an airline to get there." Although leisure travelers and those visiting friends and relatives look forward, for example, to their experience at their destination, they dread their experience on the airlines in order to get to that destination. Then on the return, the feeling is reversed. They enjoyed their experience at that destination, but now have nightmares of their trip back home.

There are, of course, some exceptions, but they are definitely just exceptions. One example of a small airline service provider that has turned to the experience brand driver is Blue Star Jets' Air Salon. Specifically, passengers booking private flights on Blue Star Jets' Air Salon may have all their grooming needs taken care of during the flight. The small, private charter service has even partnered with a plastic surgeon and a team of beauty experts, thus turning a trans-Atlantic flight into a full spa experience. While this salon is not cheap (the price list starts at US$1,000 per service, not including charter costs), this company has certainly incorporated the experience element into its initial offering.[47]

While this is only one and an extreme example of the experience brand driver, there are certainly many simple ways that airlines can focus on the experience aspect of their offerings. Think of the more than 2 dozen touch points relating to a passenger's trip, separated roughly equally by those initiated or controlled by an airline and those initiated or controlled by a passenger. The experience component does not have to be extensive. Consider in-flight service for a moment. On long-haul flights, most airlines offer in-flight entertainment at various levels. Consider what other opportunities there may be to distinguish one airline from another with just the in-flight service phase of a trip. Southwest Airlines adds to its brand in a very simple and inexpensive way by having flight attendants tell jokes, sing songs, and conduct contests, all in an effort to make the passengers' experience more enjoyable. The whole idea behind the brand experience driver is to take an everyday, sometimes even monotonous, experience and turn it into entertainment.

Consider just one simple example of how an airline's policy can impact the experience of a passenger. A passenger with a valid ticket for a 6:15 PM flight arrives early at the departure airport, and sees that the 5:00 PM flight is still there and passengers have just finished checking in. Here is how the conversation went in one case. "Do you still have an empty seat on this flight? I am booked on a later flight." "Let me see your ticket. Yes we do have extra seats but you cannot have it unless you pay US$50 more." "But you are about to close the door. Why can I not fly on this aircraft since my aircraft is expected to be delayed given that the weather is deteriorating and my flight may in fact be cancelled?" "I am sorry madam, the company policy is to let the seat fly empty rather than give it to you without the US$50. Now please step away from the counter so that I may finish the paperwork, and get this flight on its way before the weather delays this flight." How is the overall experience of this passenger impacted?

*Creativity and Innovation*

As mentioned in the second chapter on "Trends," consumers nowadays are expecting more from businesses—more value, more convenience, more speed, more efficiency, more choice of products, and most of all, more "just for me." In order to cater to an individual customer rather than to the masses, it is necessary for business executives to get out of the office or plant and find out customers' needs. Ordinary focus groups are no longer sufficient. The top brands are truly going above and beyond in terms of implementing creative research methods to anticipate and satisfy the needs of current and future customers in attempt to make a difference in their lives.

Procter & Gamble is one example of an organization that is embracing the concept of creative research. P&G launched a strategy which involved living with, talking to, and observing "real" customers around the world. Specifically, P&G sent designers and consultants to homes in Europe, Asia, and North and South America to observe people doing such tasks as cleaning their bathrooms, mopping their floors, and doing their laundry. They noticed if the products people used worked well or how they did not work, leading to frustrations occurring during these everyday experiences. These studies, in turn, allowed P&G to create prototype products that they could then take to more homes to have tested. This type of in-depth research has resulted in several successful creations, including the "Swiffer," an electrostatic floor sweeper that has become P&G's newest billion-dollar brand.[48]

Kimberly-Clark is another example of an organization striving to be creative and innovative. Kimberly-Clark, maker of Huggies diapers and other baby products, found that its sales were declining. In an effort to regain its share of the marketplace, Kimberly-Clark implemented a creative research strategy instead of relying on the traditional focus groups or surveys. The company utilized an innovative technique to truly get inside the customer experience. They mounted a camera and microphone on a pair of glasses for parents to wear as they cared for their babies at home. The system allowed the company to observe in detail how consumers use their products in real settings, rather than sitting in a conference room in a focus group. The researchers discovered that parents were struggling to open packages of wipes and pour out lotions while changing babies. This in-depth, in-home study provided valuable feedback, and the company responded by redesigning its product containers for easy grabbing and dispensing with one hand.[49]

Customer-focused innovation is not occurring just in the packaged-goods arena, exemplified above by the experience of

Procter & Gamble and Kimberly-Clark. Service businesses are also implementing creativity and innovation into their business strategy, as exemplified by Marriott Hotels. Marriott developed new design concepts for the lobbies of its Marriott and Renaissance Hotels with input from a team assembled by IDEO, a well-known design consulting organization. Specifically, IDEO sent a team of several consultants, including an anthropologist, on a multiple city tour in order to observe travelers interacting in hotels—in their lobbies, restaurants, and bars. Researchers noted positive customer experiences in these areas, as well as the improvements needed. For example, they found that few lobby spaces were comfortable for conversations, reading, small meetings, or private work sessions. Marriott, in response to these observations, is creating "social zones" for informal meetings, and work areas with ample room for laptops, papers, and coffee cups.[50]

In the airline industry, most airlines tend to rely on their own intuition of what passengers want and need. Senior executives who have never traveled in the economy class section during a 14-hour flight, and think that a 31- or 32-inch seat pitch is acceptable as long as passengers have their own six-inch monitors on which to watch movies are out-of-touch with their customers' needs and wants. There are, of course, exceptions, although very few. Virgin Atlantic has experimented with a number of creative approaches to learn about and to improve the experience of passengers such as pick up and drop off service for premium-fare passengers using such modes as motor cycles and boats in congested cities such as London. Like Virgin Atlantic, Singapore Airlines introduced an innovative in-flight entertainment system, the "video on demand" in all cabins of the plane.[51] For first-class passengers, Lufthansa not only developed separate check-in terminals in Frankfurt and Munich, but also a special ground transportation system for getting to the aircraft from those terminals. Dubai-based Emirates has developed separate compartments for its premium-fare passengers to provide privacy, and personal comfort amenities such as mini bars and meal service to suit the convenience of passengers.

While a few airlines have used some creative and innovative methods to learn about their passengers, the industry, in general, has a long way to go. Just think about a big issue that passengers are concerned about—the hassle factor relating to security at airports. One recent survey showed that 43 percent of travelers indicated that the new airport security measures implemented since the events of September 11, 2001, have made business travel a big hassle.[52] Airlines must be creative and innovative to solve this problem. They can gain significant insights not only from the companies mentioned in this chapter such as Procter & Gamble, Kimberly-Clark, and Marriott, but also from many companies profiled in the next chapter. According to both frequent and infrequent flyers, an improvement in this area would not only be highly valued, but some passengers would in fact, be willing to pay additional fare. According to informal surveys, frequent flyers would be willing to pay a significant premium, *even if their companies were not.* One passenger remarked, "If an airline wanted a US$50 premium fee for a guaranteed 15 minutes processing time, from arriving at the ticket counter to reaching the boarding gate, my only question would be, 'Would you prefer cash or a credit card?'"

*Emotion*

As with experience, emotion is a way that businesses can appeal to consumers beyond their product or service offering. Also, as with the experience brand driver, the emotion brand driver is a way to bring a product or service to life, so to speak. According to one expert, the power of a brand really comes to life when it surpasses the actual product or service features to represent an idea that comes from the "soul" of the business. Consequently, real brand power occurs when a brand is able to engage a customer not only on a *functional* level by the brand being reliable but also on an *emotional* level when the brand touches a customer's feelings and inspires them.

There are a number of examples of businesses that have successfully invoked emotion in branding. Let us start with Disney. Experts point out that Disney, for example, makes parents feel that childhood without a visit to the Magic Kingdom is not complete.[53] Next consider the auto industry. The emotional brand driver is deployed by companies such as Mercedes-Benz, who is not just trying to sell a car; the company is trying to sell a lifestyle to which a customer can aspire. They also realize that by achieving this goal, the product can, and does, command a premium price.[54] Let us move next to the upscale cooking retailers Crate & Barrel and Williams-Sonoma, both considered to be "masters at delivering an emotionally engaging brand experience." Specifically, they offer unique, high-quality products by scouring the world for new and interesting items. They enhance their product offerings by sharing stories that appeal to consumers' emotions and provide inspiration. Williams-Sonoma Grand Cuisine stores even offer customers product tastings, demonstrations, and cooking classes on specialty topics. Experts on branding note that it is the importance of experience, one that is individualized and associated with the use of a product that makes some brands unique.[55]

One way that businesses have been successful in incorporating emotion into their offerings is by finding ways to deliver new experiences, to explore situations, ones well related to travel, to acquire new skills or knowledge, or simply to collect memorable experiences.[56] In branding their products and services, some commercial airlines need to go a lot further in engaging with their customers to individualize and improve their passengers' experiences. For example, when introducing new routes, instead of just announcing the new city in the typical terms of what it offers, such as the beach, the nightlife, and so forth, emphasizing what the city offers in terms of true adventures, and portraying different activities to different segments of passengers may appeal to those segments' emotional needs to participate in and experience the unusual in terms of activities. Obviously, while the "fly and flop" mentality of just wanting to travel to a beach/resort is still a top desire of the leisure travel market, there is also a new breed of leisure travelers who seek a more adventurous, individual experience, away from the crowds and the typical vacation. Two examples of currently available and popular customized leisure trips are cycling trips and spa/wellness trips.[57] Consequently, airline brands that make a connection at the emotional level are more likely to succeed. Needless to say, this branding strategy is not for all airlines. With some low-fare airlines, it is simply, pay your fare, get on the airplane, and we will get you there safely and on time—not much different than a city bus service. There is nothing wrong with his approach to branding, and at least, there are no false promises. The airline promises nothing, other than a seat on a safe vehicle, and a passenger gets nothing additional. As one hotelier said, the best surprise is that there is no surprise.

## Leadership

From one viewpoint, when one thinks of great companies, one thinks of the strong leaders that are behind them and the characteristics that those leaders possess enabling them to get the job done. While these characteristics are certainly important, leadership branding goes beyond the characteristics of a dynamic leader or group of leaders, it encompasses every aspect of the organization; the internal employees and the external customers as well as vendors and partners. Specifically, leadership branding is about the process, not just the characteristics of the leader, and its focus is on the organization, not just the leader. However, it is leadership branding that helps to ensure that the brand promise is actually being delivered and meets customers' expectations.

Some experts think of leadership brand as the identity of a leader throughout a business that aligns customer expectations with all aspects of the behavior of the organization that affect the brand, including the employees, as discussed in the section below. The critical success factor to branded leadership is working from "the outside in," rather than the traditional "inside out." By starting at the outside, the leadership is beginning with the key reason of the business' existence; its customers. This practice involves specific, "targeted" leadership rather than traditional, generic qualities that are similar in each business. By analyzing what customers think and expect of the brand, leaders can shape the organization and its employees to create a culture that is conducive to meeting these expectations. In essence, leadership branding involves aligning customers' expectations with employees' behaviors. In addition, by focusing on customers and making the company culture customer-centric, changes in leadership become more seamless and the internal culture remains more consistent, because the focus is always on an external force, the customer, rather than an internal source, the values of the current leader. In traditional companies, the brand changes with any change in leadership.

The following are a few examples of leadership branding. At Wal-Mart, leaders focus on managing costs efficiently in order to deliver on the brand promise of "everyday low prices." At Apple, leaders aim for the development of "new products and services outside the industry norms" to meet customers' perception of the brand as innovative. At UPS, leadership branding is aligned with the brand promise of outstanding customer service.[58] Examples from the airline industry would include starting with Juan Tripp (the first leader of Pan Am), Herb Kelleher (founder of Southwest Airlines), Sir Freddie Laker (founder of Laker Airways), Sir Richard Branson (founder of Virgin Atlantic Airways), and Michael O'Leary (CEO of Ryanair). All of these leaders are considered icons who strived to "shake up" the industry and fight the "big dogs" in order to look out for their consumers.

*Employee Branding*

Leadership branding goes hand-in-hand with employee branding. The attributes that a business conveys about its brand to customers should be the same attributes that the business conveys to employees. The employees in essence need to "live the brand" to be able to deliver the brand to customers in a consistent manner.[59] Brand promises help keep employees in alignment with customers' expectations, however, while policies may be important, it is satisfied employees that are essential in terms of making the difference in delivering a brand's promise. For example, according to one expert, a merchandise return policy on its own cannot create the desired customer emotional perception. Instead, it takes empowered employees to carry out the brand's promise to the customer.[60] According to another expert, the most successful brand organizations know it requires much more than an e-mail message from the top management to get everyone involved. The leader needs to get the employees all fired up and moving in the same direction.[61] Within many airlines there are employees who say that they will continue to assist passengers out of love for this industry, despite the hurdles created by management, and the ill will toward management. Just as an unbranded product or service is a mere commodity, an unbranded employee, if you will, is a mere placeholder. All employees, especially those directly interacting with the customer, must serve as "ambassadors" for the brand, embracing the company's strategy and brand promise in order to be able to convey it to the customer and carry it out in all interactions with the customer.[62]

The RitzCarlton hotel chain is an excellent example of a company that truly embraces employee branding and truly empowers all of its employees to deliver upon the brand's promise. Specifically, the company starts, right off the bat, with spending an enormous amount on employee training and education, 10 percent of its payroll, which is four times the hotel industry average. Next, every employee, regardless of their stature, is authorized to spend as much as $2,000 in order to solve a problem of a guest staying at the RitzCarlton. RitzCarlton truly implements Rick Barrera's mantra of over-promising and over-delivering in order to gain customer loyalty. A passenger could compare this situation with a typical airline. A number of passengers miss the last connecting flight due to a late arrival and due to no fault of passengers. Given it is midnight, an airline agent decides, on her own, to provide free hotel accommodations to three passengers. One can only imagine the degree of reprimand from her supervisor the next morning. "You did what? And you did that under whose permission? You know you could get fired for such an action..." would be the probable response.

Another example is the Samsung brand. Samsung has strived to build "a corporate culture that inspires every employee to achieve both personal and corporate goals. And an essential part of that culture is a major emphasis on understanding and building the brand." Specifically, new employees receive extensive training in the values and qualities of the Samsung brand, and furthermore, Samsung monitors current employees with regards to their attitudes, feelings, and views toward the brand. Samsung offers plenty of amenities and perks, such as healthcare centers at each of its plant sites for both treating illness and promoting physical fitness, all in an effort to ensure that employees are happy and proud to be a part of the Samsung brand. The company even sponsors sports events, including the Olympics. Finally, Samsung takes great measures in terms of creating environmentally friendly products, building pollution-free workplaces, and creating accident-free workplaces. In fact, the company has been named as one of the safest workplaces in the world.[63]

*Personality*

According to Rohit Bhargava, author of *Personality Not Included*, personality can really make a company stand out from its competitors. Specifically, Bhargava defines personality in this context as "the unique, authentic, and talkable soul of your brand that people can get passionate about." This driver, in reality, is the sum of some of the drivers listed previously. This business analyst recognizes that personality can be one of a company's greatest assets, but many companies do not capitalize upon this factor. Rather, they end up hiding their personality, thus, in essence, becoming faceless in the eyes of consumers. Specifically, Bhargava describes how three companies have overcome the issue of facelessness in developing a personality:[64]

- *Target*—Kmart was the "old, reliable, chain, department store"—selling ordinary products at ordinary prices. This practice was profitable, until Target came along. Target was anything but ordinary. The company focuses on carrying the latest fashions in terms of both clothing and home goods, and the chain has even carried this image right through to its pharmacy, where it redesigned the ordinary prescription bottle into an "award-winning clear Rx bottle design." Bhargava focuses on why Target became one of the top in the discount store industry while Kmart ended up in Chapter 11 reorganization in 2003. Specifically, Target was successful for three main reasons: (1) it focused on a strategy which included developing an understanding of what consumers were purchasing and what affected their purchasing behavior; (2) it recognized that it was no longer enough to offer ordinary products at low prices; and (3) it recognized that design and style mattered to consumers. Kmart, on the other hand, did not recognize these shifts in the discount store industry, and, therefore, lost its market share.

- *Intel*—Intel has a unique business in that its product is produced to go into other products rather than to stand on its own. Intel named itself a "component brand," in order to capitalize on this unique position. Intel cleverly markets its brand with its small square seal located on each computer that contains Intel's technology. Despite these distinguishing marketing techniques, Intel still needed a means to engage with its customers—it was a "closed" company. How did Intel overcome its facelessness? It used social technology to reach out and be in front of consumers, through Internet blogs, communities, and forums. The company now even has blogs from Brazil, China, Latin America, and Russia. Implementing social technology into its strategy has helped "humanize" the brand.

- *ING Direct*—ING Direct was one of the first to offer a virtual banking business, allowing customers to have savings accounts online. The whole premise behind direct banking online is that banks can offer relatively higher interest rates as they are not bearing the typical costs associated with traditional banks such as physical branches and tellers. However, ING Direct still felt the need to further distinguish itself, especially since they are not the typical brick-and-mortar banks. One way ING Direct really "got out there" in the eyes of the public was by implementing several unique marketing campaigns. Such offerings include free commuter transit to customers in major US cities such as DC and San Francisco, the sponsoring of the New York City Marathon and other events. Finally, ING introduced the ING Café. ING realized that despite the fact that the company was offering a virtual banking service, customers still wanted to see something physical, and thus it created the ING Café. The ING Café is nothing like a traditional bank—it literally is a café, where free Internet and ING consultants are available. With all of these events and offerings, ING has managed to "exhibit the company's personality, which is irreverent, open, friendly, and genuine"— all characteristics that one would not expect from a traditional banking experience. ING's efforts have paid off—as evidenced by their 96 percent customer satisfaction rate.

The personality driver is interesting in the airline industry. In the airline industry, not many airlines have a personality to begin with, unless it is a negative one. Let us go to those precious few airlines that do have a personality and and one that is positive. In today's alliance environment, it is quite possible for a passenger to book a multi-sector flight on a brand-named airline with a highly defined personality. The passenger could end up traveling half way around the world, and never set foot on the original airline booked. How would this passenger feel?

## Managing Passenger Loyalty

While the airline industry was by no means the earliest one to offer loyalty programs, it did raise the visibility of such programs to a level that many other businesses emulated with similar customer programs—hotels, car rental companies, and so forth. Originally airline frequent flyer programs in the US were started by the larger airlines after deregulation to compete with the then new airlines (such as Midway Airlines, New York Airways, and People Express) that had low fares but limited networks and undeveloped brands. These programs allowed the established larger airlines (such as American, TWA, and United) to be able to take advantage of their competitive strengths such as:

- breadth and depth of their networks to be able to offer free seats on highly desirable leisure destinations such as Hawaii;

- massive computer systems that could keep track of all the data related to these loyalty programs;

- revenue management systems (how many seats to free up on each flight) that enabled them to charge differential fares and retain the higher-fare-paying travelers;

- brand names that were well known and, to some extent, respected.

Many new upstarts could not compete with this powerful combination strategy of a frequent flyer program and revenue management system enabled by the network and computer systems. Plus, the passenger loyalty programs allowed airlines to collect a lot of useful data on the travel habits of their higher-fare-paying passengers who traveled frequently and use this information to build loyalty. The first airline in the US to establish such a program was American Airlines in 1981. Hotels did not develop their own programs initially, but instead became partners of airlines. Subsequently, recognizing the value of such programs and the costs they had to pay airlines as partners, they decided to start their own programs. After the hotels came the car rental agencies. However, even today, while many businesses have their own loyalty programs, they still maintain membership in airline programs. It is because of the fact that the air transportation component represents the focal attraction, as it is the part that allows a customer to travel and then take advantage of a hotel or a rental car. As for other partners whose products do not relate directly to travel (say retailers of high end goods), they are interested in remaining members of airline programs because the partnership with airlines provides them access to the higher end spenders—not occasional passengers traveling at low promotional fares, but the frequent corporate travelers purchasing tickets at much higher fares. This access has enabled some retailers to acquire new customers.

While the airline loyalty programs clearly had a rationale at their inception, the question now relates to their cost effectiveness, either in their current form or in their re-designed form. Airlines are not alone in facing this question. Many other businesses face a similar question. What do their loyalty programs really mean for the companies on the one hand, and their customers on the other? As Dianne Durkin, author of *The Loyalty Advantage*, points out, buzzwords such as "customer satisfaction, customer loyalty, customer centricity, customer care" are used so much that the real meaning behind them is often forgotten. It is the existence of truly loyal customers (as opposed to those who may have limited choices) that keeps a company in business. Durkin reports that while companies talk about the subject of loyalty, there is not a lot of follow through, given that reports show that a typical company in the United States loses about half of its customers every five years. Moreover, it is reported that some surveys indicate that when consumers were polled as to the key ingredients involved to create a "good customer experience," more than 60 percent of the people surveyed had switched brands not due to the product itself, but due to "poor service and lack of personal attention."[65]

There are many factors that determine loyalty, customer satisfaction being only one. Denove and Power, authors of *Satisfaction* recount an anecdote of a husband and wife on a US airline flight, where the husband is ranting and raving about his bad experience with this particular airline. Ironically, the wife points out that he always says that he will never fly this airline again, but then always does, time after time, because that particular airline offers the lowest fare. This example illustrates that while customer satisfaction is certainly a key factor of loyalty, price is also another major determining factor. Consequently, there is an important difference between actual loyalty and intended loyalty and, of course, such a difference would vary among different businesses. Denove and Power give an example of a monopoly, the Department of Motor Vehicles (DMV) in the US, where no matter how much consumers despise their experience, there are no other choices (except to conduct their business via the online DMV site perhaps). In some ways, one could view the DMV to yield a 100 percent loyalty rate.[66]

From an airline point of view, some passengers are "forced" to choose an airline if it has the lion's share of the flights in and out of a given city (a "fortress hub"), regardless of the level of service provided. Other passengers go strictly by the schedule, and take the airline that has the best schedule, relatively speaking, regardless of the level of service provided. This is often the case, of course, for a business passenger who must travel frequently to the same city to visit an office. Therefore, an airline must not confuse these types of passengers as customers who are loyal because of its service, even though they may travel on the airline frequently. In fact, in a number of cases, passengers not only dislike the service offered but pay higher fares for services based on the lack of viable alternatives. *Consequently, loyalty (in such cases) should not be confused with patronage.* Therefore, the likelihood that a passenger will remain loyal to an airline is related to a number of factors, including availability of a viable competitor (including information about alternatives), frequency of travel, and the status earned in a given airline frequent flyer program.

Consider a couple of occasional travelers (in a major US city such as New York or Chicago) and their need to travel to India (a major city such as Delhi or Mumbai). They may know the services offered by US airlines that may even offer nonstop service (American, Continental, Delta, etcetera). They may even know a little bit about some of the European airlines that may offer connecting service through Europe (Air France, British Airways, Lufthansa, etcetera), but, how much information do they have on new carriers such as Jet Airways and Qatar Airways that may offer connecting services through Europe or the Middle East? On top of lack of information, passengers who have gathered a large number of miles on one carrier are likely to be reluctant to switch airlines (even if their airline offers a lower quality service), unless they are either members of a number of airline loyalty programs or the airline is a member of a large alliance.

To answer the key question raised above (relating to the cost effectiveness of a loyalty program), one must start with some related but fundamental questions. One important point to consider, in addition to the various aspects that factor into customer loyalty, is the information on the relationship between the loyalty of a passenger and the profitability of that passenger—if not an individual passenger, then at least a segment of passengers. Some business analysts believe that the relationship between loyalty and profitability is much weaker than originally thought, in terms of loyalty programs. V. Kumar, author of *Managing Customers for Profit*, starts the discussion by first addressing a key myth relating to customer loyalty—that loyal customers cost less to serve. Specifically, companies often tend to follow the line of thinking that although customers can be expensive to acquire, loyal customers end up being profitable over the long term because the initial costs are spread out over all of their repeat purchases with the company. However, it is quite possible that these customers are actually less profitable due to two key reasons. First, such customers are likely to expect something in return for their repeat business in terms of discounts, thus chipping away at the profit margin. Second, they tend to expect more personalized service, as they believe they have a long-term relationship with the company, and that attention also causes the company to incur additional costs.[67] There are other business analysts who support this view that not all customers generate an adequate rate of return to justify their participation in a relationship such as a loyalty program.[68]

In examining the profitability of loyalty programs there are three other issues. First, it is important to examine the cost of implementing and maintaining such programs. The issue is not just related to the administrative costs, but also the opportunity costs of giving away a free seat. There are other complications as well. For example, in the past some global airlines have tried offering perks unrelated to travel such as using the earned miles to have a private dinner party catered by an airline's chef or arranging golf outings or giving merchandise such as iPods, or 24/7 concierge service. While these alternatives are good in terms of an airline trying to differentiate itself from others in the industry, it is important, once again, to evaluate the costs of such offerings.

Second, some airlines gain a significant percentage of their revenue by selling miles to other businesses—credit card companies, hotels, car rental agencies, telephone service providers, and so forth. Specifically, these partnerships allow passengers to accrue miles with partner businesses. Partners pay a couple of cents per mile to an airline if their customers use the airline services, creating ancillary revenue for an airline. Co-branded affinity cards also play a particularly important role, for example, American Express with Delta Airlines or Citi and American Airlines. These cards allow the user to accrue miles toward a wide array of purchases, plus airline travelers can use some of the perks offered by the credit card company, such as in the case of American Express, for the ability to make reservations at certain restaurants. As mentioned later, some airlines have begun to distinguish between the miles earned by traveling verses the miles earned by purchasing merchandise/using the products or services of a partner. In fact, some airlines such as Air Canada, have actually divested their frequent flyer programs.

Third, it is important to factor in the computation about how customers feel about the loyalty programs. In the case of airlines, at least in the US, passengers feel that the value of airline loyalty programs has been decreasing year by year over the past 10 years. One reason passengers are frustrated with current loyalty programs is that they feel as if people who accumulate miles by purchasing merchandise are taking seats away from those passengers who actually earn the miles by flying. Also, passengers feel that when they first joined the programs, they were given the impression that the miles accumulated in the loyalty programs had no expiration date. Passengers also did not know that airlines would increase the number of miles required to get a free ticket. Furthermore, there are even more complicated issues. One global airline decided to keep a first-class cabin (three classes instead of two) for a number of reasons, one of which related to loyalty programs. According to this airline, many passengers purchased tickets in business class on its intercontinental flights, hoping that they would get upgraded to first class. In many markets, according to this airline, many passengers would have traveled on competitors if this airline did not have a first class, a real differentiator. How does one put numbers on such considerations? Many companies, not just airlines, simply do not have adequate metrics to evaluate the cost effectiveness of their loyalty programs, and as such, end up implementing and maintaining totally flawed loyalty programs.

In light of the aforementioned issues, how can an airline overcome these issues involved with customer loyalty? The first recommendation of some business analysts is that loyalty programs should not be offered to all customers, and the profitability factor of the customer must be considered. For example, Kumar points out that the early airline frequent flyer programs were based on the miles traveled, not the price paid for the ticket. Thus, all customers were awarded the same amount of points, regardless of whether they were profitable or not. Only recently has this trend in airline loyalty programs been corrected. Currently some airlines have begun to reward passengers on what they spend. A truly successful loyalty program should be able to generate approximately 10 percent of an airline's revenue. It is doubtful if any airline today comes close to this number, the actual number being perhaps closer to half that for a typical airline. To achieve such a goal, it becomes necessary to focus on the passenger and not the transaction. That means having the capability to correctly identify, differentiate and communicate with the high margin passenger by delivering customized services, like a free seat at the last minute or an upgrade on an exceptionally crowded flight. Based on experience within the airline industry, it is difficult to formulate a strategy based on such considerations. For example:

- Passengers who are used to getting mileage credit regardless of the fare paid will be violently opposed to such a strategy.

- Some passengers are likely to riot at a gate or in the airplane if an airline upgraded some passengers and not others even though there were seats available in the premium cabin.

- If an airline were to have a seat available on a highly desirable flight, the day before a major holiday to a particularly desirable leisure destination, how would the airline decide who gets that seat. Would the choice be based on mileage tier status or on lifetime customer value?

- Some passengers are not too happy learning that some airlines do differentiate between the miles earned by flying airplanes and those earned by buying general merchandise.

One way to resolve such strategy issues is to examine best practices, not just within the airline industry, but other businesses in general, for example the hospitality industry. In the airline industry, Southwest Airlines is considered to have a good loyalty program, as mentioned earlier. From the perspective of the airline, it is relatively simple to maintain. From a passenger's perspective, the conditions are very clear and there are no blackout dates or flights. If a seat is available, it is available for any passenger, one buying a ticket or one looking for a free seat. Outside the industry, Hilton has differentiated its Hilton *HHonors* program by not implementing blackout dates at all, a feature that plagues most loyalty programs, especially airline frequent flyer programs.

Marriott also seems to have a desirable loyalty program. One feature of Marriott's program is the ability for members to override blackout dates by utilizing more of their points, if they wish. Even though some airlines follow the same practice but, unlike Marriott, the practice is not made transparent.

Using a carefully designed program, an airline can, in fact, bring about differentiation through its loyalty program. Besides looking at best practices as described above, some business analysts suggest a slightly different approach. Sisodia, Sheth and Wolfe, authors of *Firms of Endearment*, claim that one way to gain loyalty is, in fact, to become a "Firm of Endearment" (FOE). Specifically, they describe FOEs as being "humanistic" businesses that try to maximize shareholder value from a much broader perspective, one that includes society as a whole. They also look at value with numerous dimensions—emotional, social, and financial value. Consequently, they focus on not just a much broader group of shareholders (including the general public, employees, suppliers) but also value measured from different perspectives. These analysts indicate that while many companies may be successful financially, they may lack this "emotive" quality. Consider, for example, Wal-Mart. While consumers undoubtedly enjoy Wal-Mart's "everyday low prices," some consumers may not get their "warm and fuzzies" from shopping at the superstore, and some may not want the superstore in their backyard. Some may go so far as to view it as "a company without a soul." Specifically, Sisodia, Sheth, and Wolfe address the difference between behavioral loyalty and attitudinal loyalty. While there may be people who often shop routinely at stores to which they feel no emotional attachment (customers can be loyal in *behavior* to a company without being loyal in *attitude*), attitudinal loyalty comes from emotional attachment. These authors attribute the success of Target partially due to this chain's ability to balance both of these elements, thus offering low prices, a pleasant experience, and more stylish products. Eventually, this difference does get reflected in the financials. They report, for example, that Wal-Mart's stock has been relatively stagnant for the past five years while Target's has risen nearly 150 percent. Finally, according to these writers, FOEs are able to create customer loyalty by striving for a "share of heart" that, in turn, will lead to a customer's "share of wallet." They are convinced that a strategy of implementing an "emotive" element into business will be key in surviving in the future marketplace. Examples of companies reported and their strategies are: [69]

- Whole Foods and Costco that have relatively modest executive salaries.

- Honda and Harley-Davidson that have an open-door policy at the executive level.

- Honda that views suppliers as true partners and encourages suppliers to collaborate so that Honda itself and its suppliers can improve quality and become profitable.

- Trader Joe's with its employee compensation and benefits at a significantly higher level than the standard.

- The Container Store chain that devotes considerably more time than its competitors to employee training.

- Southwest Airlines that has a much lower employee turnover compared to the industry average (the company considers its corporate culture to be its greatest asset and a primary source of competitive advantage—demonstrated by the fact that Southwest Airlines elected a "Culture Committee").

- Wegmans Food Markets that empower their employees to make sure customers leave a transaction experience fully satisfied.

- Patagonia that makes a conscious effort to hire people who are passionate about the company and its products.

- Google that humanizes the company experience for customers and employees on a daily basis, for example, by providing free gourmet meals around the clock to all employees.

It should not be surprising that many of these qualities, especially the emotive factor, capitalizing upon the emotional and experience elements of business, overlap with the brand drivers that were discussed earlier in this chapter. One writer, Durkin, in fact, ties another one of the brand drivers, employee branding, to customer loyalty. Specifically, she discusses a simple, but very powerful, criterion that she calls "the Loyalty Factor" which links employees, customers, and brands: *"Employee loyalty drives customer loyalty, which drives brand loyalty."* While this may seem like common sense, she points out that many managers either take it for granted or completely ignore it altogether. Consequently, according to Durkin, it is imperative that managements take the responsibility to create an atmosphere in which employee loyalty can flourish.

A perfect example of a company who has been over-whelmingly successful in the area of employee loyalty is Southwest Airlines. Half of its mission statement is about the airline's commitment to its employees. It keeps its costs, as well as fares, low through its employees. And how does it achieve the loyalty and satisfaction of its employees? According to Durkin, it is through Southwest's adherence to its motto: "Treat others as you would like to be treated." For example, after the terrorist attacks of September 11th, Southwest did not lay off any workers, unlike most of its competitors. According to McConnell and Huba, authors of *Creating Customer Evangelists*, companies like Southwest create "evangelistic" loyalty by hiring "empathetic people." The company wants its employees to be authentic—to talk like "real" people, to have fun on the job—they want the employees to relate to customers in a humanistic manner, instead of being a "corporate robot." This aspect ties to the discussion earlier in this chapter as well as in Chapter 5: do not talk at your customers, talk to/with them, engage your customers. Finally, Southwest, like other companies who are loyalty "evangelists," recognize that "people are loyal to people."[70]

Unfortunately, most companies do not enjoy Southwest's relationship with their employees. It is common to hear that employees do not think that their companies care about them. Specifically, according to one report, 60 percent of respondents to one survey said that employers showed less concern for employees than they did for the "financial bottom line." Ironically, employees are often the key link to both prospective and existing customers, and are therefore the single most valuable asset to a company, as discussed in the employee branding section. In order to create the loyalty factor, Durkin states that companies must go beyond the old tools of rewarding employees. Compensation and benefits are certainly important, but companies must go above and beyond in order to differentiate themselves with their employees. Eastern Bank in New England, for example, recognized this need to go above and beyond, and implemented an "on-the-spot" rewards system that empowers managers to reward employees who are "caught" providing exemplary service. These employees are allowed to choose the award, whether it be a gift certificate or an Eastern Bank item. The implementation of this employee rewards system illustrates that Eastern Bank understands that employees are key to the company's success.[71] In the final analyses, one could say that customer loyalty depends on customer service, but customer service, in turn, depends to the attitude of employees.

Relating customer loyalty back to brands and branding, a company needs to get to a position where its products and services become a brand that customers not only like, but cannot live without. According to Durkin, examples of companies that are on this track include American Express, Harley-Davidson, Waterford, Ben & Jerry's, and Victoria's Secret. These companies "sell more than products; they are part of a lifestyle with which customers can identify." These companies embrace several of the brand drivers described earlier in this chapter, and, in the case of Whole Foods, Durkin acknowledges that it exemplifies all the principles of the loyalty factor, employee loyalty, customer loyalty, and brand loyalty, all working seamlessly. Furthermore, Whole Foods even exemplifies the criteria describing a "Firm of Endearment." Specifically, John Mackey's (CEO, President, Chairman, and Co-founder) "passion about food—food that is good, fresh, ethically raised, and, in the case of animals, humanely treated," along with his "philosophy to treat people—and animals, and the earth—fairly" have won the hearts of the company's employees and customers.[72]

What about airlines? Southwest Airlines appears to exemplify all of the same principles of the loyalty factor listed previously, again, all working seamlessly. From a passenger's point of view, Southwest provides a reliable product with consistently good service, and at reasonable fares. That is it—nothing more, and nothing less. Finally, what is a good measure of customer loyalty? According to one expert, Frederick Reichheld, there is only one metric—the number of customers who would recommend your company or brand. He calls this metric, the "Net Promoter Score" which is the difference between promoters and detractors.[73] In an article also written by Reichheld, he illustrates the "net promoter" effect in terms of graphs representing the airline industry and the car rental industry. Not surprisingly based upon examples illustrated in this book, Southwest Airlines and Enterprise Rent-A-Car were the top companies, respectively, in terms of the correlation between the company's growth rate and the percentage of its customers who are "promoters."[74]

## Takeaways

- In the new world of marketing businesses must learn to engage with their targeted audiences, a tall order even for visionary businesses, let alone airlines. In the US, the quality of airline service has deteriorated to the point that according to one recent survey, 42 percent of the respondents would avoid airline travel if they could get their business done in some other manner.

- Within airline marketing, branding requires particular focus. Most airlines either do not have a recognized and respected brand, or the one that they have contains generic promises that are copies of other brands with promises that are either not delivered at all, or not delivered consistently.

- A few airlines that have succeeded in developing strong brands have, differentiated themselves, communicated effectively the difference, and delivered consistently on the promise. One of the best examples is Federal Express.

- Based on an examination of the best practices from businesses in general, the important brand drivers are distinctiveness, relevance, consistency, authenticity, transparency, experience, creativity and innovation, emotion, leadership, employee branding, and personality. With the exception of a very few, airlines have not developed their brands around even a few drivers. The only driver that does show up is consistency and, unfortunately, that shows up in the negative sense, particularly in the US.

- Loyalty must not be confused with patronage. Many passengers travel on airlines through their hub fortresses even when service is poor.

- Airlines must develop adequate metrics to measure the cost effectiveness of their loyalty programs. A truly successful loyalty program should be able to generate approximately 10 percent of an airline's revenue.

- Employee loyalty drives customer loyalty, which drives brand loyalty.

## Notes

1   Shiffman, Denise, *The Age of Engage: Reinventing Marketing for Today's Connected, Collaborative, and Hyperinteractive Culture* (Ladera Ranch, CA: Hunt Street Press, 2008), pp. 4–5, 8–9 and 9–10.
2   McConnell, Ben and Jackie Huba, *Creating Customer Evangelists: How Loyal Customers Become a Volunteer Sales Force* (Chicago, IL: Kaplan Publishing, 2007), pp. 10–14.
3   Millward Brown, "2007 Brand Z: Top 100 Most Powerful Brands," Millward Brown Optimor.
4   Quote the University of Michigan Survey as reported in the Bloomberg Press, dated 14 May, 2007.
5   Harteveldt, Henry, Forrester Research, Presentation at the OSU Conference in Turkey, September 2007.
6   Harteveldt, Henry, Forrester Research, Presentation at the OSU Conference in Turkey, September 2007.
7   Unisys Scorecard, Volume 6, Issue 7, April 2008, p. 6.
8   Unisys Scorecard, Volume 6, Issue 7, April 2008, p. 7.
9   London, Joanne, Gernstein, *FLY NOW: A Colorful Story of Flight From Hot Air Balloon To The 777 "Worldliner"* (Washington. DC National Geographic), p. 65.
10  Unisys Scorecard, Volume 6, Issue 5, February 2008, p. 3.

11 London, Joanne, Gernstein, *FLY NOW: A Colorful Story of Flight From Hot Air Balloon To The 777 "Worldliner"* (Washington. DC National Geographic), p. 170.

12 Lovegrove, Keith, *AIRLINE: Identity, Design and Culture* (London: Laurence King Publishing, 2005), p. 102.

13 Adamson, Allen P. *BrandSimple: How the Best Brands Keep it Simple and Succeed* (NY: Palgrave MacMillan, 2006), p. 18.

14 Clifton Rita, Simmons, John, and others from *The Economist, BRANDS AND BRANDING* (Princeton, NJ: Bloomberg Press, 2003), p. 98.

15 Unisys Scorecard, Volume 6, Issue 5, February 2008, p. 4 (originally from Bain & Company, The Gilford Group Limited, November 2006).

16 Knapp, Duane, *The Brand Promise: How Costco, Ketel One, Make-A-Wish, Tourism Vancouver, & Other Leading Brands Make and Keep the Promise That Guarantees Success!* (NY: McGraw Hill, 2008), p. 13.

17 Sartain, Libby and Mark Schumann, *BRAND FROM THE INSIDE: Eight Essentials to Emotionally Connect Your Employees to Your Business* (San Francisco, CA: Jossey-Bass, 2006), p. 16.

18 Cone, Steve, *Powerlines: Words that Sell Brands, Grip Fans, & Sometimes Change History* (NY: Bloomberg Press, 2008), pp. 129–30, 136–7, 228–9.

19 Unisys Scorecard, Volume 6, Issue 5, February 2008, p. 5.

20 Hatch, Mary Jo and Majken Schultz, *Taking Brand Initiative: How Companies Can Align Strategy, Culture and Identity Through Corporate Branding* (San Francisco, CA: Jossey-Bass, 2008), p. 21.

21 Davis, Scott M. and Michael Dunn, *Building the Brand-Driven Business: Operationalize Your Brand to Drive Profitable Growth* (San Francisco, CA: Jossey-Bass, 2002), p. 16.

22 Harter, Gregor, Landry, Edward, and Andrew Tipping (editors), *CMO Thought Leaders: The Rise of the Strategic Marketer*. A book published by Booz Allen Hamilton in 2007, Interview with Foster's Neville Fielke: *The Brand Equity Challenge*, p. 103.

23 Kador, John Charles, *Schwab: How One Company Beat Wall Street and Reinvented the Brokerage Industry* (Hoboken, NJ: John Wiley, 2002), p. 57.

24 "Building an Airline Brand," *Airliner World Magazine*, July 2007.

25 Kelly, Lois, *BEYOND BUZZ: The Next Generation of Word-of-Mouth Marketing* (NY: American Management Association, 2007), p. 36.

26 Kelly, Lois, *BEYOND BUZZ: The Next Generation of Word-of-Mouth Marketing* (NY: American Management Association, 2007), p. 36.

27 Davis, Scott M. & Michael Dunn, *Building Brand-Driven Business: Operationalize Your Brand to Drive Profitable Growth* (San Francisco, CA: Jossey-Bass, 2002), p. 38.

28 Bund, Barbara E., *The Outside-In Corporation: How to Build a Customer-Centric Organization for Breakthrough Results* (NY: McGraw-Hill, 2006), p. 219.

29  Simon Glynn, Lippincott, Presentation, at the OSU Conference in Turkey, September 2007.

30  Wetherbe, James C., *The World On Time: The 11 Management Principles That Made FedEx an Overnight Sensation* (Santa Monica, CA: Knowledge Exchange, LLC, 1996), p. 183.

31  Kador, John Charles, *Schwab: How One Company Beat Wall Street and Reinvented the Brokerage Industry* (Hoboken, NJ: John Wiley, 2002), p. 81.

32  Michelli, Joseph A., *The Starbucks Experience: 5 Principles for Turning Ordinary into Extraordinary* (NY: McGraw-Hill, 2007), pp. 99–101.

33  Clifton Rita, Simmons, John, and others from *The Economist, BRANDS AND BRANDING* (Princeton, NJ: Bloomberg Press, 2003), p. 70.

34  Gilmore, James H. and B. Joseph Pine II, *Authenticity: What Consumers Really Want* (Boston, MA: Harvard Business School Press, 2007), p. 3.

35  Davis & Dunn, *Building the Brand-Driven Business: Operationalize Your Brand to Drive Profitable Growth* (San Francisco, CA: Jossey-Bass, 2002), p. 109.

36  Bhargava, Rohit, *Personality Not Included: Why Companies Lose Their Authenticity—And How Great Brands Get it Back* (NY: McGraw Hill, 2008), pp. 46–7.

37  Kelly, Lois, *BEYOND BUZZ: The Next Generation of Word-of-Mouth Marketing* (NY: American Management Association, 2007), p. 74.

38  Bhargava, Rohit, *Personality Not Included: Why Companies Lose Their Authenticity—And How Great Brands Get it Back* (NY: McGraw Hill, 2008), pp. 87–8.

39  Gilmore, James H. and B. Joseph Pine II, *Authenticity: What Consumers Really Want* (Boston, MA: Harvard Business School Press, 2007), pp. 5–6.

40  Clifton, Rita, Simmons, John, and others from *The Economist, BRANDS AND BRANDING* (Princeton, NJ: Bloomberg Press, 2003), p. 99.

41  Weiner, Edie and Arnold Brown, *Future Think: How to Think Clearly in a Time of Change* (Upper Saddle River, NJ: 2006), p. 112.

42  Durkin, Dianne Michonski, *The Loyalty Advantage: Essentials Steps to Energize Your Company, Your Customers, Your Brand* (NY: American Management Association, 2005), pp. 81–2.

43  Mariotti, John L., *The Complexity Crisis: Why Too Many Products, Markets, and Customers are Crippling Your Company—and What to do About it* (Avon, MA: Platinum Press, 2008), p. front jacket flap.

44  Unisys Scorecard, Volume 6, Issue 7, April 2008, p. 8.

45  Tisch, Jonathan M., *Chocolates on the Pillow Aren't Enough: Reinventing the Customer Experience* (Hoboken, NJ: John Wiley, 2007), pp. 1–3.

46  Johnson, Lisa, *Mind Your X's and Y's: Satisfying the 10 Cravings of a New Generation of Consumers* (NY: Free Press, 2006), p. 83.

47  Johnson, Lisa, *Mind Your X's and Y's: Satisfying the 10 Cravings of a New Generation of Consumers* (NY: Free Press, 2006), p. 190.

48  Tisch, Jonathan M., *Chocolates on the Pillow Aren't Enough: Reinventing the Customer Experience* (Hoboken, NJ: John Wiley, 2007), pp. 19–20.

49  Tisch, Jonathan M., *Chocolates on the Pillow Aren't Enough: Reinventing the Customer Experience* (Hoboken, NJ: John Wiley, 2007), p. 20.

50  Tisch, Jonathan M., *Chocolates on the Pillow Aren't Enough: Reinventing the Customer Experience* (Hoboken, NJ: John Wiley, 2007), pp. 20–21.

51  Roll, Martin, *Asian Brand Strategy: How Asia Builds Strong Brands* (NY: Palgrave MacMillan, 2006), pp. 130–38.

52  Yesawich, Peter, Y Partnership, Presentation at the OSU Conference in Turkey, September, 2007.

53  Sartain, Libby and Mark Schumann, *BRAND FROM THE INSIDE: Eight Essentials to Emotionally Connect Your Employees to Your Business* (San Francisco, CA: Jossey-Bass, 2006), p. 9.

54  Harter, Gregor, Landry, Edward, and Andrew Tipping (editors), *CMO Thought Leaders: The Rise of the Strategic Marketer*. A book published by Booz Allen Hamilton in 2007, Interview with Olaf Gottgens, Vice President, Brand Communications, Mercedes-Benz, pp. 162–70.

55  Silverstein, Michael J. and Neil Fiske, *Trading Up: Why Consumers Want New Luxury Goods—and How Companies Create Them* (NY: Portfolio, Penguin Group, 2005), p. 103.

56  Silverstein, Michael J. and Neil Fiske, *Trading Up: Why Consumers Want New Luxury Goods—and How Companies Create Them* (NY: Portfolio, Penguin Group, 2005), p. 45.

57  Tom Costley, TNS, UK, Presentation at the OSU Conference in Turkey, September 2007, pp. 4–5.

58  Ulrich, Dave and Norm Smallwood, *Leadership Brand: Developing Customer-Focused Leaders to Drive Performance and Build Lasting Value* (Boston, MA: Harvard Business School Press, 2007), pp. 5, 8–9, 43, 51.

59  Sartain, Libby and Mark Schumann, *BRAND FROM THE INSIDE: Eight Essential to Emotionally Connect Your Employees to Your Business* (San Francisco, CA: Jossey-Bass, 2006), p. 21.

60  Knapp, Duane, *The Brand Promise: How Costco, Kotel One, Make-A-Wish, Tourism Vancouver, & Other Leading Brands Make and Keep the Promise That Guarantees Success!* (NY: McGraw Hill, 2008), p. 79.

61  Adamson, Allen, *Brand Simple: How the Best Brands Keep it Simple and Succeed* (NY: Palgrave MacMillan, 2006), p. 134.

62  Knapp, Duane, *The Brand Promise: How Costco, Ketel One, Make-A-Wish, Tourism Vancouver, & Other Leading Brands Make and Keep the Promise That Guarantees Success!* (NY: McGraw Hill, 2008), pp. 81 and 99.

63  Barrera, Rick, *Over Promise and Over Deliver: The Secrets of Unshakable Customer Loyalty* (NY: Penguin Group, 2005), pp. 17, 62–3.

64  Bhargava, Rohit, *Personality Not Included: Why Companies Lose Their Authenticity—And How Great Brands Get it Back* (NY: McGraw Hill, 2008), pp. 23–31, 67–8, 80–81, 169–71.

65  Durkin, Dianne Michonski, *The Loyalty Advantage: Essential Steps to Energize Your Company, Your Customers, Your Brand* (NY: American Management Association, 2005), pp. 63–5.

66  Denove, Chris and James D. Power, *Satisfaction: How Every Great Company Listens to the Voices of the Customer* (NY: Portfolio, 2006), pp. 17–19, 22.

67  Kumar, V., *Managing Customers for Profit: Strategies to Increase Profits and Build Loyalty* (Upper Saddle River, NJ: Wharton School Publishing, Pearson Education, 2008), pp. 11–19.

68  Keiningham, Timothy L. et al., *Loyalty Myths: Hyped Strategies That Will Put You Out of Business—and Proven Tactics That Really Work* (Hoboken, NJ, 2005), pp. 202–5.

69  Sisodia, Raj, Sheth, Jag, and David B. Wolfe, *Firms of Endearment* (Upper Saddle River, NJ: Wharton School Publishing, Pearson Education, 2007), pp. 4–5, 7–11, 99, 100.

70  McConnell, Ben and Jackie Huba, *Creating Customer Evangelists: How Loyal Customers Become a Volunteer Sales Force* (Chicago, IL: Kaplan Publishing, 2007), pp. 2–3.

71  Durkin, Dianne Michonski, *The Loyalty Advantage: Essential Steps to Energize Your Company, Your Customers, Your Brand* (NY: American Management Association, 2005), pp. 43, 46, 48, 52, 56–7.

72  Durkin, Dianne Michonski, *The Loyalty Advantage: Essential Steps to Energize Your Company, Your Customers, Your Brand* (NY: American Management Association, 2005), pp. 65, 68–9, 79–82.

73  Reichheld, Fred, *The Ultimate Question: Driving Good Profits and True Growth* (Boston, MA: Harvard Business School Press, 2006), pp. 18–19.

74  Reichheld, Frederick F., "The One Number You Need to Grow," *Harvard Business Review*, December 2003.

# Chapter 7

# Gaining Insights from Non-Airline Brands Around the World

In order to develop some foresight from some insight, airlines should benchmark less within the airline industry and much more outside the airline industry. This chapter can help airlines gain significant insights from other businesses, especially in the areas of strategy and branding. This chapter provides key insights relating to branding and strategy from a broad array of 20 companies in different businesses and based in different geographic locations.

## Amazon.com

Amazon.com, a US$15 billion (revenue in 2007) company based in the US, is an excellent example of a business whose online retailing systems and processes have all but replaced the need for traditional customer service, and raised consumer expectations for state of the art online retailing in all categories. Amazon enables customers to find what they need, order it, obtain a status report by e-mail, pay online, and get the purchases made by mail.[1]

Amazon developed a different business model for selling books and, within an amazingly short period of time, gained a prominent position in the US just behind the giants—Barnes & Noble and Borders. Having established itself in the field of selling creatively books online, Amazon's website is now a virtual mall selling numerous products—CDs, DVDs, electronics, videos, and more. Amazon.com has developed a unique partnership with other merchants. It hosts other retailers' websites and it allows third parties to sell their products on its website.

The merchant partnership not only helps to increase customer traffic to Amazon's website, but also broaden its brand name. Take, for example, a recent decision by NBC Universal, a television and movie media company, to download and sell television shows on the Web. Amazon plans to market NBC Universal's content through its Unbox download service, giving customers the choice, for example, of renting a movie or buying a download. The video can be viewed on a personal computer, or some portable video players, or it could even be delivered directly to television sets through TiVo devices.[2]

The key competency of Amazon, enabled by the Internet, is its ability to create and serve micro-segments—virtually segments of one for each individual purchaser. Amazon.com is at the cutting edge of acquiring and analyzing relevant information about its customers—who they are and what they buy—to create customized and relevant marketing promotions and offers.[3] Amazon.com enables its users to submit reviews of a book, for example, to the book's webpage, using a rating scale—a relevant and influential function for customers to evaluate a particular book from different perspectives of reviewers. Amazon.com also provides a *Search Inside the Book* feature on many books, allowing potential book buyers to browse the table of contents and view portions of the book as a preview.

Following are a few key takeaways from the experience of Amazon. First, the Internet can enable a business to micro-segment the market virtually to a segment of one. Second, technology can enable a business to replace the traditional customer service in a different way. Third, customers value customization, interaction (for example, the ability to read and provide book reviews), and have choice (for example, to buy or rent a video and to view it through a variety of channels). In the final analysis, Amazon rewrote the rules for the category by providing a service customers did not even know that they wanted.

*Takeaways for Airlines*

Amazon itself is a "non-asset" company. It does not own stores, warehouses, distribution trucks, and so forth. It is also a "nonproduction" company, as it does not produce any of the items it sells. It is even becoming a "non-merchant" company, as it only buys products after they have already been sold or allows others to sell on its website. Its power is the customer intimacy and the value-adding aspect of the Internet. Imagine a "Travel Amazon" where all offers, comments, and blogs for all destinations of the world can easily be found, compared, and commented as well as the management of a whole trip from purchase to the return home. Imagine also, how much bigger "in scope" an online travel agency, such as Expedia or Travelocity, could be if it also began to include charters and the proposed air taxis. Finally, imagine if an airline could also learn to use the Internet (like Amazon) to enable it to micro-segment the market virtually to a segment of one.

## Apple Inc.

Apple started its personal computer business in the mid-1970s with a vision and mission to improve the experience of is targeted market—students, educators, and creative professionals. Having started a successful revolution in the design of innovative and user-friendly personal computers, Apple continued its revolutions in other areas of consumer electronics such as digital portable media players, and smart mobile phones. The company's innovation is exemplified by its line of personal computers (the original Apple, Lisa, the first one to have a mouse, the iMac, PowerBook, the AirBook), to its iPod line of portable, digital media players, and its current iPhone, the smart phone. Its customer base is certainly devoted to its brand due, in part, to the company's focus on developing user-friendly product features such as the original graphical interfaces and advanced graphics capabilities.

Apple is a company known for understanding consumer trends and anticipating the needs of consumers. Examples include the introduction of one of the original digital cameras (the Apple Quick Take), one of the original personal digital assistants (the Apple Newton), one of the original digital audio players (the iPod), and one of the original multi-touch smart phones (the iPhone). Although some of the original products were improved significantly by competitors (for example, by Palm Pilot, in the case of personal digital assistants), the innovative culture of Apple has maintained its loyal customer base, producing even more innovative products such as the iPhone. The iPhone integrates the Internet-enabled smart phone and the Apple video iPod. Apple has also continually extended its brand, opening, for example, Apple's iTunes, a channel that offers online music downloads for less than one US dollar per song. Then there is the Apple TV, a video device that can link the sale of content from iTunes with television.

Following are a few key takeaways from the experience of Apple. First, and foremost, is Apple's ability to introduce truly new products. Second, the company followed consumer trends carefully and, accordingly, branched into relevant consumer electronics. Third, Apple has built a great customer-serving infrastructure (for example, the music store, iTunes) to support and enhance its successful product line (the iPod).[4] To achieve this, Apple has built an atmosphere of innovation-friendliness and flat hierarchies with easy access to the top management. The key insight, however, is that Apple has had the discipline to limit its focus to consumers who are willing to spend their own money and pay a premium for design and quality.

*Takeaways for Airlines*

Relentlessly search for the customer's "real" desires, do not compromise when it comes to features like function and style, and, most important, do not sell at any price. Perhaps the most difficult lesson for the airlines is that Apple has accomplished all with no "business class." Apple did not chase corporate computing, did not build up a large commercial sales force, and accepted a very low share of the business market. But, Apple executed brilliantly on a consumer-focused model. Since consumers are becoming so enamored with Apple products, such as the iPod and iPhone, could it be that the next generation of knowledge workers demand that corporate IT departments provide Apple desktops and laptops?

## Banyan Tree Hotels and Resorts

Banyan Tree Holdings, a Singapore-based brand listed on the Singapore Exchange, is a manager and developer of premium resorts and hotels in the Asia-Pacific region, with spas and retail galleries that augment the resort's hotels and extend the brand. The relatively young company (having started in the late 1980s) has developed a strong umbrella brand (with numerous subsidiary brands that target clear market segments) that allows it to charge premium prices for the product line. The company controls quality and consistency of its product line by maintaining an integrated capability—in-house design, project management, and centralized marketing.[5] There are around 20 properties in the Asia-Pacific region and plans are to expand with products in India, Greece, Barbados, and Mexico.

In the Asia-Pacific region, Banyan Tree Hotels and Resorts has grown into an enormously successful hospitality brand, winning international awards from publications such as the Condé Nast *Traveller*. It is an up-market luxury boutique hotels and resort brand that differentiates itself by (a) successfully blending its concern for the environment, (b) the unique Asian traditions and heritage, and (c) the concept of individual luxury villas that promise to provide an intimate experience.[6]

Branding has played an important role in this chain's positioning in the hospitality business, particularly within the Asia-Pacific region where competition tends to focus on lower prices, especially in the commodity business. The development of a strong brand has not only enabled the Banyan Tree chain to charge premium prices but also enabled it to maintain reasonably high occupancy rates during such crises as the financial crisis in Asia during the 1997–1998 period, the September 11, 2001 attacks in the US, the Bali bombings in Indonesia in 2002, and the SARS outbreak in 2003.[7]

There is consistency in the message within the targeted segments, for example, the "stressed-out urban dwellers." Consider Banyan Tree's themes: "Sanctuary for the senses," or a "romantic escape for couples." The characteristics of the themes are carried over in all aspects of the creation and management of the brand, location of properties (exotic and exclusive but with a good transportation infrastructure), design and type of facilities at the properties (garden spas and villas with pools), and the selection and training of staff. Examples of the length to which staff have gone to look after the guests include spelling out "welcome" on the bed with flower petals, cooking dinner on a private island, and providing in-suite massages.[8]

Following are a few key takeaways from the experience of Banyan Tree. First, customers are willing to pay a premium price if what is promised is actually delivered in a consistent manner. Second, an investment made to develop and maintain a premium brand can provide a handsome return during unforeseen events and bad times. Third, the development and management of a strong brand requires a cross-functionally integrated strategy. And, fourth, some customers do pay attention to a business that shows concern for the environment and is socially responsible.

*Takeaways for Airlines*

Airlines need to develop cross-functionally integrated strategies to develop strong brands. Just imagine an airline trying to approach the nightmare of airport handling by offering "Banyan Tree-like" terminals, from where passengers can be taken to airplanes. Lufthansa's first-class terminals in Frankfurt and Munich are a first attempt.

## BMW

BMW has achieved incredible success in the high-end segment of the automobile market by focusing and remaining focused on its targeted core customers—those seeking the ultimate in driving experience. And the decision on the targeted customer base is made by getting the information from the sources that really know customers—in the case of autos, the dealers. BMW deals with customer segmentation based on information and needs of customers that go beyond the standard socio-economic characteristics such as high incomes or one element of a need, such as "status." One way that BMW can collect more tailored information on its clients is through the "Owners Circle" program. This is a special feature offered on the BMW website, in which owners can register their vehicles as well as enter very specific data regarding their car, such as lease/own, type of lease, any customization on the vehicle, as well as enter their own areas of personal interest. This allows BMW to provide targeted, customized, and relevant e-mail communications to the owner, including everything from service notices to upcoming BMW events in the area that the customer may be interested in as well, and, of course, upcoming new products.[9] In the case of BMW, the brand is built around the needs of its core customer base, and the driving experience, thus leading to the tagline, "BMW — The Ultimate Driving Machine." Of course, other elements of the consumers' needs can also be part of the brand, in the respect that, for example, some BMW drivers not only want a certain driving experience, but they may also want to be seen driving cars that deliver such an experience.[10]

These consumers, in turn, are so enthusiastic about the BMW brand that the BMW network of "enthusiasts" has grown into one of the largest in the premium car brand sector. This network hosts events such as the annual "Bimmerfest" in Santa Barbara, California, which attracts both "current and potential brand-loyal customers."[11] There is even a magazine for the group, *Roundel*, the official magazine of the BMW Car Club of America, Inc. The company also illustrates its desire to differentiate itself in, first, its creation of the "Uniquely BMW" section on its website, and then within this section, its tagline: "Independent. Unmistakable. Unique. Admittedly, we're not the typical car company." The company believes that everything is driven by ideas, and that is what makes them unique. It is great ideas, in turn, that lead to the creation of "The Ultimate Driving Machine."[12]

Consequently there must be alignment between strategy and the brand, in that with a manufacturer such as BMW strategy cannot be price-driven. Much more important are the considerations that the brand design must not be compromised to reduce costs. And, BMW ensures that there is consistency in the brand. Whether it is the new 1 series, the traditional 3, 5, or 7 series, or even the sports utility vehicles, the core purpose remains the same: "to deliver an outstanding experience through superior car performance."[13] Moreover, BMW tries to carry some aspects of its brand even in acquired products such as the Mini, and the top-end, Rolls Royce.

The core values stay consistent in the updated designs that come out regularly to keep the brand relevant. The variances among the BMW models relate to customers' preferences for style and the amount of money they want to spend.

BMW delivers on its brand through its focus on innovation. The company maintains its four innovation centers in four countries, Austria, Germany, Japan and the United States, that are connected by satellite. In addition, the company relies on its partners (for example, suppliers), and deploys the power of the Internet to capitalize on input from a much broader community than its own four centers. Another element of innovation is to develop a comprehensive engagement process with employees. In the case of BMW, this process consists of well-defined agreements on targets, a cooperative style of management, an array of education programs, and lifetime employment.[14]

One element of BMW's global success has been to enhance its brand profile globally by establishing subsidiaries and assembly plants overseas. This strategy not only provides local knowledge of the market, and customer needs, but also enables BMW to get the market's reaction to the product. Thus, BMW has successfully achieved the strategy of being at both the global and local level, along the ranks of other great brands such as Coca-Cola.

BMW also embraces the concept of employer branding. Specifically, according to Adamson, author of *Brand Simple*, "the people in charge at BMW make sure everyone inside the organization knows the recipe for 'ultimate driving machine' and can instinctively make it happen without having to consult a brand cookbook."[15] It has been reported that right from the beginning, BMW sets the tone for recruiting individuals into its unique organizational culture by having stated on the BMW website's career page: "If you love mobility in all its many guises and want to get ahead, then the BMW Group is just the place for you." Hatch and Schultz, co-authors of *Taking Brand Initiative*, note that this theme of "mobility" links to the brand's slogan "The Ultimate Driving Machine" and creates alignment between new incoming employees and the rest of the organization, as well as the views of those outside the company about the brand.[16] According to Davis and Dunn, co-authors of *Building the Brand-Driven Business*, BMW invests extensively in training for both its dealers and its mechanics to ensure that consumers have a "low-hassle" experience in which problems are addressed quickly and on the first time they arise.[17] The BMW Group was voted in the top five (#4) most attractive employers in the United States in a recent study of undergraduates by Universum, according to Hatch and Schultz.[18]

The following are a few key takeaways from the BMW Group. First, BMW's success can be attributed to the brand's ability to hone in on their target consumer market and their ability to cater to the needs of this group, never compromising this relationship by cutting costs or corners. Furthermore, BMW's success can be attributed to its ability to maintain a "glocal" strategy, its focus upon ideas and innovation, as well as its constant focus to include every part of the organization in its quest to offer "The Ultimate Driving Machine." BMW also embraces several of the brand drivers in its strategy including differentiation, consistency, and above all, emotion and experience. The dedication of this core company-wide competency prevented the brand dilution Mercedes-Benz incurred with its merger with Chrysler, whose attitude toward cars was quite different to the luxury brand from Germany.

*Takeaways for Airlines*

To develop a brand, an airline needs time and consistency in every move that it makes. Remember, BMW (like Apple) always stays in character at every customer touch point, for example, BMW Financial Services, BMW Magazine, BMW car club, and BMW's delivery center in Munich. And the airline has to withstand the temptations of those mergers that only make sense on spreadsheets. Finally, airlines must make further investment in their employees.

## Cemex

Cemex, based in Monterrey, Mexico grew from a basically commoditized cement manufacturing plant into one of the world's largest cement producers—with an empire that now includes 50 cement works and 475 ready-mix plants in 30 countries and has a revenue base of more than US$15 billion.[19] There were four basic problems with Cemex's core business. First, the core business was a commodity. Second, ready-mix concrete was a perishable business in that the ready-mix concrete began to set very soon after it was loaded on trucks. Third, demand is unpredictable. And, fourth, customers were not happy with the delivery schedule due to tremendous variances in the weather, traffic conditions, and availability of labor and raw materials. Some were not ready to receive it and some had been waiting too long. From a customer's point of view, the value related not so much to the price but rather to the delivery that met the exact needs of a customer.[20] Consequently, the value was not in the product or even the price, but a feature of the product. In response, management decided to focus on the brand from a customer's perspective first, providing delivery as close to the customer's desired time as possible, and management's perspective second, reducing the spoilage due to the perishability of the product.

Cemex rebranded the product totally. Instead of selling concrete by the cubic yard, an industry standard, Cemex offered to sell it at a price based on windows for a delivery schedule—ranging from three hours to 20 minutes. Cemex had deployed advanced information technology previously to take advantage of industry consolidation worldwide, specifically, to gain better control over the supply chain by increasing plant utilization, reducing costs, mitigating cyclicality, and managing distribution channels. Now Cemex began to focus on the creative use of information technology to become a global player in an otherwise commodity business by focusing on the true needs of its customers. At the same time they also began making their own operations more efficient, creating true alignment between strategy, brand, and various functional divisions, in line with the discussion in the introductory chapter.

The company is reported to have deployed cutting-edge information technology, first, to integrate its post-merger global acquisitions judiciously by monitoring the global operations in real time to manage productivity, costs, and revenues and to take decisive and timely actions. Second, advanced IT was deployed to develop a brand based not only on critical need of its customers, reliable delivery, but also its own need to match supply with uncertain demand. Cemex studied the operations of numerous entities to develop its delivery schedule windows; express service couriers and ambulance routes and systems. Moreover, the company began to use a system based on satellites and the Web to coordinate with plants and trucks using the digital platform. Cemex developed an incredibly customer-focused system that worked in real time. For example, it could tradeoff the needs of customers when one customer's need was delayed while a second customer's need became more urgent. As experts put it, the system began to be known as "Dynamic Synchronization of Operations."[21] Advanced IT coupled with redesigned processes enabled Cemex not only to achieve reliability approaching 98 percent but also to offer a 5 percent discount to customers whose delivery was not made during the promised window.[22]

Other elements of developing a trusted brand at Cemex included gaining the trust and loyalty of employees and taking seriously the aspect of corporate social responsibility. In the case of its employees, Cemex commits significant resources to employee training. One report shows that Cemex provides its employees Web-based training and "mini-MBA" programs. As for social responsibility, despite the nature of Cemex's business, the company ensures that its processes are environmentally friendly. In addition, the company sponsors community outreach events worldwide.[23]

The following are a few key takeaways from the experience of Cemex. The business was characterized by four attributes: commodity business, product perishability, unpredictability of demand, and customer dissatisfaction relating to uncertainty of supply. Cemex improved the brand by focusing, first, on the customers' concern (delivery as close to the customer's desired time as possible), and, second, on management's concern (reducing the spoilage due to the perishability of the product). Technology was an important enabler of the change in strategy.

*Takeaways for Airlines*

If one accepts that the basic "product" of airlines is time savings (more than other modes of transportation), then airlines should be far more obsessed with speeding up the process in the airport (before and after the flight) and, where helpful, using IT to synchronize various service providers (from catering trucks to the extent possible, ATC controllers). A dramatic reduction in delays and holding patterns could also result in a huge reduction in fuel burned uselessly.

## Enterprise Rent-A-Car

Enterprise Rent-A-Car is the largest rental company in the world, with a fleet of more than 1 million vehicles, a revenue base of about US$12 billion, 65,000 employees, and 6,000 locations in the US as well as 900 in other countries.[24] Historically, the company has targeted its customers in neighborhood markets (cities and suburbs) who need (a) a replacement car as the result of an accident, a mechanical repair or theft, and (b) a vehicle for a special occasion. Enterprise now also serves airport locations nationwide through its acquisition of Vanguard Car Rental that, in turn, owned National and Alamo brands.

Enterprise's value proposition is fairly simple: clean, late-model cars, customer-service-focused employees, policies, and systems, good basic prices that do not include the cost of frills such as frequent flyer program miles, and social responsibility such as consideration for the environment. Like many other businesses, the car-rental business is a commodity-driven business given that major competitors tend to offer similar cars at similar prices. There is very little quantifiable differentiation. In the case of Enterprise, there is one clear distinction in the service offered, door-to-door service. Enterprise will bring the car to you, a service proposition captured in its slogan, "Pick Enterprise. We'll Pick You Up," and, as mentioned above, it is also different in that it focuses on non-airport customers, an enormously different segment of the car-rental market.

Many businesses acknowledge that a key to good customer service is to meet and exceed expectations of customers that, in turn, implies hiring the right people, then training them correctly, and finally keeping them motivated. Only in the case of Enterprise, the company actually practices what it preaches. Examples: Employee promotions are based on employee performance relating to actual satisfaction of customers. As for customer satisfaction, there are formalized and effective systems to track customer satisfaction. There are also policies in place to hold employees accountable for delivering on promises.[25] Besides employees and related systems and policies, customer convenience is another integral component of good service. In the case of Enterprise, the company will come to a location that is convenient for the customer, such as a home, or a car repair shop where the customer's car is being repaired. Even customers coming to an Enterprise location to pick up their cars are scheduled to arrive at times to minimize their processing time and avoid long lines.[26]

As discussed in the main part of the book, having the right strategy for communications is one thing, but ensuring consistency is another. Enterprise seems to pay a lot of attention to this requirement. Consider, for example, its longstanding strategy to stay away from serving airport locations. Serving the airport customer segment, despite its large size, was not only highly competitive, it was expensive and difficult to provide good service—not just fast service but also the ability to provide personalized service. If the company's brand represents excellent customer service, airport locations increase difficulty in meeting the expectations associated with the brand. Next, when Enterprise first began to add airport locations, it did so with great care to make sure that customer service was not impacted negatively. That means choosing the locations carefully, relative to downtowns, for example, and controlling growth to ensure that service did not suffer. Only when a wave of bankruptcies and consolidations made a game-changing acquisition possible did Enterprise take advantage of its balance sheet strength to make a cash acquisition of Vanguard and take over the combined business of Alamo, an innovator in the leisure segment, and National, a competitor focused on business travelers. Next, Enterprise put forth a lot of energy to ensure sustainability of the brand as it expanded in international locations taking into consideration, for example, the differences in preference for the type and color of cars and the relationships with customer referral organizations.

Finally, Enterprise exemplifies the value of social corporate responsibility. Enterprise's concern for the environment is evident from its program to provide retail customers an opportunity to offset the pollution created by their rentals by matching the customers' offset purchases. In addition to the offset program, Enterprise also pledges to plant a million trees a year, acquire more cars that run on ethanol and other alternative fuels, and print its corporate magazine on recycled paper.[27] It is also valuable to recognize the role Enterprise played in helping stranded air travelers home after the September 11, 2001 attacks. This initiative was appreciated by customers since Enterprise did not really offer one-way or drop-off rentals. Despite this constraint, Enterprise's employees took it upon themselves to provide one-way rentals to stranded air passengers.[28]

Most recently, Enterprise Rent-A-Car has implemented a "car-sharing" service, called WeCar. The program began in early 2008 on the Washington University campus, and is now available to the general public in St Louis. The company also plans to eventually expand the offering beyond St. Louis.[29] While Enterprise has already been offering hourly rentals in Chicago, New York, and Washington, D.C., the WeCar program is different in that "this is the first time that cars are strategically placed in parking spaces around the city, accessed electronically by participants, and booked online and available 24 hours a day, seven days a week." The program is in alignment with Enterprise's strategies of providing "customized solutions" to its customers, and of social responsibility, through its "Keys to Green" environmental initiative as all of the cars offered in the program are hybrids. The WeCar program is "environmentally friendly, providing convenience, flexibility, and cost savings" to downtown employees and urban residents.[30]

Following are a few key takeaways from the experience of Enterprise-Rent-A-Car. First, a business should attempt not just to satisfy its customers, but to satisfy its customers *totally*. Second, select, train, and retain employees with great care. These initiatives require effective systems and policies. Third, every element of strategy should focus on customer service, including, segments targeted, and growth of the business. Finally, recognize that social responsibility is becoming a recognized characteristic of a strong brand.

Enterprise shows that in a commodity business like travel, there are ways to innovate and differentiate. Door-to-door service is an example. Their focus on customer friendliness (especially in the core disciplines), selective staff training, and corporate social responsibility varies sharply from the standard management patterns in the airline industry where obsession for cheap labor, announcing more gimmicks than value, and focusing on the creation of fantasies for analysts than good basic products for passengers is typical.

### Federal Express

FedEx is another example of a brand that changed the way businesses manage their supply chains and how some people live. It was the dependability and the speed attributes of the service that persuaded businesses and people in the 1970s that there was a viable alternative to the US Postal Service. Some people may recall a few of the famous slogans of FedEx:

- "When it absolutely, positively has to get there overnight"

- "Relax, it's FedEx"

- "Don't panic"

- "Whatever it takes"

- "The World On Time"

Today, FedEx is a global transportation, businesses services, and logistics company with revenues exceeding US$35 billion (FY 2007), operating a fleet of approximately 670 aircraft and 75,000 motorized vehicles serving 220 countries and territories, including every address in the United States. The company employs more than 280,000 people (including contractors) worldwide. There are four major operating facilities—Express, Ground, Freight, and Kinko's (the retail subsidiary of FedEx). The company processes more than 6.5 million shipments for express, ground, freight, and expedited services. The company has been listed numerous times as one of "America's Most Admired Companies." In 2007, *Fortune* magazine listed it as No. 6 and No. 7 among the "World's Most Admired Companies."[31]

When customers think of FedEx, they think of absolute dependability and no surprises—brand attributes derived from extreme attention to detail and corporate culture and subcultures. At the corporate level, first, FedEx ensures that all employees understand the overall goal which is a high level of customer satisfaction measured through such criterion as dependability and innovation. The subcultures relate to activities at functional levels, such as customer service and hub operations. Second, the company's culture is to welcome its customers' problems.[32] A key to FedEx's success is it aims to understand its customers' problems that could be relating to inventory or costs. FedEx really does look at a problem from a customer's perspective whether it is late delivery, a damaged shipment, or lack of information, that is the outside-in thinking. Third, FedEx's corporate culture accommodates its willingness to take risks. FedEx is willing to experiment with different products. Take, for example, the case of ZapMail (to fax a document via a satellite-connected system). This product failed with the market entry of low-cost fax machines. The company has an image and it not only maintains its image, but constantly tries to expand it.

Another key to the success of the FedEx brand is internal marketing. There is definitely a correlation between brand and culture. FedEx has extended its brand from simply an express delivery service to a global transportation, business services and logistics company to meet the needs of a much broader segment of customers. It is amazing how FedEx has been able to maintain its corporate culture through all of its subsidiaries and a global workforce approaching 300,000 (including contractors and spread globally) when many companies cannot even maintain a culture within one company and a lot less employees, all based in just one location.

In the case of FedEx, all operating facilities are different units but extensions of the same brand with the same promise. Employees know and understand that they are an integral part in the service business. Many employees depend heavily on other employees to be able to deliver the FedEx value proposition so as to meet customer expectations and maintain loyalty. Call center service agents, couriers, and sorters—all FedEx employees— whether or not they come into direct contact with customers, are expected to keep the needs of customers as priority one.[33] This is an important differentiator of the FedEx brand, one that keeps FedEx from falling into the "It's not my job" trap that seems to plague so many employees of so many companies. While each employee has an assigned role, it is also the responsibility of each employee to step outside of that role "wherever and whenever" someone is in need of assistance. This "everyone-pitches-in attitude" is a core value of the FedEx brand, and it helps the company to achieve its brand promise of being on time. Consequently, collaboration and timeliness appear to be two key drivers in the FedEx culture.[34] The image of the brand is formed by customers' experience with different employees in different places—the pickup person, the website, the customer service rep, the advertisement, the drop box (relating to its stock of supplies), the tracking system. The brand is the sum of all these experiences.

In its advertisements, FedEx has consistently communicated its message that it will go beyond the call of duty to deliver outstanding customer experience. More recently, it is communicating some ways that FedEx can help customers "access opportunities in the marketplace." It shows customers how their businesses can benefit from FedEx's services. According to its website, FedEx is developing ads that show its value proposition keyed to some relevant words such as "ACCESS." For each word, the letters are grown to larger than life size and then each letter shows what happens behind the scenes, showing FedEx's infrastructure at work. In its print ads, FedEx is attempting to generate spontaneous awareness whereas through its online channel, it is trying to drive customer engagement. For example, the idea is to show how a customer can go very quickly to "a specifically dedicated website that demonstrates how FedEx behind the scenes delivers outstanding experiences at every touch point."[35] The brand appears to be promoted more to individual customer segments such as sports' events (for example, NASCAR) and online interactive marketing (for example, the television show, *The Office*) and less through general mass media.

As for technology, FedEx has been at the forefront in its deployment to improve constantly the customer's experience. It was an early user of the Internet and the Web to provide customers with an interactive capability—a product feature that added significant value to its brand. The functionality provided by FedEx enabled its customers to (a) organize a shipment (booking a pickup, printing labels, and so forth), (b) obtain rate information (including customs duties, and taxes), (c) track the status of the shipment at various times, and (d) receive a proof of delivery. FedEx's Kinko's provided customers access to Web-based printing and document management services. Now, customers can receive information via wireless devices.

FedEx takes its social responsibility seriously. Here are just two examples. FedEx recognizes peoples' concern for the environment and has implemented strategies to reduce the risks. It is experimenting with the use of hybrid electric vehicles to reduce emissions and improve fuel efficiency. It uses recycled and recyclable material for packaging. In October 2007, Safe Kids Foundation and FedEx introduced a Pedestrian Safety Program in Mumbai, India. The foundation is India's first childhood injury prevention organization with an aim to educate child pedestrians and save lives. For its part, FedEx not only provided volunteers to help the children learn about different aspects of road safety, but it also took the safety pledge along with the children.[36]

Following are some key takeaways that can be learned from the FedEx brand. First, FedEx has truly excelled in the area of employer branding. FedEx's slogan, "People-Service-Profit"—in which "people" represents both customers *and* employees— solidifies this fact.[37] FedEx has been successful at instilling "The Purple Promise" – "the FedEx pledge of excellence" in its employees.[38] Employees have a clear understanding of this brand promise. FedEx recognizes that, like many service industries, its people are its product, and therefore, "getting it right with our workforce has always been the key to our success," states Eric Jackson of FedEx. "Getting it right is all about setting expectations to get the desired behavior from your employees so the promise we make to the customer is met or exceeded every time."[39] To fulfill customer needs and expectations, FedEx understands the importance of fulfilling its employees' needs and expectations. FedEx operates with an "outside-in" philosophy—the company truly operates with a customer approach. FedEx takes the time to "listen to its customers" and even rewards its employees for going above and beyond and being risk takers—"for understanding the needs of customers and being willing to do things that competitors are not.[40] FedEx tries to "walk in the shoes of (their) customers."[41]

## Takeaways for Airlines

FedEx offers guaranteed delivery times with money-back guarantees, something that seems to be completely impossible for passenger airlines that fly basically the same airplanes in the same airspace, many times to the same airports, and in the same weather conditions. It is FedEx's attitude, processes, and IT deployment that make the difference. It would appear that FedEx's philosophy is much more focused on the customer than the constraints within the airline.

## Google

Google, a US-based company, has such strong brand recognition that people have turned it into a verb as well as an every day term: "Let's *google*..." According to David Vise, author of *The Google Story*, the company's name has not only entered the English vocabulary, but in several other languages as well; "Germans *googelte*, Finns *googlata*, and the Japanese *guguru*."[42] One often reads in the media that millions of people "*google*" every day in more than 100 different languages. Google is an interesting organization as it is not selling its consumers a product or service, but rather is providing a free search engine. Yet, the company, which was founded in 1998, was named the fifth-most-valuable US company in fall 2007—less than ten years after it came to fruition.[43]

How can a company provide a free information service to its users? In this case, the answer is through advertising. However, Google differentiates itself in the manner that it generates revenue. For example, instead of posting an advertisement from the highest bidder, Google "ranks" its ads based on a formula that takes into consideration both how much a vendor is willing to pay as well as how frequently users click on the particular ad while using the search engine (presumably, relating frequency to relevancy). Consequently, it is "consumer pull" rather than "business push" that determines the ranking of the ads. Google further differentiates itself in terms of advertising in that it places the ads to the side of the search results rather than interrupting its users' search with pop-up ads or banner ads.[44]

Besides advertising, Google also differentiates itself by its customer-centric approach in all its endeavors. For example, the original premise of creating the organization by its founders was based on the dissatisfaction with then available search technology. Google's founders wanted users of its search engine to find more relevant information online, not only faster, but also with better experience, such as by reducing duplicate entries.[45] Today, Google employees travel the globe to visit with local Googlers and local employees to get a sense of the culture, trends, and user needs.[46] The issue is related not just to satisfying user needs but also anticipating user needs. This combination calls for Google employees to be able to "learn to work—and to dream—on a vastly larger scale."

And it is the anticipated needs of current and future users that are leading Google to expand its business beyond search, media, and advertising to scientific research using "cloud computing"— a giant cluster of computers that house such quantities of data that are too large for traditional computers.[47] Another example of Google's expansion of its business while meeting the anticipated needs of customers relates to its decision to create software for mobile phones that would enable consumers more flexibility and choice in their mobile phones, wireless service providers, and specific programs. This business initiative, named "Android," involves a suite of open software and could help Google overcome phone companies that could have been blocking the use of some Google applications being used on certain phones. The new Google software is being promoted by a group of more than 30 mobile and technology companies, known as the Open Handset

Alliance. Such an open environment in the telecom industry would undoubtedly lead to a new wave of innovation.[48]

Following are a few key takeaways from the Google experience. First, Google has built a strong brand by carefully adhering to the brand drivers of consistency, creativity, credibility, differentiation, relevance, and experience/emotion. Second, Google never loses sight of its value proposition—to enable people to get answers to their questions through the relevant websites and to do so rapidly and conveniently. Finally, Google is dedicated to the creation and maintenance of a strong corporate culture. The founders "spared no expense when it came to creating the right culture inside the Googleplex and cultivating strong loyalty and job satisfaction among Googlers. The artifacts of that culture—brightly colored medicine balls, lava lamps, and assorted gadgets and toys here and there—gave the business the appeal of a vibrant college campus and a cool place to work.[49] When combined with a very careful employee selection process, the corporate culture attribute becomes part of developing "employer brand."

*Takeaways for Airlines*

An innovative environment requires a relatively small and homogeneous core group not being bothered too much with physical fulfillment and its day-to-day problems. Consequently, airlines should consider separating their creative part (network and product design, customer retention, pricing, competitive analyses) from the physical production that requires other competencies such as consistent delivery, on-time performance, and social interaction. In the final analysis, in the case of Google, it is culture, something that airlines just cannot seem to consistently create and maintain.

# IKEA

IKEA, a Swedish company offering home goods and furniture, has quietly become a global phenomenon. The IKEA group includes 90,000 employees and has a presence in 44 countries.[50] It has been listed along with other great brands such as UPS and Wal-Mart as a "role model" to those striving to build a brand-driven organization.[51] The company is best known for its modern, low-priced furniture, much of which is to be self-assembled by the customer. It differentiates its offerings by its unique Scandinavian design. IKEA has been described as "far more than a furniture merchant. It sells a lifestyle that customers around the world embrace as a signal that they've arrived, that they have good taste and recognize value."[52] IKEA's strategy was built upon the assumption that "the often young customers would value stylish furniture, sized to fit in apartments and other relatively small living spaces, at affordable prices," and would therefore accept some trade-offs such as having to transport and build the furniture themselves.[53]

The brand has been able to achieve its low-cost structure due to the fact that a majority of its operations are "self-service" — there is no delivery — consumers take their products with them. Furniture comes in kits that consumers assemble at home, thus saving labor costs and also shipping costs, as packages can be shipped in flat boxes that can be stacked, thus taking up less space, reducing the possibility of damages, and easily fitting in the customer's car. The company's cost strategy begins even before the consumer purchase phase — another element of its cost savings strategy is its global sourcing of products. Specifically, the company works with more than 1,000 suppliers in over 50 countries.[54]

IKEA has a simple brand promise: "Good design and function at low prices."[55] The company has consistently delivered on this value proposition, and that is exactly what has made the brand such a success. In addition, IKEA has also built a successful global brand by developing its brand around the drivers of differentiation as well as emotion and experience. Specifically, the brand seeks to "create a better everyday life for many people."[56] The company has done this in a few different ways. First, the store, or showroom as it is referred to, is configured differently than traditional retailers. Specifically, the showroom consists of a "predetermined path" through which customers are "gently coerced."[57] The showroom appeals to the sense of "touch" — customers are encouraged to "test out" sofas and so forth as they make their way through the showroom filled with model displays of rooms in a house, and demonstrations are given to support the construction and quality of the product—for example, "chairs are pounded with machinery to demonstrate durability." Second, the customer is offered in-store product-knowledge sessions. Finally, the store offers childcare facilities as well as a full-service restaurant featuring both Swedish traditional fare as well as local dishes, making a trip to IKEA a complete experience.[58] Through these unique elements incorporated in its store, IKEA has managed to "customize the experience even though the product is mass-produced."[59]

Most recently, IKEA has extended its offerings to include "BoKlok" homes, which are prefabricated homes. The home offering is in alignment with the brand's strategy in that it is "simple, affordable, and has good design," just as their furniture and home goods offerings. In fact, the name "BoKlok" translates to "Live Smart." IKEA gives those who purchase the homes IKEA gift certificates to help decorate and furnish their new home, thus tying in all parts of the brands offerings together.[60]

IKEA also creates a distinct experience for its customers through its unique contests, which add an element of fun and also build awareness of the brand in terms of free "buzz" advertising. For example, when IKEA was opening a new store in Atlanta, they offered a US$4,000 gift certificate to the first person in line. Another contest involved writing an essay on why contestants deserved US$2,000 in gift certificates and the contestants had to live in the store for three days before the opening, take part in contests, and sleep in the bedding department of the store.[61] The powerfulness of the brand is also illustrated in the events that took place during a recent store opening in March 2008 in West Chester, Ohio, just outside of Cincinnati. Specifically, an announcement was made that the store would allow customers to start lining up/camping out two days prior to the opening of the store. Furthermore, due to unbelievable demand starting on the opening day, which was a Wednesday, they had to establish alternate parking lots miles away and run shuttle buses back and forth, even though the store opened on a weekday. Even several months after the opening of the Cincinnati-area store, those in other surrounding cities, such as Columbus, plan "road trips" to the new IKEA store.

IKEA has also excelled in terms of employer branding. Specifically, the brand strives to "create a sense of belonging" for its employees.[62] It also instills right from the beginning its customer-centric focus, by stating "we employ people who really care about customers."[63] The founder applied the company's strategy of "creating a better everyday life" to both consumers *and* employees. Specifically, he stated, "A better life means getting away from status and conventions—being freer and more at ease as human beings." He did so by making sure that the company operated in an informal manner—employees in the office sat in an open-plan configuration, all employees address each other in a familiar and personal way, and employees are known to wear jeans and sweaters.[64] Focus is placed on simplicity and attention to detail. The founder would state, "Complicated rules paralyze," while "retail is detail" was also a key statement at IKEA. Specifically, all employees, whether corporate or store workers, are all expected to understand all functions and operations of the stores. IKEA even implemented "antibureaucrat weeks" in which all management was required to work in a store for a week each year.[65] The corporate culture is also extremely cost-conscious, in alignment with its low-cost structure for consumers—managers travel coach and are expected to take buses if possible rather than cabs, and employees are encouraged and reminded to turn off lights and computers when not in use in order to conserve electricity. "Waste (is) considered a deadly sin at IKEA."[66]

In terms of corporate social responsibility, IKEA has joined with the UNICEF organization in an effort to battle child labor. Specifically, the two organizations are working together in India to promote awareness of, and prevent, child labor. Furthermore, the program also promotes the enrollment of children in school and the two organizations have even established alternative learning centers in order to help facilitate the transition of the children to formal schools.[67]

Following are a few key takeaways from the IKEA experience. It has almost all the attributes of a great brand described in Chapter 6. It has distinguished itself from its competitors with a strong brand promise upon which it consistently delivers. It has also differentiated its brand by its unique Scandinavian design. It appeals to, and evokes, an emotion that goes beyond just the mere product—it portrays a goal—a lifestyle to which to aspire. It offers a unique experience both in-store and through its unusual contests, which draw great attention to the global brand. It ensures that its brand extensions in terms of new offerings are in alignment with the brand strategy of the company. Finally, the brand offers a strong value proposition to its customers. They do not charge customers for things that customers can easily do for themselves.

*Takeaways for Airlines*

IKEA is another example that shows that a mass consumer product can be designed, produced, supplied, and sold in a different way. IKEA's dedication to smart and less wasteful processes, empowered employees, and "happy" customer integration can be relatively easily transferred to the service-intensive airline industry.

## Nestlé

Nestlé, founded in the 1860s and headquartered in Switzerland, is truly a global company—with operations in literally almost every country in the world. The company has a portfolio of brands that include a myriad of beverages and foods—everything from coffee to water to ice cream to pet food to candies. Nestlé started out offering baby formula, and now has grown to be one of the largest providers of packaged foods. According to Sartain and Schumann, a great brand should focus on the long haul (and weather ups and downs resulting from trends and economic conditions) even as individual products and services adapt. The key insight from great brands such as Coca-Cola and General Electric is the focus on values, not just current offerings. Nestlé exemplifies this philosophy.[68]

The Nestlé company, along with all of its sub-brands, portrays several best practices which can be attributed to its success. First, the company is dedicated to providing relevant products to its consumers. Specifically, "the Company's priority is to bring the best and most relevant products to people, wherever they are, whatever their needs, throughout their lives."[69] Next, the company possesses the ability to think globally while acting locally, thus truly catering to the needs of its consumers in each local market. The company states: "We demonstrate through our way of doing business in all the countries where we are present a deep understanding of the local nature of food; we know that there is no single product for everyone—our products are tailored to suit tastes and habits where you are."[70] Third, the company has maintained a disciplined approach to business growth. Specifically, the company has grown through a strategy of both acquisition and brand building.[71] This strategy includes focusing on "growing existing products through innovation and renovation while maintaining a balance in geographic activities and product lines."[72] By utilizing this strategy, Nestlé keeps the brand fresh and alive, and of course, relevant to its consumers. Former CEO Peter Brabeck stated, "The biggest problem with a successful company is that you don't learn from success." To prevent this, Nestlé constantly revisits and revamps its strategies and goals. Brabeck recognizes this key characteristic of the company: "We see adapting, improving, and restructuring as a continuous process ... Just constantly challenging people to be better, day by day, bit by bit."[73] Finkelstein, Harvey, and Lawton in their book, *Breakout Strategy,* also recognize this as a key characteristic to success. Specifically, they recognize that "superleague" companies, such as Nestlé, stay ahead of the game due to their willingness and commitment to shift, break out, and transform—"products, markets, and ways of doing things."[74] Finally, the Nestlé brand is unique in its approach to corporate social responsibility. Specifically, Nestlé's view is not focused on meeting a set of standards, nor on philanthropy, but rather on creating value for society in the long run, such as bringing farmers and factories in developing countries up to speed to meet the standards of those in developed countries.[75]

The success of the Nestlé global parent brand can be attributed to the fact that it has consistently adhered to the following business principles in all countries, taking into account local legislation, cultural and religious practices:[76]

- Nestlé's business objective is to manufacture and market the company's products in such a way as to create value that can be sustained over the long term for shareholders, employees, consumers, and business partners.

- Nestlé does not favor short-term profit at the expense of successful long-term business development.

- Nestlé recognizes that its consumers have a sincere and legitimate interest in the behavior, beliefs and actions of the company behind brands in which they place their trust, and that without its consumers the company would not exist.

- Nestlé believes that, as a general rule, legislation is the most effective safeguard of responsible conduct, although in certain areas, additional guidance to staff in the form of voluntary business principles is beneficial in order to ensure that the highest standards are met throughout the organization.

- Nestlé is conscious of the fact that the success of a corporation is a reflection of the professionalism, conduct and the responsible attitude of its management and employees. Therefore recruitment of the right people and ongoing training and development are crucial.

- Nestlé continues to maintain its commitment to follow and respect all applicable local laws in each of its markets.

One of the most well-known of the Nestlé brands is Nescafé. Nescafé was recently named one of the top global brands according to Interbrand's rankings.[77] Nescafé, like Starbucks, is positioned as much more than just a mere cup of coffee—it is an experience. "Coffee is not just a beverage… it's an experience you create that's a reflection of who you are."[78] And, like Starbucks, this "experience" commands a premium price. For example, in Europe, Nescafé is actually listed as a separate offering from regular coffee on a menu, and is associated with a higher price than the regular cup of coffee, thus truly illustrating the premium value of the Nescafé brand. Like the parent brand, Nestlé, the Nescafé brand aims to cater to each individual consumer by offering a variety of types of Nescafé. "Nescafé coffees are available to suit all tastes and in a wide range of packaging."[79] This is also in alignment with Starbucks—catering to the individual tastes of consumers. Both companies have succeeded due to their careful attention to, and execution of, the brand driver of experience/emotion.

Another well-known brand under the Nestlé brand is Juicy-Juice, which was acquired approximately 20 years ago. According to Robert Bloom, the Juicy-Juice brand became a success for three reasons. First, the brand recognized the need to differentiate itself from the other juice drink offerings—its "uncommon offering"—the fact that it is 100 percent pure juice with no additives. Second, the brand identified its target customer—not kids, as one would expect, but rather parents who would appreciate and appeal to the healthy offering. Finally, Juicy-Juice found an appropriate, relevant way to deliver its brand message to its target customer. Instead of marketing to the masses, the brand chose channels that honed in on its target customer—the parent—such as providing educational literature at pediatrician's offices, featuring the brand in parents' magazines and programs, and distinguishing itself through "kids-to-moms" messaging in which children were used in television advertising of the brand. The brand went beyond just the product offering, the juice itself, and appealed to the emotional brand driver—providing healthy choices for your children.[80]

Following are some takeaways from the experience of Nestlé. A good brand should have a long-term perspective, with relevancy, consistency, and experience as key drivers. Global companies must act locally. Growth must be disciplined, and it can be through innovation and/or renovation. Valued brands (for example, Nescafé, in the case of Nestlé) can command premium prices.

*Takeaways for Airlines*

First, Nestlé demonstrates that consistency across borders is not only necessary but possible, a characteristic with which airlines seem to have significant difficulty. Second, it takes decades to build a brand, but it can be destroyed in weeks.

## Nokia

Nokia grew from a relatively small Finnish manufacturer of paper (wood processing plant) to a global telecommunications business.[81] Today, Nokia, the world's largest mobile phone maker by sales, is a well recognized and pace-setting brand as a result of numerous factors, including technological innovation and organizational change in the rapidly changing environment such as the deregulation of the telecommunications industry[82] and with digital, media, and social convergence.[83] The key to Nokia's success, however, seems to be its understanding that mobility is a business solution which can be achieved by addressing people, processes, and technology in a balanced way.[84] This vision appears to have been implemented by leadership that is bold—willing to reinvent itself, divest business units that no longer add value, be open-minded and be flexible.[85]

In Interbrand's list of *Best Global Brands 2007*, Nokia now ranks number 5 in today's cluttered marketplace, just behind such household names as Coca-Cola, Microsoft, IBM, and General Electric.[86] In terms of the drivers of branding discussed in Chapter 6 of this book, Nokia not only has satisfied consumer demand but appears to have *created* demand in the evolving technology-centric world through its (a) product design—sleek and stylish, easy to use, robust, and relevant, (b) the ability to make emotional connections (Internet-driven experiences through integrated access to customized content without dependency on a particular device such as computer or television), and (c) business practices that have consistency in the global marketplace while customizing products and services to meet the needs of local markets. Consumers trust the brand with respect to the quality of its technology because of the company's focus on human technology—how technology products can make people's lives easier or more enjoyable in an era in which people want to be connected to as many things as possible. The key to human technology is the "observe (values, lifestyles, attitudes, and media habits) and design" philosophy—a balance between function and form.[87] And it is this alignment between the business strategy and the branding strategy that is helping Nokia survive and thrive in competition with other giants such as Motorola, Samsung, LG, and the new product, iPhone, from Apple—identifying different forms of lifestyles and personalizing the products and services to meet the needs of each lifestyle, that is, making their lives better.

Consider, for example, the length to which Nokia goes to explore the needs and expectations of its customers. To begin with, Nokia recognizes the limitations of segmenting the marketplace on standard variables such as income, age, and gender. These variables alone provide little information about customer needs. It is much more important to learn about lifestyles and the psychology behind purchase decisions and customer satisfaction. Consider, for example, the question as to whether the younger generation buys mobile phones more to make phone calls or to send text messages. As for emerging markets, Nokia is planning to add about 2 billion customers in emerging markets—Brazil, China and India, for example. The company has established design studios in these countries to study country-specific consumer trends (how people behave and communicate), desired product features (color, user interface—for example, integrated sliding menu, services, and price), and emotional attributes (such as projection of a certain image). In the case of the latter, it could be the desire to portray that a person has moved up the economic ladder (as in India) or found a right bargain (as in China).[88]

Nokia is clearly exploring the full range of uses of the Internet relating to the capabilities of its mobile devices—transmitting photos taken on the mobile phone, finding relevant information using the Internet, and developing an online community.[89] Nokia also launched its *Ovi* brand (which in Finnish means 'door') that combines the Internet and mobility leading to a gateway to a number of services and contents such as access to customers' social networks, music, games, and GPS navigation. Consumers will no longer be restricted to their computers and televisions to access these services. Consumers can not only buy, but also try music and games and have access to maps and city guides. To capitalize on the belief that "consumers want a complete experience," Nokia is expanding its services to include online music stores, an interactive multi-player game service, and a way for Nokia product users to exchange photos, videos, and music.[90]

According to Interbrand, demand creation is a key aspect of the branding process and Nokia represents a good example of aligning its business strategy with its branding strategy—combining the Internet and mobility. How can a brand reach out and engage with targeted consumers given the enormous quantity of brands and brand messages attempting to engage with consumers? One way to succeed is for a brand to communicate not only with the targeted customer but with a message that matters to the customer (for example, experience *and* services), is welcome by the customer, and one that the customer is willing to share with other potential customers. Nokia is an example of such a brand because of its focus on human technology and its willingness to redesign its product based on input of customers—for instance, "integrating e-mail, Web, and music in a single handset."[91]

An example of Nokia's segmentation of its actual and potential customers is provided by its Senior Vice President of Strategic Marketing, Brand Management, and Consumer Relations. In this example, customers can be segmented into "Live, Connect, Explore, and Achieve." With respect to product design, there is a heavy emphasis on aesthetics for the "Live" segment, on simplicity for the "Connect" segment, tools to get things done for the "Explore" segment, and pushing the envelope of capabilities relating to mobility for the "Achieve" segment.[92] It is interesting to note that a company such as Nokia is not only a provider of technology but also a user of technology to obtain information on the purchase decisions of its current and target customers.

Given that connectivity is becoming ubiquitous, Nokia is committed fully to exploit mobility in its own business, a strategy well demonstrated by its efforts to use mobile capabilities as solutions in its own organization. It helps decision makers understand that mobility is a business solution. Nokia, for example, established a virtual team whose members, located in seven different time zones, could work with each other productively using mobile technologies, regardless of location ("corporate offices, home offices, Internet cafes, cars, airports, and hotels").[93]

Following are a few key takeaways from the experience of Nokia. First, there is a strong alignment between business strategy (that focuses on human technology that, in turn, is based on "observe and design" philosophy) and branding strategy (improving people's lives by enabling them to connect with anything they want). This alignment is evident in Nokia's emerging brands such as *Ovi* that combines the Internet and mobility to offer relevant services and contents. Second, Nokia illustrates the value of meaningful segmentation and the development of products to meet the needs of each segment. Third, Nokia practices what it preaches. It exploits the value of mobility in its own organization to implement efficiently and effectively its own business strategy. The defining difference with the development of the Nokia brand has been leadership. And, as with Nestlé, they have managed to achieve a small country-big world effect.

*Takeaways for Airlines*

Another commodity product producer shows how to stay ahead of the competition—never give up innovating, constantly listen to customers, and walk the talk. It is also interesting that Nokia shows that it is possible to have both high tech and high touch. Can an airline do both?

## The Park Hotels

The Park Hotels is a chain of premium boutique hotels in India managed by the Apeejay Surrendra Group (an Indian family-controlled conglomerate with interests in tea, shipping, and steel). Currently, the properties in this chain are located in Bangalore, Chennai, Kolkata, Navi Mumbai, New Delhi and Visakhapatnam (a resort city in Andhra Pradesh). The properties are relatively small (between 80 and 220 rooms), tend to be located downtown, have reasonable access to commercial and entertainment districts, place emphasis on contemporary design and settings in the private and public areas as well as international experience. There are 20 more properties in the pipeline. The chain's vision and philosophy is reflected in its "customer focus, product and service innovation, advocacy of environment and social issues and nurturing of art and culture." The chain provides an image of "India's first collection of luxury boutique hotels."[94]

Although the first hotel opened for business about 40 years ago (in Kolkata), it was Ms. Priya Paul who became the head of The Park Hotels in 1990 and who began the branding process. She first started by aligning business strategy (processes) with branding strategy. For example, she installed contemporary reservation systems and management training programs to get the basics right. Then came branding—"hotels with character" and the alignment with strategy—"design-led." Following are some examples. The Kolkata had a Chinese restaurant with the typical design—red-and-green and dragons. She pushed the boundaries of design and changed the design to a sleek black-and-white restaurant and the property "developed a reputation as a trendy venue for live bands;" in Chennai, she created a "Leather Bar," a dark and sexy room with leather walls and floor; in Delhi, the property showcased an outdoor yoga pavilion.[95]

Following are a few key takeaways from the experience of The Park Hotels. First, the business must evolve with the changing environment. Not only the economy of India is growing and forecast to grow at high rates but the number of globe-trotting Indians is increasing. These travelers have high expectations based on best practices. Second, there is a need to get away from one-size-fits-all strategy. And, The Park Hotels is not a chain for all customers. They cater to a different segment which is willing to pay for the product—a room rate range of US$375–US$700 a night in the Bangalore property.[96] Third, educating and branding employees is a must. In the case of The Park Hotels, the concept of boutique hotels had to be explained very carefully to employees. Fourth, it is really important to differentiate the brand. The Park Hotels chain does not have "cavernous, chandelier-lined lobbies"— features expected in some other high-end hotels. As reported in an excellent article in the *Financial Times*, it is marketing its brand to the in-crowd—"the place to see and be seen."

The real insight, however, is, once again, visionary leadership. Moreover, there is a top, perhaps one hundredth of one percent market in many different parts of the globe that if you know who your customers are and focus intently, you can offer a product they will respond to and buy. What may be remarkable to Western readers about Park Hotels is the location where it is happening. The story itself is not new. Last year Marriott International announced that it would partner with Ian Schrager, who invented the concept of the boutique hotel more than 20 years ago. Schrager created a new brand with about 100 hotels that offered a personal and unique lodging experience. Consequently, while these smaller brands gain much of their power from their locality and customers, it is usually difficult for any of them to retain this character and go global, or even beyond their region. However, there is value in partnership. In the case of Schrager and Marriott, it was Marriott, a premier lodging chain worldwide, and Schrager, the pioneer of the lifestyle boutique chain.

## Takeaway for Airlines

The Park Hotels and The Banyan Tree show that even in the luxury travel segment there are more ways of doing it right than just copying Four Seasons or the RitzCarlton (or, in the case of airlines, Singapore Airlines). Is there a lesson, perhaps, for some airlines to break new ground and push the boundaries by combining successfully two synergistic brands?

## Samsung

Samsung, based in South Korea, was ranked the twentieth most valuable brand in the world in 2005, according to the Interbrand Corporation.[97] However, this had not always been the case. A decade ago, the Samsung brand was plagued with low brand image and brand erosion. Specifically, Samsung was known for its poor quality and lack of innovation.[98] One reason for the decline of the company is that it had no differentiating factors and therefore could not command a premium price. Rather, the company was offering mere commodities—similar to those made by many other companies. Therefore, the company was forced to compete on price alone, and could therefore only offer cheap products. However, in 1997, after realizing that the company was at risk, its Chairman conducted a "brand makeover"[99]— "to reposition the company as a cutting-edge designer of high-quality electronics."[100] Before the transformation of the brand, the company was mostly known for poor quality household appliances and consumer electronics. The Chairman recognized the need to differentiate the brand, and proposed to do so by offering consumers high-end products, thus totally changing the value proposition.[101]

Samsung's commitment to being a truly global brand is portrayed in the CEO and Vice President's statement, "We need to hire and train the best talents from all over the world because we are a global company, not just a Korean company."[102] The Chairman made sure that the new focus on and commitment to quality was portrayed internally as well as externally— workers even wore headbands with the slogan "Quality First."[103] Furthermore, the Chairman had employees destroy US$50 million worth of defective cell phones at a plant in South Korea to illustrate his commitment to stopping production of substandard products.[104] Samsung's brand transformation also focused on employer branding—promoting cross-functional teams in place of the traditional silos, and implementing programs to empower employees and in turn allow them to be aligned with the goal of bringing products to market faster.[105]

The Chairman recognized "the crucial importance of innovation and speed to market as brand components in the world of consumer electronics, where new devices retain their full value for a matter of quarters or even months." Therefore, the company began to focus its resources and efforts into R&D, thus allowing Samsung to launch new products at a faster rate than competitors such as Panasonic and Sony—thus changing Samsung's status as a follower to that of a leader.[106] In order to promote and ensure the status of a leader, Samsung implemented the Innovative Design Lab of Samsung, an in-house institution to teach and study design. The leadership of the center took Samsung employees to other major cities around the world in order to immerse them in the local culture in an effort to help them understand consumer behavior around the world.[107] Furthermore, the Chairman implemented training courses which focused on design, ergonomics, and mechanical engineering for employees.[108] In an effort to ensure ongoing quality, Samsung invests in its own factories rather than relying on outsourcing operations. Furthermore, the company follows a vertical integration strategy—for example, Samsung chips and displays are placed in Samsung digital products.[109]

Samsung has also been successful in appealing to the brand driver of emotion/experience. Specifically, the CEO has stated, "Our new focus is not just about using great engineering to build new products; it is about tapping into the customer's experience with a great brand, through creativity."[110] For example, the company has created a 10,000 square foot gallery at the Time Warner Center in Manhattan where consumers can come to experience the brand's latest technology. The sole purpose of the gallery is to promote brand awareness (by offering an experience to consumers rather than trying to make a sale).[111] Specifically, the center allows consumers to engage and immerse themselves in the latest and greatest in the digital world—music, phones, video. In addition, Samsung offers consumers the chance to experience their online brand magazine, DigitAll, produced four times a year, containing interviews with those who are the drivers behind the latest and greatest innovations.[112] Samsung, who built the high-end apartment complex, Tower Palace in Seoul, is showcasing a version of its networked home in the complex in which a family can "operate appliances from washing machines to air conditioners by tapping on a wireless "Web pad" device, which doubles as a portable flat-screen TV."[113]

In terms of corporate social responsibility, "Samsung takes active strides to achieve the betterment of society on a global scale." While Samsung is involved in a myriad of projects and interests in the community, it has focused on three main areas: "the disabled, environment preservation, and "informatization" for society." For example, the company has run computer classes for the blind, and offers a scholarship for the children of disabled households. Recently, Samsung has implemented the "Student Science Knowledge Olympics" in conjunction with science institutes to help broaden students' scientific knowledge and education. Finally, the brand has developed an interesting new concept called the "Customer Volunteering Social Program," in which both the employees and the customers participate together.[114]

Following are two key takeaways from the experience of Samsung. First, the commitment to totally change the brand must come from the top. Second, the company totally aligned its brand strategy with all other major corporate functions—innovation, cutting-edge technology, world-class designs, recruiting the world's best talents, and internal branding. It is basically these two points that transformed Samsung from a failing brand into a successful global brand. Now, Samsung "stands for a brand that is known for innovation and world-class, quality products."[115] Its cutting-edge technology and world-class design have created a new "hip" image for the brand.[116]

*Takeaways for Airlines*

Again, a brand-elevation task requires commitment from top to bottom, time, and an integration of all functions. Just repainting the airplane and updating the uniforms is not enough. Remember, Samsung set up a gallery with the sole purpose of promoting brand awareness by offering an experience to consumers rather than trying to make a sale. How many airlines are prepared to do that?

## Shiseido

While Japanese brands such as Sony and Toyota are known for technology and production efficiency, Shiseido is a Japanese non-technology global brand. Founded in 1872 in Japan as a pharmacy, Shiseido has blossomed into a strong global cosmetic brand. Specifically, Shiseido has expanded through Asia, including Taiwan, Singapore, and Hong Kong, as well as in Europe, North America, and New Zealand. The company has also grown in terms of its offerings to include cosmetics, toiletries, and salons. In addition to offering products under the Shiseido brand name, the company includes other brands and subsidiaries under its umbrella. The company not only offers products and services, but is also deeply involved in culture and the arts. Shiseido supports, for example, art exhibitions at museums around the world, as well as publishes a magazine, *Hanatsubaki*, that promotes the arts, fashion, and travel.[117]

Shiseido has differentiated itself in a number of ways. One key brand driver that Shiseido capitalizes on is its cultural heritage. Specifically, it uses "the mystique and aura of a distant land, with its oriental tradition, color, smells and aesthetics." Shiseido capitalizes on being unique, in both its product offerings as well as the packaging of its offerings. Shiseido "brings together rational elements backed by scientific proof, and aspirational as well as emotional elements backed by a strong brand image and personality." Next, Shiseido also distinguishes itself by offering high-quality, relevant and exciting products.[118]

The success of the Shiseido umbrella brand can be attributed to the fact that it has consistently adhered to its Five Management Principles, established in 1921, which include promoting a "constant quest for the highest possible quality standards," customers first—"Shiseido pursuits must be thoroughly consumer-oriented," and a sense of credibility/transparency—"Shiseido business transactions must be conducted loyally, honestly, and respectfully." Also included in the five key points is the implementation of "creativity and innovation in all of its product offerings," the "unique blend of oriental mystique and sensitivity with Western fashion and values," and the "ability to customize its offerings to its different markets by constantly analyzing market trends."[119]

Following are the key takeaways from the experience of Shiseido. Important aspects of its brand are a cultural heritage, consistency, and uniqueness. The company is dedicated to the development of high-quality, relevant and exciting products. Customer focus is a reality, not just a company-stated mission.

*Takeaway for Airlines*

And again, we have the dominance of "customers and quality first" that is the prerequisite for building a successful brand.

## Starbucks

Starbucks has clearly succeeded in taking an ordinary commodity (coffee) and transforming it into a whole way of life. The unmistakable cup along with the safety sleeve has literally become an icon in our society. And it appears to be the consumer word-of-mouth rather from actual customer experience than traditional mass advertising that has propelled the expansion of Starbucks.[120] The company even achieved a stature to sell its brand to restaurants and other businesses, such as Barnes & Noble bookstores, including airlines (United and Horizon—part of Alaskan Airlines). But how did they do it? How was Starbucks able to take on the giant producers of roasted and instant coffee— the likes of General Foods, Nestlé, and Procter & Gamble. Starbucks is a truly global brand that has boomed due to a few key characteristics:

- First, Starbucks was successful because it is in tune with the current "luxury consumer"—the company caters to this segment's needs. Silverstein and Fiske in their book *Trading Up: The New American Luxury* discuss this new consumer, and Taylor Clark, author of *Starbucked* also addresses this segment, noting specifically, that consumers in this segment look for "emotional satisfaction" in the products they consume, and that is exactly what Starbucks provides.[121]

- Second, the company's initial success can be attributed to its commitment to employee training (learning history of coffee, beverage preparation, customer service, and so forth)—this emphasis on training was necessary because the company differentiated itself by offering something way beyond just an excellent product. It offered an experience, one that has changed the way we live our lives, conduct business, and socialize. Astute observers have noted that Starbucks is like a third place in people's lives—home, work, and Starbucks. While some people may stop by Starbucks to get their favorite drink on their way to work or on the run, many people use Starbucks as a place to meet, to socialize, or use the location even as an office to work remotely. Starbucks has gone to great lengths to create an atmosphere that is inviting and makes customers want to stay. According to Michelli, Starbucks' success is linked, at least in part, to the incredible ability of its servers (carefully selected, trained, and rewarded) to focus on the small details that matter greatly to customers. Starbucks even employs a "programming manager" who carefully selects the music for the Starbucks stores to create a unique customer experience. Clearly, the company is very in tune to the atmosphere of its stores—

be it the music, the layout of the seating and the fixtures in the stores, the lighting. Every detail matters, which is in alignment with one of its training principles: "Everything Matters." One server (called barista or partner) sums it up perfectly, "I want the details to reach out and say 'Come in and stay awhile.'"[122]

- Third, Starbucks differentiated itself not just by its customer service—an attention to the customer that goes way beyond mere courteous service—the company literally caters each drink to each customer. This is truly mass customization that has not been achieved successfully by many other businesses. According to Clark, there are "literally 55,000 drink combinations to choose from, thus ensuring that you can express your individuality."[123] According to Howard Schultz, the Chairman, some of Starbucks' customers are such regulars that when they come to a store, a server remembers their favorite drink. And if that server were to leave, the connection with the customer would be broken.[124]

So, what is Starbucks' value proposition? It appears to be creating an "experience" around coffee drinking—an "experience" that people can integrate into their everyday lives.[125] And, according to Clark, it is not simply the advertising (Starbucks spent the same on advertising in a decade compared to what Coke spends in a two-day period), but rather that unmatchable experience that was the key to the brand's success.[126] And the initial experience comes from employees who are branded and taught to make a "connection" with the customer through a technique called "connect, discover, and respond." These are elements of "being genuine," a characteristic that Starbucks outlines as one of the key principles, called "The Five Ways of Being," for its partners to follow. This technique encourages partners to anticipate the needs of customers and go above and beyond to meet these needs.[127] Finally, Starbucks developed and implemented a meaningful service performance measuring system that focused on such aspects as customer service (speed as well as customer contact and responsiveness), store cleanliness, and product quality.

Starbucks truly goes above and beyond in terms of training in a time where training seems to be the first thing to be cut in an attempt to reduce budgets. The company even produces a training reference guide that employees can keep right in their apron while on the job. Specifically, this training guide offers specific ideas on how to personalize relationships with customers through various types of interactions.[128] Starbucks has even created a role-playing game that can be used to train employees. Specifically, the goal of the game is to make a connection with the customer. To achieve this goal, the partner needs to understand more than just the customer's stated needs. The partner needs to try to understand a customer's unstated needs—that could be the desire for a certain experience.[129] Consequently, Starbucks teaches its employees to go above and beyond traditional customer service—to anticipate the needs of customers, to surprise them, and to delight them. This characteristic is Starbucks service-minded corporate culture—its Principle 3—"Surprise and Delight."[130] It appears that the company places an equal amount of emphasis on the employee experience as on the customer experience. It offers, for example, higher benefits than other businesses in services organizations.[131] It is therefore not a surprise that Starbucks is listed in the top 20 (#16) on Fortune's Top Places to Work.[132]

Starbucks' stance on corporate social responsibility goes way beyond merely making charitable contributions—it is literally intertwined with the entire business. As Sue Mecklenburg, vice president (of Business Practices and Corporate Social Responsibility), states, "I've seen Corporate Social Responsibility move from being a matter of philanthropy to being the way we run our business. It's transformational!"[133] While Starbucks does support such organizations as the American Wildlife Foundation, Save the Children, and Mercy Corps, it also incorporates social responsibility in the way it conducts its daily business—from where the company buys its beans to the use of recycled fibers in its beverage cups. The company considers and evaluates the environmental impact of its actions. The company's involvement is not just at headquarters either—it is apparent on the bulletin boards in the individual local stores. The company truly walks the talk. This aspect is evident by the fact that Starbucks was selected as one of the top companies.[134]

While Starbucks has certainly excelled in the area of branding, it is also important to note the importance of being cautious when growing at such an accelerated speed to protect the entrepreneurial vision and the integrity of the brand. The very things that have differentiated the company such as the barista training and the customer experience can easily be diminished or even forgotten in the whirlwind of expansion, not just relating to scale and people but also complexity. For example, are the Starbucks kiosks in grocery stores really in alignment with the Starbucks "experience" strategy? The Starbucks kiosks do not have the space like the regular Starbucks stores to offer the "experience"—comfy chairs, a place to fire up a laptop, the carefully chosen music.

External factors, such as a downturn in the economy, can also have a direct impact on non-essential luxury items such as specialty drinks. So, one question is: Is the Starbucks product recession proof? Second, one must constantly watch competition as demonstrated by the fact that chains such as Dunkin' Donuts and McDonald's are trying to find a niche market providing the specialty drinks at more economical prices. The question is that if one of the differentiators of Starbucks has been its enormous presence and convenience, then could competitors such as Dunkin' Donuts and McDonald's diminish such a competitive advantage, particularly during a recession. For example, at the beginning of 2008, reports indicated that the McDonald's chain plans to install coffee bars with "baristas" serving a myriad of specialty coffee drinks in nearly 14,000 locations across the United States. This strategy represents "the biggest addition to its menu in 30 years."[135] As of summer of 2008, the McDonalds chain has already started to introduce a few specialty coffee drinks, and has started to build the bars in some cities. Furthermore, a recent report in the media indicated that McDonald's not only plans to move into the specialty coffee business, but is also planning on mimicking the "experience" factor as well by adding upscale chairs and decor to its restaurants in an effort to encourage patrons to "stay a while." One must also add another caution—the growth of ethnic groups such as Hispanics in the US and their response to Starbucks' value proposition.

Starbucks, has in fact, hit some of these pitfalls recently. For example, on February 14, 2007, Schultz wrote to his executive staff, admitting that some decisions had been made that led to the "watering down of the Starbucks experience." Specifically, Starbucks has taken away from its experience by pre-grinding, offering less "comfy" seating, and less carpeted areas, and rather has been focusing upon boosting sales. Schultz, in an effort to get the brand back on track, resumed his position of CEO, which he had left in 2000 for a seat on the board. He is refocusing on "the start-up years" — back to selling "exemplary coffee with the kind of service and ambiance that makes a US$4 latte worth the price." Specifically, Starbucks closed more than 7,000 stores one day so that 135,000 baristas could be retrained on the whole process that goes on behind the counter.

Starbucks has spent a lot of time recently "figuring out what really matters to (their) customers." Schultz recognizes the power of Starbucks' competitors and is making sure that the company is doing everything they can to differentiate themselves, and instill customer value, from everyone else that is "attempting to be in the coffee business."[136] For example, Starbucks, in addition to offering new "goodies" to its customers such as free brewed coffee refills and free flavor shots for beverages (through its new customer loyalty card program), has established "MyStarbucksIdea.com" so customers may have dialogue with the company — suggestions about products, the store environment, operations, etc.[137] These efforts appear to be paying off — Starbucks was voted #16 in BusinessWeek's Top 50 Performers (April 2008), in which it was recognized that while Starbucks is currently in a weaker position, Schultz is on a "crusade" to restore the company's image — including strategies such as "streamlining management, closing (hundreds of) underperforming stores, and reeducating baristas."[138]

Following are a few key takeaways from the experience of Starbucks. First and foremost, is the importance of responsive customer service, appealing store ambience and experience, customer trust that is earned, and customer intimacy. Second, employees are the key to customer service and what they need is not only good training (actually, education rather than mechanical training to develop "soft skills") but also good benefits — perhaps the real enduring competitive advantage. Third, distribution is through high-traffic stores (located in retail centers, college campuses, and office buildings) that have high visibility. Fourth, rapid expansion should not get in the way of unmet customer expectations. Always revisit what made the brand great in the first place. Are those principles still being upheld in the current environment? Is the company staying fresh in order to keep up with changing consumers and ahead of industry invaders?

*Takeaways for Airlines*

Starbucks managed to describe the lifestyle of its customers much better than the airlines (who want to be everything for everybody). Focusing on a key group of well-educated, young urban professionals might pull other groups without the same self esteem. There is, however, also a caution. Starbucks began to dilute its brand by opening up tiny little areas in the corners of very ordinary grocery stores to expand the operations and appeal to much larger groups. This strategy lost the concept of providing "experience" of a third place and simply selling a cup of coffee to a person doing grocery shopping. And, for airlines, "Starbucks on board" on the airplane neither makes the experience, nor differentiates the brand, by borrowing on Starbucks equity.

## Tesco

Tesco, a UK-based grocery store, has become a global brand serving the UK, Europe, and Asia, offering non-food products and services such as discount clothes, consumer electronics, banking and insurance as well as mobile telecommunications. It is now reported to be the third largest retailer, behind the US-based Wal-Mart and France-based Carrefour. Interestingly, Tesco actually grew into a great brand through its struggles in the early 1990s. Specifically, Tesco was losing customers due to the state of the economy—due, in part, to the effects of the recession in the UK. Tesco realized that it needed to make major changes in order to gain a competitive advantage in the marketplace.

First, Tesco realized that it needed to refocus on the customer, rather than focusing solely on the competition, as had been the case. Specifically, the company used, and continues to conduct, "Customer Question Time" (CQT) meetings right in stores to identify and respond to changing customer needs. In the past year, the company held nearly 300 CQTs in the UK, involving almost 6,000 customers. In addition, more than 45,000 customers were interviewed in stores outside of the CQT focus group meetings.[139] In polling shoppers, the company found that value was still their number one concern, even though the economic conditions were improving. While low prices were important, it was value that was number one, as value includes the whole proposition—quality and variety—not just low price. The CEO of Tesco at the time realized that the company needed to offer "the best value (and) the best shopping trip," both achieved by "having a contemporary business and therefore one that remains relevant by responding to changing needs." Specifically, it evolved its superstore offering 40,000 food items as well as health and beauty items, CDs and videos, clothing, and gasoline.[140] In addition, Tesco developed a strategy to meet the needs of multi-segments of its customer base—its own brand products, the "Finest" for the up-market segment, and the "Value" for the mid-market segment. Tesco seems to have developed an innovative way to market its products in three categories—"good, better, and best." Furthermore, Tesco has used its reward scheme the "Clubcard" not only to build loyalty but also collect information on specific customer needs and to cross-sell its products and services.

Second, Tesco recognized that its success depended on people—both its customers *and* its employees. Its customer focus is evident through its core purpose statement: "to create value for customers to earn their lifetime loyalty."[141] It has been said that it is this brand promise that has been the driver in the company's ability to extend the brand into its non-food service sectors.[142] In building the new and improved Tesco brand, the company used the concept of "simplicity" as a tool in employer branding. The efforts emphasized three guiding principles: "better (for customers), simpler (for staff), and cheaper (for Tesco)." The principles were highlighted in "The Tesco Way," which made clear to employees that "they should be using their talents to simplify rather than to complicate, that Tesco should focus on simple solutions to serve customers better."[143] Tesco has also implemented a slogan called "Every little helps" in which Tesco asks customers and employees what the company can do to enhance the shopping experience and the workplace.[144] Finally, Tesco implemented a program called "TWIST—Tesco Week In Store Together" in which managers from corporate division spend time working in a Tesco store to stay relevant with the needs of both customers and employees.[145] These efforts have paid off: ideas resulting from staff feedback have yielded approximately US$15 million in direct annual savings.[146] Consequently, in building its brand, Tesco paid a lot of attention to employer branding to create value for its customers. And it was listening to its consumers and employees and simplifying its operations that helped turn a troubled company into a global giant, and one of "the most admired retailers" in the UK.[147]

Third, Tesco also recognized that growth had to come from new concepts and alternative means of distribution besides just the large stores (Tesco Extra and Tesco Superstores), and therefore it rolled out new formats of smaller and mid-size city-center stores (Tesco Metro, Tesco Express, and One Stop—a category that does not include the word Tesco in the name). This new distribution strategy allowed Tesco to compete in local markets. It focused on price, quality, variety, and service, and ensured that operations were implemented to deliver on these elements. Tesco was probably the first to launch home delivery and Internet home shopping on a significant scale.[148] Users of the online shopping distribution channel appear to cover a wide spectrum of consumer types—from the person at home with small children for whom it is difficult to get to the store, to the single professional who does not want to waste time going to the store to shop and is therefore happy to pay the delivery fee in an effort to save time.[149]

In an effort to promote "green" choices by consumers, Tesco is developing a program through their shoppers reward card, "Green Clubcard," that will reward consumers for environmentally friendly purchases such as "intelligent plugs" which turn off appliances when they are not in use. Furthermore, Tesco offers consumers incentives in terms of rewards points for recycling shopping bags. The company is also offering similar incentive programs in order to promote the recycling of old mobile phones and Inkjet cartridges. Such incentive programs have been highly successful—since the program's inception, more than 400 million fewer plastic bags were used by consumers.[150]

Following are some takeaways from the experience of Tesco. First, focusing on customers (and their changing needs) is more insightful than focusing on competition. Second, value (that includes quality and variety) is more important than just low prices. Third, in rebuilding its brand, Tesco used the concept of "simplicity" as a lever in employer branding—"better (for customers), simpler (for staff), and cheaper (for Tesco)." Finally, the key to earning lifetime loyalty is by creating value for customers through listening to customers.

*Takeaways for Airlines*

To gain a competitive advantage in a changing marketplace requires massive changes. Focus much more on customers than on competition. While low prices are important, it is value that is number one, as value can include quality, variety, price.

## United Parcel Service (UPS)

The UPS brand, which became famous for its brown trucks and uniformed drivers making reliable ground service deliveries, has transformed itself into a global supply chain management business. UPS, headquartered in Atlanta, Georgia, processes approximately 15 million parcels daily with service to more than 200 locations around the world and a revenue base of well over US$40 billion.[151] In addition to its well-known ground service, UPS owns its own airline with a fleet of about 250 aircraft and powerful hubs in the USA, Germany, and the Philippines, operates less-than-truckload (LTL) freight services, integrated financial services, as well as retail services through its 'The UPS Store' (formerly Mail Boxes Etc.).[152]

The UPS brand was built on two main principles: customer service and timeliness. The company's founder knew that "anyone could deliver a package," so in order to distinguish his business, his employees had to be "faster, neater, and more reliable." As such, the founder not only instilled the value of service in UPS' culture from the beginning, he also implanted the concept that every little detail *does* matter and that "service is the sum of many little things done well." For example, from the very beginning, the founder focused on cleanliness—relating to trucks and drivers. Vehicles were cleaned every night (with the insides being cleaned weekly). Drivers were expected to be clean and tidy (being clean-shaven, and not smoking) and in their uniforms. UPS even implemented an idea from one of its own drivers—to place mirrors and shoe shine kits in the employee locker rooms. As to timeliness, the concept went beyond getting the package to its destination on time regardless of external conditions; it also extended to office meetings. The founder did not think of timeliness as just a catchphrase at UPS; he thought of it as the core of good business practices.[153]

UPS has also distinguished itself through its culture. Right from the start, UPS started employer branding with the formation of its newsletter, *Big Idea*. While the newsletter contained the traditional messages from senior management, it also included tips/instructions on how employees should conduct business with customers and even included submissions from employees. The whole basis of the publication was to promote the mission of the company and to get all employees thinking about serving the customer. From the beginning, UPS truly followed the concept of employer branding—treat your employees as you want them to treat your customers. For example, UPS truly valued their drivers and paid them a premium wage over driving jobs with other companies in order to attract the qualities important to UPS such as "appearance, personality, and manners."[154] In turn, UPS employees promote UPS' brand promise to "make each customer feel as if they are (their) only customer."[155]

Furthermore, while everyone claims to promote from within, UPS actually strictly adheres to this policy. Employees' efforts are rewarded—moving both jobs and departments. This policy promotes employees to do their best as well as promotes constant training as employees are promoted.[156] UPS' culture has been characterized as a "strict regime," where employees are expected to comply with numerous regulations that comprise the "highly disciplined" company and are known as "the UPS way." Specifically, UPS screens potential candidates for employment to ensure that they will be able to adapt to what has been referred to as a "tribal" culture, and once onboard, the company ensures that employees have a clear understanding of what is expected in terms of meeting standards. According to Niemann, these stringent policies and procedures are rarely questioned because they work for employees as well as customers — and help make the company profitable.[157] Every motion at UPS is measured, stressing efficiency and safety. Drivers are given extremely detailed training, from the "Don't Back" rule implemented to reduce accidents to the manner in which they should exit and reenter the vehicle during a delivery. Drivers are driven by "commitments, quotas, punctuality, and performance measurements."[158]

As UPS expands into other nations, it analyzes the current culture and implements "culture-sensitive corrections and adjustments," such as when UPS first entered Germany in the 1970s.[159] For example, the UPS culture of calling coworkers by their first name did not mesh with the German culture, where they prefer to use titles when addressing an individual.[160] Furthermore, UPS was not on par with other German companies employing drivers in terms of wages, especially since UPS was requiring more from their employees than the other German companies.[161] Then, there was the disparity of the "living to work" culture from the USA versus the "working only to live" philosophy of the German culture. German laws dictated very different policies in terms of vacation time, sick time, and the standard work day and work week hours.[162] In the German expansion, UPS learned that policies and procedures that worked in the USA could not just be directly applied in a different culture — the company learned to "think global, act local."

UPS has also differentiated itself through its use of technology to enhance the customer experience. UPS believes "technology is not only beneficial to improving a company's internal operations, it is also a key component of a service culture."[163] While UPS still offers its customers the ability to track their packages via the Internet, it also provides its customers so much more in order to make conducting business easier. For example, UPS offers shipping tools which expedite the customs process, calculate rates and pricing, as well as help customers manage their product flow. According to Jordan Colletta, Vice President of Customer Technology Marketing, "We still move packages from A to B, the same as we did twenty years ago, but we've laid in value that reduces our customers' costs."[164]

Consequently, instead of "pushing" its products and services, UPS favors "pulling" its needs from the customer. This philosophy has lead UPS to focus on supply chain management, in which UPS tries to integrate its products and services with a customer's business, enabling the customer to focus on the core components of its business instead to having to deal with transportation and distribution issues.[165] It is interesting to note that even UPS, a highly disciplined business, did deviate from its core business in 1996 when the company converted some its aircraft to carry passengers when they were not being used as freighters. Five years later, the company decided to drop this line of business (even though it was an additional source of revenue) to focus on its core business and expand it in ways to help its customers focus on their core business.[166]

Finally, the UPS brand is also distinguishing itself through its corporate social responsibility initiatives. UPS has been using technology, specifically electronic processing technology, to better plan routes in order to avoid UPS trucks sitting waiting to make left hand turns. This "right turn" initiative saved UPS approximately 3 million gallons of fuel and more than 28 million miles in 2006.[167] The implementation of this initiative is win-win—it helps the environment while also helping UPS' bottom line.

Following are a few key takeaways from the experience of UPS. First, while a lot of businesses know that good customer service is an important driver of brand, the philosophy tends to be implemented at a superficial level in such areas as employee selection, training, and performance measurement. UPS follows through on this part of the mission. Second, UPS' decision to try to learn more about its customers' needs rather than push its products and services has grown its customer base. Third, UPS has used disciplined strategy to focus on its core business rather than expand in areas that might generate additional revenue but are not focused on its core customers. Fourth, UPS has deployed technology not only to improve its customer service but also to be a socially responsible company and increase its profit margins.

As airlines' staff have far more customer contacts than UPS', a strong focus on the attitude and behavior of all staff (sales, check-in, flight crews, etcetera) would certainly make a difference. Second, there is plenty of room to integrate the customer's travel needs into the airline's IT systems. Third, if UPS gave up flying passengers, why do some airlines dilute their attention by flying cargo? Fourth, UPS shows that every little detail matters and that "service is the sum of many little things done well." Can most airlines say they subscribe to this concept? Finally, just to repeat, instead of "pushing" its products and services, UPS favors "pulling" its needs from the customer. Is there a lesson for passenger airlines?

## The Virgin Group

Virgin is a globally recognized brand that encompasses a broad spectrum of products, relating, for example, to travel, finance, media, communications, health, and retailing (books, drinks, music, clothes, even bridal shops). Within the travel category, there are airlines (such as Virgin Atlantic, Virgin Blue, Virgin Nigeria, and Virgin America) and trains (Virgin Trains). In finance services, there is Virgin Money (financial cards, loans, insurance, pensions, etc.). In telecommunications, there is Virgin Mobile. In retailing, there are the Virgin Megastores. In an independent study conducted in the UK in 2007 by HPI Research, Virgin received more votes (from a sample of 2,000 adult voters) than any other brand—23 percent, Sony came in the second place with 21 percent, and Tesco came in third place with 20 percent.[168] What is the common linkage among all these businesses and products? According to one group of business analysts, the linkage is the "values of the brand and the attitude of the people."[169]

The Virgin organization was started by Richard Branson (now Sir Richard) around 1970 when he started Virgin as a mail order retailer. This business was followed by a chain of record stores, and a recording studio. The Virgin Music product was followed by a chain of travel and tourism companies, starting with the world-renowned, Virgin Atlantic Airways, founded in the early

1980s. Later, in the late 1990s, Virgin's travel group expanded by including Virgin Trains. Throughout the entire group of Virgin businesses (reported to be over 200 companies in more than 30 countries, employing over 50,000 people, and generating more than US$20 billion[170]), the core values of the brand appear to be "fun" and "value for money." The "cool" image follows the brand driver of distinctiveness. Specifically, Sir Richard is known for "(projecting) the Virgin brand as a 'cool' alternative to whatever the suits are offering."[171] Sir Richard is known for looking out for the consumer's best interest. For example, when he launched the financial services company, Virgin Direct, Branson's intention was to "shake up the market." Specifically, he stated, "The consumer has been taken for a ride for too long by an industry which has been able to hide its charges."[172] Along the same lines of this theme, Sir Richard is also known for "fighting for the underdog" in all of his business lines. For example, right from the start, the premise of Virgin Records was that the brand "sought to give struggling new bands a means to be heard when the 'fat cats' at the major labels refused to deal with them."[173] In addition, one can easily see another element in the development of the Virgin brand—competitive challenge. All of these aspects are clearly evident in the products offered by Virgin Atlantic—the Upper Class, the Premium Economy, and Economy services. And this element is also most certainly evident in the planned product Virgin Galactic, with vehicles in which passengers will fly in the suborbital space and Virgin Fuels for automobiles and airplanes that will address the environmental concern. In terms of the Virgin brand's association with society, Sir Richard Branson is known for his contributions to charities, such as his fight to make the National Lottery a non-profit-making venture with the proceeds going to worthy causes, and more recently, his concern and actions to protect the environment.[174]

Virgin aligns all its businesses and operations in terms of strategy and organizational culture in order to sustain the Virgin brand. For example, its employees are "dared" to join in on taking on new challenges—which is a core distinction of the brand.[175] Sir Richard has built the Virgin brand on people. He believes that people—both customers and employees—come first. Specifically, Sir Richard sees employees as belonging to a large, extended family. In the beginning, each new employee was even given his home phone number, with the idea that they may call him if they had any ideas or complaints. Even today, employees call him by his first name.[176] Sir Richard recognizes that consumers are key, and therefore it is "absolutely critical" to never let them down.[177]

Sir Richard is one of the key bonds that link, what otherwise seem to be, all the non-related businesses together. He has been recognized for successfully creating what is known as "the universal brand"—a brand that goes beyond an association with a particular category of product (such as Hoover with vacuum cleaners or Levi Strauss with jeans).[178] While some have questioned how such a wide spectrum of businesses can be under the umbrella of one brand, in reality, the Virgin brand is "one of the most focused brands and most intrinsically understood brands by the general public. It is a reputational brand, based on the reputation of Richard Branson and the companies he has been associated with, especially Virgin Records and Virgin Airways."[179] His passion for new things keeps the brand fresh. And his business model allows the Virgin brand to be instilled in all these new ventures—specifically, Branson calls his business method "branded venture capital," in which he starts and manages all new companies under the Virgin name while partners provide the majority of the investment. Sir Richard, who was voted as one of the 26 "most fascinating entrepreneurs" by *Inc.* magazine in 2005, states, "I keep a notebook in my pocket all the time ... and I really do listen to what people say, even when we're out in a club at 3 a.m. ... Good ideas come from people everywhere, not in the boardroom."[180]

The following are a few key takeaways from the unique Virgin brand. First, a common thread in the success of Virgin companies appears to be a focus on research into the potential to improve customers' experience by examining thoroughly the needs of customers on the one hand and the development of competitive advantages by shaking up competition in the market on the other hand. In the case of customer needs, it is not so much the importance of a feature of an actual product or service; rather, it is the "identification with an attitude toward life" that plays an important role in the development of a brand.[181] On the supplier side, it is first, the development of culture, relating to innovation, flexibility, and empowerment. And second, products or services are not only priced reasonably, delivered reliably and consistently, but created to meet customer needs. As to the challenge of shaking up the competitive marketplace by offering a new value proposition, it was Virgin Atlantic that challenged the mega carriers in the early 1980s—British Airways, Pan American, and TWA. "People connect the brand with value, quality, innovation, adventure, fun, challenge." Virgin is above all "a brand of customer service and customer experience."[182]

*Takeaways for Airlines*

With Virgin being already engaged in a number of quite different airlines, the effect of a "branded venture capitalist" can be seen. Virgin Atlantic certainly is the most innovative long-range carrier when it comes to offering new types of services. And Virgin USA successfully takes the concept of "smart low fares" to new levels. In the case of Virgin, it is leadership, exemplified by marketing done at the top, a willingness to challenge, reinvent, or turn upside down existing business models, an appetite for invading others' business space, but never for me-too or commoditized market entries. How many airlines does this profile characterize?

**Whole Foods**

Whole Foods, a supermarket based in Austin, Texas, has virtually transformed the standard retail food industry that competed, in general, on price and basic promotions such as coupons, double coupons, and even reward cards in an effort to promote customer loyalty. It took an innovative company like Whole Foods to develop a brand and an aligned strategy that not only enabled the company to sell its products at premium prices but also provided some relief from other issues facing this industry such as labor.[183] Starting in 1980, when there were less than half a dozen natural food supermarkets in the United States, Whole Foods now has more than 265 locations in North America and the United Kingdom.[184] The original goal, that is just as valid today, was to provide a full-service, natural food store for middle-of-the-road customers. Now, Whole Foods has become "the grocery store of choice for the hip and the health-conscious—the supermarket equivalent of Starbucks."[185] The company has a philosophy, "Whole Foods, Whole People, Whole Planet" which demonstrates that they go beyond merely selling groceries—they are a strong brand in terms of their commitment to the needs of both the customer and the employee as well as, the community and the environment.[186]

Whole Foods is built upon a simple brand strategy—customers will pay a premium for food that is healthy for them, tastes good, and is grown organically to the extent possible. This strategy differentiates the brand from its competitors which follow the "promotion-driven, loss-leader pricing model."[187] Whole Foods is also a good example of a company that appeals to the experience/emotion brand driver. Specifically, it appeals to the customer inspirationally, causing the customer to connect with what the brand stands for, over and above the actual product. Whole Foods literally is the "essence of natural."[188] Sartain and Schumann capture eloquently this characteristic of the Whole Foods brand in their statement, "Whole Foods make(s) you feel, as you buy organic peanut butter, that you are somehow helping to keep the world healthy."[189] According to Bernd Schmitt, author of *Big Think Strategy*, Whole Foods' CEO John Mackey showed "creativity and visionary leadership (also see Chapter 6 for more on leadership) by tapping into consumers' desire for gourmet products, home cooking, and an emotional connection to their food and health."[190]

The company also differentiates itself by offering true customization to its consumers. While most grocery stores today do offer a salad bar and a few pre-made items to either take out or eat in at the small tables and chairs area within the store, there is no customization associated with the offering—customers must choose from what is already prepared. However, Whole Foods actually offers "stations" with a myriad of hot items to choose from including ethnic foods. Moreover, they will prepare your order to your specifications, right there in front of you. For example, on certain nights of the week, a "chef" is available to prepare a pasta dinner for a customer right on the spot in the store. The customer gets to view the ingredients and hand pick what she would like in terms of the type of pasta, the type of sauce, the type of protein, vegetables, and so forth. One can literally walk around the store choosing a hot item here, a piece of fish cooked to your specifications there, a slice of pizza, a salad from one of its multiple salad bars, and then top it off with a fresh dessert.

Furthermore, the company differentiates itself by its unique hiring methods which empower employees—each store is divided into approximately eight teams—new employees are temporarily assigned to one of the eight teams for a four-week period, after which team members vote on whether the employee will gain a full-time position on the team. Specifically, a two-thirds vote is required for the associate to become a permanent team member. This practice is also used at the corporate headquarters. Furthermore, employees have a much more direct effect on both their customers and their paycheck than in a traditional hierarchical system. Team leaders, in collaboration with the store manager, have a say in what products are offered to customers. Stores are "encouraged to buy locally as long as the items meet Whole Foods' stringent standards." Moreover, just as new team members are reviewed every four weeks, Whole Foods also determines the profit per labor hour for each of the teams within the store every four weeks, and teams that exceed their goals are awarded a bonus in their next paycheck.[191] This "entrepreneurial spirit" in which associates are driven by themselves and their peers clearly differentiates Whole Foods from traditional food retailers where employees' performance is managed by superiors.[192]

The company adheres to the concept of transparency, which is a key driver to surviving in the new economy, as discussed in Chapter 6. Whole Foods has a "no secrets" management philosophy.[193] Specifically, the brand makes compensation data available to each employee, therefore each associate is aware of his/her colleagues' salaries. Furthermore, the company shares its operating and financial data to any associate who requests to review such information, with the philosophy that such data will assist them in purchasing products, determining prices, and so forth.[194] The company's unique approach to employer branding has been successful—Whole Foods was named #5 on the 2007 "Best Companies to Work For" List. The company also earned this title due to its practice of implementing an executive salary cap, its policy of covering 100 percent of employees' health insurance premiums, as well as the CEO's announcement to reduce his salary to US$1 and forgo all future stock options.[195]

In terms of social responsibility, Whole Foods believes "companies, like individuals, must assume their share of responsibility as tenants of Planet Earth."[196] Specifically, Whole Foods has been involved in such projects as the creation of the non-profit Animal Compassion Foundation, to promote practices for raising farm animals naturally and humanely. Similarly, Whole Foods is involved in The Marine Stewardship Council to promote responsible fishing practices, and even owns its own seafood facility and processing plant, Pigeon Cove Seafood, located in Gloucester, Massachusetts. Finally, the company has implemented an internal group called the Green Mission team—each store has a Green Mission team representative who collaborates with other reps at the store level as well as coordinators at the regional and national level to promote "green actions" within the company.[197]

Following are a few key takeaways from the experience of Whole Foods. First, Whole Foods has "invented a different game and a different way to play" which "creates excellent financial results in a difficult retailing environment."[198] Second, the company has become a successful brand due to its ability to create a powerful differentiation in the food business, as well as the ability to appeal to the brand drivers of experience/emotion. Third, the company has truly walked the talk in terms of its motto, in looking out for the interests of its customers, its employees, the environment, and the community.

*Takeaways for Airlines*

Check-in or flight crews are in some ways service teams like a shift in a store. Challenging new staff with the expectations and standards of experienced team members, adapting their pay to the customer experience they create, and having full transparency over everybody's income would help airlines to get relief from still powerful unions that "allege" to speak on behalf of all employees when they may only be striving for their organization's influence. Also recall, Whole Foods' practice, "a two-thirds vote is required for the associate to become a permanent team member." Would an airline ever implement such a practice?

## Zara Stores

Trend-setting clothier Inditex with its well-known brand Zara (founded by Amancio Ortega and headquartered in La Coruña, Spain) has been expanding around the world at a phenomenal rate—more than one store a day.[199] The first Zara store was launched in 1975—there are currently more than 1,000 stores in 68 countries.[200] Ortega built this company by "listening to his target customer—primarily young women, initially in Europe, who wanted absolutely current fashions at moderate prices." However, they did not want to wear exactly the same clothes as other people were wearing. The company found out that customers would make frequent visits to a store that carried things they liked and that changed its merchandise often. Although they were not willing to pay extremely high prices, they were willing to pay slightly more for fashion and timeliness. The key to the Zara brand appears to be not clever advertising, or even attractive displays in clothing-store windows, but the company's ability to meet a market need—absolutely current fashions at moderate prices by (a) collapsing its design, manufacturing, distribution cycle time, and (b) simultaneously "managing" costs at the "system-wide" level.

Traditionally apparel makers of specialty brands tend to introduce their new product lines seasonally, on an 8–12 month cycle. The apparel maker can be highly profitable if its new line happens to be on the market at a time that the consumer is willing to pay the full retail price. Unfortunately, many brands end up selling a high proportion of their merchandise at substantial discounts. On the cost side, many brands tend to minimize their costs, particularly manufacturing (cutting and stitching) by outsourcing the activity to low-cost locations. As a result most competitors end up with similar costs and similar pricing tactics— high prices at the beginning and high discounts at the end. Zara, on the other hand, works on an extremely accelerated schedule in terms of time to market to meet consumer needs. The company has reduced its cycle time (from concept stage of a product line to availability in stores) to a few weeks as opposed to months. As a result, Zara is able to sell about double the percent of product line at full retail prices compared to its competitors.[201] Consequently, the increase in shelf life of its product lines enables Zara to sell a much higher percentage of its merchandise at a full retail price. However, Zara appears to use this price advantage by selling its clothes at a lower price than its competitors but not be forced to introduce substantial discounts to move inventory because it is no longer in fashion. Zara's competitive advantage is therefore its ability to bring new items to its stores in weeks compared to about nine months for competitors such as the Gap, enabling Zara to introduce more than 10,000 items each year—with new styles coming continuously rather than seasonally.[202]

Zara appears to "manage" its costs on a "system-wide" basis by implementing an integrated strategy. First, Zara analyzes quickly and constantly what is selling, what new trends are emerging, and makes decisions accordingly. Not only are trend spotters trotting the globe to observe market trends relating to its targeted customers but store managers monitor very carefully particular styles that are moving briskly and order more units via customized handheld devices. Next, not only can the orders be placed immediately but the manufacturing and delivery part of the cycle can be reduced since Zara has made the decision to locate its manufacturing facilities in Spain (to control quality and timeliness).[203] In addition, vital information—relating to customers' needs and concerns—from the stores is constantly communicated to Zara's professional designers.[204] Store managers can make suggestions for modification to existing styles or the desire for totally new designs. The designers, in turn, synthesize this almost "real time" information and produce computer-assisted designs that are then transmitted through the intranet to manufacturing facilities.[205] The "system-wide" management of costs is exemplified in two ways. First, Zara's decision to pay higher costs in one area (for example, higher manufacturing costs in Spain) is offset by not having to introduce marked-down sales of products not in fashion.[206] Second, instead of using traditional advertising to promote the brand, Zara appears to reinvest in its business, may it be the opening of new stores or the improvement in the time to respond to changing fashion trends and customers' tastes.

Following are a few key takeaways from the experience of Zara. First, monitor and respond to the customer needs almost in "real time basis"—exemplified by the timeliness of Zara's trend spotters and the input provided by store managers. Second, meet customer needs even if it leads to higher costs—higher costs of manufacturing in Spain, in the case of Zara. The company makes up for such higher costs by less mark downs.

*Takeaways for Airlines*

Similar to traditional apparel stores, airlines have long cycle times in planning and assigning the production capacity. This practice results in long-term shifts and roster plans for the staff. As reservations come in on short-term notice, a lot of capacity has to be sold at dramatically reduced fares. With much shorter planning cycles airlines could first accept the reservations for passengers looking at lower fares (albeit with more traveling flexibility) and then assign the capacity to the routes required by real (undiscounted) demand. Try to copy Zara's ability to meet a market need—absolutely current fashions at moderate prices by (a) collapsing the design, manufacturing, distribution cycle time, and (b) simultaneously "managing" costs at the "system-wide" level.

## Takeaways

The case studies, from a broad array of industries and businesses based in different parts of the world, clearly provide evidence of the strong value of developing and maintaining brands. Brands enable businesses to differentiate their products and services, charge premium prices, and develop and maintain customer loyalty. However, as evidenced from a number of case studies, a strong brand cannot be developed either by simply handing it over to a functional vice president operating in a typical silo system or based on superficial knowledge of customer concerns, stated or unstated. The initiative requires not only insightful and timely research on actual and potential customers; it also involves everyone within the business, starting with the head of the business.

All the companies assemble behind a strong brand, focus on their customers, empower and cherish their staff, take care with regards to their social responsibilities, and, most important, put promises ahead of results. This philosophy requires a totally different management attitude (away from quarterly results), flat hierarchies, massive deployment of customer-centric IT, focus on processes instead of functions, and so forth. Instead of "management of innovations" the core competency is the "innovation of management." In the final analysis, the common thread among all these case studies is first, leadership, whether it is Sir Richard Branson (Virgin), or Fred Smith (FedEx), Steve Jobs (Apple), or Howard Schultz (Starbucks). Somehow, these leaders have managed to develop a strong culture, avoid labor strife, and non-standard, rather than me-too business models. The second commonality is the focus on the customer, way beyond mere courteous customer service. These companies put the customer at the heart of everything they do—in essence, the customer is their reason for being. These companies truly understand that the goal is "to create customer value," whether it be Apple's iPhone "creating a user-friendly and cool mobile entertainment," or Whole Foods' "natural food with an emotional connection," or Tesco's numerous programs, all established and implemented to get at the core of the customer's needs.[207] Third, these companies all understand the importance of treating employees well so that they will in turn do the same for the customers. This seems like common sense, but yet many businesses either fail to see the connection, or even if they do, they fall short in carrying the concept through. These companies all show how much has to be changed to become really different. If existing airlines, particularly the large legacy carriers, will not be able to dramatically change, as some of the companies described did, they are likely to fall prey to format invaders that will design the "new airlines" from scratch. They could also be acquired by private equity groups and broken up for the higher value of their parts.

## Notes

1    Barrera, Rick, *Over Promise and Over Deliver: The Secrets of Unshakable Customer Loyalty* (NY: Penguin Group, 2005), p. 18.
2    Barnes, Brooks, "NBC in Deal With Amazon to Sell Shows on the Web," *The New York Times*, September 5, 2007.
3    Capon, Noel, *THE MARKETING MAVENS* (NY: Crown Publishing Group, 2007), pp. 49–50.
4    Slywotzky, Adrian J with Karl Weber, *UPSIDE: The 7 Strategies for Turning Big Threats Into Growth Breakthroughs* (NY: Crown Publishing Group, 2007), p. 46.
5    For more on Banyan Tree Hotels and Resorts, see: www.banyantree. com
6    Roll, Martin, *Asian Brand Strategy: How Asia Builds Strong Brands* (New York: Palgrave MacMillan, 2006), p. 227.
7    Roll, Martin, *Asian Brand Strategy: How Asia Builds Strong Brands* (New York: Palgrave MacMillan, 2006), p. 228.
8    Wu, Ming, "Banyan Tree: branching out," *Brand Channel*, November 15, 2004 appearing in www.brandchannel.com/features_profile. asp?pr_id=206
9    Davis, Scott M. and Michael Dunn, *Building the Brand-Driven Business: Operationalize Your Brand to Drive Profitable Growth* (San Francisco, CA: Jossey-Bass, 2002), p. 185.
10   Bloom, Robert H., *The Inside Advantage: The Strategy that Unlocks the Hidden Growth in Your Business* (NY: McGraw-Hill, 2008), p. 22.
11   Hatch, Mary Jo and Majken Schultz, *Taking Brand Initiative: How Companies Can Align Strategy, Culture and Identity Through Corporate Branding* (San Francisco, CA: Jossey-Bass, 2008), p. 23.
12   For more on BMW, see: www.bmwusa.com
13   Clifton, Rita, Simmons, John, and others from *The Economist*, *BRANDS AND BRANDING* (Princeton, NJ: Bloomberg Press, 2003), p. 66.
14   Yoshihara, Hiroaki and Mary Pat McCarthy, *Designed to Win: Strategies for Building a Thriving Global Business* (NY: McGraw-Hill, 2006), pp. 44–5, 66, 112, 238.
15   Adamson, Allen, *Brand Simple: How the Best Brands Keep it Simple and Succeed* (NY: Palgrave MacMillan, 2006), p. 134.
16   Hatch and Schultz, *Taking Brand Initiative: How Companies Can Align Strategy, Culture and Identity Through Corporate Branding* (San Francisco, CA: Jossey-Bass, 2008), p. 23.
17   Davis, Scott M. and Michael Dunn, *Building the Brand-Driven Business: Operationalize Your Brand to Drive Profitable Growth* (San Francisco, CA: Jossey-Bass, 2002), p. 185.
18   Hatch and Schultz, *Taking Brand Initiative: How Companies Can Align Strategy, Culture and Identity Through Corporate Branding* (San

Francisco, CA: Jossey-Bass, 2008), p. 23, and http://universumusa. com/undergraduate.html

19   Finkelstein, Sydney, Harvey, Charles, and Thomas Lawton, *Breakout Strategy: Meeting the Challenge of Double-Digit Growth* (NY: McGraw-Hill, 2007), pp. 87, 271.

20   McGrawth, Rita Gunther and Ian C. MacMillan, *Market Busters: 40 Strategic Moves that Drive Exceptional Business Growth* (Boston, MA: Harvard Business School Press, 2005), p. 87.

21   McGrawth, Rita Gunther and Ian C. MacMillan, *Market Busters: 40 Strategic Moves that Drive Exceptional Business Growth* (Boston, MA: Harvard Business School Press, 2005), p. 89.

22   Barwise, Patrick and Sean Meehan, *Simply Better: Winning and Keeping Customers by Delivering What Matters Most* (Boston, MA: Harvard Business School Press, 2004), p. 79.

23   Finkelstein, Sydney, Harvey, Charles, and Thomas Lawton, *Breakout Strategy: Meeting the Challenge of Double-Digit Growth* (NY: McGraw-Hill, 2007), pp. 270–71.

24   Stein Wellner, Alison, "Nothing But Green Skies," *INC. Magazine*, November 2007, pp. 114–20.

25   Kazanjian, Kirk, *Exceeding Customer Expectations: What Enterprise, America's # 1 Car Rental Company, Can Teach You About Creating Lifetime Customers* (NY: Currency, Random House, 2007), p. 2.

26   Kazanjian, Kirk, *Exceeding Customer Expectations: What Enterprise, America's # 1 Car Rental Company, Can Teach You About Creating Lifetime Customers* (NY: Currency, Random House, 2007), pp. 3–4.

27   Stein Wellner, Alison, "Nothing But Green Skies," *INC. Magazine*, November 2007, pp. 116–17.

28   Kazanjian, Kirk, *Exceeding Customer Expectations: What Enterprise, America's # 1 Car Rental Company, Can Teach You About Creating Lifetime Customers* (NY: Currency, Random House, 2007), p. 22.

29   *The Wall Street Journal*, February 7, 2008, "Car Rental Companies Learn to Share," by Darren Everson, page D1.

30   For more on Enterprise's WeCar initiative, see: http://aboutus. enterprise.com/file/171/Downtown_WeCar_Feb08.pdf

31   FedEx website, Fact Sheet. 31 December 2007.

32   Wetherbe, James C., *The World On Time: The 11 Management Principles That Made FedEx an Overnight Sensation* (Santa Monica, CA: Knowledge Exchange, LLC, 1996), p. 18.

33   Wetherbe, James C., *The World On Time: The 11 Management Principles That Made FedEx an Overnight Sensation* (Santa Monica, CA: Knowledge Exchange, LLC, 1996), p. 16.

34   Wetherbe, James C., *The World On Time: The 11 Management Principles That Made FedEx an Overnight Sensation* (Santa Monica, CA: Knowledge Exchange, LLC, 1996), p. 43.

35   For more on initiatives at FedEx, see: http://news.van.fedex.com/ node/6004 (31 October 2007).

36   For more on initiatives at FedEx, see: http://news.van.fedex.com/node/5476 (31 October 2007).

37   Wetherbe, James C., *The World On Time: The 11 Management Principles That Made FedEx an Overnight Sensation* (Santa Monica, CA: Knowledge Exchange, LLC, 1996), p. 23.

38   Glenn, T. Michael, "Absolutely, Positively Entrepreneurial," in *CMO Thought Leaders: The Rise of the Strategic Marketer* (edited by Geoffrey Precourt and published by Booz Allen Hamilton, 2007), p. 148.

39   Sartain Libby and Mark Schumann, *BRAND FROM THE INSIDE: Eight Essential to Emotionally Connect Your Employees to Your Business* (San Francisco, CA: Jossey-Bass, 2006), p. 29.

40   Glenn, T. Michael, "Absolutely, Positively Entrepreneurial," in *CMO Thought Leaders: The Rise of the Strategic Marketer* (edited by Geoffrey Precourt and published by Booz Allen Hamilton, 2007), p. 149.

41   Glenn, T. Michael, "Absolutely, Positively Entrepreneurial," in *CMO Thought Leaders: The Rise of the Strategic Marketer* (edited by Geoffrey Precourt and published by Booz Allen Hamilton, 2007), p. 151.

42   Vise, David A., *The Google Story: Inside the Hottest Business, Media and Technology Success of Our Business* (NY: Delta Trade Paperbacks, September 2006), p. 146.

43   USA Today, Money Section, "Google's Power Grows with Stock Price," by Matt Krantz, page 1B.

44   Vise, David A., *The Google Story: Inside the Hottest Business, Media and Technology Success of Our Business* (NY: Delta Trade Paperbacks, September 2006), pp. 87–90.

45   Vise, David A., *The Google Story: Inside the Hottest Business, Media and Technology Success of Our Business* (NY: Delta Trade Paperbacks, September 2006), pp. 59, 69.

46   Levy, Steve, "Google Goes Globe-Trotting," *Newsweek Online*, November 12, 2007.

47   Baker, Stephen, "Google and the Wisdom of Clouds," *BusinessWeek*, December 24, 2007. pp. 49, 51.

48   Ante, Spencer E., "Tim Wu, Freedom Fighter," *BusinessWeek*, November 19, 2007, pp. 88–90 and Paul Taylor, Richard Waters, and Andrew Parker, "Google Unleashes Android on the Mobile Phone Sector," *Financial Times*, November 6, 2007, p. 21.

49   Vise, David A., *The Google Story: Inside the Hottest Business, Media and Technology Success of Our Business* (NY: Delta Trade Paperbacks, September 2006), p. 94.

50   IKEA corporate website: www.ikea.com

51   Davis, Scott M. and Michael Dunn, *Building the Brand-Driven Business: Operationalize Your Brand to Drive Profitable Growth* (San Francisco, CA: Jossey-Bass, 2002), p. 248.

52   *BusinessWeek* (online version), November 14, 2005, Cover Story, "IKEA How the Swedish Retailer Became a Global Cult Brand."

53  Bund, Barbara E., *The Outside-In Corporation: How to Build a Customer-Centric Organization for Breakthrough Results* (NY: McGraw-Hill, 2006), pp. 105–6.
54  MIT Sloan Management Review, Fall 2006, Volume 48, No. 1, SMR 229, p. 82.
55  IKEA corporate website: www.ikea.com
56  Sartain, Libby and Mark Schumann, *BRAND FROM THE INSIDE: Eight Essential to Emotionally Connect Your Employees to Your Business* (San Francisco, CA: Jossey-Bass, 2006), p. 13.
57  "IKEA Invades America," *Harvard Business School* Case No. 9-504-094, September 14, 2004, p. 5.
58  Clifton Rita, Simmons, John, and others from *The Economist, BRANDS AND BRANDING* (Princeton, NJ: Bloomberg Press, 2003), p. 70.
59  Clifton Rita, Simmons, John, and others from *The Economist, BRANDS AND BRANDING* (Princeton, NJ: Bloomberg Press, 2003), p. 70.
60  Slywotzky, Adrian J with Karl Weber, *UPSIDE: The 7 Strategies for Turning Big Threats Into Growth Breakthroughs* (NY: Crown Publishing Group, 2007), pp. 198–9.
61  *BusinessWeek* (online version), November 14, 2005, Cover Story, "IKEA How the Swedish Retailer Became a Global Cult Brand."
62  Sartain, Libby and Mark Schumann, *BRAND FROM THE INSIDE: Eight Essential to Emotionally Connect Your Employees to Your Business* (San Francisco, CA: Jossey-Bass, 2006), p. 133.
63  Sartain, Libby and Mark Schumann, *BRAND FROM THE INSIDE: Eight Essential to Emotionally Connect Your Employees to Your Business* (San Francisco, CA: Jossey-Bass, 2006), p. 145.
64  "Ingvar Kamprad and IKEA," *Harvard Business School* Case No. 9-390-132, July 22, 1996, p. 4.
65  "Ingvar Kamprad and IKEA," *Harvard Business School* Case No. 9-390-132, July 22, 1996, p. 4.
66  "IKEA Invades America," *Harvard Business School* Case No. 9-504-094, September 14, 2004, p. 3.
67  IKEA corporate website: www.ikea.com
68  Sartain, Libby and Mark Schumann, *BRAND FROM THE INSIDE: Eight Essential to Emotionally Connect Your Employees to Your Business* (San Francisco, CA: Jossey-Bass, 2006), p. 10.
69  Nestlé corporate website: http://www.nestle.com/AllAbout/AtGlance/Introduction/Introduction.htm
70  Nestlé corporate website: http://www.nestle.com/AllAbout/AtGlance/Introduction/Introduction.htm
71  Finkelstein, Sydney, Harvey, Charles, and Thomas Lawton, *Breakout Strategy: Meeting the Challenge of Double-Digit Growth* (NY: McGraw-Hill, 2007), p. 102.

72   Nestlé corporate website: http://www.nestle.com/AllAbout/
     AtGlance/Introduction/Introduction.htm
73   Apgar, David, *Relevance: Hitting Your Goals by Knowing What Matters*
     (San Francisco, CA: Jossey-Bass, 2008), pp. 162–6.
74   Finkelstein, Sydney, Harvey, Charles, and Thomas Lawton, *Breakout
     Strategy: Meeting the Challenge of Double-Digit Growth* (NY: McGraw-
     Hill, 2007), p. 77.
75   For more on initiatives at Nestlé, see: http://www.nestle.com/
     SharedValueCSR/Overview.htm
76   For more on Nestlé's business principles, see: http://www.nestle.
     com/AllAbout/AllAboutNestle.htm
77   *BusinessWeek Online*, August 6, 2007.
78   Nestlé corporate website: http://www.verybestcoffee.com/default.
     aspx?seg=VBC
79   For more on Nescafé, see: http://www.nescafe.com/nescafe/
     My+favourite+Nescafe.htm
80   Bloom, Robert H., *The Inside Advantage: The Strategy That Unlocks
     the Hidden Growth in Your Business* (with Dave Conti) (NY: McGraw-
     Hill, 2008), pp. 24–5, 29, 79–81, 127, 163–4.
81   Meridden, Trever, *Cold Calling, Business the Nokia Way: Secrets of the
     World's Fastest Moving Company* (Hoboken, NJ: John Wiley, 2001).
82   Häikiö, Martti, *Nokia: The Inside Story* (Upper Saddle River, NJ: FT
     Prentice Hall, 2002).
83   Pardy, Keith, "The Human Approach," in *CMO Thought Leaders:
     The Rise of the Strategic Marketer* (edited by Geoffrey Precourt and
     published by Booz Allen Hamilton, 2007), p. 256.
84   Gopalakrishnan, Vishy, Korhonen, Antti, and Michael Lattanzi,
     *Work Goes Mobile: Nokia's Lessons from the Leading Edge by Nokia*
     (New York: John Wiley, 2006).
85   Häikiö, Martti, *Nokia: The Inside Story* (Upper Saddle River, NJ: FT
     Prentice Hall, 2002).
86   Interbrand website: www.interbrand.com/best_brands_2007.asp
87   Pardy, Keith, "The Human Approach," in *CMO Thought Leaders:
     The Rise of the Strategic Marketer* (edited by Geoffrey Precourt and
     published by Booz Allen Hamilton, 2007), pp. 250–67.
88   Lakshman, Nandini, "Nokia: It Takes a Village to Design a Phone
     for Emerging Markets," *Business Week*, September 10, 2007, pp. 12
     and 14.
89   Chapman, Matt, "Nokia plots mobile future," www.vnunet.
     com/2201814
90   Schenker, Jennifer L., "Nokia Aims Way beyond Handsets," *Business
     Week*, September 10, 2007, p. 38.
91   "Interbrand: All Brands are not Created Equal" *Best Global Brands
     2007*, pp. 5 and 22.

92  Pardy, Keith, "The Human Approach," in *CMO Thought Leaders: The Rise of the Strategic Marketer* (edited by Geoffrey Precourt and published by Booz Allen Hamilton, 2007), p. 258.

93  Lattanzi, Michael, Korhonen, Antti and Vishy Gopalakrishnan, *Work Goes Mobile: Nokia's Lessons from the Leading Edge* (Upper Saddle River, NJ: John Wiley, 2006), front jacket.

94  Website of The Park Hotels, www.theparkhotels.com/park/abt%20us.html

95  Yee, Amy, "India's hotelier with an eye for the unconventional," *Financial Times*, October 24, 2007, p. 12.

96  Yee, Amy, "India's hotelier with an eye for the unconventional," *Financial Times*, October 24, 2007, p. 12.

97  Roll, Martin, *Asian Brand Strategy: How Asia Builds Strong Brands* (NY: Palgrave MacMillan, 2006), pp. 151–2.

98  Slywotzky, Adrian J with Karl Weber, *UPSIDE: The 7 Strategies for Turning Big Threats Into Growth Breakthroughs* (NY: Crown Publishing Group, 2007), p. 17.

99  Slywotzky, Adrian J with Karl Weber, *UPSIDE: The 7 Strategies for Turning Big Threats Into Growth Breakthroughs* (NY: Crown Publishing Group, 2007), pp. 144–9.

100 Schmitt, Bernd H., *Big Think Strategy: How to Leverage Bold Ideas and Leave Small Thinking Behind* (Boston, MA: Harvard Business School Press, 2007), p. 147.

101 Finkelstein, Sydney, Harvey, Charles, and Thomas Lawton, *Breakout Strategy: Meeting the Challenge of Double-Digit Growth* (NY: McGraw-Hill, 2007), p. 209.

102 Roll, Martin, *Asian Brand Strategy: How Asia Builds Strong Brands* (NY: Palgrave MacMillan, 2006), p. 154.

103 Slywotzky, Adrian J with Karl Weber, *UPSIDE: The 7 Strategies for Turning Big Threats Into Growth Breakthroughs* (NY: Crown Publishing Group, 2007), p. 146.

104 Schmitt, Bernd H., *Big Think Strategy: How to Leverage Bold Ideas and Leave Small Thinking Behind* (Boston, MA: Harvard Business School Press, 2007), p. 19.

105 Schmitt, Bernd H., *Big Think Strategy: How to Leverage Bold Ideas and Leave Small Thinking Behind* (Boston, MA: Harvard Business School Press, 2007), p. 19.

106 Slywotzky, Adrian J with Karl Weber, *UPSIDE: The 7 Strategies for Turning Big Threats Into Growth Breakthroughs* (NY: Crown Publishing Group, 2007), pp. 144–9.

107 Schmitt, Bernd H., *Big Think Strategy: How to Leverage Bold Ideas and Leave Small Thinking Behind* (Boston, MA: Harvard Business School Press, 2007), p. 147.

108 Roll, Martin, *Asian Brand Strategy: How Asia Builds Strong Brands* (NY: Palgrave MacMillan, 2006), p. 154.

109 BusinessWeek, *Strategy Power Plays: How The World's Most Strategic Minds Reach the Top of Their Game* (NY: McGraw-Hill, 2007), p. 83.

110 Schmitt, Bernd H., *Big Think Strategy: How to Leverage Bold Ideas and Leave Small Thinking Behind* (Boston, MA: Harvard Business School Press, 2007), p. 20.

111 Roll, Martin, *Asian Brand Strategy: How Asia Builds Strong Brands* (NY: Palgrave MacMillan, 2006), p. 157.

112 Samsung corporate website: www.samsung.com

113 BusinessWeek, *Strategy Power Plays: How The World's Most Strategic Minds Reach the Top of Their Game* (NY: McGraw-Hill, 2007), p. 88.

114 Samsung corporate website: www.samsung.com

115 Roll, Martin, *Asian Brand Strategy: How Asia Builds Strong Brands* (NY: Palgrave MacMillan, 2006), pp. 153–4.

116 Kumar, V., *Managing Customers for Profit: Strategies to Increase Profits and Build Loyalty* (Upper Saddle River, NJ: Wharton School Publishing, 2008), p. 193.

117 Shiseido corporate website: www.shiseido.com

118 Roll, Martin, *Asian Brand Strategy: How Asia Builds Strong Brands* (NY: Palgrave MacMillan, 2006), pp. 145–51.

119 Shiseido corporate website and Roll, Martin, *Asian Brand Strategy: How Asia Builds Strong Brands* (NY: Palgrave MacMillan, 2006), pp. 145–51.

120 Koehn, Nancy, "Howard Schultz and Starbucks Coffee Company," *Harvard Business School* Case, 9-801-361, Revised, September 30, 2005, pp. 1 and 2.

121 Clark, Taylor, *STARBUCKED: A Double Tall Tale of Caffeine, Commerce, and Culture* (NY: Little, Brown and Company, 2007), p. 76.

122 Michelli, Joseph A., *The Starbucks Experience: 5 Principles for Turning Ordinary into Extraordinary* (NY: McGraw-Hill, 2007), p. 56.

123 Clark, Taylor, *STARBUCKED: A Double Tall Tale of Caffeine, Commerce, and Culture* (NY: Little, Brown and Company, 2007), p. 72.

124 Koehn, Nancy, "Howard Schultz and Starbucks Coffee Company," *Harvard Business School* Case, 9-801-361, Revised, September 30, 2005, pp. 16 and 17 and originally appearing in Neff, Thomas J. and James M. Citrin with Paul B. Brown in *Lessons from the Top* (New York: Currency/Doubleday, 1999), p. 127.

125 Moon, Youngme and John Quelch, "Starbucks: Delivering Customer Service," *Harvard Business School* Case Number 9-504-016, Revised July 10, 2006, p. 3.

126 Clark, Taylor, *STARBUCKED: A Double Tall Tale of Caffeine, Commerce, and Culture* (NY: Little, Brown and Company, 2007), p. 88.

127 Michelli, Joseph A., *The Starbucks Experience: 5 Principles for Turning Ordinary into Extraordinary* (NY: McGraw-Hill, 2007), pp. 25–6.

128 Michelli, Joseph A., *The Starbucks Experience: 5 Principles for Turning Ordinary into Extraordinary* (NY: McGraw-Hill, 2007), p. 21.

129 Michelli, Joseph A., *The Starbucks Experience: 5 Principles for Turning Ordinary into Extraordinary* (NY: McGraw-Hill, 2007), p. 67.

130 Michelli, Joseph A., *The Starbucks Experience: 5 Principles for Turning Ordinary into Extraordinary* (NY: McGraw-Hill, 2007), p. 84.

131 Koehn, Nancy, "Howard Schultz and Starbucks Coffee Company," *Harvard Business School* Case, 9-801-361, Revised, September 30, 2005, p. 16.

132 For complete list of 100 Best Companies to Work 2007, see: www. money.cnn.com/magazines/fortune/bestcompanies/2007/full_list/

133 Michelli, Joseph A., *The Starbucks Experience: 5 Principles for Turning Ordinary into Extraordinary* (NY: McGraw-Hill, 2007), p. 154.

134 Starbucks corporate website: www.starbucks.com

135 *The Wall Street Journal*, January 7, 2008, "McDonald's Takes On A Weakened Starbucks," by Janet Adamy, cover page.

136 Kiviat, Barbara, "Wake Up and Sell the Coffee," *Time Magazine*, April 7, 2008, pp. 46–50.

137 Adamy, Janet, "Starbucks Moves Aim to Revive Brand, Shares," *The Wall Street Journal*, March 20, 2008, p. B5.

138 "How the 50 Made the Cut," *BusinessWeek*, April 7, 2008, p. 63.

139 Tesco corporate website: www.tesco.com

140 Barwise, Patrick and Sean Meehan, *Simply Better: Winning and Keeping Customers by Delivering what Matters Most* (Boston, MA: Harvard Businesss School Press, 2004), pp. 89–96.

141 Tesco corporate website: www.tesco.com

142 Clifton Rita, Simmons, John, and others from *The Economist*, *BRANDS AND BRANDING* (Princeton, NJ: Bloomberg Press, 2003), p. 234.

143 Bund, Barbara E., *The Outside-In Corporation: How to Build a Customer-Centric Organization for Breakthrough Results* (NY: McGraw-Hill, 2006), pp. 135–6.

144 Tesco corporate website: www.tesco.com

145 Bund, Barbara E., *The Outside-In Corporation: How to Build a Customer-Centric Organization for Breakthrough Results* (NY: McGraw-Hill, 2006), p. 258.

146 Barwise, Patrick and Sean Meehan, *Simply Better: Winning and Keeping Customers by Delivering what Matters Most* (Boston, MA: Harvard Business School Press, 2004), p. 96.

147 "Tesco Plc." *Harvard Business School* Case 9-503-036, October 16, 2006.

148 Barwise, Patrick and Sean Meehan, *Simply Better: Winning and Keeping Customers by Delivering what Matters Most* (Boston, MA: Harvard Business School Press, 2004), pp. 89–96.

149 "Tesco Plc." *Harvard Business School* Case 9-503-036, October 16, 2006, p. 9.

150 Tesco corporate website: www.tesco.com

151 Hough, Bill and Ben Wang, "UPS: How 'Brown' Did It," *Airliners*, March/April, 2007, pp. 35–9.
152 The UPS Corporate website, www.UPS.com
153 Brewster, Mike and Frederick Dalzell, *Driving Change: The UPS Approach to Business* (NY: Hyperion, 2007), pp. 20, 21, 33 and 49.
154 Brewster, Mike and Frederick Dalzell, *Driving Change: The UPS Approach to Business* (NY: Hyperion, 2007), p. 21.
155 Sartain, Libby and Mark Schumann, *BRAND FROM THE INSIDE: Eight Essential to Emotionally Connect Your Employees to Your Business* (San Francisco, CA: Jossey-Bass, 2006), p. 7.
156 Brewster, Mike and Frederick Dalzell, *Driving Change: The UPS Approach to Business* (NY: Hyperion, 2007), pp. 285–6.
157 Niemann, Greg, *Big Brown: The Untold Story of UPS* (San Francisco, CA: Jossey-Bass, 2007), p. 70.
158 Niemann, Greg, *Big Brown: The Untold Story of UPS* (San Francisco, CA: Jossey-Bass, 2007), pp. 7–8.
159 Niemann, Greg, *Big Brown: The Untold Story of UPS* (San Francisco, CA: Jossey-Bass, 2007), pp. 162–5.
160 Niemann, Greg, *Big Brown: The Untold Story of UPS* (San Francisco, CA: Jossey-Bass, 2007), p. 164.
161 Brewster, Mike and Frederick Dalzell, Driving Change: The UPS Approach to Business (NY: Hyperion, 2007), p. 104.
162 Niemann, Greg, *Big Brown: The Untold Story of UPS* (San Francisco, CA: Jossey-Bass, 2007), pp. 163–4.
163 Brewster, Mike and Frederick Dalzell, *Driving Change: The UPS Approach to Business* (NY: Hyperion, 2007), p. 177.
164 Brewster, Mike and Frederick Dalzell, *Driving Change: The UPS Approach to Business* (NY: Hyperion, 2007), pp. 278–9.
165 Hough, Bill and Ben Wang, "UPS: How 'Brown' Did It," *Airliners*, March/April, 2007, p. 38.
166 Hough, Bill and Ben Wang, "UPS: How 'Brown' Did It," *Airliners*, March/April, 2007, p. 36.
167 Website: sustainableindustries.com, article: "UPS gives green light to right turns" by Sarah Crespi, 6/11/07 and "UPS ramps up 'green' fleet" by SI Staff, October 12, 2007.
168 www.virgingroup.com and www.hpiresearch.com. HPI is the UK's largest full service independent research agency and the research study was conducted during February to April of 2007.
169 Finkelstein, Sydney, Harvey, Charles, and Thomas Lawton, *Breakout Strategy: Meeting the Challenge of Double-Digit Growth* (NY: McGraw-Hill, 2007), p. 194.
170 For more on Virgin, see: www.virgingroup.com
171 Dearlove, Des, *Richard Branson Way: 10 Secrets of the World's Greatest Brand Builder* 2nd ed. (Oxford, UK: Capstone Publishing Limited, 2002), p. 39.

172 Dearlove, Des, *Richard Branson Way: 10 Secrets of the World's Greatest Brand Builder* 2nd ed. (Oxford, UK: Capstone Publishing Limited, 2002), p. 25.

173 Hatch and Schultz, *Taking Brand Initiative: How Companies Can Align Strategy, Culture and Identity Through Corporate Branding* (San Francisco, CA: Jossey-Bass, 2008), p. 111.

174 Dearlove, Des, *Richard Branson Way: 10 Secrets of the World's Greatest Brand Builder* 2nd ed. (Oxford, UK: Capstone Publishing Limited, 2002), p. 7.

175 Hatch and Schultz, *Taking Brand Initiative: How Companies Can Align Strategy, Culture and Identity Through Corporate Branding* (San Francisco, CA: Jossey-Bass, 2008), p. 112.

176 Dearlove, Des, *Richard Branson Way: 10 Secrets of the World's Greatest Brand Builder* 2nd ed. (Oxford, UK: Capstone Publishing Limited, 2002), pp 45–6.

177 Dearlove, Des, *Richard Branson Way: 10 Secrets of the World's Greatest Brand Builder* 2nd ed. (Oxford, UK: Capstone Publishing Limited, 2002), p. 86.

178 Dearlove, Des, *Richard Branson Way: 10 Secrets of the World's Greatest Brand Builder* 2nd ed. (Oxford, UK: Capstone Publishing Limited, 2002), p. 4.

179 Capon, Noel, *The Marketing Mavens* (NY: Crown Business, 2007), p. 84.

180 Inc.com, "26 Most Fascinating Entrepreneurs," April 1, 2005, (http://www.inc.com/magazine/20050401/26-branson.html).

181 Finkelstein, Sydney, Harvey, Charles, and Thomas Lawton, *Breakout Strategy: Meeting the Challenge of Double- Digit Growth* (NY: McGraw-Hill, 2007), p. 182.

182 Capon, Noel, *The Marketing Mavens* (NY: Crown Business, 2007), p. 84.

183 Schmitt, Bernd H., *Big Think Strategy: How to Leverage Bold Ideas and Leave Small Thinking Behind* (Boston, MA: Harvard Business School Press, 2007), p. 7.

184 Whole Foods corporate website: www.wholefoodsmarket.com

185 Hamel, Gary (with Bill Breen), *The Future of Management* (Boston, MA: Harvard Business School Press, 2007), p. 71.

186 Whole Foods corporate website: www.wholefoodsmarket.com

187 Hamel, Gary (with Bill Breen), *The Future of Management* (Boston, MA: Harvard Business School Press, 2007), p. 71.

188 Schmitt, Bernd H., *Big Think Strategy: How to Leverage Bold Ideas and Leave Small Thinking Behind* (Boston, MA: Harvard Business School Press, 2007), p. 95.

189 Sartain, Libby and Mark Schumann, *BRAND FROM THE INSIDE: Eight Essential to Emotionally Connect Your Employees to Your Business* (San Francisco, CA: Jossey-Bass, 2006), p. 9.

190 Schmitt, Bernd H., *Big Think Strategy: How to Leverage Bold Ideas and Leave Small Thinking Behind* (Boston, MA: Harvard Business School Press, 2007), p. 8.

191 Hamel, Gary (with Bill Breen), *The Future of Management* (Boston, MA: Harvard Business School Press, 2007), pp. 72–3.

192 Schmitt, Bernd H., *Big Think Strategy: How to Leverage Bold Ideas and Leave Small Thinking Behind* (Boston, MA: Harvard Business School Press, 2007), p. 152.

193 Schmitt, Bernd H., *Big Think Strategy: How to Leverage Bold Ideas and Leave Small Thinking Behind* (Boston, MA: Harvard Business School Press, 2007), p. 152.

194 Hamel, Gary (with Bill Breen), *The Future of Management* (Boston, MA: Harvard Business School Press, 2007), p. 74.

195 For detail on Whole Foods' ranking as #5 on the list of 100 Best Companies to Work 2007, see: http://money.cnn.com/magazines/fortune/bestcompanies/2007/snapshots/5.html

196 Sartain, Libby and Mark Schumann, *BRAND FROM THE INSIDE: Eight Essential to Emotionally Connect Your Employees to Your Business* (San Francisco, CA: Jossey-Bass, 2006), p. 152.

197 Whole Foods corporate website: www.wholefoodsmarket.com

198 Slywotzky, Adrian J. with Karl Weber, *UPSIDE: The 7 Strategies for Turning Big Threats Into Growth Breakthroughs* (NY: Crown Publishing Group, 2007), p. 131.

199 BusinessWeek.com, August 6, 2007, p. 62, The 100 Top Brands (Interbrand article).

200 Parent Company, Inditex, website: http://www.inditex.com/en/who_we_are/concepts/zara

201 Shelton, Bertrand, Thomas Hansson and Nicholas Hodson, "Format Invasions: Surviving Business's Least Understood Competitive Upheavals," *strategy + business*, Booz Allen Hamilton, Fall 2005, pp. 48–9.

202 Bund, Barbara E., *The Outside-In Corporation: How to Build a Customer-Centric Organization for Breakthrough Results* (NY: McGraw-Hill, 2006), pp. 134–5.

203 Silverstein Michael J. and Neil Fiske, *Trading Up: Why Consumers Want New Luxury Goods—and How Companies Create Them* (NY: Portfolio, Penguin Group, 2005), pp. 65–6.

204 Parent Company, Inditex, website: http://www.inditex.com/en/who_we_are/concepts/zara

205 Silverstein, Michael J. and Neil Fiske, *Trading Up: Why Consumers Want New Luxury Goods—and How Companies Create Them* (NY: Portfolio, Penguin Group, 2005), pp. 65–6.

206 Shelton, Bertrand, Thomas Hansson and Nicholas Hodson, "Format Invasions: Surviving Business's Least Understood Competitive Upheavals," *strategy + business* (Booz Allen Hamilton, Fall 2005, p. 49.

207 Schmitt, Bernd H., *Big Think Strategy: How to Leverage Bold Ideas and Leave Small Thinking Behind* (Boston, MA: Harvard Business School Press, 2007), p. 17.

# Chapter 8

# Preparing for Tomorrow

Recall a question that was raised in the introduction by some readers of the draft contents of the first seven chapters. "OK, I understand some of the trends and scenarios presented as well as the need to transition from traditional management to integrative management. Also, while I do not agree with the relevancy of all the case studies presented, since the airline business operates in a different framework, I do see that it is possible to improve in a number of areas. My question is: "Where do I start?" This closing chapter is an attempt to answer this question.

First, let us reiterate a couple of dilemmas faced by airline top management. Most airline CEOs are frustrated that, while they are literally working around the clock, most of their time and talent is consumed in dealing with issues relating to finance, unions, government regulators, shareholders, vendors, airport authorities, and so forth. When the 14-hour executive work day is over, often there has been no time to even think about what really matters, namely customers and optimization of current business models, let alone think about the challenges of competing with airlines about to enter the marketplace with totally new business models or being prepared for any of the imminent crisis situations facing the airline industry.

Some airlines have survived in the past without focusing on what really matters to their business, but in the future it will separate the real winners from those who while they will continue to stay in business, will either become much more dependent on governments or they will simply become irrelevant. Second, most airlines can no longer deny the reality that their business model is either broken to various degrees or vulnerable to format invaders. Take the case of the major network airlines in the US. The financial performance of these airlines has never compensated their shareholders for their investments. They are continuing to lose market share to low-fare airlines. As shown in a recent survey, more people would prefer to fly low-cost airlines than legacy airlines. In addition, if many are finding it difficult to survive with a fuel price around US$130, what will happen when it reaches US$150 a barrel, or even higher?

Shouldn't management take a few relevant initiatives and execute them relentlessly as opposed to taking on dozens of initiatives and making incremental changes? What does your airline stand for, and are all decisions made consistently with that stated value proposition? While BMW stands for the ultimate performance, it does not mean that BMW does not care for customer service or the ergonomics related to comfort. What differentiates such benchmarking companies from most airlines is that they make hard decisions and trade-offs without compromising in areas that affect their value propositions. What is needed from individual airlines is the focus and dedication to attain success in those areas. In response to the question, "Where do I start?," this book suggests the CEO start with a focus on three initiatives:

1. Airlines can no longer deny that consumer demographics, tastes, and incomes are changing. Also, political, economical, and environmental crisis situations can break out at any time with immediate and strong implications for airlines. Let us not overlook the possibility that new and strong competitors can appear with business models never heard of before in the airline industry. Therefore, management must simultaneously focus on corporate strategy for long-term competitiveness (for example, strategy for brand), and the capability for short-term reactions (flexibility, agility, and planning tools).

2. Long-term competitiveness and development have to be based on a viable value proposition (for example, "What makes our airline unique?"). The value proposition then needs to be translated into an emotionally appealing brand, developed around customers and employees, as well as around appropriate business concepts and processes that

efficiently and flawlessly turn promises into experiences. There must also be an intimate communication platform with customers to share good and bad experiences to enable further improvements. The Internet and the social network communities are new and excellent communication tools. Airlines should no longer accept the excuse that their business is a commodity business, and that profits cannot be achieved through differentiation. Airline CEOs should ask what constraints, such as labor, technology, and government regulations, stand in the way, and how they can be overcome. Just remind yourself of the establishment and success of FedEx. In the current environment, there are examples of global airlines that have succeeded in differentiating themselves: examples include, Lufthansa, Virgin Atlantic, Singapore Airlines, and Cathay Pacific. Where is the evidence that a strong brand can lead to higher margins in the airline business? Singapore Airlines obtains at least 50 percent of its revenue from first- and business-class passengers![1]

3. Agility for short-term reactions is what translates the horsepower of a powerful car into a race winner, and airlines need maneuvering ability more than ever. Both sharp turns and short braking distances will be required to avoid suddenly appearing obstacles. Consequently, airlines need to be prepared for those appearances at any time, and they need to react immediately. This capability requires not only flexible capacities, but also planning and operations tools able to deliver results within hours. These changes will require management to move much more quickly, and to have a much more flexible business model. Such business models must be totally integrated and analytically driven, as exemplified by the jetEngine™ O/S integrated business platform developed by Airline Intelligence Systems Inc.[2] The required technology must be able to respond dynamically and strategically to competitive market forces in real time, to maximize profits, increase operating efficiencies, and mitigate enterprise risks. Airlines really do have more information about their businesses than many other businesses. Most airlines have used the available data

to report on history, or, at best, project the performance of their businesses. Airline CEOs can enjoy the flexibility of being able to re-plan their businesses in real time if they lay out strategic requirements from their technology. Recall the business approaches of Cemex and Zara.

Within a more strategic framework, airlines must overcome their market share or volume obsession. While most CEOs agree that the goal is profit and not market share, their actions do not support this statement. They must also overcome their dependence on a particular competency that may be extremely detrimental. This is particularly relevant for some large, network carriers who have been dependent on their protected networks or alliance partnerships. Look what happened to traditional travel agents. Finally, airlines must not define competition too narrowly. Could fractional ownership and VLJs or Internet-enabled travel become new competitors? If these format invaders find new ways of doing business (just as Google did with search-based advertising and MySpace did with GenY[3]), then the existing airlines must stop their perceived core competencies from blinding them to new opportunities being created by the "flattening" world.

In closing, it is suggested that the reader go back and try to determine if there was one clear theme that stood out of the 20 businesses discussed. One answer would be leadership. In light of the way other businesses have been managed and newer businesses are likely to be managed in the "flattening" world, one could ask: "Is airline management flying ahead of the airplane?"

## Notes

1   "Singapore Airlines: The push into China," *Aviation Strategy*, June 2008, p. 14.
2   For more on Airline Intelligence Systems, see: www.aisystems.org
3   Evans, David S. and Richard Schmalensee, *Catalyst CODE: The Strategies Behind the World's Most Dynamic Companies* (Boston, MA: Harvard Business School Press, 2007), front jacket.

# Index

# About the Author

**Nawal Taneja** has more than 35 years' experience in the airline industry. As a practitioner, he has worked for and advised major airlines and airline-related businesses worldwide in the areas of strategic and tactical planning. His experience also includes the presidency of a small airline that provided scheduled and charter services with jet aircraft, and the presidency of a research organization that provided consulting services to the air transportation community worldwide. In academia, he has served as Professor and Chairman of the Aerospace Engineering and Aviation Department at the Ohio State University, and an Associate Professor in the Flight Transportation Laboratory of the Department of Aeronautics and Astronautics of the Massachusetts Institute of Technology. On the government side, he has advised civil aviation authorities in public policy areas such as airline liberalization, air transportation bilateral and multilateral agreements, and the financing, management and operations of government-owned airlines. He has also served on the board of both public and private organizations.

Nawal Taneja authored four books for practitioners in the airline industry: (1) *Driving Airline Business Strategies through Emerging Technology* published in 2002; (2) *AIRLINE SURVIVAL KIT: Breaking Out of the Zero Profit Game* published in 2003; (3) *Simpli-Flying: Optimizing the Airline Business Model* published in 2004; and (4) *FASTEN YOUR SEATBELT: The Passenger is Flying the Plane* published in 2005. All four books were published by Ashgate Publishing in the UK.

# PREFACE

*The Healthcare Customer Service Revolution* is an outgrowth from the experiences that we have seen first-hand through our professional assignments and experienced personally as patients, wives, husbands, parents, daughters, and sons.

We have surveyed thousands of patients and interviewed dozens of employers throughout the country to get their reactions to their personal experiences in healthcare situations. They all confirm that what needs to be improved in the healthcare arena is the human element.

The fact is that most people in healthcare entered their profession to give something back—they had a driving need to help humanity and make a difference, but somewhere they became disconnected. We need to shed that superiority complex and rediscover that keen desire to work for a noble goal and get back to the basics of human dignity.

As a mother of a large family, I have the opportunity to get into hospitals, doctors' offices, and clinics on a regular basis. Although my experiences at many of them have been positive, I can almost always cite problems relating to customer service. Rarely does a healthcare facility treat me as a customer and not just another patient.

Attitude is everything; indifference breeds anger and hostility. The basics of good human relations coupled with excellent medical care can create a special kind of synergy.

People have a great thirst for smiles. They have an enormous longing for cheerfulness and encouragement. Each day we encounter a good number of patients who await that momentary gift of our joy. They are extremely grateful for small acts of human kindness.

Gratitude is a human virtue that adds a great deal to social life. It consists of affectionate recognition when a favor is received. This virtue contributes remarkably to a more friendly environment.

Throughout the course of our professional work we should sense the importance of friendship, cordiality, temperance, love for the truth, understanding, loyalty, optimism, and sincerity. These social virtues make daily life more pleasant. In my opinion, these are the critical ingredients that are missing in an otherwise exceptional healthcare system in this country.

Our incomprehensible advances in medicine have given the medical profession the "Midas touch." What is needed now is the "human touch."

**Peggy Zimmerman**

# **A**CKNOWLEDGMENTS

**O**ur thanks to those who spent many hours to assist us in this project: Sandee Klopfer, Tim Malaney, Chris Mroz, Bruce Nelson, Elizabeth Ridley, Christy Zimmerman, and Mike Zimmerman. Our gratitude to the many who shared their personal experiences as patients in our nation's healthcare providers. Finally, to those hospitals that allowed us to learn from them what successful customer service can mean to the public, we are extremely grateful.

# CONTENTS

**CHAPTER**

**Managed Care's Monetary Measures**                        **27**

**CHAPTER**

**Competing Means Satisfying Patients**                      **41**

# 5 CHAPTER

# 6 CHAPTER

# 7 CHAPTER

# 8 CHAPTER

# 9 CHAPTER

## Unleashing Customer Service through Servant Leadership                    117

# 10 CHAPTER

## Focus on Customer Service                    135

# 11 CHAPTER

# 12 CHAPTER

# 13 CHAPTER

# 14 CHAPTER

## An "Aloha" Approach to Patient Relations: The Queen's Medical Center                    183

# 15 CHAPTER

## Customer Service Commandos: Holy Cross Hospital's War to Improve Patient Satisfaction          195

# CHAPTER

# The Revolution
# Has Begun

**A** physician was recently confronted by a 40-year-old female patient detailing the mistakes that the physician's
office staff had made. The doctor responded, "Well, you can
go somewhere else if you want to." This scenario exemplifies
the attitudes of many healthcare providers regarding customer service.

When we asked this patient what aspects of customer
service from a healthcare provider were important to her,
she answered, "I expect them to see me as a person . . . that
they use my name, look at me, and show a certain amount
of empathy. I also expect a sense of personal service regarding the bills and the reduction in long delay times." These
are certainly not unrealistic expectations for patients to
have from their healthcare provider. However, patients say
their expectations are not being met.

The revolution for improved customer service by
healthcare providers has begun. For years, Americans have

told opinion pollsters that they felt disenchanted, disenfranchised, and alienated from healthcare providers. Every available study indicates that patients no longer view providers as angels of mercy.

Until recently, patients had no formal mechanism to voice displeasure with the way they were treated by the apathetic hospital staff or the pious, egocentric physician and his cold, indifferent staff. Managed care, which is rapidly taking over the industry, is changing all of that. Now patients are being asked by HMOs and PPOs to score their hospitals and physicians on customer service issues. Employers and managed care organizations are evaluating patient feedback and taking action.

Within the past several years, the nation's employers have gained control of the way healthcare is delivered in this country. Their choice of controlling the delivery system is primarily through the managed care concept. During the 1990s, controlling health costs has been the major objective of employers. In fact, in 1994, the average healthcare cost per employee actually dropped slightly. The 1.1 percent decrease U.S. employers realized in 1994 reflected the first decline in healthcare costs in 20 years. Justifiably, employers feel they have begun to control their healthcare costs and are now turning their attention to quality of care. Under the heading of "quality of care" falls customer service or patient satisfaction.

For instance, in the summer of 1995, a group of representatives of some of the country's largest employers and purchasers of health insurance agreed to pursue a fundamental shift in emphasis in the nation's managed healthcare systems: Now that costs have begun to be controlled, they want the primary focus to be placed on measuring the quality of care. The broad-based agreement was reached at Jackson Hole, Wyoming, by 30 officials of federal, state, and local public employees' organizations, consumer groups, and officials of such major employers as American Express, the Minnesota Mining and Manufacturing Company, the

Ameritech Corporation, and Pepsico. All together they represented an estimated 80 million consumers of health insurance.

"Monitoring quality will be the next battlefield," said Tom J. Elkin, assistant executive director of the California Public Employees Retirement System, which represents more than 800,000 state and local government employees and their families. He predicted that only health plans and providers that demonstrate high quality would still be in existence by the year 2000. Two elements of the consensus that emerged were regarded as significant by leaders in healthcare. One was that purchasers of healthcare for such large numbers of consumers with great potential power in the marketplace were united in their desire for greater attention to quality. The second was a decision to put into motion a plan to gather data in a more uniform and comprehensive way than ever before on the medical outcomes for various methods of treating patients for major illnesses.[1]

More employees are now grouped together through managed care companies than ever before. Those employees who become patients now have a unified voice and their perceptions of their healthcare are being heard. Employees now have a method of expression. More important, the employers care about what their employees think about their healthcare service. How patients are treated as human beings is now becoming an issue the employer tracks, evaluates, trends, and communicates to the managed care companies and providers.

## CUSTOMER SERVICE WILL IMPACT REVENUE

Customer service, long given a low priority by providers, now becomes so important that it can affect their cash flow and revenue. Employers are saying to providers and managed care companies, "Score well in customer service or

---

1. *The New York Times,* July 5, 1995.

you'll get your knuckles wrapped, you'll be scolded, or worse yet, your bonus will be stripped, or you'll lose our patients altogether." Providers who flunk the customer service test will lose patients. It won't be a few disgruntled patients who take their business somewhere else because of the poor service they received from the provider—it will be large numbers of patients taken away through the managed care network. They will turn to the provider who knows what customer service is all about and can provide it successfully.

Customer service has indeed become the new battlefield for providers in this day of the new paradigm in healthcare delivery. Cost control and excellent customer service will go hand-in-hand. Employers with newfound leverage in healthcare will make certain it happens. And make no mistake about it: Patients and their families are the customers for providers. Customers are no longer the medical staff, or payers for hospitals, or the payers for physicians, but the people receiving the care or their relatives.

When the three of us decided to write this book, we put together a research plan in early 1995 that called for personally interviewing a large number of Fortune 500 companies and a good sampling of managed care companies. The objective was to learn their attitude and approach toward customer service of providers to their employees and subscribers. We wanted to learn whether providers' customer service was important enough for them to track and evaluate and what they would do with the data once collected. If they did track that aspect of healthcare delivery, what would they do about the providers who did not score well?

During the summer months of 1995, we personally interviewed more than 25 large employers representing millions of employees in locations all across the country. Included were: Boeing, Borden, Coca-Cola, First Chicago Bank, General Electric, Hallmark Cards, Hershey Foods, Hewlett-Packard, Johnson Wax, Kellogg's, Kimberly-Clark,

Marriott Corp., McDonald's, Nike, Inc., J. C. Penney, Procter & Gamble, Sara Lee, Sherwin-Williams, Time-Warner, Toys 'R' Us, UPS, Walgreen's, Walt Disney Co., Warner-Lambert, and Wrigley Co. Nearly half of these corporations ranked in the top 100 most-admired companies in *Fortune* magazine's recent listing of "America's Most Admired Corporations."[2] These companies will set the pace for the rest of America's employers in demanding improved patient satisfaction and customer service from the nation's healthcare providers.

We also conducted personal telephone interviews with large- and mid-sized managed care companies representing more than 25 million enrollees, to determine their approach to tracking and evaluating customer service at the provider level. Included in the interviews with managed care organizations were the following: Kaiser Permanente, Beech Street of California, Health Service Network, Preferred Care, ConnectiCare, Medica Primary, The Prudential, Virginia Health Network, FHP of Colorado, Humana, Cigna, American Lifecare, Choice Care, IHC, and King Co. Medical.

We also conducted interviews with nearly 50 hospitals to determine their approach toward customer service. We made on-site visits to a half dozen of those hospitals in order to obtain a better feel for their customer service approach. Some of interviews lasted a day or two; others covered a week or more. We were attempting to discover specifically what facilities were doing to improve their patient relations and what their future customer service plans might include. We also asked the hospitals and medical groups what they thought were the most important factors in excellent patient relations; how they tracked customer satisfaction; and *who* (in their opinion) is the customer: community employers? payers? their medical staff? the patients and their families?

---

2. *Fortune,* March 1995.

## PATIENT DISSATISFACTION WITH CUSTOMER SERVICE BY HOSPITALS AND PHYSICIANS

We also wanted a good sense for what the patient thought about customer service at the provider level in healthcare. We conducted written, mailback surveys with former patients (patients within the last six months from the date of service), as well as hundreds of personal interviews with former patients. The patient interviews and survey included nearly 2,000 people in 17 states who had received care from 30 different hospitals and hundreds of physicians' offices within the last year. Our investigation also included in-depth discussions with such well-known patient survey organizations as Press-Ganey, Healthcare Research Systems, and The Picker Foundation.

The hundreds of hours of interviews and painstaking research led us to the observations you will find in the succeeding chapters. We feel it is the most up-to-date look at the organized patient revolt against poor customer service by healthcare providers and at the growing trend of the employer to tie cash to customer satisfaction. The revolutionary trends we uncovered revealed that employers are placing a higher emphasis on employee/patient satisfaction than ever before and that patients are fed up with indifferent, cold, uncaring service they receive from hospitals and physician offices. The employers and patient both want a change and they will get it.

We found nearly 60 percent of the Fortune 500 employers we interviewed presently survey and track employee satisfaction for provider customer service issues; another 21 percent of them told us they plan to start tracking soon. That means nearly 80 percent of the nation's largest employers will be tracking customer service issues. Nearly 100 percent of the managed care companies said they survey and monitor provider patient satisfaction with their enrollees. Over 50 percent of the employers and managed care companies said they will drop providers who flunk the customer service standards they set. In fact, some have switched providers already for that very reason: poor customer service.

Our surveys and interviews of more than 2,000 former patients showed they are not satisfied with customer service in hospitals or medical offices. Although 90 percent of those surveyed said customer service was *extremely* important to them, they reported that both their hospital and doctor fell far short of their expectations. On a 10-point satisfaction index, hospitals scored a low 7.4 and their physicians only slightly better at 8.1. These findings of ours coincided with the results of a University of Michigan research project designed to measure the quality of American goals and services. That study of 46,000 customers scored hospitals only a 74 on a 100-point satisfaction index—just above the postal service and just behind long distance telephone services.[3]

Amazingly, our survey revealed that 6 percent of the patients who responded said the customer service aspect was so bad they would not return to that hospital, and 8 percent said they would tell the world how badly they were treated so others would not be faced with the same "poor service and humiliation." "Lack of human respect," was a complaint they often reiterated. Patients told us that they defined good customer service by the provider as good old-fashioned actions such as communicating with them, showing compassion, fast service, and (the old stand-by) friendliness. There were no surprises there; certainly such actions are not difficult to provide. However, patients reported in no uncertain terms it's not happening nearly often enough.

---

3. *Modern Healthcare,* December 19–26, 1994, p. 38. This and all similar subsequent references are reprinted with permission from Modern Healthcare, copyright Crain Communications, Inc., 740 N. Rush St., Chicago, IL 60611.

We asked former patients to describe the term *customer service;* following are some of the responses:

Fast and friendly check in and out; compassionate and friendly treatments from nurses and doctors.

Adequate parking; wheelchair availability at the door; prompt, courteous, and cheerful customer relations.

Courteous and helpful. "In tune" with patients' needs.

Registration and admittance without long delays and with courtesy.

Being taken care of and having questions answered in a quick, friendly manner.

Answering questions, giving information, showing directions, making people understand.

Courteous treatment by personnel. It is important to make their patient feel that she is important and her needs will be met.

Having the staff listen to your questions or complaints and also discussing your bill later. I guess I equate "customer service" with communications.

## HOSPITALS' APPROACH TO CUSTOMER SERVICE SHOWS LITTLE INGENUITY

We also spoke with nearly 50 hospitals having bed sizes ranging from 46 to 949 in various geographical regions regarding their approach toward improved patient satisfaction. Most of what we found has been going on in the industry for years. Almost every hospital has some kind of a patient survey or questionnaire to determine how patients felt about the customer service aspect of their visit. About one-third of the hospitals we talked to use an outside firm such as Press-Ganey to conduct the patient survey and report the findings. The rest have their own in-house patient survey process.

Nearly one-third of the hospitals said they had some kind of customer service training program for their employees. Again, such programs have been fairly common practice for years. The other most common practices we uncovered were focus groups (16 percent), specific process changes to cut waiting time (16 percent), patient-focused care reengineering or restructuring (14 percent), development of a special department (usually called the patient representative department) (16 percent), formation of a special committee or task force (9 percent), and development of specific standards of customer service excellence (9 percent).

Most experts interviewed by *Modern Healthcare* magazine last year didn't think hospitals were serious enough about improving customer satisfaction. However, an increasing number are starting to document satisfaction for payers, employers, and the public out of fear they will lose patients and revenue. Industry leaders in customer satisfaction, such as the Marriott Corp., are far ahead of hospitals in developing programs to reward employees for treating their customers well, experts told *Modern Healthcare*.[4]

Although the vast majority of hospitals said the patient or family was their customer, another 63 percent told us their medical staff was also their customer, another 50 percent said the payers were also their customer, and 22 percent told us their community employers were also considered their customer. In our opinion, this may be part of the problem for providers in their attempt to focus on improved customer relations. Because of their confusion about who their target of service really is and trying to be all things to all people, they fail altogether in many in-

---

4. *Modern Healthcare,* July 18, 1994, p. 30.

stances. When we asked each hospital its plans for the future regarding upgrading their customer service, we generally got more of what the facility is already doing with a few exceptions.

Providers will have to face up to the negative image many Americans have of their healthcare service, then do something about it. This includes every area of human contact within every healthcare institution in the country. Hospitals and medical groups can no longer compete on the strength of their clinical expertise alone because the industry is having to react to competition that can and will provide the care for less cost. What sets providers apart today is the success of their "service" efforts.

More and more, the service and patient relations context that surrounds the medical care given will give providers added value and will differentiate them from the competition. Patients are up in arms, believing that they are treated with a lack of dignity, respect, and compassion. They are mad, and now that they can voice their displeasure, their anger will hit providers at the bottom line. Future business in the form of patient volume will swing in the balance, based a great deal on provider customer service.

It's a new battlefield that providers themselves have created by their apathy toward customer service. Dissatisfaction has been festering in patients' minds for a long time, fueling the revolt for improved customer service. And today patients are leading it.

CHAPTER

# Customer Service
## The Next Battleground

Since the mid-1980s, dramatic changes have occurred in the healthcare delivery system. The concept of managed care is rapidly taking control of the industry. Ten years ago, 15 million Americans were enrolled in health maintenance organizations (HMOs). That number skyrocketed to 47.2 million as of July 1994, according to a report by *Interstudy*. More than 100 million Americans are enrolled in HMOs or preferred provider organizations (PPOs). Managed care, with its emphasis on controlling treatment and containing costs, is changing the way healthcare services are delivered. Gone forever are the simpler days of fee-for-service healthcare. Today's managed care world of medicine is more complex, and ultimately more controversial, than anything that has gone before.

The vast majority of people who participate in managed care programs are enrolled through their workplace, which means that the employers themselves have been

suddenly and dramatically thrust into the role of interme-
diary in the formerly sacrosanct provider/patient relationship. As a result, the employer has gained the leverage of
control from the providers and payers. "We've had a revolution in this country in terms of the accountability of
healthcare purchasers," says Helen Darling, manager of
healthcare strategy and programs for Xerox Corp. "There's
been a paradigm shift in terms of who's in charge that
began in the early 1980s."

"The biggest news story missed in the last decade has
been business' impact on healthcare," echoes David
Langness, vice president of the Healthcare Association of
Southern California. "Employers have had the largest impact
on healthcare costs—not physicians, hospitals, or health
plans."[1] Large employers represent huge patient bases.
Managed care companies are feeling that pressure, and as
a result have recognized the need to woo, win, and keep the
contracts of large, powerful employers. The best way to do
that, of course, is for the managed care companies to make
sure that their subscribers—the employers' employees—
are satisfied with their healthcare experiences.

Managed care offers the potential patient fewer choices
in terms of the who, what, when, where, and why of seeking
medical treatment. In exchange, it promises lower premiums, caps on out-of-pocket expenses, and potentially better
service. But better service as judged by whose standards?
Employers expect efficiency and quality from their providers, and are beginning now to demand statistical evidence
to prove that their healthcare choices are meeting the needs
and desires of their employees. This statistical evidence
comes from two primary sources: the surveys done by a
company overall among its employees, and the survey results provided to the employer by the managed care company. The results illustrate the measured level of satisfaction
among enrollees in a particular HMO or PPO. Regardless

---

1. *Hospitals & Health Networks,* May 5, 1995.

of the source of the information, the bottom line issue is and will continue to be to an even greater extent, *whether the patient is satisfied with the care he or she receives.*

## MOST OF THE NATION'S LARGEST EMPLOYERS WILL BE TRACKING CUSTOMER SERVICE BY PROVIDERS

As noted in Chapter 1, nearly 60 percent of the companies we interviewed presently survey their employees to determine the level of their satisfaction with their managed care company and their providers, and another 21 percent stated that they were going to start surveying and tracking their employee satisfaction with providers. Eighty percent of the nation's largest and most progressive employers will be tracking customer service issues.

As hospitals and physicians compete for patients, and employers shop around for the best benefit packages to offer their employees, patient satisfaction and customer service are suddenly major concerns for everyone in both the healthcare industry, and in industry overall. A revolution is underway in the healthcare world: Employees are telling their employers what they want and need in healthcare services, and the employers in turn are pressuring the managed care companies to find providers who measure up.

Nowhere is this equation clearer than at First Chicago Bank in Chicago, Illinois. First Chicago employs 18,500 people, which translates into 18,500 potential HMO enrollees. Robert Bonin, First Chicago's manager of benefits administration, says his company's two HMOs are eager to work with First Chicago on issues related to employee/patient satisfaction. "We are the flagship employer for both of our HMOs," Bonin explains. "It's not a question of how open are they, but how quickly will they do it? I would say they are totally open because the alternative is, I dump them, take my $20 million and give it to someone else," he says. "We've done that. We've canceled our largest network and made our smallest local network our largest local network because we were unable to come to terms. So they [managed care companies] are well-motivated to look at things."

Many major U.S. employers are starting to realize the importance of good customer service in healthcare and have begun to pay more attention to the care and kindness received by their employees as they use healthcare benefits. To many people, it just makes good sense. "The more you move into managed care and the less choice an associate has regarding where he or she goes, it becomes more incumbent upon the employer to be sure that what their choices are, are making them [the employees] at least moderately happy," says Marcia McLeod, manager of benefits program development at J.C. Penney's corporate headquarters in Dallas.

Bill Greer, the director of benefits for Kellogg's Company in Battle Creek, Michigan, agrees. His company recently surveyed one-third of its 7,000 employees about healthcare. "Because we're putting in managed care, we want to track what's going on. We hope to be able to show that our managed care plan is a higher quality than our other plans. We don't know if that will happen or not," he admits.

This sentiment is echoed by Robert Wittcoff, director of employee benefits for McDonald's Corporation in Oak Brook, Illinois. His corporation is also beginning to get more involved with tracking employee/patient satisfaction. "We're a service business and we've learned that, for a business, it's very important to keep our customers happy; and if you take that to the next logical step, you've got to keep employees happy. We're spending gobs of money on healthcare, and it doesn't make sense to spend that money and not have satisfied employees," he says. "Healthcare, whether we like it or not, is becoming part of our business."

## QUALITY BECOMES KEY STRATEGY

In addition to keeping their employees happy, companies have a huge financial interest vested in their employees' healthcare. A 1994 survey by Foster Higgins found that total healthcare benefit costs averaged $3,741 per employee per year. The importance of improving the quality of the care received for those precious healthcare dollars is recognized by many corporate executives.

"We wanted to drive quality in terms of healthcare as a very key strategy towards healthcare cost management. We're trying to improve the value for the dollar," says Richard Dreyfuss, director of employee benefits at Hershey Food Corporation in Hershey, Pennsylvania.

"Looking at what you're getting for the dollar is something that I think companies need to focus on more, particularly as it relates to outcome measurement and patient satisfaction," Dreyfuss says. Hershey Foods recently surveyed all 6,500 of its employees with a written questionnaire on healthcare. The company then used the results to help design a better health plan and to work with individual providers to improve their services. "That's valuable data when you walk into someone's office and you try to address a specific issue. There's just no substitute for having facts," he says.

And those facts help Hershey's employees to make better healthcare choices for themselves and their families. Hershey Foods offers its employees choices among four HMOs and its own point-of-service plan. "I think people are more accommodating or more accepting of the managed care way of buying healthcare now. Price is an issue, but I don't think it's as big an issue as everybody thinks it is. They [the employees] may select the most expensive option if that's the way it comes out in terms of their values."

One common concern voiced by employees pushed into managed care by their employers is that such strict attention to cost control on the part of the insurers will automatically translate into a compromise on the quality of the care they receive. Not so, insists Bill Ruoff, leader of insurance benefits delivery for GE headquarters in Schenectady, New York. "One of the things we work really hard at, in terms of our communication with the employees, is to assure them that yes, we are in fact trying to save money, no question about that; on the other hand, saving money doesn't mean that we're going to short-change the quality of the care that you receive. And we have actions, things that we do to back up that claim," Ruoff says.

Employers will force their managed care companies to make customer service a part of the contractual negotiations with providers. For instance, to encourage HMOs to improve customer satisfaction and the quality of their care, a business group negotiated agreements in which the HMO could lose 2 percent of its premiums if it failed to achieve specified improvements in customer satisfaction and quality of care.

A group of large companies in California recently negotiated an average price cut of 4.3 percent in 1996 for their employees' healthcare from a group of 13 HMOs in the state. It was the second consecutive year that companies belonging to the Pacific Business Group on Health have obtained price reductions. For 1996 the HMOs offered contracts that ranged from no price increase to a decline of 13 percent.[2]

Patricia Powers, head of the California business coalition, said 13 of the 15 HMOs working with her group agreed to cut their rates. A major reason, she told *The Wall Street Journal*, is that health plans themselves can negotiate lower prices from providers of medical care. "There's an oversupply of hospitals and physicians."[3] "It's a buyer's marketplace right now," according to Glenn Meister, a Foster Higgins & Co. health-insurance consultant. "As employers head into renewal negotiations for 1996, we're seeing expectations of a zero percent increase, or even a decrease."[4]

---

2. *The New York Times,* June 22, 1995.
3. *The Wall Street Journal,* June 22, 1995.
4. Ibid.

## EMPLOYERS BECOME THE PATIENT'S CHAMPION

From an employee/patient standpoint, one of the great advantages of having the employer suddenly so involved in their healthcare decisions is the chance to have a powerful ally on their side when confronting the HMO or PPO. Robert Bonin calls the employer the patient's "champion" in any healthcare debate and offers this illustration from his own experiences at First Chicago:

> We had an employee with a great big lump on his head. HMO member. Cosmetic surgery. How would you like to go walking around with a lump two inches long and an inch and a half wide and about three centimeters thick, on your forehead? That's cosmetic? But it is. Two doctors say it is cosmetic. But don't you think we should use a little judgment here? Without a champion, the system would say no. "Go in peace. Just don't lay on it." So we caused them, I think, to be a little more rational, or patient-oriented in their thinking. Without our focusing on the patient, there would be less focus by the health plan on the patient, believe me.

This added pressure by the employer on obtaining health benefits can manifest itself in several ways. For many companies, it means first surveying employees on healthcare, and then requiring the HMO or PPO to survey its members and provide those results to the company, and to account for any discrepancies. "With our managed care plans, we measure employees both through the company and through the supplier. Most of the managed care plans, as a requirement for contracting with us, are compelled to survey customers on various service-oriented parameters. We make that part and parcel of their job," says Bill Ruoff of GE. "We do that for one of two reasons. To measure something very specific that we're interested in knowing about, or basically, to keep our suppliers honest, to make sure that the feedback we get is correlating with the feedback that they're giving to us."

But most employers are quick to add that in most cases, the managed care company is as concerned about getting accurate information as the employer is. "I made it sound like we bludgeon people, and we're certainly willing to do that if we need to, but I don't think there's going to be a need to bludgeon anybody," says Bonin of First Chicago. "I think that they (managed care companies) are seriously interested in the results and what they may do to improve themselves."

## EMPLOYER'S PERSPECTIVE: WHAT DO PATIENTS/ EMPLOYEES REALLY WANT?

So what do healthcare patients want? Care. Compassion. Concern. Those are things so basic providers might just take them for granted. But even the simplest issues like friendliness, cheerfulness, and privacy will become more important as employees rate their healthcare experiences and make their choices for future care. And because these issues are so important to employees, they will be important to employers as well, in the long run.

"There are other ways to measure quality, but certainly it's the more subjective issues that you want to look at, too. Do you feel like you're being treated with respect, in a timely manner, do they feel like they're getting quality care? That's an important piece of it," says Marcia McLeod of J. C. Penney's.

Sensitivity on the part of the provider is an important issue too. "One of our most important concerns is a doctor who shows sensitivity to the employee's needs," says Ronald Kastler, human resources manager for benefits, education, and communication, at Johnson Wax in Racine, Wisconsin. Also important is the doctor's awareness of the patient's "life events."

"A young person with a family has different concerns and healthcare needs than a single person with elderly parents, and a sensitive doctor or hospital staff should be aware of those differences," Kastler says.

The best employers also realize that the job an employee does may affect his or her conception of customer service from the provider. Marcia McLeod of J. C. Penney's recognizes the connection; her employees are required to perform to a high standard of customer service, and they expect the same level of service when they are on the receiving end of care: "Their main job in life is going out and smiling at people and trying to be nice to them and provide customer service. They expect the same from others," she explains.

## HOW EMPLOYERS USE THE DATA THEY RECEIVE

Our research has shown that most major U.S. companies do survey their employees, right down to the specific level of satisfaction with individual providers. But what happens to that information once it is gathered? Is it filed away in a locked cabinet, never to see daylight again, or do employers actually use that data?

"They use it," says Melissa Kennedy, vice-president of HealthCare Research Systems, a healthcare surveying and consulting firm at Ohio State University that has performed surveying for several major employers, including Xerox, GE, Digital, and GTE. "People that we talk to in hospitals get these huge reports and they sit on someone's desk for months and months and months. Employers and health plans are dying for this data because they're using it at the negotiations table constantly," she says. "They're using it a lot because when you're on the employer's and the managed care side of things, there's a direct relationship between what can be drawn from these results and the money that can be saved by using these data."

For many employers, the first way the survey results are used is to change the plans themselves according to what employees have indicated they wanted. For example, when many second- and third-shift workers at S. C. Johnson Wax in Racine, Wisconsin, complained on their surveys about no doctors being available during the hours they were off work, Johnson Wax worked with its HMO and arranged for one of the doctors in the plan to reschedule some hours to be available at more unusual times, for example, from 11 AM to 7 PM. The company saw great improvement in the survey results the following year. Here is a clear example of an employer gleaning information from a survey, data not obtainable any other way, then using that information on behalf of the employee. Ask yourself whether the typical American assembly line worker could phone the doctor and persuade him or her to schedule an appointment for 7 PM on a Friday night. But that's precisely what the employer has succeeded in doing.

There are other uses for survey results, too. Kellogg's uses its survey results to target both educational and intervention efforts. The company also uses the data to risk-adjust the company's healthcare costs. At J. C. Penney's, survey information is used as feedback for the managed care plans, so managed care managers know how associates perceive them. The company may also eventually use those survey results for negotiations when it comes time to renew contracts with specific managed care plans and their network of providers. "We plan on using that information for whatever good reasons there are to use it," says Marcia McLeod.

In a slightly different vein, First Chicago Bank publishes the results of its surveys and makes that information available to employees as they decide which plan to join. "I don't know if anybody changed his or her mind based on the information, but the plan that consistently got the highest scores is our biggest plan, and also our least expensive plan. So it had the highest satisfaction, lowest cost, and highest membership," says Robert Bonin.

## THE PROBLEM OF LOW-SCORING PROVIDERS: WHAT WILL EMPLOYERS DO?

In worst-case scenarios, doctors and hospitals that score low on patient satisfaction surveys among employees may be dropped from the healthcare network at the insistence of the company itself. Although most companies told us they would rather work with a provider over a period of time to help the provider improve low scores, over half of the large employers we surveyed said if customer service issues continued to be a problem, the providers would be dropped.

"We tend not to be a company that quickly fires our vendors, whether that's in purchasing underwear or purchasing healthcare. We like to work with our vendors, sit down, tell them how we feel, what the problems are, and give them an opportunity to respond. But I think if it [poor scores] went on for a period of time that was unacceptable, then we'd probably fire them," McLeod of J. C. Penney's says.

Although it has not happened yet, Johnson Wax told us that providers who consistently score low in patient satisfaction would not have their contracts renewed.

Giving low-scoring providers the opportunity to improve is important to other companies too. "I can't envision us just saying, 'Gee, here are the criteria and if you don't make it this year, even though you've been with us 15 years, you're out in the cold.' That's not traditionally how we do things," says Robert Wittcoff, director of employee benefits at McDonald's Corporation. "When we develop a partnership, not necessarily only within healthcare, if something goes wrong with that, before we drop vendors we want to help them improve. If the improvement doesn't come, then we'll drop them."

Robert Bonin of First Chicago stresses that dropping a provider, for whatever reason, is not a decision to be entered into lightly, and certainly not without the cooperation of the managed care company itself.

We've taken a role in individual cases where a number of problems have come to our attention. We have done it in the HMO world and have caused people to be decredentialed. The one case I'm thinking of, the HMO wanted to do it anyway. It was a total joining of minds here. We don't know what the doctor was practicing, but it wasn't medicine. Even though he was a big provider for us, he was becoming too expensive. Patients loved him because basically he'd say, "Stay home and complete bed rest for a month or so." Normally we would not get involved at the physician level; we would if it were an exceptional case.

In other instances, employers don't yet have the right or the responsibility to hire or fire a healthcare provider in the system, although that doesn't preclude the company from staying actively involved in the relationship between employee/patient and healthcare provider. At GE, the health plan administrators are required by contract to deal with this issue. "But we expect them to take swift and immediate action." says Bill Ruoff. "From a liability standpoint, we can't add or delete providers." However, he does add that, "If it's a serious complaint, we'll be on the phone with the administrator wanting to know what's happening and explaining that we want an answer on this pretty darn fast. We do give it a sense of immediacy and urgency, but do we control the ultimate decision? No."

## THE OTHER SIDE OF THE COIN: COMPANIES DISINTERESTED IN EMPLOYEES' SATISFACTION WITH HEALTHCARE

Although our research shows a clear trend toward greater employer involvement with healthcare customer satisfaction, not every company we interviewed sees the urgent need to get involved. Hallmark Cards, headquartered in Kansas City, Missouri, doesn't survey its employees about healthcare. "We don't do it now and don't plan to do it in the future. Our medical plan means employees have total choice of providers," says Connie Zimmer, insurance benefits manager. Hallmark employees don't report back to the company with their good or their bad healthcare experiences, and if employees become unhappy with the care they receive they simply switch providers themselves.

Another company that doesn't track employee satisfaction with healthcare is Borden, Inc., headquartered in New York City. Borden doesn't survey its employees on healthcare, and has no plans to start doing it in the future, according to Victoria Fortman, director of medical benefits. The company also has no way to track which providers are unpopular among employees. "We would expect the profit centers to let us know, and we would exclude them from future efforts," she says.

The Sara Lee Company in Chicago is another employer that doesn't track employee satisfaction with healthcare. The company may, however, begin tracking that information in the future, according to Jim Clousing, director of employee benefits. He realizes the responsibility employers have to make sure their employees are happy with the care they receive.

And what does he anticipate doing when providers score poorly? "I imagine we'll have to deal with it. I guess we'd have to find out why the remarks are low," he says. For now, a third party deals with it; for example, Aetna Insurance investigates complaints against their providers. "Our employees haven't made many complaints," Clousing says. "In the HMOs and PPOs, they have the choice to go to another doctor."

## EMPLOYER INVOLVEMENT IN HEALTHCARE: FUTURE TRENDS

According to Melissa Kennedy, quality issues will become increasingly important as employers delve deeper into the area of employee satisfaction. "Satisfaction is very important to the industry, it's very important to the hospital administrators, it's very important to the employers and the health plans, but they're also becoming more and more interested in the outcomes of these people, not just satisfaction," she says.

From the employers' perspective, it's more than cost that drives their choice of health plans, according to the study's participants. The quality of care offered was ranked highest in terms of priority by employers, followed by access to physicians and cost, a 1995 study found. The study, initiated by the Chicago Business Group on Health, polled 7,000 workers who receive employer-sponsored health insurance through some sort of managed healthcare plan.

Because how much an employee pays for health insurance is largely controlled by employers, not health plans, employers could use results of the study to set pricing strategies, Mindy Kairey, a consultant with Hewitt Associates, told the *Chicago Tribune*.[5] In other words, employers won't simply be asking, "Did you like your hospital and doctor, did you have to wait too long," etc., but questions like, "Are you as active socially now as before your surgery? Can you engage in your social life as much as you used to?" Employers are realizing that patient satisfaction goes beyond what happens in the clinic, physician's office, or hospital.

"This is something that's very important on the part of health plans and employers," says Melissa Kennedy. "They're saying, OK, I know my patients are satisfied and that's great, but is what you're doing to them really helping their quality of life? You replaced their hip, they're satisfied with the hip replacement, but can they walk up and down the steps easier now? And there are tools that allow people to make that assessment," she adds. According to Kennedy, as employers become more involved in employee healthcare, they will eventually do away with the middleman of the

---

5. *Chicago Tribune,* July 5, 1995.

managed care company altogether. For now, employers are most concerned with which plans employees like best. That will change as the employers begin to survey more specific providers. "The employers are not necessarily yet responsible for that [questions about specific doctors]. They just want to find out what health plans are making their employees more satisfied. I don't know that employers are going to be interested in specifically what hospital or doctor until employers have direct relationships with providers, which will happen sooner rather than later, and in effect eliminate the whole health plan/insurance company side of the coin," Kennedy says.

This shift will be the result of integrated health systems, Kennedy says, a concept that has already taken hold at several major corporations. "We've already got very large employers—for example, GTE—who own their own clinics and things, who don't go through insurance companies at all, and they're saving a whole lot of money doing it," she says.

Employers have made quality their next target to improve in healthcare. The momentum has begun to build over the past year and if healthcare costs per employee continue to be as low as they were in 1994 and 1995, employers will focus even more on quality issues. Customer service and patient satisfaction with their providers, based on feedback from their employees, have become their new focus.

# CHAPTER

# Managed Care's Monetary Measures

**N**o aspect of the healthcare revolution has affected more lives, more dramatically, than the introduction of the managed care approach to medical treatment. Since 1985, the number of people enrolled in health maintenance organizations (HMOs) and preferred provider organizations (PPOs) has more than tripled. About 33 percent of the population is covered by an HMO or PPO according to industry research.[1]

A managed care "takeover" of healthcare in the United States will occur between the years 1996 and 2000. Already, about 100 million Americans are enrolled in an HMO or PPO. By the beginning of 1995, every state except Alaska and Wyoming had medical offices of at least one HMO. That marks a dramatic transformation to managed care. For instance, two out of three insured Americans who work in

---

1. SMG Marketing Group, *SMG Market Letter,* August 1993, p. 4; *Estimates for Year 2000* by The Health Forecasting Group.

larger organizations now are enrolled in HMOs and managed care plans, according to a study by KPMG Peat Marwick of companies with more than 200 employees. For-profit HMOs grew so rapidly in 1993 and 1994 that they now enroll more members than do nonprofit plans; and three-fourths of all physicians have contracts with HMOs and managed care plans, and 89 percent of physicians employed in group practices are working under managed care agreements.[2]

Government health programs will be rapidly converted into HMOs within the next five years. Medicare and Medicaid will be market targets for HMO enrollment. An estimated 7 percent—or 2.2 million—of the approximately 33 million people eligible for Medicare will have signed up with HMOs by the end of 1995.[3] As employers push employees into more tightly managed programs and offer increasingly limited choices for healthcare, the issue of ensuring patient satisfaction has become tantamount to good business. Employers, in exchange for providing such limited choices, realize they must be able to offer documented proof to their workers that the benefit plans they are offering to them will make the employees and their families happy. That proof comes in the form of customer satisfaction survey results, designed to illustrate what is/is not working among healthcare providers. Not so long ago, patients followed their physicians to hospitals. But today, pressure to change hospitals is coming from employees enrolled in particular health plans.

More frequently health plans are finding that employers listen to their employees as managers choose providers. Managed care organizations are paying increased attention

2. Eric Eckholm, "While Congress Remains Silent, Healthcare Transforms Itself," *The New York Times,* December 18, 1994, pp. A1, 22.
3. SMG Marketing Group, *SMG Market Letter,* August 1993, p. 4; *Estimates for Year 2000* by The Health Forecasting Group.

to subscribers' satisfaction with the providers they've chosen. If subscribers aren't happy, they'll likely jump ship to another plan, says Stephen Pew, Ph.D., senior director of improvement information at VHA Inc., Irving, Texas.[4]

During our 1995 research, we spoke with numerous large and midsized managed care organizations that represent more than 25 million employees to determine their approach to tracking and evaluating customer service by their plan providers. The managed care companies themselves are feeling the heat from two sides: the employers, who are demanding good customer service for their employees; and from the patients themselves, who are bonded together in greater numbers, to ensure that their voices are heard. Their message is: *We demand better customer service from our healthcare providers.* One patient told us, "We are getting sick and tired of being ill treated!"

## COMPETITION'S FOCUS ON CUSTOMER SERVICE

The directors of managed care companies have seen this trend developing and are realizing how important customer service is, and will continue to be. "That's going to be one of the number one things—trying to maintain your patient base," acknowledges Nan Wallis, executive director of American Lifecare in New Orleans, a PPO with an enrollment of 340,000. "With as many health plans as there are out there, everyone's going to have to improve on customer satisfaction, service, and everything else."

The principle reason for this new focus, quite simply, is price. "I think the price of healthcare, proportionately, will continue to fall. In other words, as everyone is tightening their belt and delivery of medical care becomes locked into cap rates, and premium prices don't continue to rise

---

4. *Hospitals & Health Network,* December 5, 1994, p. 68.

the way they were, I think you're going to see people fighting to stay in line, pricing-wise, to stay competitive. The differentiating factor is going to be customer and client service," says Wallis.

Paul Gardetto agrees. "The way we've decided to differentiate ourselves within this market is through service, because somebody else is setting the prices. So we take this stuff very seriously," says Gardetto, service assurance manager at Humana Wisconsin Health Organization in Milwaukee, Wisconsin, an HMO with 100,000 subscribers. "Customer-satisfaction scores will be a very important piece of the decision making process," says David Epstein, MD, Prudential's vice president of medical services for its southern group in Atlanta.

Dr. Epstein says customer satisfaction will become even more important in managed-care selection when hospitals competing for contracts standardize their measuring tools. Currently, HMOs find it difficult to compare hospital scores because different survey techniques are used, he says.[5]

Everyone in the managed care arena seems to agree that change is in the air. But not everyone in the medical community is so quick to embrace this brave new world. "It's very difficult because if there is a profession that's couched in tradition and won't budge, it's medicine," says Robert Herek, director of customer service for Cigna Healthcare of Arizona, an HMO with half a million members, located in Phoenix. "Really, it's embarrassing sometimes how we are set in our ways. When we look at ourselves we don't think so, but when others look at us, it's big-time."

The healthcare revolution of the past decade has affected each component of the healthcare equation: consumer, provider, and payer. One major result of this change has been the increased interaction of the employer with the health plan itself, which may be a factor of increased customer awareness, according to Tom Beggs, senior research

---

5. *Modern Healthcare,* July 18, 1994, p. 30.

associate for IHC-Inter-Mountain Health Care, an HMO/ PPO of half a million members in the Salt Lake City area.

> I think that with the competitiveness of the industry, consumers are awakening to the fact that they need to be more involved in the consumption of this product. Average Americans know more about their toaster than they do about their healthcare plan. And that's coming to the front, and the big companies are saying, "Gee, we can't afford to continue to keep paying $X$ number of dollars in premiums a year. What can we all do together to help contain the costs?" Part of that is the insured waking up and saying, "Well, I really don't need to see a specialist for this. I'm going to go to my GP first and see if this ear infection is anything other than swimmer's ear." Rather than running off to an ENT at three or four or five hundred dollars a pop; or worse yet, going to the emergency room on the weekend to do it because you don't want to wait until Monday morning.

This increased consumer awareness goes hand in hand with increased pressure from the employer, who is asking for information about specific providers within the health plan network. Says Beggs:

> Client companies are saying to us, "What information do you have about this plan, that plan, and the providers in those plans?" We are saying internally, "Hmm, I wonder, why does one physician have a full service, the other doesn't?" One sees $X$ number of patients a day, the other sees $2X$ patients a day, and so forth. So we're just sort of digging around, looking at that information. It's information that we need in order to be more efficient in management.

## HOW MANAGED CARE COMPANIES MEASURE PATIENT SATISFACTION

A full 100 percent of the managed care companies we interviewed in the summer of 1995 either survey their members or plan to do so in the future. The methods they use to measure patient satisfaction vary. For instance, 76 percent of those interviewed use mail-in surveys, 65 percent do phone surveys, 6 percent use a file of complaints, and 6 percent use focus groups.

Many managed care companies realize that the issue of customer satisfaction within a health plan can be broken down into two components: clinical quality and service quality. Says Gardetto of Humana:

> To satisfy the member, which is the customer, both the provider customer and the member customer, there are really two ways that they measure quality. One is, "Is the doctor nice? Does the receptionist treat me well? Did I get seen in a reasonable amount of time, and was the care appropriate?" That kind of thing. But it's also, "Do my claims get paid on time?" "Do I get put on hold when I call Humana?" So it's, "How am I treated as a customer?" So we split it into service quality issues and clinical quality issues.

Many managed care companies make this distinction in tracking and analyzing their survey results. Traditionally, surveys focused more on the service quality side of satisfaction, but more managed care companies today realize that the two issues go hand-in-hand: Good service quality impacts good clinical quality, and vice versa.

Many of the managed care companies we interviewed have only recently begun to track patient satisfaction information down to the level of satisfaction with individual providers. But to many people in the industry, it makes sense for managed care companies to elicit the most specific information possible when the companies survey their members about satisfaction. "Think about the stakeholders and their different perceptions," offers Melissa Kennedy, vice president of HealthCare Research Systems at Ohio State University. "The health plans want to know who the providers of care are that make people happy, because they want those providers on their panel, and they want providers who don't make patients satisfied off their panel, so I think insurance companies are asking more and more those types of questions," Kennedy says.

Because the customer service revolution in healthcare is just warming up, it does mean that long-term statistics about patient satisfaction trends are nonexistent. For many managed care companies, this translates into some uncertainty about which programs are the most, or least, successful. "You don't really know until you can look back on 5 or 10 years and say, 'Yeah, that helped here,' or, 'We need to do more of this there,' or whatever it happens to be," says Tom Beggs. "But you have to try. You can't just sit back and say, 'Gee, I hope we're doing the right thing.'"

Some industry experts feel the managed care industry manipulates the data from enrollees to make themselves look better and misses the valuable points altogether. Roberta Clarke, an associate professor of healthcare management at Boston university, says managed-care organizations are losing enrollees at a rate of about 20 percent a year, a rate she says would be "truly horrendous" in other industries. Moreover, she states HMOs, PPOs, and point-of-service plans aren't tracking data that could help stop the dramatic customer loss.

Clarke called about 25 managed care organizations for an ongoing study, but most lacked precise disenrollment figures, including voluntary versus involuntary disenrollment.

She also accuses managed care organizations of "playing footsie" with customer-satisfaction data. "In every ad I've ever seen for a managed-care organization, the customer-satisfaction rate is always in the high 90s", she says. "It makes you wonder: Where are all those managed care organizations that people are complaining about?" She urges managed care organizations to empower their marketers to study and track disenrollment and customer satisfaction and to focus on access, coverage and customer service rather than promotion.[6]

## MANAGED CARE'S USE OF PATIENT FEEDBACK TO IMPROVE CUSTOMER SERVICE

The results of patient satisfaction surveys are often used to counsel hospitals and individual physicians, and a growing percentage of the managed care companies we spoke to use satisfaction scores as part of a physician's contract negotiation or as part of a bonus package. For example, in FHP of Colorado, top-performing providers receive an incentive of 40 cents per member per month, according to Lori Muneta, research analyst. In 50 percent of the companies interviewed, a provider may be dropped from the network for continued poor scores.

In other cases, managed care companies use their survey results as the impetus to help devise new and better programs for customer service. For example, Humana has recently begun a new initiative for hiring customer service representatives called Care Coordinators. In this new program, every person who answers the telephone at Humana will be a care coordinator, and every one of them will be a college graduate who will be considered part of the management team. "In the past, usually the person answering the phone was the lowest-paid person on the totem pole," explains Paul Gardetto. "That just doesn't make sense. Now they'll be some of the highest-paid people. Because that's how we interface with our customer. It's going to be expensive, but hopefully it will pay off."

In other cases, managed care companies use their survey results to solve problems that they might never have known about if it hadn't been brought to their attention through a survey. For example, the Provider Relations

6. *Modern Healthcare,* July 17, 1995.

Department at Health Service Network in Cincinnati, Ohio, recently came across a survey filled out by a young man whose wife had died during childbirth. "When he filled out the survey, he indicated that he had no clue what had happened medically," explains Barbara Kauffman, director of marketing for the 1.5 million-member PPO. "Now, we're not sure if the doctors and the staff failed to share that information with him or if he was too distraught to understand it. He never received his wife's autopsy report. Our advocate worked with him to direct him back to the physician to get some of those answers, and to work with the physicians to facilitate that response. The issue was ultimately resolved," she says.

Some managed care organizations will use their data to impact provider compensation and or bonus programs. A study of 200 HMO medical directors was conducted in 1995, by National Research Corp., a Lincoln, Nebraska-based market research firm. Of the HMOs collecting physician data, 60 percent are using the scores as part of a physician compensation/bonus program. Extrapolated over the entire sample of HMOs, 36 percent are assessing patient satisfaction with individual physicians and using the findings to help determine physician pay.

The larger the HMO, the more likely the data will be used as part of a compensation/bonus program. Some 70 percent of HMOs with 50,000 or more enrollees use the information for compensation programs. At HMOs with fewer than 50,000 enrollees, it drops to 50 percent.

## THE MANAGED CARE PERSPECTIVE: WHAT DO PATIENTS WANT?

As our research demonstrated in Chapter 1, when it comes to good patient relations and customer service, the simplest issues are by far the most important. A caring, compassionate hospital staff and physician will always rank highly in patient satisfaction surveys. This simple truth is realized by the people at the Cigna Healthcare headquarters in Bloomfield, Connecticut. "The satisfaction levels are highest with those providers who take the time to treat patients like individuals, not treat them like just one more file," says Sali Bonazelli, director of Cigna Healthcare Marketing.

That personal touch is important to patients, managed care companies realize. But along with that comes a growing realization that the customer comes first; that the doctor works for the patient, and not vice versa. Says Herek of Cigna in Phoenix:

> I think a lot of us give lip service to the statement, "We must know the needs of our customers, and provide service either at those expectation levels or greater than that." But look at something as basic as operating hours. If you go back to when those hours were originally set as being from eight to five, those hours were set for the convenience of the physician, way back when. And now we, the customer, believe that those are the hours we set, and we believe that we are asking for favors if we say, "Couldn't you keep your clinics open later than five o'clock?"

To Herek, those old standards no longer make sense in today's two-career, nontraditional family world. "When you look at the economy and the two bread-winner families, with both spouses working to put weenies and beans on the table, we realize we better start paying attention to customer service. And if we're going to ask the questions, we better be prepared for the answers," he says.

Survey results have shown that a big concern for members in an HMO or PPO is the fear of not having the opportunity to choose your own doctor. But that isn't as much of a problem as many people may think, according to Tom Beggs of IHC in Salt Lake City.

> There are a lot of misperceptions out there. There's a general perception, even in our company, that people are less satisfied with the more tightly managed program

with an HMO. That in fact is opposite. Both in national surveys and in the surveys we do here, we find out that people are much more satisfied who are on HMO plans than people who are on PPOs or indemnity plans. After you drag them into the HMO kicking and screaming, complaining that there's only 600 physicians to choose from on the panel, they get in there and 99 percent end up with a doctor that they like. Some of course just never will, and they'll keep hopping around from doctor to doctor. But they get in there, they get to know that person, and they get to like him or her. As long as we don't take off the wrong leg, like they did in Florida, we've got smooth sailing. They [members] know that whenever they go, it's going to be a ten-dollar copay or a five-dollar copay, or in some cases, no copay, and that's that. And these plans all have out-of-pocket caps, usually $1,000 per person, $2,000 per family. So you know that in a worst-case scenario, you're going to have to come up with $2,000 over the course of a year. We rarely ever have to deal with that. And if your doctor isn't there, there are emergency considerations, urgent care considerations. It's one-stop shopping. And it works.

## THE PROBLEM OF LOW-SCORING PROVIDERS: WHAT WILL MANAGED CARE COMPANIES DO?

Although many managed care companies are willing to take drastic action with low-scoring providers—even terminating them when necessary—most stress the educational aspect of working with providers, and giving them every possible opportunity to improve their performance before such radical actions are undertaken.

Nearly half of the managed care organizations we interviewed stated that they would drop providers who flunk the customer service standards they set. Two of the largest, Kaiser Permanente and Humana, said they would drop providers if necessary. Kaiser, which serves 6.6 million enrollees in 16 states and the District of Columbia, indicated that in some markets, a consistently low-scoring provider is dropped from the group. Humana, with 3.3 million enrollees, said the organization will try to find out what's wrong, educate the provider, but drop him or her if the need dictates.

Prudential currently is less likely to change providers, but that may change. "Right now, we wouldn't change a provider unless there were serious questions about customer service," Dr. Epstein says. "But with newly created networks or realigned networks, customer satisfaction could be an important piece of information that differentiates one hospital from another."[7]

"When we attack an issue, we don't attack the 'who,' we attack the 'what,' " says Gardetto of Humana. "Providers want to do a good job. Ninety-nine percent of them don't have an agenda other than treating their patient." However, problems do sometimes occur. "If the providers are subaverage performers, we either need to educate them or get rid of them. And we'll do any one of those actions. We do put pressure on the providers for price, and for what we expect of them. So they obviously have got something invested in this, too," Gardetto states.

At Preferred Health Care Inc., in Wichita, Kansas, low-scoring providers receive two warnings before being dropped from the network. But providers have a strong incentive not to let that happen, and once again that incentive comes down to dollars and cents. "Once they get one or two warnings, they don't want out of our network because we're the largest network in the Wichita area. They can't afford to lose our business," says Gaylee Dolloff, vice president of program services at Preferred Health Care, an HMO with an enrollment of 108,000 and a network of 900 physicians.

Beech Street of California, which tracks customer service issues like "friendliness and cheerfulness" of providers

---

7. *Modern Healthcare*, July 18, 1994, p. 30.

staff, told us that if low marks continue with a provider they will be dropped from the program. Bob Gerger, controller for the PPO, which has 8.8 million enrollees said, "Negative responses weigh a great deal. If that [negative feedback from the patient] continues, then it becomes an issue with us as to whether we want to keep that provider in the network." The Prudential said they will terminate providers who do not improve, whereas FHP of Colorado will deny bonus fees to low scorers.

Although tracking patient satisfaction is something most managed care organizations have been doing for years, the major difference now is they are going to do something more drastic with the data. More and more, as pressure mounts from the employers, they will use the customer service information to choose providers, in contract negotiations, and to help determine provider bonuses. Customer service performance by providers will undoubtedly be tied to monetary rewards more and more as the patient satisfaction revolution gains momentum.

# CHAPTER 4

# Competing Means Satisfying Patients

**"A** poorly designed patient satisfaction survey can be worse than not measuring patient satisfaction at all, it can actually be harmful to a provider, particularly if it gives them false-positive results. They'll swear they're doing well until the day they are forced to close their doors due to unresolved patient satisfaction issues." Irwin Press, PhD and co-founder of Press-Ganey, Inc., doesn't mince words, and he believes that developing a patient satisfaction survey is both art and science.

"Slowly the industry is realizing it has to compete, and successfully competing in healthcare means satisfying patients," says Dr. Press. His firm helped Mercy Hospital Medical Center in Des Moines, Iowa, identify problems in its emergency department (ED) and has worked actively in the healthcare industry measuring patient satisfaction since 1985. Press-Ganey, Inc., currently serves more than 500 clients. "If you satisfy patients, they're less likely to sue you, they're more likely to come back, and they're more likely to recommend you to others." Press believes that it's essential that hospitals find out where they can improve, and then take action. "Survey data is meaningless unless you use it and when you use it, you can make a difference."

Management at Mercy Hospital Medical Center understood that people don't usually go to hospital emergency rooms by choice; what they didn't understand was that extended wait times made patients feel as though they were "being ignored." Most of us know the feeling. It's frustrating, but getting angry just doesn't seem like the appropriate response. And for some reason, you start to notice negative details you might otherwise overlook.

That was exactly what was happening at Mercy. In January 1992, managers reviewing patient survey data noted that long waits and limited medical staff scrambling to care for the sickest patients were taking their toll on Mercy's patient satisfaction ratings. There was no significant increase in complaints, just increasingly frustrated patients. The patterns were clear, and after reviewing alternatives, hospital managers concluded it was time to make a change. As a result, the hospital opened a minor care unit to treat patients with less serious conditions and regrouped nurses into teams to make them accountable for certain patients. Those actions raised scores on subsequent surveys and boosted staff morale. "Obviously, satisfaction and quality are in the eyes of the user," says Pat Spurlock, administrative director of the emergency department. "Until you listen to your patients, you're not going to know whether you're meeting their needs."

Patient satisfaction surveys like the one for Mercy summarized in Table 4.1 not only help target improvements in services but can become a part of continuous quality improvement efforts. But now, increasing managed care penetration is changing old assumptions about patient choice of hospitals and underscoring the importance of the patient satisfaction survey as an important tool.[1]

---

1. "Are Patients Happy? Managed Care Plans Want to Know," *Hospitals & Health Networks,* December 5, 1994, p. 68.

**TABLE  4.1**

Selected Results from Mercy Hospital Medical Center's Patient
Satisfaction Surveys

|  | Satisfaction Rates | |
| --- | --- | --- |
| **Factor Surveyed** | **January 1992** (%) | **July 1994** (%) |
| 1. Courtesy of the hospital's nurses | 79 | 88 |
| 2. Technical skill of the nurses | 84 | 86 |

Source: "Are Patients Happy? Managed Care Plans Want to Know," *Hospitals & Health Networks,*
December 5, 1994, p. 68.

## MANAGED CARE FIRMS LISTEN TO PATIENTS

"Not so long ago, patients followed their physicians to
hospitals. But today, pressure to change hospitals is coming
from employees enrolled in particular health plans. Managed care organizations are paying increased attention to
subscribers' satisfaction with the providers they've chosen.
If subscribers aren't happy, they'll likely jump ship to
another plan," says Stephen Pew, PhD, senior director of
improvement information at VHA Inc., in Irving, Texas.

According to Melissa Kennedy at HealthCare Research
Systems, a patient satisfaction survey company affiliated
with Ohio State University, "Employers and health plans
are dying for this data because they're using it at the
negotiation table."

Patient satisfaction surveys not only help target improvements in services but can become a part of continuous
quality improvement efforts. The Joint Commission on
Accreditation of Healthcare Organizations (JCAHO) has
incorporated requirements to measure patient satisfaction
and "meet its expectations" within their 1995 standards. As
a result, there is a lot of activity in the patient satisfaction
survey business. Some hospital patient surveys are done in-
house; others are conducted by outside firms. The VHA,

with its 1,000 affiliates, is developing a patient satisfaction survey for its hospitals. The alliance is exploring a variety of survey methods: telephone calls, mailback forms, and computerized systems. The Agency for Health Care Policy and Research recently hired a research institute to develop a model instrument for a consumer survey. The goal was to develop a consensus on which kinds of consumer satisfaction and consumer perception information should be collected and surveyed. The research involves exploring questions that look at hospitals and how hospitals choices interact with a choice of health plans.

We looked closely at three firms, all using different formats, client bases, and research approaches to get a better idea of a provider's alternatives:

> Press-Ganey, considered one of the pioneers in the industry, with more than 500 participating clients, recommends that surveys be mailed to patients within a few days of discharge. Their base survey contains 49 questions, but hospitals can customize the survey to meet their specific needs. The surveys are designed for different specialties, such as day surgery, emergency departments, ambulatory care, and home care.

> HealthCare Research Systems, a group of professionals affiliated with Ohio State University, believes the firm has two sets of clients: employers and providers. Although the firm conducts conventional surveys, similar in format to those employed by Press-Ganey, it also performs "quick assessments" for employers (like Xerox, Digital, GTE, and GE) and health plans (recently the firm completed a survey of more than 30,000 patients for Kaiser-Permanente). They use mailback, telephone, and computer-based survey formats.

> The Picker Institute, a nonprofit affiliate of the Beth Israel Corporation, adopted a mission to promote

healthcare quality assessment and improvement strategies that address patients' needs and concerns as defined by patients. The institute has surveyed more than 45,000 patients and their families, and has worked with more than 200 healthcare institutions and community healthcare coalitions. In addition to global ratings using a four or five point scale, Picker/Commonwealth surveys also ask patients to report whether specific events took place. The institute staff believe these simple reporting variations provide managers with the ability to identify problems without having to analyze time variations in ratings.

Finally, we reviewed dozens of surveys designed internally by healthcare institutions. Although formats were sometimes similar, each seemed to have unique characteristics that reflected the particular focus of the institution involved. Their uniqueness may have been both their greatest strength and most significant weakness. Although they provided specific data—excellent for providing a time series comparison—it was not possible to compare the data to other institutions of similar size, patient base, or regional dispersion.

## Survey Format

Clearly, all surveys prepared by the three companies we reviewed recognized the need to specialize survey questions based on the services used:

- *Inpatient surveys* designed for the areas of medicine, surgery, childbirth, and pediatrics.
- *Ambulatory / outpatient surveys* designed for all aspects of ambulatory care.
- *Emergency services surveys* that identify the unique aspects of urgent care.

- *Homecare surveys* detailing issues like care instruction and coordination of services.

Press-Ganey has developed a coordinated and complete set of instruments, whereas the Picker Institute is still in the development stage for all but the inpatient and ambulatory survey products.

HealthCare Research Associates will design an instrument based on the specific needs of the client, and many times the client is not the hospital. When the consultants work with employers, they start by asking questions about the overall benefits package, then move to the specifics of their patient care. Beyond specifics of delivery of care, consultants also focus on these three areas:

- Do employees have access to the doctors they want?
- Can they get an appointment at their PCP (primary care provider) when needed?
- Do they feel that the dollars paid for coverage is appropriate?

All these things create the employee's or member's perception of satisfaction with the health plan *before* they even see a doctor!

## All Questions Are *Not* the Same

Stephen Strasser, PhD and executive director of HealthCare Research Systems, feels it is essential that survey questions be absolutely balanced. Here is a sample question from an HCRS survey:

*Parking was not a problem.*   a. *Strongly Disagree*
b. *Disagree*
c. *Neither Agree*
   *nor Disagree*
d. *Agree*
e. *Strongly Agree*

Strasser points out that each response has a balanced "contraresponse"— "Strongly disagree" is the exact opposite of "strongly agree." "Disagree" is the opposite of "agree." "Neither agree nor disagree" is a neutral response.

Strasser adds, "We would not use a term like 'excellent,' because it can produce a false positive response. There is not an obvious 'contraresponse' to 'excellent' and as a result, questions are often structured with more positive responses than potentially negative responses." For example, the following question was taken from a survey developed in a 400-bed facility in Pontiac, Michigan:

*The compassion shown by the staff was*      *a. Excellent*
                                             *b. Very Good*
                                             *c. Good*
                                             *d. Fair*
                                             *e. Poor*

Of the five available responses, four are generally favorable. Strasser's perspective is that a question like this is much more likely to produce a positive patient response than a balanced response. He points out that although that may be good for an administrator's ego, it does little to identify real patient satisfaction issues within the organization.

## Survey Methods: Timing Is Everything

After exploring a variety of survey methods, the 1,000-member VHA hospital alliance believes that the optimal moment to survey patients is 14 to 30 days after discharge. The VHA asserts that it is still recent enough for the patient to recall most aspects of his/her experience but long enough to provide perspective to the incident requiring healthcare services. Press-Ganey recommends that its clients mail surveys one to three days after discharge. HealthCare Research Systems is less specific but has actually developed "point-of-service" computer survey systems that enable patients to comment on service levels almost as the services are provided.

Patient satisfaction survey data is collected by consulting firms through three primary methods:

- Mailback surveys.
- Telephone interviews.
- On-site surveys and computer systems.

Given the same questionnaire, former patients will go easier on the provider if their comments are taken over the phone or face to face, rather than on a mailed survey. The scores for telephone surveys not only fail to capture the extreme dissatisfaction that may be out there but may also yield a narrower spread of opinion than with a written survey that's mailed back.

The choice of data collection method can mean a deceptively rosier and less detailed picture for healthcare providers, which can complicate efforts to fix problems before they result in customer defections. Melvin Hall, PhD, author of the study that disclosed these findings, cautions providers not to be lulled into false confidence. To be effective, a survey must be able to ensure two things: that the sample is representative of the population being targeted and that the survey procedure encourages open and honest evaluations.

Those who promote the phone method say it usually yields a much higher response rate, which reduces the likelihood that the results are unrepresentative of the target population. However, phone surveys contain an "acquiescence bias" or a tendency to agree with what's being asked by a phone interviewer. "Patients are intimidated by healthcare and caregivers," according to Hall. "They are less inclined to criticize the hospital when contacted in person." Mailed responses showed a wider range of responses—more results at the lower end of the scale but also a good representation of former patients who were extremely satisfied. The diverse scores reflect a greater degree of thought that leads to more elaborative and useful feedback. In addition, "The mailback method seems more likely to garner opinions of those most critical of the care received." The value to the institution is that administrators have a better chance to hear those who have reservations about their care, giving them an opportunity to improve.

## Trending Reports, Summary Reports, and Reports on Reports

All survey companies provide for extensive and comprehensive summary reports. However, volume and value are not synonymous. The Picker Institute stresses the "actionable" nature of their reports. While most patient satisfaction instruments are designed to generate global impressions of various aspects of care, Picker/Commonwealth survey questions are designed to generate information that managers can act upon. Their questions differ from the other two survey companies in that in addition to perception ratings, they detail whether specific events took place (that is, information provided about medication side effects, follow-up visits, or delays in scheduling). This type of response reporting can sometimes make it easier for managers to identify problems without having to analyze variations in ratings.

Press-Ganey's extensive client base offers the most flexible peer groupings, providing meaningful normative comparisons. Perhaps the most useful tool in its quarterly report package is an executive summary that identifies major changes (both positive and negative) from previous periods. Clients are able to quickly focus on potential problem areas.

HealthCare Research Systems has a unique reporting/database analysis tool that enables clients to "interact" with patient responses. HCRS has the ability to correlate patient medical records with patient satisfaction responses. As a result, it is feasible to identify which floors, physicians, nursing stations, and procedures (as well as virtually unlimited analysis groupings) produce the most positive and negative results.

## ARE WE MEASURING THE RIGHT THINGS?

Clearly, providers, employers, and health plans have access to sophisticated patient satisfaction instruments that are statistically valid and useful in determining whether healthcare institutions are providing a reasonably high quality of services. However, the instruments consistently measured only the level of satisfaction associated with the current provider's procedures and services. In other words, it is generally communicated to the patient that "these are the things we do (or are supposed to do); please tell us how you think we did those things." Therefore, this approach is likely to produce the same potentially "false positives" we are attempting to avoid by carefully structuring our questions.

The next step may be to "break out of the box" and ask patients what they expected, or perhaps more importantly, what they wanted. Then, based on their response, we can ask how close we came.

Only then can providers truly determine whether they are meeting their patients' needs.

**CHAPTER**

# Angry Patients Want Dramatic Improvements

**B**ecause almost every person surveyed in our 1995 study said that customer service by their hospital and physician was "extremely important," we asked patients to define customer service in a healthcare setting. We got a passionate response, with answers ranging from the emotional to the profound:

- "They should treat you like a human being—like you matter."
- "Just listen to the patients. Listen to what they say, as well as what they don't say."
- "Have empathy for my feelings, my confusion, my fears, my pain."

But we also heard another message. Many told us loudly and clearly that they are angry. Patients said they are sick and tired of being treated like they are an intrusion in a healthcare worker's day. A pet peeve is endless wait time spent in emergency rooms, registration areas, radiology departments, and doctors' offices. And while patients wait, they are observing what they believe to be inefficiencies and inappropriate employee activities.

We interviewed and surveyed nearly 2,000 people in 17 states who had received care from 30 hospitals and hundreds of physician offices within the last year. We asked how important customer service was to them. Not surprisingly, 90 percent of those who responded said it was "extremely important" in physicians' offices. We also asked them to define customer service in their own words, as well as rate their recent experiences with all types of healthcare providers. When we asked patients to rate their most recent hospital stay, the average score was 7.4 on a 10-point scale. On its surface, this is a respectable, "average" rating, until you look a little closer. Unfortunately for hospitals and clinics, many patients don't grade customer service on a "curve."

Nearly a third of the patients gave their hospitals a "failing grade" of less than 5 on that 10-point index. Patients are not expecting perfection. When asked what the rating should have been, the same patients replied that the score should have been as high as 9.4 on a 10-point scale. Sometimes it was simply a matter of courtesy that patients found lacking in a hospital staff. "Every morning they would get me up at 5 AM to weigh me. I could always hear them coming down the hallway, even though they tried to be quiet. But to this day, I can't understand why it was necessary to wake me up at that hour, just to weigh me. I don't think I got a good night's sleep the entire time I was in the hospital."

And at other times, the lack of communication created more serious concerns: "I was asked to sign a consent form without a clear explanation of what I was authorizing. In my opinion, 'informed consent' means exactly what it says. I was not informed and did not understand the biopsy procedure that was subsequently performed. I was upset and angry."

A less frequent complaint, but one cited sufficiently to evidence concern by patients, is related to the technical competence of the staff: "I repeatedly observed inappropriate actions by one of the nurses: one person, not the entire staff. However, both my wife and I observed the same person. I asked that he not come to my room. Unfortunately, he was sent anyway."

Although clinics and physician offices fared slightly better, they still only averaged an 8.2 rating, with more than a quarter of their patients rating them at 5 or less. The clear frustration in physicians' offices is excessive wait time: "Had to wait two hours to be seen at a local clinic. When I complained, I was told they had misplaced my records and were 'working on it.'" Sometimes the wait time can be more than frustrating; at times it can impact the level of care provided to the patient: "I will never forget waiting in the OB/gyne examination room, stripped down—cold and frightened—for more than an hour. Finally, I simply got dressed and left. I never even saw a physician."

## MANY PATIENTS WILL NOT RETURN TO A HOSPITAL

Hospital patients from across the country indicated that almost 4 out of 10 are unhappy with the billing and collection process. The survey revealed that 6 percent of the patients were so disappointed with billing and collection procedures that they would not return to the same hospital for future care or recommend it to others. This means hospitals are losing more than 6 percent of future revenue for reasons that could be avoided.

From simply understanding hospital charges displayed on the bill to explanation of insurance, more than 35 percent of the patients were dissatisfied. Of these, 10 percent were extremely dissatisfied. Low patient satisfaction levels heavily contribute to a hospital's archnemesis: delayed cash flow and patient complaints.

So, why are so many patients so disenchanted about billing and collection? A common excuse is that healthcare billing is too complex and certainly not user-friendly. Regarding requests for further information about billing questions or problems, about 30 percent of the respondents said they were not happy with the assistance they had received. Patients were not satisfied with the ability of the billing representatives to understand their questions and provide answers or solutions; many former patients complained about the speed with which an answer/solution was given. The unfriendliness of the representative was also a cause for discontent. In analyzing patient responses, poor perception of the billing and collection process was closely related to the lack of up-front information about the reimbursement process. More than one-third of all patients received no information about insurance billing during the registration process, at time of discharge, or during insurance billing.

## YOUNGER PATIENTS HAVE THE HIGHEST EXPECTATIONS AND LOWEST PERCEPTION OF SERVICE

As we tried to understand the patient's perspective, we observed another interesting phenomenon. As Table 5.1 shows, older patients (over 55) are less likely to be critical of their healthcare provider than middle-aged patients (36 to 55). Not only did older patients rate hospitals and physicians higher overall, they were significantly less likely to score the provider five or less.

Younger patients (those under 35) have the highest expectations and lowest perception of healthcare delivery. This data, summarized in Table 5.2, suggests that employers and managed care providers have good reason to be concerned about future customer service ratings.

**TABLE 5.1**

Rating of Customer Service by Age Group

|  | Older Patients | Middle-Aged Patients |
|---|---|---|
| Rating of last hospital experience* | 7.9 | 6.8 |
| Ratings at less than 50% | 27% | 32% |

*Rating scale 1 = low, 10 = high.

**TABLE 5.2**

Rating of Customer Service by the Under-35 Age Group

|  | Younger Patients (Under 35) |
|---|---|
| Rating of last hospital experience: | 6.7 |
| Where it should have been: | 9.6 |
| Rating of last clinic experience: | 7.7 |
| Where it should have been: | 9.4 |

Leading the "customer service revolution in healthcare" are younger and middle-aged patients—those currently in the work force, ultimately paying the bills. They are dissatisfied with current service levels and have their own perception of what is "appropriate" care.

A February 1995 study by *Consumer Reports* pointed to one other dimension of patient satisfaction. That organization's database related the condition being treated to the patient's happiness with care, service, and personnel. Table 5.3 shows the percentage of patients who were dissatisfied with their healthcare provider. Interestingly, the ailments topping the list are not necessarily the most serious, but instead those for which a clear treatment program is often lacking. When questioned, respondents stated

**TABLE 5.3**

Percentage of Patients Dissatisfied with Provider—by Ailments

| Condition Treated | Patient Dissatisfaction (%) |
|---|---|
| Chronic Headache | 23 |
| Lower Back Pain | 20 |
| Broken Bones, Torn Ligaments | 18 |
| Anxiety, Depression | 17 |
| Arthritis | 15 |
| Intestinal or Stomach Problems | 15 |
| Pregnancy | 13 |
| Allergy | 12 |
| Respiratory Problems | 11 |
| Cancer | 11 |
| Prostate Problems (not cancer) | 10 |
| Heart Condition | 10 |
| Diabetes | 8 |
| High Blood Pressure | 8 |
| Cataracts or Glaucoma | 8 |
| High Cholesterol | 7 |

*Source: "How Is Your Doctor Treating You?" Copyright 1995 by Consumers Union of U.S., Inc., Yonkers, NY 10703-1057. Reprinted by permission from *Consumer Reports*, February 1995, p. 82.

they often felt "left out" of the treatment program. They didn't understand what the physician and/or caregiver was trying to accomplish, and didn't know how to become more involved in their own care.

A clear message of the analysis seems to be the value of ongoing communication between the patient and the caregiver. The importance of communication was confirmed by our own survey results.

## SURVEY RESULTS FOR ASPECTS OF CUSTOMER SERVICE

We asked patients to describe "customer service" within a hospital in their own words. We then attempted to classify their responses into major categories shown in Table 5.4.

**TABLE 5.4**

Patient Definition of Customer Service by Hospitals

| What Patients Want | National Average | Older Patients (over 55) | Middle-Aged Patients (36 to 55) | Younger Patients (under 35) |
|---|---|---|---|---|
| Compassion | 40.5% | 39.5% | 38.7% | 40.0% |
| Communication | 40.5 | 31.6 | 58.1 | 26.7 |
| Shorter Wait Time | 39.3 | 50.0 | 22.6 | 46.7 |
| Friendliness | 36.9 | 36.9 | 29.0 | 53.3 |
| Professionalism | 25.0 | 15.8 | 22.6 | 46.7 |
| Efficiency | 15.5 | 21.1 | 9.7 | 13.3 |
| Accuracy | 7.1 | 10.5 | 3.2 | 6.7 |
| Privacy | 4.8 | 7.9 | 3.2 | 3.1 |

Patients were able to identify more than one area, so totals exceed 100%.

Interestingly, core competencies like efficiency, accuracy, and privacy appear to be expected, and they did not often represent a significant aspect of a patient's customer service perception.

## Communication

At or near the top of the list for nearly all age groups were communication and compassion. For some, they were characterized by simple consideration for another person's time: "The hospital took the time to call us and say they were running a little behind, and suggested we come later, so we wouldn't have to wait." For some, the feeling is just as strong, but not nearly as positive: "My wife was treated like a 'customer' instead of a 'patient'—and that's exactly the problem. Hospitals seem to be run by people with business degrees, with an eye on making a profit first instead of combining patient care with cost." And many others acknowledged a special person who was able to communicate a high level of compassion or professionalism: "I had wonderful service, especially from a wonderful, kind RN on the second shift." "Dr. Green performed knee surgery on me. He was so professional but yet made me feel so comfortable. He had excellent bedside manner, second to none." "Had good, qualified nurses in intensive care area, continually watched my progress and made me feel they were really concerned about me."

As indicated in the first portion of the chapter, it is clear that patients from different age groups have different ideas of the most important aspects of customer service. Middle-aged patients mentioned the importance of communication in almost 60 percent of their responses (Table 5.5), significantly higher than any other age group.

A lapse in communication, regardless of how subtle or unintended, can have a disturbing impact on patient care and is likely to remain in the patient's memory for a long time: "There was a miscommunication between me and the doctor regarding the medication used after delivery. I ended up in tremendous pain for three to four hours. He thought he was saving me money; he may have saved money, but I paid for it differently."

One of our respondents pointed out that good communication doesn't always mean telling the patient everything: "I really didn't want to know all the details. I told the doctor I'd ask if I wanted to know; otherwise, he should just tell me what he wanted me to do. We're all different you know. He respected my wishes, and I appreciated that."

## Wait Times

We weren't surprised to see that elderly patients were concerned about excessive wait time (Table 5.6): "I was told to come in at 1 PM, to find out that 12 other patients had been told to arrive at the same time."

**TABLE 5.5**

Percentage of Patients Mentioning Importance of Communication

|               | Average | Older | Middle | Younger |
|---------------|---------|-------|--------|---------|
| Communication | 40.5%   | 31.6% | 58.1%  | 26.7%   |

**TABLE 5.6**

Percentage of Patients Mentioning Importance of Wait Time

|           | Average | Older | Middle | Younger |
|-----------|---------|-------|--------|---------|
| Wait Time | 39.3%   | 50.0% | 22.6%  | 46.7%   |

(Elderly patients also commented frequently regarding the difficulty associated with accessing a facility's services; parking, valet service, and long hallways without hand rails.)

Perhaps more interesting is how often wait time was cited by younger patients (46.7 percent) as a key aspect of customer satisfaction. "At Children's, even when left in a waiting room for a short time, we were told 'your wait will be. . . .' It was great knowing we hadn't been forgotten."

When wait time was excessive, it often resulted in an unsatisfactory rating of the entire experience: "I was left for hours in a waiting room in ER while doctors and nurses were sitting, doing nothing."

As Table 5.7 shows, wait time becomes one of the most important dimensions of customer service when patients consider their expectations at a clinic or physician's office.

**TABLE 5.7**

Patients' Definition of Customer Service by Physician

| What Patients Want | National Average | Older Patients (over 55) | Middle-Aged Patients (36 to 55) | Younger Patients (under 35) |
|---|---|---|---|---|
| Shorter Wait Time | 52.3% | 60.0% | 43.3% | 46.7% |
| Friendliness of Staff | 41.9 | 42.5 | 33.3 | 60.0 |
| Communication | 44.2 | 37.5 | 56.7 | 40.0 |
| Compassion | 38.4 | 35.0 | 43.3 | 46.7 |
| Professionalism | 19.8 | 17.5 | 16.7 | 33.4 |
| Efficiency | 10.5 | 15.0 | 6.7 | 6.7 |
| Accuracy | 7.0 | 12.5 | 3.3 | 6.7 |
| Privacy | 3.5 | 5.0 | 3.3 | 3.1 |

Patients were able to identify more than one area, so totals exceed 100%.

## Staff's Friendliness

In addition, "friendliness of staff" takes on additional importance, particularly for younger patients. One recent clinic patient summed up these feelings effectively: "People need to be treated as people, other human beings; not insurance claims. And being left for hours in waiting rooms is just unacceptable."

## What the Results Reveal

We wondered what characteristics of customer service were the most likely to cause a strong reaction, good or bad. We asked patients to relate the best and worst example of customer service, and then we looked for common elements. Table 5.8 provides some insight indicating the most common "worst" experience.

Once again, "wait time" is at the top of the list. How often does a patient's contact with a hospital or clinic begin

**T A B L E   5 . 8**

Patients' Most Common Complaints in Their Hospital Experience

| Worst Examples | National Average | Older Patients (over 55) | Middle-Aged Patients (36 to 55) | Younger Patients (under 35) |
|---|---|---|---|---|
| Excessive wait times | 40.8% | 28.6% | 52.4% | 64.7% |
| Lack of professionalism | 28.9 | 40.0 | 19.1 | 5.9 |
| Not enough communication | 26.3 | 28.6 | 33.3 | 17.7 |
| Lack of compassion | 25.0 | 20.0 | 33.3 | 23.5 |

Patients were able to identify more than one area, so totals exceed 100%.

with a long wait in registration, an examination room, or diagnostic staging area? "I was in the emergency room after having almost severed two of my fingers and waited for over an hour. Finally, I ended up going to another hospital, and they took care of me right away."

Patients are telling us that efforts to reduce healthcare costs are unacceptable if they have resulted in extensive staff and service reductions without making necessary operational adjustments or improvements in technology. Patients also expect professional, effective support operations and will not accept less: "I wasn't billed until 11 months after a brief hospital procedure. Even though I was upset, I mailed a check. But then they didn't record the payment, so I had to go in and 'fix' the situation in person. The hospital I go to now doesn't have those kinds of problems."

But what are the most likely things to cause a positive patient reaction? The answers, reported in Table 5.9, are more fundamental than you might think.

When combined, human compassion (47.1 percent) and friendliness (38.2 percent) were the key aspects of the "best"

**TABLE 5.9**

Patients' Best Experiences in a Hospital Related to Customer Service

| Best Examples | National Average | Older Patients (over 55) | Middle-Aged Patients (36 to 55) | Younger Patients (under 35) |
|---|---|---|---|---|
| A showing of compassion | 47.1% | 42.9% | 59.1% | 36.4% |
| Friendliness by staff | 38.3 | 37.1 | 36.4 | 23.4 |
| Professionalism | 26.5 | 31.4 | 27.3 | 9.1 |
| Communication | 25.0 | 11.4 | 40.9 | 16.4 |
| Shorter wait time | 23.5 | 14.3 | 27.4 | 45.5 |

Patients were able to identify more than one area, so totals exceed 100%.

customer service experiences in 95 percent of the respondents' comments. The solution almost sounds too obvious. "When I had to have an MRI, I was very frightened. The technician talked me through the procedure and kept encouraging me and talking to me so I would know someone was with me. It made all the difference in the world." "I will never forget one very special RN. She brought me a much needed box of Kleenex and gave me a hug while my husband was in a treatment room. He died recently of cancer, and that was one of my 'low days.' "

## KEY FACTORS IN HEALTHCARE CUSTOMER SATISFACTION

So what are the key factors in customer satisfaction? We think patients have made their opinion clear. We broke their responses down into three categories:

- **Compassionate, friendly, and committed staff with excellent communication skills.**

    The most unique characteristic of any healthcare institution is its team of professionals—physicians, nurses, and nonmedical staff. The quality of care they provide, as well as their ability to work together, will create the longest-lasting impressions of customer service in the patient's mind. Unfortunately, this is no small feat. Healthcare professionals are under great stress at many facilities. Most are ill equipped to handle the additional pressures of shrinking resources, aging facilities, and uptight co-workers. The foundation of any customer service improvement program appears to be a compassionate, upbeat, committed, and motivated staff trained in human relations.

- **Professional and high-quality services, provided efficiently, at hours convenient to modern work schedules.**

  In our consulting practice, we have repeatedly identified the cause of "extended wait time" as inefficient scheduling of procedures and ineffective admission procedures. Emergency rooms and other waiting rooms are all too often "clogged" with patients seeking nonurgent healthcare, because they can't access services during conventional schedules. Many hospitals have far too many patient processes that take patients from one waiting area to another with unnecessary long delays in each. Extended wait times can be fixed, and have been, at many healthcare facilities. If the patient (the customer) wants service during times at which providers currently do not provide them, providers should consider changing their schedule.

- **Adequate information, provided in a timely fashion, in understandable terms.**

  Patients want an explanation of procedures and medications. They want thorough instructions when they are discharged. They want to know about their treatment program. They want a bill they can understand and someone to explain the charges to them. Patients want healthcare providers to take the time to talk to them, listen to their concerns, and then provide them with information they can understand. These needs are too often not being met by providers today.

A recent editorial in *Modern Healthcare* put it this way:

> Wake up, Mr. and Mrs. Administrator. As an industry, healthcare just doesn't get it. Jack West, chairman of the American Society for Quality Control, put it best: "Quality is not what the quality professional says it is. It's not what the engineer says it is. It's what the customer says it is."[1]

---

1. *Modern Healthcare,* December 19–26, 1994, p. 38.

**CHAPTER**

# Indifference Causes Its Own Kind of Pain

The words themselves are enough to make us stop, step back, and pause: *Blood. Pain. Fear of the unknown. Surgery. Anesthesia. Long, drawn-out illness. Death.* These are powerful words and powerful images too, images most of us would rather not think about for ourselves and for our loved ones. But no matter how much we close our eyes, close our hearts, and close our minds to those powerful and frightening words, the sad reality is that we all must face pain, illness, and death at some point in our lives. And someone, somewhere, right now, is facing it, even as you read these words. Maybe it's your mother or father. Maybe it's someone you know from work or someone who lives down the street. Maybe it's a total stranger, but someone is experiencing those things right now. Someone in a white paper gown walks down a long, lonely corridor. Meanwhile, a man clutches the hand of his wife of 40 years, watching for movement behind the eyes that will never again slip open and never again smile to see his face.

A skinny 12-year-old boy waits quietly to start his chemotherapy, a stuffed toy under his arm and a baseball cap pulled over his pale, bald head.

A young mother weeps for joy as she cradles her hungry daughter, only six hours old, against her breast, and her proud husband's hands shake as he steadies the camera, ready to immortalize the moment forever.

Two teenage boys sit quietly in the waiting room, grim-faced and firm as they wait to hear the results of their father's biopsy.

A middle-aged woman brings a bunch of pink roses for her elderly mother who, stricken with Alzheimer's disease, no longer recognizes the child she raised, but thanks her anyway, and inwardly marvels at the kindness of strangers.

A young woman on her knees in the hospital chapel prays fervently for her three-year-old niece, struck by a hit-and-run driver now entering her eighth hour of surgery.

These are our stories; yours, mine, and everyone's. Many of us have been there and all of us will all be there again, racked with worry, pacing the waiting room floors waiting for news about our mother. Or father. Daughter. Son. Sister. Husband. Friend. But if we are lucky, we will look up and find a kind face there to greet us, a warm smile and a pat on the shoulder, a few soft words of comfort and encouragement. It may be a busy doctor who takes time to explain exactly what went wrong, shows us the X-rays, and tells our loved one what to expect in the next few hours. It may be the head nurse who offers a tissue to dry those tears and a squeeze of the hand to let you know you're not alone. It may be the lab technician, who, instead of pointing to the cafeteria and saying, "Down there," takes our arm and walks with us, steadying our trembling steps along the way. A hospital can be a sad, scary, lonely place to many patients, but much less so when staffed by people who care. And that, ultimately, is what the customer service revolution in healthcare is all about: putting the human touch back into the healthcare system; restoring compassion to its rightful place at the start of the medical equation.

In purely clinical terms, the United States leads the world in medical miracles. Diseases once considered incommutable death sentences—tuberculosis, diabetes, leukemia, breast cancer, and kidney failure—can now be successfully treated, and in some cases, even cured. Procedures that formerly would have been considered the stuff of science fiction are now so commonplace that we don't even notice when we meet someone who has had a lung removed, a heart transplanted, or given birth through artificial insemination. We have become somewhat overconfident about our nation's medical potential, expecting that nearly everything in the human body that can break down can be fixed or replaced. The United States is the envy of the world in this respect, and patients travel from all over the world to seek treatments and cures at our world-renowned hospitals and institutions.

## THE HUMAN ELEMENT HAS BEEN LOST

But there is, of course, a downside to our amazing achievements in medical progress. Somewhere along the line, the human element has become lost or forgotten. Or perhaps it was only misplaced, its luster tarnished among the gleam of all the ventilators, the vaccines, the dialysis, and the heart-lung machines.

The medical community has also become overconfident, even arrogant, in its assertion that it can treat any ill. Medical personnel are often accused of acting as if they themselves had the power of life and death. They often take on the arrogance of some celestial deity. It seems as if the entire medical profession has adopted a superiority complex about all facets of the delivery of healthcare in this country. Staff have gotten so good at saving lives, putting people back together again, and healing that the little niceties of life such as acts of kindness, thoughtfulness, and going above and beyond normal procedures are somehow beneath the personnel. Sometimes you get the feeling if the staff of hospitals and physicians' offices displayed acts of charity and compassion they would betray some medical oath of their profession. Indifference by those with whom the public comes in contact has become what patients have come to expect. A patient's physical well-being is the bottom line, indeed has become the only concern, and the only means of measuring success. A patient's mental, emotional, and psychological well-being all take a back seat.

Nearly everybody has at least one personal horror story to share; an example of professionals' behavior that goes beyond indifference to that of rudeness, insensitivity, blatant unconcern, or even medical malpractice. Such behavior results from the medical community's failure to *put the patient first*. Through our 1995 surveys and interviews, we talked to nearly 2,000 former patients about their healthcare experiences. Following are just a few brief examples of some of the more disturbing stories told to us by ordinary Americans, people who could be your family, co-workers, or friends, or patients.

A chief of nursing at his own hospital, Bill York of South Springs, South Dakota, told us of a humiliating experience with his pregnant wife:

> My wife, also a registered nurse, and I had preadmitted her and completed a "dry run" prior to her going into labor with our daughter. We were told to go to the emergency department of the hospital and ask for a wheelchair and an escort to labor and delivery. On arriving in the emergency department, no one even could find a wheelchair in the area. We were also rudely greeted by a male RN who asked, actually shouted at us, in front of the entire ED waiting room, "Honey, has your water broke yet?" I was so upset, I wrote the V.P. of nursing,

complimenting the labor and delivery care and recounting the above situation, but I never even received a response.

An elderly man from Alabama described how a lack of compassion by the hospital staff led him to digust:

They let me lie on bloody sheets, with blood all over my pajama top, to the point that it had dried on my skin. Now if someone had checked on me during the night, they might have seen this. I had in two IVs and was unable to get the pajama top off by myself. In postsurgery, they plopped me in the bed and did not take my vitals for 55 minutes. They said they were "busy." If it had not been for my family who stayed with me, I might not even be talking to you now.

A 40-year-old woman from Kailua, Hawaii, reported how the rudeness of a physician's office staff could have had disastrous implications:

When the doctor was confronted with several mistakes made by the office staff (waiting days to report vital lab results to patient, etc.), the doctor responded, "Well, you can go somewhere else if you want to." One other very bad memory I have is the physician's response at another facility a couple of years ago. When I suspected my child had Down's Syndrome (she did), right after delivery at 9 PM, the OB/gyne told me to wait until morning to have a pediatrician check her out! Luckily I insisted that my pediatrician be called, because a heart defect surfaced soon after and the baby was transferred to NICU at another facility within hours.

As disturbing as these stories sound, the most concerning aspect may be that these situations do not appear to be isolated incidents. Examples such as these appear to be all too common at hospitals and clinics around the country. One man who knows how widespread this kind of treatment is, Dave Gorden, is a Tennessee businessman and professional "mystery patient," whose undercover experiences as a patient in 49 different hospitals during the past 11 years have given him a unique insight into the state of healthcare services and patient satisfaction. The most significant thing that his experiences have taught him is that a little compassion can go a long way.

> In the hospital, you're a prisoner. I like to say that they give you a private room and a public gown. And they take control away from you. They tell you if you can go to the bathroom, when you can go to the bathroom, and what to do with it after you go to the bathroom. So when someone is kind, in what you and I, in a day-to-day situation might think is no big deal, in a hospital setting, it really makes a big impression.

## HAIR-RAISING EXPERIENCES

As a mystery patient, Gorden has had his share of hair-raising experiences. At one hospital, where Gorden was under observation after pretending to have suffered chest pains, the phlebotomist had trouble drawing blood from his vein, so she decided to take it from his finger. She was in the process of doing that when an EKG technician came in to perform a test, which made the phlebotomist nervous. She proceeded to squeeze two vials of blood out of Gorden's finger, which he found quite painful. When she finished with the second vial, she started looking around because she had misplaced the first vial. The EKG technician helped her look for the vial, as did Gorden, who climbed out of bed with his IV still attached because, as he says, "I didn't want to go through this again."

The three of them looked everywhere and could not locate the vial, so the technician said, "It must be in the sharps disposal unit, in a locked box on the wall." The phlebotomist got the key to the box from the nurses' station, opened the box, and proceeded to dump the contents into the sink in the patients' bathroom. She said she found a vial of blood, which may have been the one she misplaced,

but could easily have been somebody else's. The phlebotomist took that vial away and never came back to clean up
the mess in the bathroom. Gorden tried to clean it up but
worried about possible HIV contamination from the used
needles among the refuse left in the sink. "I didn't know
what to do," he admits. "That was the closest I ever came
to calling the hospital administrator at home and saying,
'I'm out of here.'"

Several times Gorden has been a patient in a hospital
for three or four days and never had a bracelet put on his
wrist, which means the doctors and nurses didn't know
whether they had the right patient for blood work, tests,
and so on. Many times he has been presented with the
incorrect medication. For example, he was once given a pill
which is given to nonbreast-feeding new mothers to dry up
their milk supply. "I didn't take it because I challenged the
nurse and said, 'What is this?' And she went out and came
back and said, 'Oh, I think that wasn't really meant for
you,'" Gorden says. The result: The hospital still charged
him $42 for that pill.

So what do patients really want from their healthcare
providers? Are their expectations too high? Do they unrea-
sonably expect the Ritz Carlton treatment from people who
are often overworked, stressed, and in trying situations?
Are they asking doctors, nurses, and technicians to go above
and beyond the call of duty? Our research suggests not. The
patient survey we conducted revealed that although customer service is extremely important to them, patients
expect a 9.4 rating on an index scale where 10 is highest.
The most important issues to patients revolve around simple,
basic concepts like waiting time, privacy, and compassion.
Following are some of the features of care that patients told
us they want from their healthcare providers:

> "As a paying customer, I expect prompt, professional
> attention regarding my procedure, with a full
> understanding of what is going to be performed."

"No one wants to be neglected, ignored, or wait for unreasonable lengths of time."

"Familiarity with your insurance; no blame for the type of insurance you have."

"Patience and warmth."

"I want them to listen to my problem."

"Respect! To be treated as timely as possible, and with a friendly atmosphere."

"Explanation and discussion of treatment, symptoms, future expectations."

"Quick and still caring."

## PATIENTS' EXPECTATIONS NOT UNREALISTIC

These issues hardly sound like unrealistic or unreasonable expectations. They reflect the level of service you would expect in a department store, a restaurant, or a car repair shop. Is it too much to ask for doctors, nurses, technicians, and other healthcare employees to supply the same level of customer service? Based on our research, the problems with customer service in healthcare can be divided into the four main areas that concern patients: communication, friendliness and warmth, compassion, and wait times.

### Communication

A director of patient relations of a hospital in Albany, New York, told of how a lack of good communication by the hospital staff impacted his father:

> In October 1993 my father was a patient in a hospital in downstate New York. The staff—including nurses, physicians, nurse managers, and a VP—refused to answer his questions about his care. Even after I revealed my profession and my sister's, who is an attorney, the hospital refused to explain a nursing care plan, to tell us

why specific tests were ordered, or to tell my father what his diagnosis/prognosis was—and he's an alert and oriented 59-year-old! They stated that they have a patient representative on staff. It took me two days to find out that their patient representative is a volunteer who works on Thursday afternoons only!

A young mother from Graysville, Alabama, told us how a lack of communication caused her concern and pain:

> Having my first child by C-section after 17 hours of labor was exhausting and painful. Afterwards I was given a small amount of medicine and was told to, "Make it last, that's all you're getting." I lay there all night hurting until a new nurse took over and gave me the medicine I was supposed to get. I didn't know any better, I just accepted it . . . I think my first pregnancy and delivery were so bad that everything about the second one seemed better, even though I had another C-section after 14 hours . . . I also had a bad experience the second time, which was due to miscommunication between me and my doctor about the method of medication used after delivery. I ended up spending around three to four hours in tremendous pain. He thought he was saving me money. He did, but I paid for it differently.

## Friendliness and Warmth

An elderly man from Lombard, Illinois, has bitter memories from his experiences in hospitals:

> The hospitals today are run by people with business degrees, with making a big dollar profit first instead of combining patient care with cost care. . . . My wife spent 75 days in a hospital in Arizona, 65 days of them in intensive care, and received a range of care from indifferent to bad. If I would not have been present, my wife could have died several times if I hadn't intervened.

A young woman from Nashville, Tennessee, described how she was treated for her weight problem:

I was treated as ignorant and fat. Most, if not all, of the information about my condition and my surgery was given to me in a handout in the hospital. I did not know what was in the future for my health until it was over. Please, please, inform doctors and hospital staff to treat their patients with respect. Tell them about the illness, the treatment, and the recovery.

## Compassion

A 60-year-old woman from West Hartford, Connecticut, described how a lack of compassion by the hospital left her with bad memories:

Being left unwashed for hours in a pool of blood after surgery. The aide was afraid to check the surgical area. . . . Having the nurse give me less pain medicine than ordered by the doctor. . . . Being very cold after surgery, both in the recovery room and on the floor, and having to wait a long time for someone to bring me a blanket.

A lack of simple compassion was often the complaint from patients we spoke with during the research. A 30-year-old mother from Oklahoma told us:

Our one-year-old son choked on some popcorn. We did the Heimlich maneuver on him and he breathed again, but then little red spots broke out on his chest. We took him into the emergency room and we were scared to death. The nurse yelled at us, "Don't you know not to do this?" in a very rude way. We were so mad at her, we didn't care to ever return.

A man from Bisti, New Mexico, described an incident similar to ones we heard from many patients: "When I had a broken leg, the doctor just marched into my room and cut my stitches, then started cleaning my wound without telling me what he was doing."

The last days of her husband's life were characterized this way by a woman from Bloomfield, New Mexico:

> My husband was very sick with acute leukemia and one
> of the nurses refused to do anything for my husband. I
> asked for service and she didn't come, so I reported her.
> My husband had a night nurse who wouldn't change him
> for his terrible rash. My husband died that week. He had
> such a poor nurse that night. I reported her. You wouldn't
> believe how much my husband suffered.

## Wait Times

A retired Navy veteran voiced an often-heard complaint.
"Much of the time patients get little time with the doctor,
and the doctors are often quick to diagnose and slow to
listen to the patient's questions and listen to the patient's
answers. I've been a heart patient since 1984, and when I
had emergency chest pains, many pertinent questions were
not asked. The doctor left the unit to go home three hours
early because he missed lunch. The doctor involved in
reviewing and I assume, responsible overall, never saw me.
Two weeks later he still had not yet advised me of the
results. The charge for about 30 minutes was $3,900."

Although our research with patients uncovered some
horror stories about customer service and patient *dis*satisfaction about practitioners within the healthcare field, the
news is not all bleak. The American public has spoken.
Patients are making their feelings known, through their
employers and their managed care organizations. Slowly
but surely, the customer service revolution has begun.
Patients are demanding better services for their healthcare
dollars, and hospitals and clinics have heard the alarm bells
and are heeding their call.

## PATIENTS DEFINE CUSTOMER SERVICE IN HEALTHCARE

As part of our patient satisfaction research, we asked the
people we surveyed how they define the term *customer
satisfaction* in healthcare. Their responses tell the story
well:

"Customer service in a hospital means making the patient feel as relaxed as possible, and as comfortable, and letting the patient know that you're there to help him or her get well again."

"Be sensitive to your patients' needs, have empathy for patients' feelings of loss of control, confusion, illness, or pain. Customer service is based on understanding."

"Admitted quickly, procedures fully explained. People listened when questions were asked and showed support. Customer service is smiles, sincerity, patience, and support."

"A smile means the world to someone entering or leaving a hospital or doctor's office."

How simple and yet how profound; a smile, a hand-shake, a pat on the back. What do patients want? A reas-surance that yes, I am dealing with a fellow human being. For instance, Carrie Angus, a caregiver, says, "I got tired of being a pill-pusher." An internist by training, Angus faced a crossroad in her medical career. She decided on a less-traveled path that emphasizes a holistic/homeopathic approach to practicing medicine. Sometimes it's a smile or a touch, a look of concern, or the sound of doctor and patient laughing. However it is delivered, the message is clear. Angus cares deeply about people and helping them get well. She will hug them or rub their backs—anything to jump-start them on their way to wellness. "I treat them like they are my friends," she explains. "It enriches my life to be sincere. I couldn't do it any other way."[1]

Dave Gorden, the mystery patient we described earlier in this chapter, has had many positive hospital experiences as well as his horror stories. He has experienced the full, broad spectrum of treatment within hospitals, from horrific

---

1. *Milwaukee Journal/Sentinel.*

to wonderful. "I would say hospitals are, generally speaking, consistently inconsistent. When you are a patient, you are touched by 40 to 60 people a day, both directly and indirectly. You are directly touched by nurses, technicians, dietary, housekeeping, etc., and indirectly touched by the pharmacy, lab workers, food preparers, and others," he explains. This creates a broad potential for things to go right, or to go wrong:

> Nursing services may do a wonderful job, but the lab is slow in running the tests, or the phlebotomist is rude; therefore my overall impression of the hospital is affected. You can't average a hospital experience. That would be like standing with one foot in a bucket of ice water and one foot in a bucket of boiling hot water. On average, that wouldn't be very comfortable. When a patient is discharged from a hospital, especially after three or four days, they don't say, "The lab did a good job, the pharmacy did a good job, nursing was OK, dietary was not so terrific, and environmental services was lousy." That's not what they say. What they say is, "I had a miserable time in that hospital," and it's because one nurse didn't respond quickly enough to the call light, or some other such thing. I believe that it's imperative that every hospital discharge happy patients, because they don't ever tell the good stuff. But you miss one meal, or one thing's not right, or your medication doesn't come on time, and you go home and call folks long distance to tell them about it.

Gorden, in the guise of the mystery patient, does not go beyond asking for what any ordinary patient might request. He stresses that he does not go into the hospital as a "bad guy" trying to catch someone in the act of practicing bad customer service; rather, he tries to exemplify the needs and concerns of the "typical" patient and let the hospital staff respond accordingly. One example of a very good experience that he has had came at a certain hospital when he asked a volunteer for a copy of *USA Today*. The volunteer not only brought him the paper for free, but came to work 10 minutes early each day during Gorden's stay just to have time to pick up the paper and give it to Gorden personally, and still have time to get to her volunteer position without being late.

## TRUE TEST OF PATIENT SATISFACTION LIES WITH PHYSICIAN

As important as management's role is in patient satisfaction, the true test of patient satisfaction is the interaction between doctor and patient, a thought echoed by leaders in the field. "The doctor-patient relationship is probably the single most important dimension of medical care," says sociologist Richard Frankel, director of the Center for Human Interaction at Highland Hospital in Rochester, New York.[2]

*Consumer Reports* magazine's comprehensive 1994 survey of 70,000 of its readers asked about their healthcare impressions and experiences. The results closely mirror our survey results from the summer of 1995. Both surveys found that the quality of communication between doctors and patients was perceived as a big problem. Respondents reported that their doctors were not open to answering questions, did not appear to listen to the patients' concerns, and didn't give their patients any advice on making healthy lifestyle choices or changes. The *Consumer Reports* study also found, alarmingly, that the patients of doctors who didn't communicate well were less likely to follow instructions and were overall less likely to take their medication or follow the proposed treatment plan, which in some cases lead to the continuation, or the worsening, of the patient's medical condition. This study crystallizes the issue: Good communication between doctor and patient is not just good

2. "How Is Your Doctor Treating You?" *Consumer Reports,* February 1995, p. 81.

business or some touchy-feely good PR issue; it can spell the difference between sickness and health. And in some cases it goes deeper even than that: a study published in 1994 in the *Archives of Internal Medicine* found that patients cited communication issues in 70 percent of malpractice depositions.[3]

This emphasis on good communication is a sentiment echoed by our survey respondents. One middle-aged woman from Alabama said it best. Customer service is "having the staff listen to your questions or complaints and also discussing your bill later. I equate customer service with communications."

## BEING TREATED LIKE A HUMAN BEING, NOT JUST ANOTHER PATIENT

Our interviews yielded some feedback of good customer service and patient satisfaction that we share with you here as an encouragement, perhaps even as a beacon of light. Perhaps someday all patients will be able to echo the words of Richard Barnes of Empire, Alabama: "I was treated like a human being, not just another patient."

A 60-year-old woman reported, "I had excellent, smooth, emergency room care when I was admitted with a severe fracture. The doctor came quickly. I've had very smooth admissions and discharges on my previous two or three visits, including one-day surgery. I think that care in hospitals has improved greatly over the years. The service is much more organized, including admission and discharge, meal service, and all other supplies."

A patient's husband commented on a particularly caring nurse: "A nurse came from another station to comb my wife's hair after weeks of neglect. Another nurse who was not attending my wife went out of her way to wash my wife's hair, comb, and braid it for her. That's what I call caring."

---

3. Ibid., p. 83.

Some former patients remembered kindness:

"The emergency people were very kind and sympathetic to me and my concerns. They talked to me and calmed me down, all the time explaining to me what was going on."

"Most nurses are all attentive, kind, and helpful. Good nursing care is half the battle."

"At the hospital, even when we were left in a waiting room for a short time we were told, 'Your wait will be. . . .' The doctor answered all our questions and did not rush us out."

"The RN/receptionist who brought me a box of Kleenex and gave me a hug while my husband was in the treatment room."

"My care and treatment at the hospital was superior. My family and friends commented often on the compassion and exceptional care the staff exhibited. I have not stopped talking about the wonderful treatment I received and the efficiency of the hospital to my friends and business associates."

"In the time I was at the hospital I encountered many employees; janitorial, food services, doctors, technicians, etc., and no one was less than pleasant, helpful, and concerned about customers."

As many of these examples prove, the American public has become accustomed to the "medical miracles" and the never-ending medical advances with which this country has improved outcomes. However, they have never grown accustomed to the providers' indifference or cold, uncaring, rude treatment. They have griped about it for years to their neighbors, friends, and family members. Now their voice of displeasure is growing louder and being heard by those who will do something about it.

# CHAPTER 7

# Patient Satisfaction as a Low Priority for Most Providers

As we waded through our research on how hospitals are responding to patients' demands for improved customer service, I was reminded of an old story about Earl Weaver, the legendary manager of baseball's Baltimore Orioles. Weaver was known for his colorful remarks about the wisdom of various umpire's officiating calls, particularly if they were not favorable for the Orioles. One evening, Weaver was upset about what he believed was an inappropriate strike call. He placed himself inches from the umpire's face as he shouted: "Buddy, you're doing a lousy job tonight, and I sure as h--- hope you're going to get better. But I've got a sick feeling this may be as good as it gets."

We interviewed, visited, surveyed and analyzed dozens of hospitals and clinics of various sizes and specialties from all regions of the United States. Our objective was to determine what actions were being taken to improve customer service. We were on a mission to locate innovators and visionaries, and find examples of "prototype facilities." At one point in the process, all three of us were depressed by what we perceived to be a mediocre response by providers to this equivalent of a revolution in the healthcare marketplace. More than once, we wondered, "Is this as good as it gets?" However, we did find a few shining stars. Hospitals exist like Chapman General in Orange, California, which provides a level of customer service not unlike a fine hotel. Chapman General hired Debbie Firsker as the concierge manager and is modeling itself as the "Nordstrom's" of healthcare. She stated, "There is one person—that's me—designated to get to know all patients—visit with them every day—make sure their needs are met, and that's all I do."

Chapman General is a small facility, operating in a highly mature managed care market that has to differentiate itself to survive. It's not just surviving, it's flourishing.

We were awed by the attitude and commitment of the entire staff at Bradley Memorial, a 250-bed hospital in Cleveland, Tennessee. According to Lynn Dunlap, assistant administrator for nursing, things have never been the same since Dave Gorden was admitted in 1991 as a mystery patient. "I did not want our staff or physicians to think we were merely trying to catch things being done wrong. That was not our objective. Our objective was to lay the groundwork for changing the hospital's culture." And change they did. Today the culture of this facility makes it absolutely unique. Every employee, from the CEO, to the nursing staff, to the third shift housekeeper, is "engaged" in the Bradley guest relations philosophy.

We discovered that Holy Cross Hospital on Chicago's near south side took a unique approach to determine its patients' "wants" as they relate to customer service. The hospital's new management team wanted to improve hospitalwide patient satisfaction. The team looked at the whole organization and decided to develop specific standards of behavior for interacting with customers (both internal and external). To help the team determine the proper standards of behavior, members enlisted the help of customer focus groups. Using findings from the focus groups, the team defined a clear set of standards and expectations for interacting with customers. By articulating the standards and rewarding staff who consistently exceeded the expectations, the hospital found their "patient satisfaction" scores improving dramatically, and the facility has been able to sustain the improvement. Holy Cross recently was named one of the winners in the Hospitals & Health Networks and Coopers & Lybrand Fourth Annual Great Comebacks contest. Chicago Mayor Richard M. Daley also proclaimed July 22, 1994, "Holy Cross Hospital Day in Chicago."

## CQI TO IMPROVE CUSTOMER SERVICE

Community Hospital of Anderson-Madison County in Anderson, Indiana, used the continuous quality improvement (CQI) process to improve their customer service.

Although this was an early CQI project, Community Hospital showed clearly how much a facility can accomplish by focusing on an issue and using many resources for problem-solving ideas. The hospital used data from Press-Ganey quarterly and special reports, interviews with selected patients, and consultations with other Press-Ganey client hospitals during their investigative process. By combining the information garnered through all of these channels, the hospital came up with several ideas for improving patient satisfaction with home care advice. Considering the changing focus in healthcare, the facility's decision to work on this issue was a timely one. The team realized that home care is of increasing importance to patients and their families and that to take care of the patient both in and out of the hospital, improved communication is essential. In the short time since implementation, patient satisfaction scores have gone up significantly.

St. Luke's-Roosevelt Hospital Center in New York City formed a patient relations group, the purpose of which was to find ways of improving patient satisfaction at the hospital. One of the group's many ideas was to create the Adopt-a-Floor program. Each unit was adopted by a physician and a member of the administrative staff. They formed (and worked closely with) a multidisciplinary team on each inpatient unit. The teams were charged with the mission of increasing patient satisfaction, resolving any problems that might arise, and improving the experience of being a patient. Each team continues to work to resolve the issues most important to that unit. The program has met with success as a result of the unit-specific solutions implemented by the teams.

Emergency rooms are hot spots for patient complaints in hospitals throughout the nation. Mercy Hospital Medical Center in Des Moines, Iowa, found a solution. Its busy emergency department (ED) noticed a dramatic dip in patient satisfaction as overcrowding became a serious issue. As staff frustration and patient complaints both increased, management made the bold decision to restructure the emergency department. The managers changed staffing patterns and rules regarding visitors. They also added space to the ED by moving some adjacent departments to other parts of the hospital, thereby making additional space available for the ED. They used the space to create separate areas for patients experiencing chest pain and for those needing "minor care." Since implementing these changes, Mercy Hospital has realized an increase in staff morale and has seen patient satisfaction climb.

A simple and effective approach taken by the Dannenfelser, Litwak, and Shasno Pediatric Clinic in Abingdon, Maryland, established a model for physicians groups that is built on developing a personal relationship with their patients' parents. The clinic established support groups for new parents, where complete information and answers to questions are provided by the medical staff. Emily Fleming, clinic administrator, summed up the approach, "We try to put ourselves in the mother or father's position . . . we try to understand it from their perspective. We try to treat them the same way we'd like to be treated."

## MOST PROVIDERS DRAG THEIR FEET IN CUSTOMER SERVICE

We are convinced that intensified competition for patients covered under managed care plans has shocked a number of healthcare facilities into taking customer satisfaction more seriously. However, most are being dragged reluctantly into the new era of "customer friendly" healthcare.

It's disturbing to read the results of a University of Michigan research project designed to measure the quality of American goods and services. Surprisingly, the maligned manufacturing sector of the economy actually scored higher in a study of 46,000 customers than did service industries. The real scorcher was that on a 100-point satisfaction index, hospitals scored only a 74, somewhere between the 60 of the U.S. Postal Service and the 82 of long-distance telephone service.[1]

The good news is, this *is not* as good as it gets. The customer service revolution in healthcare is just underway. A few hospitals and clinics are developing innovative ways to "connect" with their customers. Facility managers are asking questions and listening to what the patient is saying. They are beginning to understand that if they don't adapt to meet the patient's needs, someone else will.

## PROVIDERS HAVE TROUBLE IDENTIFYING "CUSTOMER"

If we've learned anything in our consulting practice, it's that sometimes asking the most obvious questions produces the most startling responses. That's what happened when

---

1. *Modern Healthcare,* December 19–26, 1994, p. 38.

we asked hospitals who their customer was. We thought the answer was obvious. As Table 7.1 reveals, it wasn't.

To say there was some confusion about this issue is to understate the passion with which the facilities responded. In fairness to the hospitals, many identified the patient as their primary customer but then went on to expound in great detail about how they also saw their customer as the medical staff, insurance companies, and employers. The medical staff was a recurring theme. Clearly, hospitals see the physician as their customer. Unfortunately, in the process, the patient's needs have too often been considered as a secondary issue. Undoubtedly, this is one reason the customer service revolution has taken hold: Patients have learned to harness the power of stating their expectations.

If ever there was evidence that many facilities just don't know who their customer is, it was provided by the 17 percent of respondents who told us it was "everyone." Most hospitals are trying to please everyone they encounter. This is a noble objective, but is it possible to achieve?

Facilities that have established a focused and successful customer satisfaction program have clearly identified the patient as their customer. James Killian, COO and executive vice president at Lake Forest Hospital in Lake

## TABLE 7.1

Who Does a Hospital Consider to Be Its Customer?

| Response | Hospital's Perceived Customers |
|----------|-------------------------------|
| 39% | Patients and their families |
| 20 | Medical staff |
| 17 | Everyone |
| 14 | Employers |
| 10 | Third-party payers (insurance companies) |

Forest, Illinois, summed up his facility's perspective, "We know that the patient is our customer, and we will do whatever it takes to meet and exceed their expectations. We actually provide patients with a guarantee. We'll go so far as to credit their account if they're not satisfied. Obviously, we can't guarantee the results of their medical treatment, but every other aspect of our service is included."

Bradley Memorial, a model for hospital guest relations programs, has the right approach. The facility exudes a culture in which all employees, volunteers, physicians, visitors, and patients are will be provided the finest personal care and surroundings. But all personnel are focused on the single objective of providing their guest—the patient—with the finest service possible.

Participating hospitals and clinics in our survey were queried as to whether they held a general consensus as to what constituted "the most important" factors in patient satisfaction. With the exception of patient wait times, we were somewhat surprised at how consistent their answers were with what patients had told us, as illustrated in Table 7.2.

**TABLE 7.2**

What Hospitals Believe Are the Most Important Characteristics of Customer Service

| Response | Hospitals' Perceived Primary Customer Service Characteristics |
|----------|---------------------------------------------------------------|
| 55% | Compassionate staff with excellent communication skills |
| 33 | Professional high quality care and responsive staff |
| 12 | Choice of treatments, physician, facilities (including extra amenities) |
| 6 | Efficiency of operations, including minimal delays in service |

## WHAT PROVIDERS WILL DO TO IMPROVE PATIENT SATISFACTION

The issue seems to be this: If providers know *what* is important in customer service, what will they do to *make it happen?* With the exception of the low priority hospitals afforded cutting down patient wait times, the facilities' managers were on target with what patients want. Most facilities seem to have an understanding of the importance of their human resources. Jane McManus, director of patient financial services at Tompkins Community Hospital in Ithaca, New York, stated that key staffing decisions were at the core of their patient satisfaction program. "Hiring the right people, in the right spots, particularly in registration and other 'up-front positions' is critical. Having customer-oriented people who have the ability to consistently smile and be personable with a real positive attitude has been a key to our success."

Glen Treml, vice president of finance at St. Agnes Hospital in Fond du Lac, Wisconsin, said that his CEO had established a hospitalwide philosophy of attentiveness to patient needs. "We found that as we improved operations, customer satisfaction improved. We also began to take the time to talk to our patients and listen to what they wanted."

Like Chapman General, St. Agnes operates in a highly competitive and fairly mature managed care environment. Even though the number of hospitals in Fond du Lac is limited, larger metropolitan markets like Milwaukee are only an hour or so away. Jim Sexton, CEO, summed it up, "Patients have more choices than we'd like to think. We've learned from experience that if we don't provide what they need, or if we make them angry in the process of providing their service, they'll go somewhere else. We can't afford to take customer service lightly."

## The Role of the Patient Representative

One of the customer service initiatives that has been around a long time is the concept of a *patient representative*—one employee or an entire department that serves as a liaison between patient and staff, to make that link even stronger. Although this is often proven to be a very successful program, in some hospitals the patient advocate exists in name only. The mystery patient and customer service consultant, Dave Gorden, has learned this is often the case.

> Many hospitals have patient representatives. But if you were to ask, "Dave, do you think it's effective?" I would say, most of the time I think it's window dressing. If you represent that you have it and you really don't, you'd be better off not saying you had it in the first place. For example, if you put a card on the nightstand that says you have a patient representative on duty 24 hours a day, and then I call that number seven times and get no answer. That often happens.

In some hospitals, a patient representative is only available a certain number of hours a week. "That would be like saying, 'Oh yeah, we have a surgical suite, but it's only open on Thursday.' Well, then you're not a hospital," Gorden says.

## ANOTHER OVERNIGHT SENSATION?

At times during our research, we wondered if the "customer service revolution in healthcare" might just become the latest buzzword or "management trend of the month." Then we discovered another interesting perspective. Attention to customer service is not a new initiative for many of the industry's "innovators." As Table 7.3 indicates, almost a quarter of those we interviewed who are actively involved in a customer service improvement program have been active for over a decade.

**TABLE 7.3**

Years Hospital Involved in Customer Service Improvement Programs

| Response | Length of Involvement |
|----------|----------------------|
| 22%      | More than 10 years   |
| 19       | 6 to 9 years         |
| 26       | 3 to 5 years         |
| 22       | 1 to 2 years         |
| 11       | Less than 12 months  |

Florida Medical Center in Fort Lauderdale, Florida, pioneered the concept of a "Patient Satisfaction Improvement Group" back in the late 80s. The center established a formal patient complaint mechanism and continues to use patient service coordinators to conduct specialized surveys. This modified CQI team provides critical quality information to managers throughout the Fort Lauderdale facility. Attention to the specific needs of our older patient demographic is essential. In addition to the high concentration of elderly patients, Florida hospitals work with many transient middle-income patients. To complete the picture, Florida has been a battleground for managed care contractors and complicated Medicaid regulations.

The revolution has continued to pick up steam as hospitals have gotten involved in the quality improvement initiatives of the Joint Commission on Accreditation of Healthcare Organizations (JCAHO). Many of the facilities we interviewed identified customer service objectives in conjunction with CQI and total quality management (TQM) initiatives in the early 90s. The JCAHO has recently added additional customer/patient service standards to its review process. The standards explain that these services are designed to respond to patient and family needs. The examples of implementation are as follows: a concurrent and retrospective survey of patient satisfaction is conducted.

Patients are asked questions about the hospital's performance through telephone interviews, questionnaires, or
interviews. The hospital reviews the information it collected in relation to its major clinical care activities and
support functions. In particular, dimensions of performance—appropriateness, availability, continuity, effectiveness, efficiency, safety, and timeliness of services—are
reviewed. Based on the results of the reviews, the hospital
refocuses its services or redesigns the existing process of
providing services, as appropriate.

The scoring of this standard indicates whether or not
the hospital's planning process considers the needs, expectations, and satisfaction of patients and their families and
adjusts the plan for services accordingly.[2]

## SO WHAT *ARE* HOSPITALS DOING?

The hospitals we surveyed were asked to identify their
primary customer service programs. We grouped their
response activities into six major categories, shown in Table
7.4.

**TABLE 7.4**

What Hospitals Are Doing

| Program Type | Facilities Using Approach |
| --- | --- |
| 1. Survey patients by mail or phone | 56% |
| 2. Customer service training programs | 32 |
| 3. Focus groups | 16 |
| 4. Process improvement to reduce wait time | 16 |
| 5. Special department of patient reps | 16 |
| 6. Patient focused care restructuring | 14 |

2. Source of this information is *1996 Comprehensive Accreditation Manual
for Hospitals.*

## Patient Satisfaction Surveys and Focus Groups

Within the broad realm of surveys and focus groups, we have included all types of customer inquiry/interview programs. This includes telephone surveys, patient focus groups, and other patient contact activities. Although virtually all facilities have implemented some form of hospitalwide patient satisfaction survey, 72 percent of the hospitals we reviewed have implemented specialized programs that focus on particular service lines, or include patients in "focus groups." These focus groups consist of former patients invited together as a group to provide personalized feedback to the hospital.

The most common survey method used appears to be mailback surveys, although telephone and computer-based assessment tools are gaining popularity. There seems to be little uniformity in distribution methods. Some hospitals place reply cards in the service areas being reviewed; others send questionnaires out to patients 3-to-30 days after discharge. But a number of facilities have come up with unique ways to use customer surveys to resolve specific concerns or problems.

Brandywine Hospital and Trauma Center, a 208-bed hospital in Coatesville, Pennsylvania, is a good example. Faced with three seemingly competing objectives—increase collections, reduce collection expense, and improve patient satisfaction—Joseph Mannion, director of patient accounts, decided to develop a proactive customer service program. Patients were contacted by telephone immediately after they received their first statement. The sole objective of this call was to offer to answer any questions patients might have about their bill and identify any potential errors or inaccuracies in registration and billing information. Although some patients received additional follow-up calls, at no time was any patient asked to pay.

In addition to identifying and resolving problems with the hospital's billing system, Mannion got a bonus. Through extensive control testing, the hospital discovered it had improved patient satisfaction levels, as well achieving a significant increase in prompt patient collections.

Another example of using patient surveys was found at the Albert Einstein Medical Center, Philadelphia, Pennsylvania. Management's commitment to gather patient satisfaction results led to a concerted effort to solicit patient feedback. Members of the management team of the center were asked to call one patient daily to request their opinions. At the same time, the team saw responses to patient satisfaction questionnaires increase.

Clinton Memorial Hospital in Wilmington, Ohio, used a "patient satisfaction tool" as a measurement to improve quality. A significant cultural shift is usually required in any organization that implements CQI, and Clinton Memorial Hospital was no different. The hospital's director of customer services enlisted the help of the hospital's president and other managers to communicate the importance of improving services at the hospital. Together they worked to keep staff motivated and to prevent complacency when survey results demonstrated above-average customer satisfaction. Their dedication and foresight led them in the right direction, as they passed their JCAHO survey under the new standards with flying colors.

At Saint Joseph's Hospital of Atlanta, improving customer satisfaction is one of the goals in the 356-bed facility's strategic plan. It's also part of the hospital's employee incentive plan. Over the past four years, Saint Joseph's has conducted various patient, employee, community, and medical staff surveys. But, unlike many hospitals that conduct surveys and then shelve the results, Saint Joseph's uses the information contained in such reviews to set goals for positive change. To coordinate surveys and to improve accuracy, four years ago Saint Joseph's switched from written surveys to telephone surveys conducted by the Gallup Organization.

Gallup's sophisticated statistical analysis of data allows Saint Joseph's to identify areas that make a difference in a patient's hospital experience.

## Patient-Centered Care: Asking Patients about Their Needs

Patient-centered care means more than just being nice to patients. It requires the development of patient care programs that meet patient needs as patients perceive them, not as professionals or hospitals do. The Picker/Commonwealth Institute has developed a patient survey instrument that allows patients to go beyond *rating* their care to *reporting about* their care. "The emphasis is not on the technical aspects of care but on whether the patient received the attention he or she felt was needed," according to Margaret Gerteis, program coordinator. Thomas Moloney, vice president of the Picker Institute's Commonwealth Fund points out, "Assuming good technology and good doctors, more patients are basing their choice (of a hospital) on what they can understand, which are mainly substantial differences in personal service."

So by definition, any hospital actively pursuing a patient-focused care program should also have in place a compatible patient satisfaction survey instrument. Improved patient satisfaction is the foundation of a patient-centered program for 124-bed Pomerado Hospital in Poway, California, a suburb of San Diego. Staff call the program "Patient First." The hospital received the 1994 Marriott Service Excellence first place award.

*Modern Healthcare* and Marriott Health Care Services sponsor these annual awards to reward programs that exhibit innovation in patient service, teamwork, and cost efficiency. The backbone of the first phase of Pomerado Hospital's project, Patient First, was the creation of a new

3. *Modern Healthcare*, July 18, 1994, p. 32.

position called "administrative partner." Improved patient satisfaction is the cornerstone of the program. It takes patients an average of 5.4 minutes to proceed from arrival to bed assignment, which is down from a minimum of 15 minutes. Patients now go directly to the appropriate nursing floor when they arrive at the hospital. An administrative partner greets them at the elevator and takes them to their room where the registration process takes place. A mobile wireless phone system allows administrative partners to be in continuous contact.

The Queen's Medical Center in Honolulu, Hawaii, has actively used patient focus groups to identify patient needs and monitor satisfaction levels. Lindsey Carry, director of patient relations, reported that the program was facilitated by a private research company and identified 25 "quality indicators." The research was validated through a telephone follow-up survey of 450 patients, and the indicators are now used on an ongoing basis to monitor performance throughout the hospital. Results are communicated to all levels, and a Performance Improvement Team dedicated to improving patient satisfaction has been set up to develop action plans based on their research.

## It's Not Enough to Ask What I Want; You've Got to *Do* Something

The problem with sophisticated survey programs and focus group structures is that it is fairly easy to lose track of your original objective. We get so wrapped up in collecting data and ensuring data integrity that we forget why we asked the question in the first place. The objective starts to become more one of analyzing information and explaining variations than improving customer service. So we asked our provider respondents one more question about the survey process; what they do with the survey data. Table 7.5 summarizes their responses.

**TABLE 7.5**

What Hospitals Do with Survey Data

| Responses | Action Taken |
|---|---|
| 36% | Route to department heads |
| 21 | Route to quality committee |
| 12 | Route to "everyone" |
| 12 | Route to CEO |
| 3 | Route to marketing |
| **85** | **Route to someone** |
| 6 | Determine "plan of action" |
| 6 | Set and/or monitor performance targets |
| 3 | Post on the bulletin board |

The hospitals' responses speak for themselves. Most of the institutions we talked to are primarily "routing" quality information around the hospital. In some facilities, it's an accountability issue. Everyone is interested in patient satisfaction, but too often no one has primary responsibility for ensuring it. We asked survey "guru" Irwin Press, PhD and cofounder of Press-Ganey, Inc., why so many hospitals don't seem to act on the data they collect. "It has everything to do with management philosophy. Survey data should not be used to discipline or rank one department against another. We encourage our clients not to focus on raw scores, but to identify and reward improvement trends."

Press believes that it's essential that hospitals *find out* where they can improve, then take action. But he points out that providers have to be willing to acknowledge their shortcomings. "Survey data is meaningless unless you use it, and when you use it, you can make a difference."

Determining the customer service problem or patient complaint and doing something about it has more than one ramification for hospitals. The JCAHO's *1994 Accreditation Manual* requires hospitals to improve performance. One of nine measurements of performance is patient satisfaction. Also, The National Committee for Quality Assurance development of the Health Plan Employer Data and Information Set (HEDIS) includes patient-satisfaction components in its 60 measurements. HEDIS is designed to help consumers and employers compare the performance of managed-care plans. Some 21 major HMOs—including Kaiser Permanente, Prudential Health Care System, TakeCare, and U.S. Health-care—plan to use HEDIS to standardize consumer health information on satisfaction. Combined, they have 9.6 million enrollees, or 20 percent of the nation's total.[4]

## Achieving Hospitalwide Buy-in to Patient Satisfaction Data

Many hospitals find that getting all departments to appreciate the full value of patient satisfaction data is somewhat difficult. Pennsylvania Hospital in Philadelphia, Pennsylvania, was no different. The marketing department and patient, guest and volunteer services teamed up to help other departments understand the data and make it work for them. To do this, they presented inservices with various departments periodically to review the data and to explain its value. Within months, the other departments began using the data and advanced to rapidly that they even began requesting more sophisticated analyses. As a result of the efforts by these two departments, the hospital is now getting more value from its reports.

Sinai Hospital of Detroit, Michigan, has made patient satisfaction a primary concern for the entire hospital. To encourage staff participation and acceptance of patient satisfaction as an important part of the services provided,

---

4. Ibid., p. 30.

the hospital has taken a number of steps. Managers reward staff who are mentioned favorably on patient surveys and recognize units that perform well. Their commitment has paid off in terms of greater patient satisfaction and lower costs.

Almost a third of the hospitals said they used employee education as their primary method of improving customer satisfaction. Training spanned a wide range of topics, from basic job skills to human relations and team building concepts. Albert Einstein Medical Center in Philadelphia, Pennsylvania, uses an institutional "values" program instituted in the early 90s to train staff to deal better with patients and each other. The program is mandatory for all employees, from the top to the lowest level.

Once again, Bradley Memorial Hospital in Cleveland, Tennessee, "set the pace" as it unveiled a comprehensive management training program in October 1994 referred to as "Bradley University." The curriculum is quite extensive, featuring 7 core courses and 11 management courses, but the customer service theme is woven throughout each class.

Effective training and education programs need to be focused, but should not be conducted only for a select group of managers, supervisors, and key employees. Our research indicated that the entire staff benefits from improved human relations, communications, and team building skills. In addition to improving day-to-day operations, each program made a notable positive impact on employee morale.

## Specific Patient Satisfaction Programs

A number of innovative programs are designed to meet specific issues identified through surveys, patient interviews, and focus groups. The most effective are often the result of a hospitalwide, CEO-led initiative. Mineral Area Regional Medical Center in Farmington, Missouri, was facing increased competition from the major St. Louis healthcare providers. After the center's local competitor was acquired, the center's managers found themselves scrambling to differentiate themselves from the larger, more aggressive multihospital corporations.

The CEO immediately instituted hospitalwide meetings in which he communicated his vision of a "hospital without walls." He convinced the staff that they were in a superior position to service the needs of the community, because they were part of that community. He told them that by interacting with their friends, neighbors, co-workers, and associates, expressing concern for their needs (and when the opportunity presented itself, telling people about the hospital), the staff would market their facility more effectively than the billboards and TV ads purchased by their competitor.

Outside firms were brought in to bolster the center's marketing skills and provide human relations training for all employees. Consistent with the hospital-without-walls vision, Mineral Area Regional Medical Center instituted a community outreach program that involved major employers in their service area. The hospital went out to local employers' facilities and conducted free blood pressure and cholesterol screenings, in conjunction with preregistration informational sessions. The director of registration met with the various benefits administrators and communicated the value of facilitating the insurance verification process. After one year of "head-on" competition, the center has experienced little if any loss of market share. But the CEO reports that the positive impact on the staff has been even more satisfying. "We are truly a team, depending on each other's strengths, compensating for each other's weaknesses."

In an effort to achieve staff buy-in and emphasize the importance of patient satisfaction to an organization, St. Luke's Medical Center in Phoenix, Arizona, created a bit of healthy competition among nursing units. Department heads wanted to raise patient satisfaction with nursing overall, and they knew they needed staff buy-in to achieve it. They developed a series of "scoreboards" for display. The

large, colorful, easy-to-read boards provided staff with the
scores and relative standings at a glance. As a result of fun
competition (including some good-natured wagering among
department heads), staff have not just accepted the results,
they look forward to each new report and the posting of
their scores, and they are motivated to continue improving
service.

In another example, the teamwork and dedication of
staff and management at Wilmington Hospital, Wilmington,
Delaware, skillfully created a more patient-satisfaction–
oriented culture through the use of Press-Ganey's patient
satisfaction surveys and results. Significant improvements
were made in the areas of visitor and family issues, cheer-
fulness/decor in patient areas, diet/meals, information to
patients, and overall emphasis on caring and courtesy in
every interaction with patients and visitors. The improvements were based directly on patient and employee
suggestions.

There are numerous other examples, some of which are
detailed in the following case studies. But the most impressive common denominator was that someone inside each
facility took action. The action was based on a deficiency
identified by getting in closer touch with patients.

## Facilities Improvement

As healthcare profit margins have declined in the last 10
years, hospital plant and equipment have suffered. Although
most facilities have done a good job maintaining existing
resources, many institutions have found themselves with
buildings no longer suited to the current marketplace. As
lengths of stay have declined and providers have shifted to
more performing ambulatory, outpatient procedures, large
inpatient "monuments" have become an unnecessary
overhead expense creating a logistics nightmare. Providers
have found themselves in the position of being "forced" to

remodel and invest in new facilities. The patient-focused care concept that most often requires a restructuring of some or all of the patient floors was mentioned frequently by hospitals as a means to improve patient satisfaction.

Some of our respondents told us that their primary "customer service improvement program" included renovation of a specialty area or emergency department. The William Beaumont Medical Center in Royal Oak, Michigan, is a good example.

- Emergency departments are being expanded to provide for more immediate triage as well as 24-hour, nonurgent medical needs.
- A comprehensive women's center provides mammography, maternity, and other OB/gyne diagnostic procedures in a low-stress, high- service-level environment.
- The ambulatory surgery unit is freestanding and provides for easy access and immediate service.

Other facilities are expanding less dramatically, but with the same objective: to serve the patient more efficiently.

Perhaps most dramatic is the development of entirely new facilities, designed from the ground up to meet patients' needs. A good example is the Austin Diagnostic Medical Center that opened in Austin, Texas, in July 1995. In addition to inpatient diagnostic procedures, it is designed to handle more than 15,000 outpatients per month. The center established customer satisfaction/patient satisfaction as its primary goal. According to Charles Pearce, the medical center's chief operating officer, the facility intends to make customer service "more encompassing."

Patient service representatives will act as greeter/hostesses to escort patients from arrival to bed. The same person will be there each weekday. Discharges will be prearranged using an integrated computer system. Reps will be "linked" to physician offices, and key information will be shared to better facilitate patient care. The "business side" of the hospital admission will be largely transparent to patients during their stay.

Starting from the ground up has its advantages. In preparation for their opening, the Austin Diagnostic Medical Center focused on identifying the best staff, then provided them with clear expectations on performance. Pearce thinks communication and staff training will be key to "making good" on his commitment of superior customer satisfaction.

The McCamy Hospital and Convalescent Center in McCamy, Texas, operates 16 acute and 30 long-term care beds, because they've listened closely to their community, and have adapted their operations to meet the community's needs. Dr. Ronald Freake, administrator for laboratory and home health services, told us that the facility has an active patient communication program, including an ongoing column in a local newspaper. According to Freake, "We're here to serve the community—period. But the way we accomplish that has changed. Once a hospital was simply supposed to provide medical services. Now, you've got to market those medical services or you won't survive."

Healthcare professionals in general need to understand that the patient is in fact their customer. Today, more than ever before, it's a competitive marketplace. Patients no longer have to go to a hospital for many medical procedures. Patients are much better educated now than before and react much more like consumers. Healthcare has become a consumable item.

## CQI/Quality Teams

One of the best examples of a "customer service based" CQI/Quality team was headed up by Dave Albrecht, vice president of finance at Bellin Hospital in Green Bay, Wisconsin. Albrecht was attempting to merge two internal units (registration and patient accounts) that had not always seen eye to eye. "The managers from both areas were very dedicated but too often focused on their specific organizational responsibility. The challenge we faced was to harness their individual commitment and high standards in a way that better met the ultimate needs and desires of our patients," he said.

His strategy included site visits of facilities unrelated to healthcare that had similar "service" objectives. He focused on the financial and hospitality services industry. He believes this was a critical step: "We were able to 'step out of the conventional box' we'd placed ourselves in. By looking at other industries, we felt less ownership and defensiveness for the way it was always done," Albrecht recalled.

## HOSPITALS' PLANNING: MORE OF THE SAME

If the customer service revolution has in fact just begun, it's reasonable to assume that healthcare providers will accelerate their improvement initiatives during coming months. That is not the case based on what our results showed. We asked respondents to provide us with a preview of their plans. The responses, listed in Table 7.6, showed that their contemplated actions are primarily a variation of what they are already doing.

Responses typically centered around conducting patient surveys, setting up focus groups, training staff in customer service techniques, and setting up special committees or task forces to address customer service issues. It appears that providers are planning on pretty much continuing their existing approaches with some fine tuning here and there. Repeatedly we recorded their response as, "Keep on with what we're doing," or "Nothing additional." The word *continue* came up in more than one-third of the hospitals we interviewed.

Many of the other responses in terms of facilities' plans for the future to improve patient satisfaction were new to them, but not to the industry, such as surveys, training, and

**TABLE 7.6**

What Hospitals Plan to Do to Improve Services

| Responses | Activities Planned |
|-----------|--------------------|
| 40% | **Operational Programs**<br>• Internal customer relations divisions such as patient representative departments<br>• Reorganize and expedite registration functions<br>• Institute "patient-focused care" applications<br>• Evaluate and revise discharge planning and procedures<br>• Customer service training for employees<br>• Form special committees |
| 33 | **Surveys, Tracking, and Focus Groups**<br>• Additional, more focused tracking and monitoring<br>• Direct patient contact programs<br>• Institute new patient focus groups |
| 27 | **New Equipment and Facilities Improvement**<br>• New, expanded computer systems<br>• Improved ERs, outpatient facilities |

focus groups. Some additional alternatives were hiring a consultant; uniforms for the clerical staff; remodeling some of the units; creating "core" committees; going to the patient-focused care concept; and starting a concierge-type program.

In summary, our distinct impression from the 1995 study was that providers don't get the message about customer service. We sense they are not tuned into the movement toward the demand for improved medical services. Most providers do not seem to sense this customer service revolution on the horizon.

In our opinion, more of the same isn't enough. The demand for a higher level of patient satisfaction will mean providers must go far beyond their past actions. Patients have told providers that they want better customer service. Employers are now in the act and they will ensure that providers get the message. In short, those providers who score high by patients in the customer service issues will become the providers of choice in the managed care network. Those who score low will lose patients and revenue.

# 8

**CHAPTER**

# Excellence through a Cultural Conversion

## A Case Study: Bradley Memorial Hospital

There are numerous approaches to improve customer service by healthcare providers. None is more thorough and successful than what we witnessed at Bradley Memorial, a 251-bed hospital in Cleveland, Tennessee, serving a five-county region that offers a vast array of specialized medical, surgical, and diagnostic services through its more than 160 physicians, 1,000 employees, and 250 volunteers. Their service area has a total population of approximately 180,000. There are 15 hospitals operating in Bradley Memorial's service area with its primary competition located in nearby Chattanooga.

We have isolated Bradley Memorial to profile in a detailed case study because we felt this midsized hospital in a community of 80,000 located 30 miles north of Chattanooga exemplifies how customer service should work at its highest level. This facility not only excels at customer service but practically every other aspect of service that a hospital typifies or should typify in today's healthcare environment.

But first, let's consider customer service. The proof of the level of customer service always lies with patients' perceptions. Bradley Memorial ranks in the top half of all hospitals surveyed in overall patient satisfaction, based on the standard items in the Press-Ganey survey. Nursing service ranks in the top 14 percent of the nearly 500 hospitals whose patients are surveyed by Press-Ganey. Bradley's nursing department scored an excellent 91 out of a 100 index by their patients in the most current quarterly ratings. Service ranking doesn't get much better.

Based on other internal patient satisfaction measurements—such as hundreds of complimentary letters from their patients, their own patient satisfaction survey, and our interviews and talks with hospital employees as well as people in the community—Bradley comes across as an exceptional hospital that lives and breathes excellent customer service.

Dave Gorden, the healthcare guest excellence consultant working with Bradley who also consults for corporations including Hallmark, McDonald's and Walt Disney World, stated,

> In three years, this hospital has made incredible progress. You can feel it in the halls. Other hospitals come here and visit and say, "I don't know what it is about this place." I have a friend whose mother died in this hospital. Before she died, he told me, "There's something about this place." I said, "What is it?" He said, "People care. You walk through the halls and you feel people care."

## CUSTOMER SERVICE PERSONIFIED

During our week-long, in-depth visit to Bradley Memorial, we witnessed the staff members' unique display of warmth and sincere caring attitude toward patients and toward each other. As we interviewed employees, roamed the patient floors, sat in waiting areas, ate in the cafeteria, and talked to the nursing staff, we experienced customer service personified.

But customer service is not the only area in which Bradley Memorial excels. In 1994, the hospital was selected one of the Top 100 Hospitals in America through the Benchmarks for Success study conducted jointly by HCIA Inc. and Mercer Health Care Provider Consulting. In 1995, the hospital received honorable mention. Bradley was one of only three Tennessee hospitals chosen in 1994. Only one Tennessee hospital was chosen as one of the Top 100 in 1995.

The dramatic announcement of the Top 100 in the faxed message that landed on the desk of Administrator Jim Whitlock at 5 PM one Friday aroused more skepticism at the time than excitement. "I thought it was a gimmick by a consulting firm," confesses Whitlock of the notification in January 1995 that Bradley Memorial had been chosen as one of the 100 top-performing hospitals in America. "I almost threw it in the garbage." It wouldn't have mattered; the award was for real. An official letter and description that arrived the following Monday named Bradley Memorial 1 of only 3 hospitals in Tennessee, 1 of only 19 hospitals in the South, and 1 of only 25 rural hospitals in America to make the exclusive list of 100.

Now, after accepting the prestigious award and after being recognized by peers, the community, and the media, the selection seems not at all surprising. For all along, Bradley has been sowing the seeds for unusual success. "We have an attitude of caring enthusiasm that permeates our organization, and that has to make a great hospital even better," beams Whitlock. "When you nurture this kind of spirit, it flows to the patient rooms and shows up in the indicators that measure the level of care."

Underlying the success by Bradley is the attitude staff members bring to their jobs each day. They seem to have employees who see beyond their job descriptions to the broader needs of the hospital. You can sense and see the value placed on teamwork, and the self-motivating sense of pride in what employees have developed. The basic measure of success or failure for any organization is individual attitude. The shaping of positive attitudes is an ongoing, high-priority process at Bradley.

In the midst of all of this, the hospital is in the middle of an ambitious multimillion dollar improvement plan. In 1993 the hospital embarked on the second and third phases of its 10-year expansion program. The $22 million construction project included development of an outpatient medical mall, a new women's center, a parking garage, education facilities including a public auditorium, advanced diagnostic imaging facilities, and a cardiopulmonary center. What is so striking is the fact the hospital embarks on the unusual to maintain their unique approach to customer service. For instance, the facility boasts its own hospital mascot and employees purposely try to catch one another doing something "beyond the demands of their job as it relates to customer satisfaction." Last year, they had their own parade down the streets of Cleveland.

In 1992, Bradley introduced the hospital's first mascot, to the community at the annual "Teddy Bear Clinic" hosted in the hospital's pediatric unit. The Teddy Bear Clinic, now in its seventh year, is designed to lessen the fear most children endure when told they need to go to the hospital. Employees set up a mock operating room where doctors, nurses, and other staff members perform surgery on stuffed animals. The volunteers sew up holes, fix fractures, bandage boo-boos, and even create limbs. For the sake of the children, they triage, admit, care for, and discharge their stuffed animals much like staff do daily for real patients. While their furry friends are in surgery, the children play games, win prizes, enjoy refreshments, and learn a great deal about the hospital and the people who might one day take care of them.

## A HOSPITAL WITH ITS OWN MASCOT

The mascot for the hospital, *Brad Lee Bunny*, is a truly southern bunny named after the bunny's home county. Brad Lee was one of the hospital's strategies for making new friends and customers. Brad Lee lent the hospital a personality and identity, particularly in terms of the hospital's relationship with children. Brad Lee Bunny visits area schools, entertains at hospital events, participates in community sponsored parades and events, and appears at other select public events. Additionally, Brad Lee is featured in the hospital coloring book and serves as the focus of the Guest Excellence Get Caught promotion material and specialty items.

Somewhere along the way, the hospital developed a special program designed to "catch" employees and volunteers who exemplified the guest excellence philosophy by doing more than the daily demands of their job. Initially, the "catchers'" mission was to identify and catch employees and volunteers worthy of recognition. If caught, the individual was awarded a certificate that could be turned in for food in the hospital cafeteria or an item in the gift shop.

In order to keep the catcher program alive, the Guest Excellence Task Force changed the rewards, expanded the number of catchers, and enhanced the value of the rewards. Bunny Bucks, featuring the slogan "Get Caught" with the Guest Excellence logo, and Brad Lee Bunny were created. Bunny Bucks can be awarded by any catcher. The first time a person is caught he/she receives five Bunny Bucks and a Get Caught T-shirt. Each consecutive time someone is caught the ante goes up 10 Bunny Bucks, which can be spent in the hospital gift shop to buy specialty items such as baseball caps, umbrellas, tote bags, and coffee cups. Each person who is caught is eligible for a monthly cash drawing ($50) and every person caught is included in a drawing at the end of the year for a trip of their choice to the Smokey

Mountains, Panama City Beach, or Myrtle Beach. Approximately 60 people are caught each month by the 25-plus catchers representing numerous departments on all shifts. Each month on the front page of the hospital newsletter, "The Pulse," all caught persons are featured by name and department.

Bradley is also big on employee education and management development, with an overall view to also improve their customer service. Mickey Mouse has "Disney University." Ronald McDonald has "Hamburger University." And Bradley has Bradley University, a comprehensive management training program. Developed by the hospital's Guest Excellence Task Force during the past two years, Bradley University offers managers and aspiring managers the opportunity for professional and personal growth and development.

"To my knowledge no other hospital offers a program like Bradley University," Jim Whitlock told us. "We have committed the resources and time to our managers, and staff members who want to become managers. What they need to develop managerial skills is provided on-site on a regular basis and extends well beyond what most organizations would consider a training program."

The curriculum at Bradley University is extensive, featuring 7 core courses and 11 management courses. All courses are taught by members of the hospital staff who have either masters-level training or a bachelors degree and experience in the field of study for which they were selected as instructors. All hospital managers are required to attend Bradley University and must successfully complete all core courses within 6 months and all management courses within 18 months.

## A FACILITY THAT CELEBRATES EVERYTHING

Staff celebrate everything at Bradley, from the traditional award banquets to each phase of the new building project.

When the hospital completed its first phase of construction, employees positioned a large balloon replica of a space shuttle on the canopy of the main patient tower facing the street signifying "space exploration." For the celebration, they had a cookout for employees and their families under a large circus tent on the hospital campus. Another special event was a black-tie, invitation-only program for donors, physicians, board members, political leaders, and other dignitaries. Held at night in the tent, the event attracted more than 250 people who were given the opportunity to have their photo taken with space aliens as they toured the new floors. An afternoon presentation for all members of the Cleveland/Bradley County Chamber of Commerce was held followed by an open house for the public.

When staff kicked off Phase II of the construction project in 1994, they knew there were mixed feelings among the staff members and former hospital employees about the demolition of the hospital's original 1952 wing. There was a strong sentimental attachment to this wing for those who had cared for patients on this unit. Through the magic of paint, wallpaper, costumes, and music, they took a make-believe step back in time. On the night of the celebration, staff and guests traveled back to 1952 when the hospital first opened. One room was transformed into a local cafe complete with jukebox, kitchen table, and soda fountain. In another room staff created a family living room circa 1952 with furnishings purchased from local shops specializing in vintage merchandise. The room was authentic down to the style of wallpaper and black and white television. Actors in vintage costumes circulated throughout the unit, talking to people about the hospital in its early days. Old photographs of the building and employees were available in scrapbooks and photo albums for all to review. Guests paid tribute to those employees from the past, something you seldom see nowadays.

During the new construction Bradley designed and built a new $1.4 million emergency center and reorganized the personnel in order to give better customer service. The facility even gave the center a new name: Super Department. The staff developed a new operational philosophy in ER in an attempt to create an environment where employees feel empowered to make decisions that affect the way services are provided.

The department was given four guest service ambassador positions whose primary functions include:

- Greeting guests in accordance with the hospital's Guest Excellence Creed and Philosophy when they enter the emergency center lobby.
- Notifying triage (evaluation) nurse of each new patient.
- Providing directions to patients and visitors searching for other hospital departments.
- Assisting persons who need help getting from the vehicle into the lobby.
- Monitoring the lobby for cleanliness and order.

Dressed in teal green blazers, white shirts/blouses, and either navy/khaki skirts or pants, the ambassadors try hard to exemplify the "Bradley image" in both appearance and action. The ER ambassadors are scheduled for three-hour shifts, seven days a week and are currently under the direction of the Super Department's administrative director.

Bradley also impacted the community with the formation of the Bradley Healthcare Foundation, created in 1991. It is composed of citizens of the community, and its primary purpose is to involve the community in a variety of ways, all designed to have a favorable impact on customer service.

## CONNECTION BETWEEN PATIENT AND EMPLOYEE SATISFACTION

We have detailed many of the actions Bradley has taken during the past several years to convey the distinct impression that the facility is a successful provider where employees have fun on their jobs. And that's a key point to remember in making the connection between excellent customer service and employees enjoying their work. These employees do enjoy their jobs and have fun doing it. It pays off in the way they treat their customers, the patients. This success didn't just happen. Jim Whitlock worked long and hard over his five-year tenure as CEO at Bradley to develop a culture in which employees get a kick out of high performance regardless of their department.

The question that demands to be asked is, "How did this hospital reach this pinnacle of customer service and turned-on employees?" We'll attempt to answer that in the next few sections devoted to Bradley. We have chosen to illustrate Bradley because we feel its approach to customer service is one to be imitated by hospitals around the nation. If this model could become a prototype for other hospitals, not only would their customer service improve, so would their overall organizational management.

Dave Gorden, the guest excellence consultant, noted, "There is a hunger for what we're doing here. It's an exciting place. I've been a mystery patient 49 times now. I live 2 hours and 20 minutes from here, but if I can make it, this would be my hospital of choice of all the hospitals I have worked with the past 11 years. There are two or three hospitals that would be my last choice. I'd rather go to a veterinary clinic than go to one of those places. There's a big difference. It's come a long way in a short period of time because there's commitment and there's vision."

Bradley illustrates many of the traditional approaches toward customer service. The managers use the Press-Ganey surveys to follow up on complaints and to improve patient satisfaction. The facility created a special task force that comes up with ideas for customer service improvement and training programs aimed at improving employees' skills in customer service. Bradley invokes a variety of techniques to keep the customer service theme alive.

But Bradley's leaders go far beyond the traditional approaches. More importantly, they have changed the way employees *think* about their jobs. They have changed the way the employees think and act toward one another. They have changed the way the employees think about *their* hospital (and they truly feel it is *their* hospital). Leaders have managed to develop an entirely newmind set and culture at this hospital, one built around relationships. Relationships thrive among themselves, from top management through department heads, through supervisors and down to each staff member in each department. And, most importantly, relationships thrive with Bradley's patients. Customer service has become a "state of mind" at Bradley.

You won't find the real answer to improved customer service in patient survey surveillance, canned training programs on customer service, special departments set up to police customer service throughout the organization, or any other of the many and usually ineffective plugged-in approaches. What exists at Bradley are employees who practice excellent customer service because they feel it is the "right thing to do and they want to." In fact, staff seem not even to know they're performing some kind of customer process or procedure. They do what comes naturally. They care about each other and their patients. The caring is sincere and it shows.

That was not always the case at Bradley. The culture began to change when Jim Whitlock assumed the administrative reins in 1990 and began his cultural change. Everyone has come to call it a *culture conversion* because we liken it to a *spiritual conversion* that involves drastic change in *belief*. During the past five years this hospital incorporated a new belief system built on personal relationships, trust, believing in themselves, and believing in the role they play in their jobs.

Over the next three chapters, we will take you through this cultural conversion and the positive impact it had on Bradley's customer service. It is worth studying because the *conversion* can be emulated in most healthcare environments.

CHAPTER

# Unleashing Customer Service through Servant Leadership

**C**ustomer service becomes a reality when employees in an organization virtually become permeated with an attitude of caring for the well-being of others. The key is in their attitude toward others. Their attitude reflects how the employees see themselves and the importance of their role in the success of the organization.

When employees view customer service as an inherent part of their performance, it becomes a natural act, not a "program" based on "technique" or reacting to patient grievances by running down patient survey complaints or nasty letters to the CEO. Good customer relations delivered by all employees all the time is more effective than an effort headed up by a special guest relations department in the hospital whose main task is often to police customer service throughout the organization. Customer service task forces, committees, and focus groups can only identify problems, analyze them, and create ideas to solve them. They cannot *implement* good customer service. Only the employees throughout the organization can actually make it happen day in and day out, month after month, year after year.

A powerful impact is generated in an organization when enough individuals are unified under a common cause such as commitment to customer service. A critical mass is built as individuals catch on to the idea. Soon it seems that more and more employees have the spark of customer service, and the idea spreads throughout the organization. It is at this point that employees question outdated processes and system limitations that everyone could always point to as an excuse for not doing better. Even employees who seemed unmovable in their resistance to change can be won over. Their laments of, "I've been here over 20 years and we've always had the same problems," and "We've been through this before and nothing ever changes," begin to fade when significant improvements are made. Winning resistors over only builds strength to the commitment.

How do managers achieve this employee attitude toward customer service throughout the organization? It starts at the top and works its way down through every department. But it must begin at the top, with the CEO, then to the rest of top executives, on to the department heads, supervisors, and then all the other employees. It begins with a management philosophy and a leadership style that creates openness, trust, and an environment in which employees know they have a voice in the decisions that impact their job. It begins with a CEO that possesses *servant leadership*. In Bradley's case, that person was Jim Whitlock, who joined the hospital as an assistant administrator before becoming the CEO in 1990. Now in his mid-50s, Whitlock cut his teeth on hospital administration with 17 years in the hard-nosed, bottom-line–oriented, for-profit chain of hospitals, Hospital Corporation of America.

However, Whitlock is anything but narrow-minded, hard-nosed, bottom-lined–oriented. He's proven to be firm and acutely tuned into the financial well-being of the hospital with his ability to make tough decisions when he has to and the fact that Bradley has been a highly profitable hospital in the past five years. However, he's much more than a professional at hospital finance. Whitlock's leadership style could best be described as subtle, participative, and patient with a strong, unyielding belief in his fellow human beings. Couple that with a large dose of optimism and the ability to visualize the future, and you might summarize his style as *servant leadership.*

## TAKING SERVANT LEADERSHIP THROUGHOUT THE HOSPITAL

The key issue to address about leadership at Bradley is how Whitlock got his servant leadership mentality beyond himself and his senior staff and implemented throughout the entire hospital. It took several years. He started with his team of senior executives that reported to him. His first objective was to convert their attitude and thinking toward themselves and those who reported directly to them. Whitlock desperately wanted a more participative management style to permeate the organization to replace the stagnating and repugnant autocratic management approach that had prevailed at the hospital for nearly 40 years. Although he didn't know it at the time, his management philosophy and servant philosophy would pave the way for excellent customer service.

Jim stated that he began by developing a close relationship with his senior management team:

> The only thing that really changed in early 1990 was the fact that I was the new administrator and we seemed to meet a whole lot more. In retrospect, I think this was very important. I didn't say we agreed a whole lot more or worked a whole lot more or differently; we just met a whole lot more.

When he met with selected members of his senior staff, Whitlock had identified a core group of seven people: Michael Willis, Lynn Dunlap, Jeannie Roark (ex-controller), Dan

Cooper, Dan Gilbert Dewayne Belew, and Larry Ingram. With the exception of Dewayne Belew, all had preceded him at Bradley by at least four or five years. Although Dan Cooper was hired about the same time Whitlock joined Bradley, he knew there were at least three staff who didn't want him there, three who weren't sure, and one (Dewayne) that he could count on. He had some odds to overcome at senior staff level.

First, Whitlock recommended consistency. Every Tuesday morning senior staff would gather in a conference room at 8:00 AM. They had no agenda beyond what they wanted to discuss. From the beginning, Whitlock took the seat at the head of the table. "In retrospect, I think that was a good move. I considered an alternative position, but decided this gesture of authority was not only traditionally acceptable but was a nonverbal way of ensuring, for their security and peace of mind, that someone would always be there to protect them from themselves and each other."

Although other cumulative meetings were called on somewhat of an ad hoc basis, the Tuesday morning gathering was sacred. It would last four hours and frequently go beyond or even through lunch. It became the "tie that binds." To make it more informal, staff had breakfast served and the first 15 to 20 minutes were dedicated to socializing. Various staff members selected their positions and reported to them each week religiously. No one challenged their selection, but it was obvious to Whitlock that there were some hidden agendas along with a "pecking order" left over from the previous administration.

In retrospect, the benefit of this weekly gathering, unstructured as it was, was that it launched the long trek toward team building. Staff began to evaluate their specific roles and how they blended with each other. They began to "pick their friends" and confide in them outside the system. "I know they evaluated and speculated on my management style and personally, that is essential for an effective leader," Whitlock told us.

Dewayne Belew, the creative, high-energy, young director of marketing and public relations recalled his impression of the beginning of the team-building process under the new CEO.

> I wondered how much things were going to change. Although Jim had been here as associate administrator, he was now *the* Administrator. Right off the bat Jim started pulling the senior management team together as often as possible to discuss a variety of issues. Initially Jim was a strong advocate of Management By Objective and we followed this course of action. Eventually, we discovered that MBO was not the most effective management strategy for us. In all likelihood, we would not have discovered a management style unique to our team had we not committed to spending so much time together and valuing each other's input.

Belew was not sure anyone could calculate the number of hours they spent together in the south conference room on the first floor of the main tower. "The closest guess would be a gazillion hours." In this case, time together meant enhanced awareness of each other's personal style and professional strengths and weaknesses. Senior staff were able to identify the unique talents of their management group as a whole and as individuals. For them, the sum of the whole was truly greater than the parts. They jelled. The chemistry was right. There was synergy. "Any way you want to put it, we were able to bottle the magic," Belew recalled.

## TUESDAY MORNING MEETINGS BECAME LEGENDARY

The Tuesday morning meetings, now legendary throughout the organization, still operate without a formal agenda four years later. Generally speaking, each manager creates his or her own agenda and presents each item for discussion and review when the staff circle the breakfast table.

For the first few months, the meeting was akin to wading into the water with no one wanting to jump in until he/she knew how deep it was. Each of them had things to discuss but needed time to gauge how far to go with each item. The team members came from different academic backgrounds, trained in various schools of management theory, and worked at different levels in their careers.

Today there are no limits, except that senior staff do not allow personal attacks and inconsiderate comments. Each member of the team knows they have the same rights and privileges at the meeting. Each expects the others to discuss each item in a fair and unbiased manner that will allow the team to make the best decision possible. They do not vote on items, although sometimes they talk about each person having one vote. They primarily do this to emphasize the fact that each of them has the same responsibility when it comes to evaluating proposals and the same responsibility for supporting a group decision. Their goal and commitment is to conduct discussions, as heated and passionate as they need to be, and then walk out of the room supporting the team's consensus and the mission of the hospital.

Those Tuesday morning breakfast club meetings were instrumental in the development of a servant leadership style at Bradley Memorial Hospital. The meetings also served as a microstudy of strategies that would foster the development of a hospitalwide management team. As time wore on, other collective meetings were scheduled, not always with the full team but frequently as circumstances warranted. The many issues that had traditionally been passed to the administrator were handed back to the complaining party with directions to meet and consider alternatives and solutions, and report back to "the management team" on Tuesday morning. Everything that affected the operation of the hospital was sent to that Tuesday morning meeting. It became so automatic that staff began to finish a sentence by saying, "I know, bring it to the team on Tuesday."

So senior staff collectively met for specific reasons and not always or solely for the purpose of solving day-to-day problems or for presetting next month or next year's management plan.

## THE BENEFITS OF THE TUESDAY MORNING MEETINGS

Benefits of the consensus-building team sessions were these:

- Exposure.
- Consistency.
- Communication.
- Socialization.
- Group interaction.
- Development of self-confidence and elimination of the fear of failure.

There were other benefits, but these were the necessary elements for team building, developing relationships, and creating the servant leadership among the senior staff. In addition, there were individual meetings. It has been our experience that most hospital CEOs hold collective meetings but only practice making decisions during individual meetings. It is not difficult to see the negative implications of this double standard. And if not watched carefully, the individual meetings soon sabotage the collective meetings and destroy the integrity of the team.

## ELIMINATING EMPLOYEE FEAR

So how did Whitlock structure individual meetings the first year of his administration?

> Very carefully. You see, some people were beating the door down to see me privately, while others avoided me in the hallway. Why? I would ask myself. The answer was—*fear*! You should recall that I had been exposed to all of these individuals for at least two years and most for three-and-a-half before becoming CEO. You would

think this to be a plus for them. How many staff members have three years to evaluate an individual who suddenly becomes the "Boss." If I had only just arrived, I could have understood their fear. In my mind I was no different than before I got the job. Why were they so afraid of me?

Eliminating this fear was a high priority for Whitlock. Although he wanted the team to feel comfortable making decisions without his input and to increase their confidence, he realized this could pose great hazards in certain circumstances. So they agreed the following rule of thumb would be applied. When an individual was placed in the position of making a major decision, by their definition of *major* (what was their comfort level in making the decision), they would ask themselves one question, "What's going to happen if I don't do anything right now?" The emphasis was placed on "right now." This was the philosophy on which Whitlock based his individual meetings. It began to give credit to the team in the eyes of the employees and it began to give credit and self-confidence to individuals on the management team. Fear was beginning to fade.

Here's a summary of Whitlock's steps during his first six to nine months on the job as CEO that would set the foundation for successful customer service later on:

1. Identification of the management team; who the players would be.
2. The mechanism by which they would communicate. What meetings they would have, and when they would have them; how they would be conducted.
3. The development of an annual management plan and a financial budget.
4. The coordinated efforts to continue the strategic plan that had been to a superficial level developed in 1989–90 and was now ready to be incorporated into the annual budget and management plan. It

now needed to be expanded to a site facility and a financial feasibility level.

5. A change in the relationship with the members of the board and the reporting of the management team at the regular board meeting. It also involved development of a unique relationship with department heads and supervisors to support and endorse the work that lay ahead for the long range plan.

At this point in the management development process, there was never any consideration as to how care would be delivered. There was never any consideration realistically of cultural change or philosophically changing how things were done. The evolution was just a matter of taking positions and letting team members learn more about each other. That took six to nine months to accomplish, but by the end of that period, every person on that senior team knew what Whitlock's style was; what his management philosophy was; and that it was probably credible.

## DEVELOPING RELATIONSHIP WITH THE COMMUNITY

It was now time for Whitlock to begin developing a second relationship. That was the relationship with their community and with their county commissioners. In late 1989, the concept of a foundation became much more interesting to the board of trustees than it had ever been before. In late 1990, Jim began to pursue a formal foundation effort. Between July 1990 and the spring of 1991, formal efforts to create a foundation began to take place and ultimately an executive director, initially hired in a consulting capacity, was brought on board and made a permanent member of the management team.

By the end of the first year, a group of fairly comprehensive community representatives had been selected to help with the foundation and the board's enthusiasm over-flowed to the foundation's enthusiasm, and this group began to grow. This was an extremely important part of the customer service program. By early 1991, the foundation was beginning to grow, the strategic plan and its affiliated plans of financial feasibility and space planning were in place, architects and engineers had been selected, and team members were prepared to go to the county commission to begin this process.

At the end of several months, a collective meeting of all the county commissioners, the county executive, the local press, Whitlock's management team, his board members, and others launched what would be ultimately a $34-million major renovation and building plan for the hospital. Shortly thereafter, the county commission approved the largest bond issue in the history of the county at $6.7 million for the first phase of their project.

By early 1991, a third relationship began. Bradley leaders began talking about *guest services,* a new customer service culture, and how it could be achieved. Members of Whitlock's board, and specifically their board chairman, were motivated by the concept of guest services and had even expressed interest in having a mystery patient come to the hospital to evaluate the quality of their service and report to the management where the facility might improve. "He encouraged us to locate people who might do this. Quite honestly, that was difficult to do, but over a period of four to six months we were able to locate that individual; as you know this mystery patient was Dave Gorden," Jim told us.

The senior staff also began to talk about how much progress they, as a management team, had made in their relationship. They began to openly talk about the credibility of their relationship, the strength of working together, the trust they had developed, and all the important things that came along with this long-range strategic plan and the meetings associated with it. The weekly Tuesday sessions had been the medium within which they could work to develop this trust and this credibility. But their concern now was, how do they get this to the department head level? It was at this point Whitlock realized the issue was not how they *should* do it, but what was *keeping them* from doing it.

## "BURYING ADMINISTRATION"

It occurred to Whitlock one day that the problem was *administration*.

> No matter where I went throughout the facility, it was not difficult to learn that "We can't do that because *administration* won't approve it," or "If we do this, *administration* may not like it" or "*Administration* doesn't allow this or they won't approve that or we can't do this, we can't do that because of *administration*," and it became apparent to me that we needed to get rid of *administration*.

Whitlock needed to effectively "bury administration." The next day he talked with Dewayne Belew about his crazy idea of "burying administration." Whitlock said, "Why don't you guys get together and think of a good way we could bury administration and make our point that we don't want administration to be a barrier any longer to our success?" Dewayne and Dan Gilbert, assistant administrator, came back to Whitlock with an idea that is probably not unique, but it was certainly a turning point in their relationship with those department heads and supervisors who worked with senior management. They decided they would videotape a funeral and bury administration in the process and that they would allow Whitlock the privilege of explaining to everyone why they had to bury administration as it now existed.

In order to present this "funeral," they had the first management retreat/educational conference of the hospital. Approximately 40 employees were invited to attend that first management retreat, and the attendees had absolutely no idea why they were being invited out of town for three days by senior management. When they arrived in Gatlinburg in 1991 and sat down to attend the opening presentation, they were greeted by a large-screen television set. On that the screen suddenly appeared an image of a graveyard with the administrator Jim Whitlock and funeral music being played in the background while the CEO walked through the graveyard.

As he stopped at an appropriate grave marker, Whitlock began to explain to the department heads and managers that the administrator could not join them today because he had to stay behind and conduct a funeral process that should not be perceived as sad, but rather be celebrated as a wake in the changing healthcare environment. He began to explain the need for change, the need for the redesign of the way staff deliver healthcare, and a change in the attitudes they have among those with whom they work. At the end of this presentation, the entire senior management team (eight of them) marched from behind a screen dressed in football uniforms and other appropriate garb and proceeded to pantomime a prerecorded rap demonstrating their various roles and responsibilities as senior management and projecting the need for team work, how they work together, and what they're going to do.

Basically they satirized themselves while making a point. Whitlock described it:

> We brought ourselves down to a level of humanness that this group of department heads had never experienced. At the termination of our presentation each one of us reached into a basket located at the front and we sailed tiny footballs labeled as the Bradley Memorial Management Team and we solicited their support in the development and growth of that team. To suggest that this was an ice breaker would be a significant understatement! For the remaining two days, they concentrated on the importance of team work and team building and

working together and it began an avalanche of opportunities among this group of people that has never slowed.

Lynn Dunlap, assistant administrator of nursing, remembers that management retreat as the turning point for the hospital:

> I believe the rapid changes started with that management retreat in 1991. At that meeting the administrative team decided that we wanted to be the preferred employer for healthcare in our region and we wanted to be the regional medical center! That's when we started to work toward the goal of employee buy-in. We worked on benefits and salaries. We started working with managers to develop their talents. We started involving employees in decision making. TQM began to be in vogue and we started developing our own version of TQM. TQM matched our management philosophy.

Craig Taylor, associate administrator and CFO, joined Bradley just as the new culture evolved in 1990:

> When I arrived in 1990, I found a culture that I perceived to be in transition. The most obvious to me was the change from a "not-for-profit" hospital to a hospital that strove to increase its profitability without sacrificing its mission. In order to achieve our profitability goals, we had to bring our employees into a new management philosophy that allowed participation in decision making. We began to accomplish this change gradually, but it began with our first management retreat when we buried administration.

Staff were truly becoming a family at Bradley Memorial Hospital. Barriers that created the fears and affected the creativity that reduced the productivity were slowly melting away along with the exterior facades that were so human to each of their personalities. They also began to expose this administrative staff to the new concepts of management being tossed about in the industry, specifically TQM/CQI, and the team-building concept itself. These strategies created a forum around which the staff could continue to develop this team-building attitude, this cultural relationship with the employees of the hospital, at least at the administrative staff level.

## THE SAGA OF THE MYSTERY PATIENT

At about this time, the mystery patient paid a visit and a format was established for Customer Service Excellence through the Guest Excellence Task Force. The Guest Excellence Task Force provided an opportunity to develop some programs that would also satisfy the management goal of trying to promote this culture more deeply into the organization. Bradley's managers had spent the remainder of 1991 and all of 1992 concentrating on the administrative staff and supervisors at the department head levels, getting the team-building concept more or less adopted. They felt comfortable this was on its way. The team wanted to look at ways to further penetrate the organization with this culture.

The employee reorientation process gave Bradley's leaders an opportunity to bring all of the employees to a common point and discuss with them the mission of the hospital, pointing out the goals and objectives of the hospital. Managers also began to meet with selected employees, not at any supervisory level but just employees at a level of care giving and invite them to lunch with the administrator. They covered this on all three shifts throughout 1993 and early 1994. This was an effective way of using the grapevine to communicate the philosophies of not only the hospital but also the administrator, and this move gained attention and perhaps established some credibility in their relationship as a management team.

The task force came up with a concept used by staff trainers at Walt Disney World for employees, and from that picked up on the possibility of developing Bradley University, which would serve as a vehicle by which leaders would not only teach management skills but also communicate their vision of a serving culture and their team-building philosophy. "You may recall that my philosophy about management is that a manager has one responsibility and that is to identify what people do well and to give them an opportunity to do it," Whitlock explained. Bradley University offered the opportunity to take employees at the care-giving level, expose them to opportunities of promotion, opportunities of transition that would be more suited to their personalities, and ones more suited to their personal development needs. Although it's early in the implementation of Bradley University to confirm outcomes, there is marked enthusiasm among those who have completed the courses.

As it turned out, 1993 was a year of transition with employees as well as administrative staff. "I felt a much stronger relationship for the department heads. Our budgeting processes were much smoother. Our projections on budgeting were very accurate. We continued to reserve cash. We did an excellent job with our financial indicators. We were gaining strength with our board, our community, our foundation; and there were numerous celebrations with all of these groups," Whitlock explained.

Philosophically, staff were shedding the management-by-objectives (MBO) cloak. They were emphasizing the TQM task force concepts. They were training facilitators, talking about Bradley University, working into the Guest Excellence relationship, and reorienting employees to these concepts. All of 1993 was designed to bring the employees in the relative departments up to speed with administrative management, the department heads, and senior supervisors. By 1993, the one-day brainstorming session that began as the management team retreat had moved to a two-day session. This made the opportunity to build their team even stronger.

## TRANSFORMING THE EMERGENCY ROOM INTO A "SUPER DEPARTMENT"

In 1994, Bradley's leaders began to talk seriously about the reengineering concepts of the hospital. Although managers really didn't know what reengineering was, they began to use terms like *Super Department;* began to look for people within the administrative management team who could help design and develop relationships to support a Super Department. Their educational efforts were directed toward rethinking their management plan, getting away from MBO and even possibly TQM/CQI concepts, and modifying them or customizing them a bit more (but most assuredly in budgeting).

As 1994 came to a close, the renovation of the emergency department (ED) was high priority. This department had demonstrated the opportunity for team building and working together. They were forced to remodel 10,000 square feet of the second busiest emergency center in the southeast United States. Task forces that had been trained to function and operate under the previous TQM systems pulled it off without a hitch. As 1995 began, leaders continued to see the benefit of their early efforts developing their management team. Whitlock summed it up:

> We also see some problems that we are having to address as we become more and more accustomed to working in this environment with each other and we become more used to each other. We begin to take each other more for granted and we also begin to second guess each other in terms of what we do and what we don't do. These are things we've had to transition to as well.

So now, after five years of learning how to work together, Bradley's leaders now emphasize how they *keep* working together and how they *remain* supportive team members as well as friends in this whole relationship.

Craig Taylor, associate administrator, looks at it this way: "The key to this change in culture basically boils down to relationships. If you can develop an honest, trusting, mutually beneficial relationship with your staff, then there is nothing your organization can't accomplish. The key to our success has been relationships."

We told Jim Whitlock we were going to try to explain how his servant leadership style laid the groundwork for successful customer relations at Bradley. We told him we were going to try to "put a box around" the concept so the readers of this book could determine how to emulate what worked so well at this hospital. His response was,

> You have asked me on more than one occasion what the cookie cutter concept is that has created the environment you experienced during your visit, which has resulted in the successes we have enjoyed at Bradley Memorial Hospital over the past five years. My response to you has been consistently *relationships*. I understand this is not what people want to read in a book. It's really too simple. It's also at the same time too complex to be a good answer, but it must begin there. As we talk about penetrating culture, what we're really talking about doing is developing relationships so that they can in effect change the culture. Unfortunately, the need to transition and to change culture takes a great deal of time, and providers in healthcare don't have a great deal of time.

CHAPTER

# Focus on Customer Service

About the same time Bradley Memorial Hospital was changing the management culture and beginning to empower the employees in a variety of ways, their focus also zeroed in on customer service. It was like two major culture conversions going on at the same time: internally with employees and externally with healthcare customers. Actually, the nudge toward the customer service focus came from the hospital board chairman, Sam Bettis. While driving home together from a meeting in early 1991, Bettis suggested to Jim Whitlock that the hospital look into finding someone to pose as a patient and investigate the facility's customer service first hand. Whitlock, in turn, turned the project of finding someone who did such investigations over to Lynn Dunlap, assistant administrator and director of nursing. She found that someone in Dave Gorden, a healthcare consultant specializing in customer service.

In June 1991 a patient was routinely admitted to the hospital. As far as everyone at the hospital was concerned, his admission was no different from any of the thousands made throughout the years. However, this patient was actually a hired professional who had been a mystery patient in some 35 hospitals (a total now exceeding 50) throughout the United States for more than 11 years. "It was very difficult to keep this a secret, but we knew the entire purpose of his hospital stay would be defeated if too many people knew," said Dunlap. The imposter's mission at Bradley was to evaluate every aspect of the hospital from finding the correct place to park, to discharge arrangements, and discussion of his final bill. The "sting" operation would conclude on the Tuesday following his weekend stay with the patient's true identity revealed and a full report presented by the mystery patient Dave Gorden to all hospital department heads and managers at an off-site retreat. "My only concern was that I did not want our staff or physicians to think we were merely trying to catch things being done wrong," Dunlap said. "That was not our objective. Our objective was to lay the groundwork for changing the hospital's culture."

While at the hospital, the mystery patient encountered the same types of experiences that happen every day in hospitals everywhere. To document his stay, Gorden took copious notes when staff members were not present. Although he found isolated areas in need of improvement, he also discovered exceptional examples of customer service. "We found some departments that were doing a superb job," Dunlap stated. "At the same time, we discovered some areas where there were opportunities for changing our systems and providing additional training for our employee."

Gorden recalled what led up to the hospital stay and his three-day inpatient experience:

> I always tell a hospital administrator I'm not going to tell you what you want to hear, I'm going to tell you what you need to know. Jim was very open to that. When I was discharged three days later, as is my practice, the CEO and I go out to lunch somewhere and talk about the

experience. I asked Jim, "How do you want me to handle it at the department head meeting tomorrow?" He said, "I want you to handle it the way it happened. I want them to hear it and I want you to share it."

Gorden presented his findings in a positive, upbeat manner to the senior staff and department heads at a management retreat, never skirting the negative experiences but discussing them as *systems* problems, not *individual* shortcomings. At the conclusion of the meeting, the senior staff and all department heads agreed that the next step should be creating a culture where all employees, volunteers, and physicians were treated like "guests." The theory behind this was if the staff and volunteers were well treated and recognized for their efforts, patients would be the ultimate beneficiary, because the treatment would be repeated. It set the foundation for what would follow— improved employee relationships and improved customer service.

## DEVELOPMENT OF THE GUEST EXCELLENCE TASK FORCE

Based on the consultant's report and information gained at the retreat, the hospital put together a special group of employees they called the Guest Excellence Task Force. Department heads and supervisors who wanted to volunteer for the Task Force were asked to submit a one-page letter stating why they wanted to be a member. From the letters submitted, 10 people from various departments were chosen. Jim Whitlock was not a member of the task force, which turned out to be a good decision.

Dave Gorden explained Whitlock's nonrole on the task force:

> Jim really wanted to be on this task force. But let me qualify this—there was nothing that ever went on—that a conclusion was reached that Jim does not know about. When we had discussions and a little dynamic tension, I said the group recommends that, or we'd like to do such

and such. We certainly never excluded him, and he did
get a report on every meeting. However, it would hamper
the procedure if the administrator were in the meeting.
Jim trusted us, but he's a hands-on kind of guy—he
really wanted to be there.

At the task force's first meeting, a consensus was
reached that internal guests—employees, volunteers, and
physicians—initially would be the primary focus of all task
force work. This was a key decision and in keeping with the
culture change going on with the employees. "If we do not
treat each other with respect and show courtesy toward one
another, how can we expect to change the hospital's culture? By focusing on our internal guests, we would make
dramatic changes in the way we serve our patients. You can
still feel how things are improving," Dunlap explained.

During the course of the first year, the task force
implemented four Guest Excellence focused projects:

• In the first month, task force members conducted
the enormous task of reorientation sessions for 1,159 hospital employees and volunteers. During the three-hour
sessions, participants were informed about the hospital's
mission, the new 12-point Guest Excellence creed, and asked
to complete a 24-question fun-but-educational quiz about
the hospital.

Near the end of each session, each participant was
presented with a new hospital name badge that featured
the employee's or volunteer's face, their full name, title, and
their first name in print large enough to be seen from 20
feet away. "Putting our names out there for everyone to see
does two things. First, anyone we encounter can quickly
identify us. Second, when you realize that everyone knows
who you are there is incentive to do the best you can,"
Dunlap explained.

Reorientation turned out not to be a one-time event.
The task force regularly evaluates the program's content so
when presented to new employees and volunteers each

month, the information is current and consistent. Additionally, a hospitalwide reorientation for all employees and volunteers was conducted again by the former mystery patient.

Prior to concluding each session, each employee was asked to sign a large sign that stated in bold letters, "I Am Committed to Guest Excellence at Bradley Memorial Hospital." Following the classroom reorientation, each group was taken on a one-hour tour of the hospital, with special emphasis placed on areas of new technology and departments not usually seen.

• To immediately recognize true Guest Excellence, Applause-A-Grams were produced. It was determined that this award could be passed to anyone who was deemed worthy of recognition. The second program, called Bunny Bucks, recognized Guest Excellence and included a financial reward. Anyone who received Bunny Bucks (similar to Disney Dollars and featuring the hospital's mascot, Brad Lee Bunny) could cash them in for a free meal in the hospital cafeteria or a discount in the hospital giftshop. Catchers were identified on each shift throughout the hospital. These were the individuals who observed and rewarded employees they caught in the act of some aspect of favorable customer service. Additionally, all persons who were caught each month were eligible for a cash award. At the end of the year, the names of all "caught" persons were placed in a drawing to receive a vacation of their choice.

• The hospital began hosting grassroots meetings between the hospital administrator and 12 employees randomly chosen from different departments.

## IMMEDIATE IMPROVEMENT IN GUEST EXCELLENCE

Was Bradley's work over the first year successful or worth the workhours spent brainstorming, developing, fine tuning, implementing, and monitoring this Guest Excellence process? Morale was up (based on a SESCO employee opinion survey). Patient complaints were down. The hospital had its best financial year since it opened in 1952. The facility completed the largest construction project in the hospital's history. More new physicians joined the hospital staff in 1991–92. By many standards, the answer was an astounding yes.

Lynn Dunlap explained to us that the focus on improved customer service was triggered by the mystery patient experience:

> Part of all this activity was the mystery patient experience. I was fortunate to find someone with a positive attitude, motivational speaking skills, and the ability to help us develop customer service programs to sell our philosophy. If the mystery patient experience had been presented in a negative fashion or the "I've got you attitude," the outcome would have set us back five years.

However, the customer service programs are just a small piece of it. Programs are just a way of internal marketing. Internal marketing is very important but pales in comparison to living the philosophy. *Living* the philosophy is the key. Employees are valued and are considered to be team members. How can that not help but spill over to customers? Most people are in the healthcare field because they really want to help people. Bradley has proven that if you create the environment for employees to do that, the customer service naturally follows.

In 1994, the Guest Relations Task Force unveiled Bradley University. Bradley University is a comprehensive management training program—the only one of its kind at a healthcare organization as far as Bradley has been able to determine. The program offers managers and aspiring managers the opportunity for professional and personal growth and development. Dave Gorden recalled the birth of the idea for the Bradley University:

It was something that Jim Whitlock had seen as a need, and I think this is true everywhere in healthcare. What we tend to do in healthcare is we take good clinicians and technicians and promote them to management, but we don't *train* them to be management. And so, many times they fail. We do that in industry as well, but it's really rampant in healthcare. We take someone who was a good technician and we make him a manager. Now they no longer get to do the technical aspects, but they have to manage other people and get results with and through other people. They don't know how because we never trained them.

We asked Jim Whitlock at what point he realized who the hospital's customer is. Did he know that from the beginning?

You know something? And I said this to the president of HCA one time. HCA's mission statement way back when I started 11 years ago, was to have a fair return to the shareholder. That was it. I believe you do what this hospital does. They talk about quality of care, they talk about commitment to their team members, internally first, and then externally, they talk about guest excellence. Some organizations say, the way we're going to make a profit is we're going to cut your hours back, we're going to lay you off. Now go out there and take good care of our patients. It won't happen. The commitment has to be internally to employees first.

The bottom line is that Bradley understood that until staff take care of the internal customer, they can never take care of the external customer. And the commitment here is to the internal customer.

## PUBLIC RELATIONS PRIMARY STRATEGIES

With the hospital's commitment to enhancing customer service within the organization, managers have allocated about 40 percent of the marketing and public relations budget to internal education, marketing, communications, and celebrations. Although they focused a great deal of effort to the development of their internal market, at the same time managers enhanced their efforts in the external market. The primary strategies they followed included improved media relations, paid advertising, and community outreach programs and education. All of these strategies had one objective: heightened awareness about the Bradley Memorial Hospital staff, facility improvements, state-of-the-art technology, role in the community as a "good" neighbor, and healthy growth of the medical staff.

The hospital positioned itself through a major marketing campaign as being the medical center that is "Miles Ahead. Minutes Away." In these four words Bradley attempted to take advantage of its centralized location in the market (minutes away). Through Miles Ahead the staff attempted to communicate the fact that their people are advanced in training and compassion and their facility and technology are state-of-the-art. This campaign has served as the basis for all of Bradley's advertising since 1992. For the campaign the marketing people created a musical identity that says a great deal about Bradley. The tune is up-tempo with instrumentals and vocals:

> Something is happening,
> Medicine's moving at a rapid pace.
> Technology's changing.
> A better Bradley is built today.
> Bradley Memorial Hospital. Miles Ahead. Minutes Away.
> Caring for your family.
> Bradley Memorial,
> Miles Ahead. Minutes Away.

By focusing on customer service in a variety of ways and by having two "customers"—the employee and the patient—Bradley certainly seems miles ahead of most providers in excelling in customer relations.

## GUEST EXCELLENCE CREED AT BRADLEY MEMORIAL

1. I am a team player. As a member of the team, I provide with care and concern the professional service that my guests deserve.

   Guest Excellence takes the effort of all team members at Bradley Memorial Hospital. You are a very important player on this team. No matter what your job title may be, it takes all of us, working together, every day, in every way, to provide the very best service.

2. I speak to my guests with my voice and my eyes. I handle complaints without becoming defensive.

   Every complaint is an opportunity. It means that something is not just as it should be and we have a chance to make it right. A pleasant tone of voice goes a long way in helping our guests know that we really do care.

3. I smile at my guests to show that I welcome them and to help put them at ease.

   A friendly smile lets everyone know that we want him/her to feel good. It also tells others that we are happy to be there to help them. (By the way, you burn up 10 calories every time you smile.)

4. I listen to my guests with my ears, my eyes—in fact with all of my body, except my voice. Even if it's "Not my job," I will *help* or *find someone who can.*

   Our guests don't always tell us exactly what is bothering them; we should always look at them when they are speaking to us. We must always do whatever it takes to make our guests happy.

5. I introduce myself to my guests and explain what I am doing and why, to reduce anxiety.

   People are often afraid of what they don't understand. By telling a guest who you are and what

*(Continued)*

you are going to do, it helps them know that you are a concerned professional.

6. I am always considerate of the feelings of my guests, and I don't talk about my guests or their case in public places. I do everything in my power to respect their dignity.

   A guest who overhears part of a conversation may think that you are talking about them or someone in their family. We always want everyone to know that we respect his/her privacy.

7. I am courteous to my guests by allowing them to go first through doors and into elevators and by keeping the halls as quiet as possible.

   The Golden Rule really does work; "we should always do unto others as we would have them do unto us."

8. I am alert to give service, directions, and assistance. I anticipate the needs of my guests.

   If we see people who look like they need help, let's smile at them and offer to assist them. Remember, our hospital is very large and it is often difficult to find certain areas.

9. I always call guests by name, because they deserve my personal attention.

   A person's name is the sweetest, most important sound he/she hears. Let's call our fellow team members by name whenever possible. Look at their ID badge and use their name; you will be surprised at how good we can make each other feel.

10. I project a caring attitude.

    We are in the healthcare profession because we sincerely care about other people. We must always do everything we can to let people know we care. "People do not care how much you know, until they know how much you care."

*(Concluded)*

11. I look the part by dressing professionally in a manner appropriate to my position.

   We must demonstrate the pride that we feel for our hospital and the pride that we take in ourselves with the image that we project. Our outside appearance projects the image of our team.

12. I always treat my guests with care, imagining that I am on the receiving end. I will care for my guests as though they were my family or friends.

   Once again, the Golden Rule applies. Always ask yourself, if this were my mother or father, brother or sister, what would I do? That goes for all of our guests, including our fellow team members.

## SPECIFIC CUSTOMER SERVICE ACTIONS AND TIME FRAMES

### Before the Mystery Patient

1985: Get Nice classes: A video was shown about a patient named Joe Green. A facilitator led a discussion about what a difference staff could have made in his hospital stay. Was not a big hit with the employees. Too superficial.

1987: Get Nice classes held for the emergency department. Outside facilitator attempted to aid staff in dealing with upset customers, but the employee evaluations of the program were generally stated: "You don't understand what we are dealing with."

1990: Emergency department held group therapy sessions with an outside facilitator to deal with problems related to ER guest relations and supervisor relations on a feeling level. These were termed somewhat successful in that at least the staff did feel "heard."

## After the Mystery Patient

| | |
|---|---|
| March 1991: | Management retreat: First formal efforts at team building and making managers feel special. |
| June 1991: | Mystery patient entered hospital. Retreat held with department managers to discuss findings. |
| July 1991: | Requested letters from managers interested in Guest Excellence Task Force. |
| August 1991 through February 1992: | Task force developed guest excellence creed and reorientation program. |
| March 1992: | Task force worked on catcher program. |
| April 1992: | Management retreat, continued to focus on team building, cooperation, and front-line involvement. Reinforced that Guest Excellence must begin with each other and it will naturally flow to external customers. |
| May 1992: | Implemented catcher program. |
| June 1992: | Visited by another hospital to review Bradley's rapid progress. |
| August 1992: | Implemented grassroots meetings. |
| September 1992 to March 1993: | Task force changed the catcher program. Balloon bouquets were the reward for getting caught beginning in July. |

| | |
|---|---|
| July 1993: | Reorientation in July to keep the momentum up. |
| | The task force began developing Bradley University in order to give managers the tools to enable them to be even better managers. |
| September 1993: | New catchers oriented and in place. New Bunny Bucks program in place by July 1994. |
| April 1994: | Bradley University concept presented to department heads at Educational Conference. |
| August 1994: | Developed float design for ER parade. |
| October 1994: | Bradley University began classes. |
| March 1995: | Objectives for guest relations outlined for upcoming year. |
| May 1995: | Action plan developed for objectives. |

CHAPTER

# Sanction Employees to Serve—Mind, Body, and Soul

The beauty of the success of customer service at Bradley Memorial Hospital is the way it is "practiced" by employees throughout the organization. During our week-long visit at the hospital, we interviewed all the senior management staff, most of the department heads, some supervisors, several board members, and many nonmanagement employees. We walked the halls, sat in the waiting rooms, ate in the cafeteria, and lingered in the lobby. What we found was a genuine fixation about patient satisfaction and how important it was in employees' roles.

They live it mind, body, and soul.

Our conclusion is that truly successful customer service can be accomplished when employees feel good about themselves and their jobs *first*. Attempts to sandwich customer service around disgruntled, uninspired, unenthusiastic employees will likely fall apart. Employees will see the sandwich approach as another flavor-of-the-month or view customer service as another "program" hospital administration is pushing on the employees. They say, "Take care of me first and I'll take good care of the patient and all aspects of customer service for you. I'll do it because I want to, not because you want me to." What employees universally want from their employer and senior management is a chance to have input into the decision-making process, and acknowledgment of their contribution; in short, to be needed, heard, and cared about. They want to be listened to and have action taken on their concerns.

When that's accomplished, employees fall all over themselves to provide excellent customer service—particularly if the organization shines its headlights on customer service and repeats over and over how important it is and the reasons why. The employee actually becomes *sanctioned* to or empowered (there's that overused word again) to serve the patient in a fashion that goes far beyond the norm. Customer service becomes something that comes naturally. It is a natural extension of their thought process, and their actions play out their beliefs.

These conclusions really don't sound complicated. Achieving customer service goals does take time, though. It is definitely not a quick-fix approach. It is not complicated; however, it's not practiced at most of the hospitals and clinics in which we worked as consultants. This approach may not be described as the "normal" path most providers take to improve customer service, but it certainly is effective. More providers should concentrate on empowering or sanctioning employees to exercise care and concern for their customers on their own terms so employees develop an ownership in the process. It is the truest form of customer service.

## HOW GOOD CUSTOMER SERVICE PERMEATES THE ENTIRE HOSPITAL

In preceding chapters we have spelled out the process that led to excellent customer service at Bradley—how it started with a management cultural conversion coupled with a concentrated focus on customer service. But the final piece of the puzzle is how the practice of good customer service permeates through the employees in the organization. The many interviews we had with department heads, supervisors, and employees reflect the notion that good customer service takes place at all levels. We sensed employees felt empowered to do what had to be done. We have chosen a few representative interviews that best reflected the employees' responses.

## Nursing Manager

Edna Shepherd, RN, nursing supervisor of 4N at Bradley, told us, "That was one of the things when we first started: that they were talking about empowering the managers, that we had to be educated to begin to realize that this really is our niche; that we are really responsible, really are in charge, really have some authority, and really have a voice." A nursing veteran, Shepherd told us she slowly began to change the way she managed. "I think our staff had to see it from us . . . it changed the way I manage . . . I mean, literally. Because I have a strong personality, I'm an authoritarian, and I thought, do I really want to be the kind of person who treats my staff that way?"

We asked Edna Shepherd to tell us about the transition for her as a manager and her approach toward her employees and theirs to the patients and their families. What promoted the transition, and how did it change her management style? She replied, "I think part of it was the change of philosophy from upper management. There was a whole change of philosophy. Suddenly they are sharing things with us that they had never shared before. They were looking at me as capable of doing more than I had ever done before . . . they were looking at me differently . . . so I began to look at myself differently."

Shepherd thought the feedback from the patient surveys also had an impact on the employees' focus on patient satisfaction. "Another thing that helped us perceive was the patient survey . . . when they started to put out the patient survey and we started to get back what people were really saying about us. It was a little startling, but it had a big impact on me. All of a sudden I'm looking at this differently . . . because you can hear rumblings and my staff saying, 'They just drove us crazy the whole time they were here.' Now we were hearing it for the first time from our patient's perspective or their family's perspective," she explained.

Shepherd described her feelings about what the patients were saying:

> In the beginning it was hard for me because I was still in this codependent management relationship style that I was responsible for everybody, and it made me feel as if I was a really poor manager because my staff wasn't "at par," they weren't doing what they should do. In the beginning it was mind-boggling for me. But, as I really got to look at it—it's really funny because I teach over-coming codependency classes—I had never placed codependency in the workplace. All of a sudden I'm saying to myself, "You made a lot of changes in your home or whatever, but you're as codependent in the workplace as anything I've ever seen."

We inquired how she perceived that she was codependent in this situation. "Because I took on total responsibility for the actions of my staff. As long as I took on total responsibility nobody else could grow. I couldn't grow as the middle-manager as long as upper-management had total responsibility. People can't grow unless you take down some walls. You have to be able to make mistakes, you have to be able to learn, and I've made some. I've made some good ones. But I'm still here." As her management style changed, the defensive barriers toward patient criticism came down. Shepherd and her staff began to look at patient complaints in a different light:

I think our staff meetings changed. We started to talk about the comments in the patient surveys and going over them. Then we would talk about situations and we began to really look at what we can do to improve. We actually started to look at it in a different way, trying not to be so defensive. You can never see your own mistakes in an accurate light as long as you're defensive.

We asked Shepherd how she and her employees conquered defensiveness and resistance to change:

In the beginning I think my staff thought I was kind of cruel, because what I would do is play devil's advocate. For instance, if they started griping about patient complaints, I'd say, "Yes, but look at it from their side." I think it was a matter of education. In some cases we actually sent nurses to the pharmacy to visit for three or four hours. They watched them work and saw what they had to do. They had to cross over those lines so they could better understand each other. We sent some nurses to admitting, watching the process, watching what happens there. Those were some of the things that were done. I really think it was like a gradual education-type thing.

Another (nonmanagement) nursing employee told us, "When all the changes in guest excellence were going on, I was still a staff person at that time and it was no big flash for me. I remember when the emphasis on Guest Relations first came out it was kind of a joke—we had the first 'revival' meeting. As things kept on, there was a gradual change. We stopped looking at the patients as causing us problems."

## Nursing Staff

One of the more direct, open discussions we had was with Gary Thomas, a recovery room RN. A large, well-built man with a dark beard speckled with gray, Thomas told us he had been with the hospital a long time and had seen the change in culture and attitudes toward fellow employees and patients. We asked him to discuss customer service and patient satisfaction from his point of view.

> I know if you treat people with respect and treat them how you would like to be treated it works a lot better and you get things done. The families feel better and the patients feel better, but sometimes it's still hard for me to do this.
>
> If you are going to do this, you have to gain the patients' confidence, you have to gain their trust. You have to be nice. I think sometimes you can even fake it. If you have to do that, fine. It gets to be a habit and gets to be where you are sincere. I'm not a cheerleader, but I have reached the stage if I decide to stay in nursing, I'm going to have to change.

We asked Thomas why he thought he had to change:

> To be able to exist and have a job and to even have a hospital we're going to have to change and that scares me . . . and that has to do with money, job security, and all of that. Now things are changing to where I might not get to work five days a week if our census is low. I've got to remember I've been told to be flexible, and as I get older I'm not that flexible. So I'm going to have to change. The big difference we've seen and learned is that through guest excellence we can get our work done a lot better if we just take families in on the front line, teach them what they need to know, try to settle their fears and deal with it from there. Patients are so much more aware of things they weren't two to five years ago. They expect a certain amount of things and a certain amount of information and help.

We wanted Thomas' thoughts about how the value of the employee was increased. The organizational culture at Bradley indicated that if the employees feel good about their jobs, feel that they have a lot more input in decision-making processes, and have bought into the culture as far down as senior management can take it, that employees will do the tasks that they sense are important, not only clinically but also in customer service. Thomas summarized it:

> It will work. It took us a while . . . this is so new, and nurses do not want to change. At first I thought it was a bunch of hooey and sometimes I still do, but I think it's one of those things you really believe in, even if we do have to fake it for a while until it starts working.

Thomas reflects the whole idea that if employees feel better about their jobs as employees in the front-line, customer service improves. He concluded: "I think it filters down . . . and you start to develop that feeling, an attitude toward your work and kind of the spiritual, emotional thing. You show it, other people sense it."

## Medical Records and Laboratory Staff

As we tried to get the employees to describe their experiences during the culture conversion, we had an interesting exchange with Nancy Dees, medical records director, and Gail Ownby, cardiac cath labs.

Here are the highlights of that interview:

*Q:* If you were to compare the customer service that you had five or six years ago (10 is high, 1 is low), what would the score be then, and how would you score it today?

*A: Probably a 4 and a 9.9.*

*Q:* How do you go from a 4 to a 9.9? Can you tell me in a paragraph? Summarize it? What are the major ingredients?

*A: I think Guest Excellence starts with an intelligent person who recognizes potential in employees.*

*Q:* But how did it go from a 4 to a 9.9?

*A: I think one of the things was establishing relationships. Walls came down.*

*Q:* What does it have to do with guest relations,
though? You're saying generally the difference is
that administration is open, the walls came
down. But what does that have to do with guest
relations?

*A: If all of us are happy, challenged, doing a good
job . . . we are more capable of practicing good
customer service. You can't do it in steps, you
can't one–two–three it. You can't give, step one
this will happen. Step two this is what happens.*

*Q:* Did you feel differently? Did you, yourselves,
others around you, your peers, feel differently
toward the patient, in a sense?

*A: Well, I think part of it is giving ownership to
the employee. Remember, Guest Excellence is
everyone's responsibility. Suddenly, we're allowed
some freedom. You could speak your mind. We
were given ownership. The first thing you do is
give employees ownership of their lives. Once you
give them ownership of their lives, leadership is
easy. You set parameters, you set the deadlines,
you tell them what has to be done, when, and how
many days you've got to get it done, and give
them ownership of it. Now this is the end product.
However you get to that, once you're trained, is
your choice.*

*Q:* Help me with some confusion. Okay, you're
saying what separates you from others is that
there's a new management philosophy, and that's
great. But I want you to help me understand how
opening up—and this participative management
where you were given freedom, and you were
given input and you were not afraid to make
mistakes because you didn't get your head
chopped off—is really customer service. Help
me see that.

> *A: I think that before, we tried to make things work*
> *more efficiently; we tried to take good care of our*
> *patients. I care for the patients the way I've*
> *always cared for them. That hasn't changed. But*
> *I wasn't given the freedom or the empowerment*
> *or autonomy to go ahead and do the extra. For*
> *example, a surgeon wasn't going to get this*
> *patient in on time, we had some scheduling*
> *problems going across the board, and maybe we*
> *could provide this family with breakfast in our*
> *cafeteria. You would think of these ideas, but you*
> *wouldn't say anything because years ago that*
> *would have been nipped in the bud, "No, we can't*
> *do that. That's unheard of!" Now, you say*
> *something about that and they do it. When you're*
> *full of fear, maybe we didn't serve these people as*
> *well as we should have, or, at least the nurses*
> *section; this is reality to them. If we can go ahead*
> *and do this, you're not stifled in your ideas on*
> *how you can better care for that patient.*

## Nursing Supervisors

We asked many of the nonmanagement employees their impression of the cultural changes and what impact they thought CEO Jim Whitlock or his senior management team had on the transition. Responses that rather typified most of the replies were from Beverly Dunn and Dorothy Phillips, both nursing supervisors.

> *Q:* What do you sense in your position, and you've
> been here for a long time, what difference did the
> CEO Jim Whitlock make?
>
> *A: He had a different approach to the whole*
> *management system. I think his approach was a*
> *hit: He said it's okay to have fun; we've got*
> *business to do, but we can have fun doing it. He*

*also stretched our paradigms to think. He told us we're not just this little entity. As a hospital, we have to reach out to the community. He's talked about that from almost day one. What you do or say when you leave here makes a difference. We want you to be visible in the community, because we've got people here that have a lot of expertise that can help in the community.*

*I think that Jim is a true leader because he was able to lead us toward knocking down those administration walls that existed for so many years. He believed in that slow, patient approach, which I think helped us. I think employees have to see you, know you, and sense everything's okay before they start to trust you. I think he allowed us to have our own dreams and our own visions, even though he had his own. Somehow, we meshed those together. He didn't take away our self-worth while he was building what he called his new environment. We all had a part in the building process. He allowed us to be a part of that, and to feel a part of that. I see him as a leader because he's our administrator, but he's also our friend.*

*Q:* You made an interesting comment earlier: It flows down hill; guest excellence has to flow downhill. What did you mean by that?

*A: Well, no matter what I do as a nurse manager, if my staff or my patients see Lynn (my administrator of nursing) as being off-limits, untouchable, unapproachable, not touching, not friendly, whatever, it stops right there. If you have this same focus all the way down the organization it makes it stronger. If some part of that ladder is broken, then it weakens the whole ladder. So basically, it has to be strong to flow down.*

*Q:* What does customer service mean to you? What do you look for? What are the factors that make up good guest excellence?

*A: For me, it goes beyond how my nurses, or my nursing assistants, or my attendants treat the patient and the family. It's how staff put them at ease, make them feel comfortable, let them know that we're here to serve them. That's what we do— we serve—and we're going to use the word serve in the element it should be. We're here to take care of their needs. It goes beyond that. It's how they treat each other as employees. Because if they are not cohesive as a group, it's not going to be reflected in your overall care for the patient. That's the key for me. For me, patient satisfaction is that family environment, where everyone has a part and a role to play. It's not a role you're playing, that's you. You become that person that is patient satisfaction.*

*Even things as small as seeing a piece of paper on the floor—before, I've seen people just walk on by and it's no big deal. For the longest time, we had a lot of cigarette butts on the front steps of the hospital. It was so interesting to have our staff complain that it just doesn't look right, it's not a good image for us. Now, anyone and everyone picks up those cigarette butts and paper on the floors. It's also the little things that go toward good customer service. For us, we began to see everyone here receiving the treatment and the care you would give to your family—your mom, your dad, your brother, your sister. That's what Guest Excellence is all about.*

*We've always had it ingrained in us to give patients good quality care, but we didn't have ingrained in us how important we were to the hospital. When they came out with Guest*

*Excellence, they presented it to the employees that*
*you're guests too. We want you to be happy,*
*because we want you to stay with us and be part*
*of our family. Everyone felt better . . .*
*immediately.*

*Q:* In your minds, what are the most important
factors in customer service? What are the key
ingredients that would identify excellence in
patient relations?

*A: It's like providing satisfaction, a satisfied*
*customer. You know when you get, we call them*
*warm fuzzies sometimes, when they come back,*
*they call you, they send you flowers, they send*
*letters to your employer telling you what a nice*
*unit the hospital has.*

*Q:* What do you do, though, that creates this?

*A: Showing that you truly care about patients.*
*You're not there just to do a job, to do the*
*procedures. You go that extra mile. You care*
*about them as people. Touch individual people.*
*Let them realize that we know that they have*
*needs and we want to help meet those needs.*

*Q:* Let me ask you a few final questions. If
somebody said, "I want to develop a better
customer service program in my hospital," would
you tell them that one of the first things you've
got to do—I don't want to overuse this word—
empower or develop ownership, get your
employees to see all aspects of the job? As you
get employees to take ownership in all aspects,
and they feel good about what they're doing, all
the things you've talked about here, what it takes
to develop this ownership on the job, that one of
the things that spins off is their concern for all of
the things that make up good customer service.
Say that somebody came in and asked you, "If I

want to develop a customer service program, where do I start?" Do they start with the employees? Not the patient, not the customer?

A: *Yes, I think so. I think the emphasis is already there in healthcare—of taking care of the patient. I would say in most facilities, the place that they would need to look into is taking care of their employees. The natural follow-through is they're going to take care of the patient.*

That's where customer service begins and it never ends.

## SUMMARY

It's difficult, if not impossible, to capture the process and experiences that led to successful customer service at Bradley Memorial Hospital, to create some kind of script that other providers could follow. Don't misunderstand, Bradley is not perfect in all aspects of customer service. The facility still has some warts, like every institution does. A few employees still don't get it. Problems with patient complaints still crop up. But this hospital is far more advanced than most of the nation's providers, based on our recent research and our many years spent as employees and consultants in hospitals. We feel Bradley's success in developing improved patient relations is worth studying and emulating.

First, based on Bradley's successful approach, customer service should be considered a *state of mind*. Employees should see it as a *mindset* so that providing good service comes as naturally as possible. It should not be seen as a program, policy, or some kind of be-nice-to-patients platitude that is thrust upon the employees by senior management. The employees will see through those approaches and chuckle at the idea behind your back. They laugh because the emphasis on customer service doesn't make sense unless the *employees feel cared for first*. Employees have to know they come first in terms of concern, compassion, being listened to, communicated with, become part of decision making, and—most of all—trusted.

The ostentatious walls of arrogance that administration often builds around itself must come down to develop this new culture. This haughty behavior manifests disdain by the employees and creates an environment of superficiality and disgust. It creates a lack of trust between the employees and administration and bottles up the serving, sharing attitude so necessary in successful patient relations. Outstanding service in an organization starts with servant leadership at the top.

Chuck Lauer, publisher of *Modern Healthcare*, spelled out his thoughts on good leadership in one of his publisher's letters:

> It all starts with humility. By that I mean not taking yourself too seriously. Too many executives think their organizations would fall apart were it not for their talent and dedication. They don't want to share power because they're too insecure about their own abilities. Even more important is the desire to treat your colleagues and customers with a gentleness that inspires confidence and loyalty. For some people that's hard to do because they feel vulnerable when they show their emotions. It's all very easy, but it requires the leader to be with his people, not in some office on the top floor where there's no noise and no laughter and where everyone is afraid to say anything for fear of being criticized or ridiculed. Good leaders know where their people are and what they need because they're good listeners.[1]

Developing an attitude of serving others has to run downhill. The example must be set by the CEO and the entire senior staff, particularly the director of nursing and vice-presidents of all the ancillary departments. Employees

---

1. Charles Lauer, publisher's letter, *Modern Healthcare,* November 1993.

will need to see this servant attitude consistently played out before they will be receptive to serving patients and their families in the manner that could be identified as excellent service. Employees have to "feel" it first. Great customer service starts with an organizational culture that stresses relationships and cultivates trust among all levels of employees, from the CEO through the executive staff, department heads, managers, supervisors, and each employee. The CEO has to initiate this process of nurturing relationships and service to one another throughout the organization, consistently and continuously.

The CEO also has to paint the vision for the future of the organization for the employees and breathe the passion of organizational pride into their very souls. Pride in the place you work is important. It is a key link in creating employee desire to excel at customer service. Once the culture of the organization has impacted the employees to the point where they feel like "guests" in their own organization—where they feel good about their organization, their contributions and their relationship with each other—then they will be receptive to excelling in customer service. This would be the time to throw in specific customer service activities, such as task forces, training, and developing specific ideas for improving patient relations. In fact, in this environment employees themselves will take patient relations to a level no other process could properly achieve. Employees will see themselves as a family and patients as guests in their "house." And a family treats guests as special while they are visiting in their "house." The more the internal "guests" feel the warmth, caring, sincere relationships with one another and administration, the more they will be able to give of themselves to the patients.

It's pretty much as simple as that. But as Jim Whitlock stated, that's not what readers want to read. But that's where it starts—building relationships with employees—and ends in developing relationships with patients who will be coming back again and again. Following is our attempt at fitting Bradley's experiences to a step-by-step process that may enable others to mirror the "process" used there:

### Developing Guest Excellence at Bradley Memorial

**1. Convert the Organizational Culture.**

- If you're not there yet, begin to develop a servant leadership style. Start it at the top and weave it throughout the organization.
- Paint the vision for the future for the organization. The CEO communicates it over and over in a multitude of ways to develop employee pride in the organization.
- Concentrate more on developing employee relationships; create opportunities for employees to interact frequently and consistently. Start with the senior staff. Follow Bradley's Tuesday morning meeting philosophy.
- Develop a "family" atmosphere in the organization. Encourage it in as many ways as possible within the management style. Tear down walls between departments and among all levels of management.

**2. Sanction Employees to Serve.**

- Bury administration. Knock down the walls. Develop an organizationwide management team. Encourage participative management. Hold annual management retreats.
- Treat employees as guests. Listen to them, develop their talents, pay them well, and give them opportunity to provide input to organizational decisions. Trust them but hold them accountable. Provide training and

educational opportunities. Empower them to act on their own and then back them up.

## 3. Focus on Customer Service.

(After Step 1 and 2 have begun and when the employees are more receptive to the idea.)

- Get employees together from a wide range of departments on a special task force (adding a consultant is optional, but in many situations it can be a big help). Create hundreds of ideas for improving patient satisfaction in your organization.

- Create your own customer service creed and promote it constantly.

- Reorient all employees to the emphasis of excellent customer service. Impress new employees with the organization's stance on customer service.

- Set up a reward system for employees for good customer service.

- Talk customer service up. Communicate it in as many ways as you can. Keep the interest keen within the organization.

- Get constant feedback from patients through surveys and focus groups. Follow up with specific action where indicated. Give employees feedback on how they are doing based on survey results.

- Train and educate all your employees on all aspects of customer service. Make it continuous, fun, and practical.

- Make patient relations issues part of all employees' salary reviews. Make it constitute as much as 25 percent of their performance score.

- Create an organizational mascot and use it in as many ways as possible.
- Form community groups from citizens around the hospital to help promote the hospital and the staff's commitment to excellent service. Seek their ideas.

**CHAPTER**

# Guaranteed Service

## Lake Forest Hospital's Approach to Customer Satisfaction

**W**hen we heard the term *guaranteed service* being applied to a healthcare setting, we were pretty skeptical. Candidly, we expected to see another well-intended customer relations "sensitivity" strategy: nice words, but little if any action. We weren't even sure we knew what *guaranteed service* meant.

That was before we met with Jim Killian, executive vice president at Lake Forest Hospital, a 250-bed facility in Lake Forest, Illinois, one of Chicago's most affluent suburbs. Killian outlined the facility's position:

> Like most hospitals that operate in this very competitive market, we are very concerned about what our patients think. About a quarter come from Lake Forest, another 30 percent come from the surrounding northern and western suburbs. The rest come from throughout the area. We take nothing for granted about our patient base—they have high expectations and no shortage of alternatives if we don't meet their needs.

First impressions can be deceiving, but as we walked around the facility, it quickly became apparent that this was not a "run-of-the-mill" hospital. As we stood in the main entrance, we were immediately impressed by its home-like atmosphere: gleaming floors, accented with green marble; rich-looking cherry furniture with solid fabric upholstery throughout the waiting rooms and community areas; patient rooms decorated with paintings and floral wallcoverings. The decor is simple, but elegant. But that doesn't fully describe what is unique about Lake Forest Hospital.

"I don't think bricks and mortar and a beautiful property have anything to do with it." Killian summed up what each of us had observed as we walked throughout the hospital. "It's really all about people." Clearly, our perception of the staff at Lake Forest was that they were every bit as unique as the attractive surroundings. We saw it in the way they greeted patients, responded to fellow workers, and accommodated visitors' requests.

Their promotional brochure makes the following bold commitment: "At Lake Forest Hospital . . . we will do whatever it takes to meet the needs of our customers and exceed their expectations." The staff promise their "customers" that they will be treated with respect, compassion, and caring. The guarantee goes on to state that staff will "respect your time, your privacy, your fears, and your need for information and reassurance."

## EMPLOYEES EMPOWERED TO RESPOND

But the customer service commitment doesn't stop at a brochure. If someone reports that "their expectations" were not met, all employees who have received "guaranteed service" training are empowered to respond. Stated Killian:

> Employee empowerment is great, if you give them the education and the knowledge to use the empowerment

effectively. Our goal is to react appropriately if things have not gone as positively as we would hope. You can't just pass a wand over somebody's head and say "Thou shall be empowered"; they need to know how to identify the other person's true concerns.

The program was the brain child of CEO Bill Reis, who had always held to an overriding management philosophy of "guaranteed service." Killian reported:

Bill applies the concept of "exceeding expectations" to every aspect of his life. As a result, the management staff of the hospital has adapted similar standards. A few years ago he suggested that "we make it more and more obvious to the public that we are willing to stand behind our service." Bill often reminds us that our employees provide Lake Forest with our "competitive edge."

According to Bill Reis, "Anyone can have a building, anyone can buy the equipment, but not everyone can have the employees and the customer service we provide here."

The facility's first attempt at formalizing the concept was a canned guest relations program called "Hospitality" initiated in 1986. It was largely a training program that focused on human relations skills—telephone answering, communication techniques, and other common courtesies. Ultimately, Lake Forest devoted six or seven trainers to expose their staff to human relations skills. But the skills training was just a foundation. Within a few years, the program evolved into the customized "guaranteed service" program, piloted in the day surgery unit in 1989.

Gail Okon, RN, P.A.C.U./day surgery unit manager, was one of the pioneers. "We drifted into it naturally," explained Okon. "Because we had an established tradition of quality care, it was not that big of a deal to guarantee it." The staff was consulted at the outset to ensure their commitment to the program. "We clearly expressed to all staff members that they would work collaboratively with the patient to decide what would be done to rectify an unsatisfactory situation." Kathy Conley, one of the unit's RNs, continues to be enthusiastic about the program. "I like the idea that when a situation arises, each one of us has the authority to do something to better it. I think it gives Lake Forest Hospital the edge over other healthcare institutions."

## ANALYZED IMPACT

Before the program was taken hospitalwide in 1992, Lake Forest analyzed the impact on the facility.

- Of more than 3,100 annual day surgery cases, only 10 resulted in "guaranteed service" payouts.
- The percentage of credits to revenue was less than 0.0004 percent.
- Many patients use the program to voice concerns and refuse monetary compensation: "they just want to be heard."
- During the pilot, only two patients truly "abused" the program. Their comment upon a subsequent visit was, "What can I get this time?"

Okon summarized the analysis:

Once we began to talk about "guaranteed services" our thinking patterns changed, which influenced our behaviors. Our goal is no longer to meet expectations, but to exceed them. Lake Forest Hospital is a noncontentious atmosphere; we are all working together to ensure the best in patient care.

Interestingly, Okon's comment identifies one of the subtle dimensions of the "guaranteed service" program. On its own, it is only a "Band-Aid" for service problems. If all the employee does is react to the patient's complaint, no improvement is noted. Lake Forest uses the information gathered from guaranteed service payouts as input for its active CQI initiative. Jim Killian agreed: "Guaranteed service is a good tool to find out where you fall down, and when things don't go well, you have the ability to take immediate action for the patient. Unfortunately, if you don't fix the problem, if you're constantly apologizing for cold meals or late surgery schedules, you're not getting to the root of the problem. That led us into CQI as the next step."

The staff's reaction to the program is not exactly what Jim Killian expected:

> On its surface, the program didn't seem to threaten anybody. However, we needed to make sure that we could provide what we were guaranteeing, and that we could identify where we were coming up short. Predictably, there was some concern about the concept of employee accountability. We hadn't always done a good job of recognizing employee contributions—positive as well as negative. They simple weren't comfortable that we'd be any more successful this time. We thought that was valid, and as a result took extra steps to ensure we were responsible in our actions. On the other hand, they were also given the authority—from line employees to board members—to take care of a situation when it happened. We were empowering people for the very first time, and in some cases, managers were very threatened by that. I think some of the managers had a harder time than most of the general staff.

## PHYSICIANS INITIALLY PANICKED BY PROGRAM

But managers weren't the only ones feeling threatened. Physicians were initially panicked by the program. They thought the focus was on medical outcomes, which obviously no one could control. As a result, even the promotional brochure carries the disclaimer that *"Because of the nature of illness, we cannot guarantee the results of your medical treatment."* But Killian immediately interjected that "we can guarantee that people would be treated in a courteous manner." Killian said, "We've had a couple of our larger practices adopt the same standards of service, and have actually asked to have their staff go through the same training program that we've done here."

## TRAINING REQUIREMENTS

The training is impressive. Two distinct "tracks" (one for line employees and another for managers) have been developed. The employee workshop initially focuses on the conceptual aspect of quality service and customer needs. Staff are provided with key customer concerns, as well as factors that impact "perception" of quality. But the material is based on the realities of day-to-day experiences, requiring participants to identify "moments of truth" from a patient's point of view.

Time is spent on identifying internal and external customers. Although the patient is the primary focus, the needs and expectations of fellow employees, physicians, and other organizations are identified and analyzed. An assessment of current quality levels is made to provide a basis for "goal setting" and action planning.

Finally, skill-based training is provided in human relations techniques—problem solving, verbal and nonverbal communication, active listening, and dispute resolution.

The management program provides the same basic level of training provided in the employee track but combines it with an introductory "attitude adjustment." Managers are sensitized to the changing business paradigm of the healthcare industry, as well as specific information regarding the JCAHO's principles of quality improvement. Clearly, the objectives of the Guaranteed Service program, as well as the employee and management workshops, speak directly to the JCAHO's new standards for quality assessment and improvement (see box).

## NEW JCAHO STANDARDS FOR QUALITY ASSESSMENT AND IMPROVEMENT

1. The organization's leaders set expectations, develop plans, and implement procedures to assess and improve the quality of the organization's governance, management, clinical, and support processes.

2. The leaders undertake education concerning the approach and method of continuous quality improvement.

3. The leaders set priorities for organizationwide quality improvement activities that are designed to improve patient outcomes.

4. The leaders allocate adequate resources for assessment and improvement of the organization's governance, managerial, clinical, and support processes through:

    *a.* The assignment of personnel, as needed, to participate in quality improvement activities.

    *b.* The provision of adequate time for personnel to participate in quality improvement activities.

    *c.* Information systems and appropriate data management processes to facilitate the collection, management, and analysis of data needed for quality improvement.

5. The leaders ensure that the organization staff are trained in assessing and improving processes that contribute to improved patient outcomes.

6. The leaders individually and jointly develop and participate in mechanisms to foster communication among individuals and among components of the organization, and to coordinate internal activities.

7. The leaders analyze and evaluate the effectiveness of their contributions to improving quality.

Jim Killian pointed out that a recent JCAHO accreditation survey—often a traumatic event for a hospital and its staff—actually presented an opportunity for the concepts of "guaranteed service" to be highlighted in an unconventional way:

> One of the "hero stories" involved our physicist for radiology and radiation oncology, who happened to be in labor the first day of the survey. The physician surveyor had a number of technical questions about radiation safety documentation that only she could answer. In true "guaranteed service spirit" she'd said, "Call me if you need me." So we did. In between cleansing breaths, she answered the surveyor's questions, and when everything was answered, she promptly had a healthy baby girl.

The JCAHO team was astounded by the staff's commitment to the organization, their fellow employees, and the patients.

## EMPLOYEES GIVEN "HOW-TO"

Employees are provided with specific "how-tos" on fulfilling guaranteed service promises. The guidelines are straightforward:

- Out-of-pocket expenses are reimbursed through the normal employee expense reimbursement system. (Immediate reimbursement will be arranged if necessary.)
- Cash is available 24 hours a day from a nursing supervisor for immediate patient payouts.
- Flowers and other items are available from the gift shop—all that employees need to do is identify themselves and briefly describe the situation.
- The dietary supervisor provides guest trays and complimentary meal passes based on employee requests.

- Credits to patients' bills can be made directly from an employee's terminal.

Sound expensive? Killian reports that the program cost less than $10,000 last year and produced immeasurable patient and employee relations benefits.

But perhaps the best place to look for evidence of the program's effectiveness is through the patient's eyes. Lake Forest publishes a bimonthly newsletter called "The Record" that regularly reports examples of guaranteed service in action, and we reviewed some back issues. The newsletter's intent is to recognize and reinforce positive action. Here are some examples noted in the newsletter:

> An indigent patient was ready for discharge, but the unit nurse noticed that his clothes were badly soiled and tattered. Although she arranged to have the clothing repaired and laundered in the hospital's laundry, when two laundry employees saw the condition of the clothing, they decided that what the patient really needed was new clothes. They bought the patient new clothing out of their own pocket—the guaranteed service checkbook would have covered the expense, but the employees refused any reimbursement.

> Although delays are inevitable, an extended wait time caused an oncology patient significant discomfort. True to the instructions of the preadmission clerk, he'd left all valuables at home, including his wallet. When lunch time came and went, he felt pretty helpless. In the spirit of guaranteed service, the oncology secretary apologized for the delay and treated the patient to lunch in the coffee shop.

The hospital has collected several stories that illustrate guaranteed service in action. Senior management believes the program is nothing more than a formalization of what the staff do naturally. "But now they know we support their efforts and appreciate how it contributes to our unique atmosphere."

CHAPTER

# CQI and Patient Satisfaction

Irwin Press, cofounder of Press-Ganey, Inc., summarized it as well as anyone we talked to: "Patient survey data is meaningless unless you use it—and when you use it, you can truly make a difference." So we looked for a good example of a facility that took action based on the data they received in their patient surveys and found ourselves in Evansville, Indiana, at Deaconess Hospital, a 590-bed facility.

## CQI EMPLOYED AT DEACONESS

Deaconess is an active participant in Press-Ganey's patient survey network and was recognized in 1994 for work it has done reducing noise levels on patient floors to minimize the disturbances to patients. Solutions included staff education and enclosing nurses' stations. Although the hospital is "still working on the problem," Deaconess claims early results are promising. We were actually more intrigued by the method used than by the results. Recent survey results have been mixed and candidly inclusive. But the hospital provides a textbook example of how CQI methods can be employed to investigate problem areas and identify potential solutions.

Deaconess jumped head first into the continuous quality improvement (CQI) wave of the early '90s. Their early initiatives included a number of site visits, as well as many hours of seminars and training. Joni Rahman, marketing analyst for the facility, told us, "We want to be one of the leaders in healthcare and we realize the methods and processes in place today may not be appropriate in the future. Change is a constant, and we are interested in any feedback that will help us to adapt to our patients' needs." During initial development, Deaconess created a CQI Task Force, a Quality Improvement Council, a quality coach position, and a quality improvement specialist position. The hospital's mission statement was rewritten to incorporate CQI. During the four years Deaconess has been actively involved in CQI, they have developed more than 20 Quality Advantage Teams (QATs). The noise level project was selected in the "second wave" of team creation.

## ADDRESSING PATIENTS' COMPLAINTS ABOUT NOISE LEVEL

The hospital became concerned about excessive noise in June of 1992, when it found itself ranking in the 59th percentile for hospital noise levels. As a result, Deaconess established a problem statement for one of its CQI teams to "reduce the impact of noise level on nursing units as measured by patient satisfaction surveys."

### FADE Process

The Noise Level QAT included members from administration, engineering, and maintenance, and used Organizational Dynamics, Inc., CQI process. ODI's approach consists of the *FADE* process: *focus, analyze, develop, and execute*. During each of these stages, the team achieves certain goals in order to continue to the next stage. An opportunity statement is developed in the *focus* stage; data is collected and analyzed in the *analyze* stage; a prospective solution is the result of the *develop* stage. Finally, during the *execute* stage, the solution is implemented and measured for improvement.

During the focus stage, the team brainstormed to generate a list of possible causes of excessive noise. With this information, a fishbone diagram was developed. This diagram was divided into four sections, each representing a different type of cause: people, method, material, and machines. To provide additional information, patient interviews were conducted, along with random observations of the nursing units.

A Pareto chart, which visually represents the distribution of occurrences being studied, identified

- Night shift activities
- Nurses stations
- Construction

as the top three sources of potential excessive noise.

During this early data collection phase, some "low-hanging fruit" opportunities (obvious, low-risk, high-impact, easy-to-implement changes) were identified to immediately reduce noise levels. On the list were repetitive weather announcements made over the hospital's public address system, noise generated from newspaper stands located throughout the hospital, and miscellaneous loud doors.

Multivoting, a CQI technique that helps to prioritize the team's position and potential actions, was used to identify three significant "opportunities for improvement": Employees at nurse's stations; patient visitation; and night noise. The team went on to develop an opportunity statement:

An improvement opportunity exists in reducing the noise level generated at the nurses station during the late evening and night time hours. This causes dissatisfaction among the patients as reflected on patient surveys. Reduction of the noise level should result in increased patient satisfaction.

As the team entered the analyze stage, additional data was collected from Press-Ganey patient satisfaction surveys. Surveys were correlated to specific nursing units, in order to determine nursing units with lowest scores. Three units were identified, and two were selected as test sites.

## Input from Employees

Input was solicited from employees to help identify potential sources of excessive noise as well as to determine what they had been told by patients regarding noise levels. This phase concluded that the top five reasons for excessive noise were:

1. Talking and laughing by employees, visitors, and other patients.
2. Noise associated with shift changes.
3. Night shift nursing activities.
4. Evening shift nursing activities.
5. Day shift nursing activities.

With this information, the team entered the develop stage. Although a number of approaches were used to identify potential corrective action, the top three solutions ultimately determined through the multivoting process included:

1. Glass-in the nurse's station.
2. Use soundproofing materials/insulation on unit areas.
3. Provide headsets for patients.

Some additional ideas included using silent paging systems and employee awareness programs.

Once these solutions were discovered, additional data gathering occurred, and the team concluded that the noise cancellation technology associated with the second solution was cost prohibitive. The team once again multivoted and decided to proceed with glassing in the nursing station. The team used a number of approaches to gain buy-in and support from the staff, physicians, and administration. Ultimately, final approval was received, and construction began the execute stage in September of 1993.

The process took slightly more than 16 months. This is relatively fast by CQI standards but still painfully slow in terms of actual impact on patient satisfaction. Although the hospital did not disclose the cost of the initiative, any facility involved in its own CQI program is well aware of the investment of time and administrative support required just to complete the associated studies, surveys, and analysis. Deaconess concluded that the glassed-in nurse's stations were a positive way to reduce noise and protect patient confidentiality. However, the facility now has a hospital-wide reengineering initiative underway, and as a result has suspended further implementation of the team's recommendations.

The noise-reduction plan effectively illustrates our concern with this approach. The thoroughness associated with problem definition and methodical research associated with potential problem resolution are both its strongest asset and its weakest link.

The process simply takes too long. By the time you've identified the problem and implemented the solution, the problem may have changed. Or worse, the patient may have gone to your competitor.

**CHAPTER**

# An "Aloha" Approach to Patient Relations

## The Queen's Medical Center

Top-quality patient relations practices come in many different forms for the nation's hospitals, as you have seen in previous chapters. We saw another unique example of this at The Queen's Medical Center. Anyone entering The Queen's Medical Center (530 beds) in Honolulu, Hawaii, will notice immediately that something here is different. Patients are welcomed to the hospital by the scent of tropical flowers and the sound of ukeleles. Greeters meet the patients and provide valet service for their cars at no charge. Based on Hawaiian tradition, there's a strong influence of family. This creates the same kind of aloha you would feel in island hotels.

Lindsey Carry, director of the patient relations department, says the hospitalwide focus on patient relations is championed by the hospital's president, Arthur A. Ushijima. Carry says Ushijima and employees throughout the hospital consider quality patient relations to be a top goal of The Queen's Medical Center. The Queen's Medical Center has a unique background: It was founded by Hawaii's Queen Emma and King Kamehameha IV in 1859. Queen Emma went door-to-door soliciting funds to build an emergency clinic on the island, which had been devastated by several major epidemics that had wiped out a huge portion of the population. As a result, the hospital has a special mission of caring for all Hawaiians (and Pacific Islanders).

Measuring patient satisfaction is something that The Queen's Medical Center considers to be important. In many ways, the measurements have become a real science. The science is to do more, to go further in-depth and find out what patients really thought about their healthcare experiences, and to determine what issues are most important to patients. Originally, Carry told us The Queen's Medical Center used the Press-Ganey written surveys for its patients. She said they found them too mainland-oriented and not really geared to reflect the unique concerns of their patient population. Realizing the need to create a scientific survey that was right for them, Carry hired an outside research group, based in Hawaii, to help them work through the process.

## SURVEYING FOR QUALITY INDICATORS

To begin revamping the survey process in April of 1994, the consulting group conducted eight hours of focus groups. The focus groups consisted of four different groups of 10 to 12 people who had recently been admitted as inpatients at The Queen's Medical Center. These groups were videotaped behind a one-way mirror, and staff members attended the sessions. From these focus groups, the consultants were able to identify 25 "quality indicators," or issues which the former patients deemed most important. From these 25 indicators, the consultants redirected their research to determine the 15 most important "quality indicators" among inpatient admissions.

A telephone poll was conducted with 450 discharged patients to validate the top 15 quality indicators. Then the patients were asked how well the hospital rated on each of the indicators during their last hospitalization. These results were then communicated to all levels of the organization. The quality indicators identified as most important to patients are as follows:

1. Care team is knowledgeable—patient feels he/she is in good hands.
2. Care team is well-informed about patients' medical condition.
3. Staff sensitive to patient's medical condition—makes him/her as comfortable as possible.
4. Staff respects patient's rights.
5. Patient and family informed about medical condition and treatment.
6. Staff treats patient professionally.
7. Patient feels he/she has say in decisions about his/her medical care and treatment.
8. Staff listens to patient.
9. Staff conveys warmth and friendliness.
10. Staff responds quickly to assistance requests.
11. Staff treats patient with compassion.
12. Patient is informed about self-care at home.
13. Staff shows respect for patient's privacy.
14. Staff gives patient encouragement and reassurance.
15. Staff anticipates patient's needs for comfort.

## SET UP SPECIAL TEAM

The next step was to set up a "Performance Improvement Team" dedicated to improving patient satisfaction by setting up action plans based on the research. A 10-minute video called "What Our Patients Are Saying" was developed from the focus groups and is shown to all new hires, as well as to all ancillary department and nursing unit staff. After this process was completed, a new written survey was developed based on the quality indicators indicated as most important to their patients. The first part of the survey consists of 15 questions, asking respondents to rate their experiences on a scale of 1 to 10, 1 being strongly disagree and 10 being strongly agree. In keeping with The Queen's Medical Center's philosophy, the emphasis here is caring. For example, the survey asks patients to respond to such statements as: "My care team was knowledgeable, making me feel I was in good hands." "The staff was warm and friendly." "The staff was encouraging and reassuring."

The second part of the survey asks about overall satisfaction. Respondents are given five choices and asked to check the one that most fits their impression, from, "Queen's fell far short of my expectations," to the top choice, "Queen's far exceeded my expectations." The survey also asks two open-ended questions with space for a reply: "What aspect of your hospitalization at Queen's impressed you the most?" and "Please tell us if there are any areas where Queen's can improve."

Reflecting the overall trend in the healthcare world toward measuring medical outcomes as a factor in patient satisfaction, the third part of the survey asks for "other thoughts" regarding medical outcomes. Respondents are asked to check one of five responses, from "Very dissatisfied with my medical results," to "Very satisfied with my medical results." Next, patients are asked, "If you needed hospitalization again, would you return to Queen's?" And finally, patients are given the chance to give the name, unit, and comments of any special staff members they would like to acknowledge.

Just as important as the survey process itself was communication to hospital employees about patient satisfaction. Carry says all results of the survey process, that is, "What do patients want?" have been communicated to all levels of the organization. This means every employee of The Queen's Medical Center in theory should understand more about the patient population he/she serves. This, of course, sounds great. The question is, do employees really pay attention to things like a patient survey? Another equally valid question is this: What incentive do employees have to care about patient concerns?

The answers to those questions are usually found in continual sharing of information (survey results) and consistent communication from senior management on the issue of patient satisfaction. This, in turn, should then be championed by department managers and staff members themselves.

## CUSTOMER SERVICE BECOMES CONTAGIOUS

So, is every employee at The Queen's Medical Center excited about the mission of improved patient relations? Probably not. But the emphasis put on the subject by hospital management is designed to capture the vast majority of employees. This, in turn, becomes contagious. As one staff member goes out of his/her way, it is noticed by other employees. When this is noticed by co-workers, it is much more likely to happen again with others. So when the hospital constantly talks about quality patient relations, it is setting up an environment where it is appropriate to go out of your way for patients.

The final piece of the puzzle to get employee buy-in on patient relations is the management environment itself. If employees think senior management is merely expressing platitudes, then there is a small chance the program will be successful. If, on the other hand, employees sense a genuine caring for patients, a solid patient relations program has a real chance. So senior management's role at The Queen's Medical Center is key. These managers set the overall tone. When hospital employees consistently experience evidence from management that patient relations is important, they get a signal that it is appropriate for them to take it seriously themselves. We saw an abundance of evidence of this when we were on-site at the medical center.

For example, when a patient looks lost, do staff go out of their way to help out? Or if staff are having a bad day, do they go out of their way to avoid letting the patient know about it? It's the little things that contribute to quality patient relations. Senior management's role at The Queen's Medical Center plays a major part in making it happen.

## HOW THE PATIENT RELATIONS DEPARTMENT WORKS

According to Carry, one key aspect of "managing" patient relations is the patient relations department. Carry has a staff of nine in her department. Six are patient relations representatives including three volunteers. Two work on the off-island housing program and there is one administrative secretary. To promote use of the patient relations department, a Patient Visitation program was initiated. Patient relations representatives are assigned to nursing units and meet with newly admitted patients to proactively address any concerns.

A colorful, easy-to-read brochure highlights the Patients' Rights and Responsibilities. If the patient is not in the room when the representative visits, an attractive tent card, similar to those used in hotels, is left informing the patient whom to contact should there be a complaint. The in-house television channel also promotes patients' contacting the department regarding issues they feel need resolution. Carry says she encourages patients to complain or bring up issues to her department. "We can assist patients with issues ranging from patient rights to parking. Should they have any questions, concerns, or special needs, they are encouraged to call their patient representative."

Carry says this approach of asking patients to work with patient representatives is good business. "Malpractice lawsuits are less likely to happen. We like to deal with issues as they come up," says Carry. In fact, Carry says an *increase* in patient complaints may actually be a positive sign, meaning that the patient representatives are relating to more patients. It also means the design of the system is sound, because it funnels patients into the patient relations department.

Carry added that results for improving patient relations do not rest alone with the patient relations department; "results of patient satisfaction are communicated to all levels of the organization." She described how the patient relations assistant positions are key to controlling patient complaints. The organization setup is fairly simple:

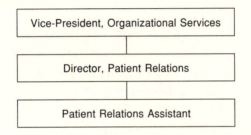

Carry said the primary contacts for the patient relations assistant are patients and their families, physicians, nurses, and clinical and nonclinical staff. The primary focus of the patient relations assistant is patient advocacy, problem resolution, and education. Carry also outlined the job description of the patient relations assistant, listing 11 of the major duties and responsibilities:

1. Identifies, assesses, and makes recommendations to director regarding situations in which preemptive intervention will result in reduced numbers of patient complaints and problems.
2. Informs patients, families, community, medical staff, administration, and employees on the role and function of patient relations as directed or required.

3. Provides counsel to patients and families regarding patient rights within the medical center.

4. Assists and participates in facilitating the grievance mechanism for patients exercising their rights; refers problems/concerns to appropriate staff and provides follow-up and advocacy for appropriate resolution under the direction of the director.

5. Assists patients with needs not routinely met in other medical center areas such as special parking rates, meal vouchers, VIP services, and so on.

6. Provides ongoing support and assistance to the patient relations volunteers as required.

7. Performs duties in a courteous and friendly manner that fosters superior customer service.

8. Participates in providing information on issues of patient rights, informal counsel, and community and hospital resources to the community, medical center, and medical staff.

9. Establishes and maintains working relationships with community health, welfare, and social agencies; maintains department resources on file.

10. Serves on committees and attends meetings as directed and required.

11. Maintains records and prepares statistics as required.

When you analyze the duties and responsibilities of the patient relations assistant, you will see that the position is designed to help patients with virtually any problem they may encounter.

One question you might ask in reviewing the duties of the patient relations assistant is, does it really work? And if it works, how do you know it? In this area, The Queen's Medical Center has done extensive research.

The patient relations department collects information regarding complaints for the following reasons:

- To maintain a comprehensive record of allegations, interventions, and resolutions of cases investigated.
- To determine patients' and families' needs and expectations.
- To identify trends throughout the medical center.
- To identify targets for performance improvement projects.
- To meet JCAHO and Department of Health standards.

The medical center also tracks complaint resolution. It breaks the complaint resolution into three categories:

1. Resolved.
2. Unresolved.
3. Unfounded.

One area of potential problems for the medical center is that often complaints are received and resolved directly by the departments receiving the complaint. Consequently, the statistics tracked by Queen's represent only those complaints received and investigated by the Patient Relations Department. Complaints are also categorized by area of concern. At Queen's there are nine major categories, illustrated in Table 14.1.

According to Carry, the extensive tracking of patient complaints helps The Queen's Medical Center better understand patients. Carry also told us about her role. She said her job has 10 major functions:

1. Formulation of department vision.
2. Ensuring that medical center staff support patient rights.

**TABLE 14.1**

Types of Complaints

| Accessibility | Food | Physical Environment |
|---|---|---|
| • Received Inaccurate Information<br>• Wait for Service | • Taste/Preparation/ Appearance<br>• Correct Diet Plans | • Noise Level<br>• Patient Unhappy with Room<br>• QMC Property<br>• Roommate Problems |
| **Clinical Staff (Non-MD/RN)**<br>• Courtesy/ Communication<br>• Efficiency/Service<br>• Medical Care | **MD**<br>• Courtesy/ Communication<br>• Efficiency/Service<br>• Medical Care | **Property**<br>• Damaged<br>• Misplaced<br>• Stolen |
| **Dissatisfied with Policies and Procedures**<br>• Billing Policy<br>• Department Policy<br>• Nonparticipation with Insurance<br>• Queens Medical Center Policy | **Nonclinical Staff**<br>• Courtesy/ Communication<br>• Efficiency/Service<br>• Patient Care | **RN**<br>• Courtesy/ Communication<br>• Efficiency/Service<br>• Medical Care |

3. Involvement in housewide performance improvement activities.

4. Resolution of patient and family complaints with emphasis on potentially litigious cases.

5. Inpatient and outpatient patient satisfaction projects:
   • Focus groups.
   • Telephone surveys.
   • Mail out surveys.
   • Quarterly and annual patient satisfaction reports.

- Analysis and trending of data.
- Patient satisfaction video.
- Patient satisfaction presentations throughout medical center.

6. Ensuring that JCAHO standards relative to patient rights are satisfied.

7. Strategic planning relative to healthcare reform.
- Focus on outpatients/Pacific Rim.

8. Development of proactive patient-focused activities.
- Patient visitation program.
- Volunteer patient relations representative.

9. Collaboration with nursing in "transforming and enhancing the health paradigm."

10. Reporting on patient relations activities (compliments, complaints, and so on) to all levels of the organization.

These duties are all geared toward ensuring that the patient relations department runs smoothly and stays relevant into the future.

## COMMITTED TO PATIENT RELATIONS

Our visit to The Queen's Medical Center showed a group of people committed to helping patients. Staff are also willing to track and measure results far beyond what average employees would do. As a result, they have put an effective program in place.

Entering The Queen's Medical Center and learning about its approach to patient relations, we had one initial reservation. Can accountability for patient relations rest with one department? In reality what we observed was something a little different. Although The Patient Relations Department is squarely in the middle of the effort to help patients, the overall program is much wider in scope. The entire medical center is tuned into the patient relations effort. This begins at employee orientation and continues with consistent feedback on the issue to all employees. So what we observed was an overall patient relations program that blends well with the unique patient population served by The Queen's Medical Center.

The program is geared to Hawaiians and Pacific Islanders, but the basic process staff are using could be emulated by any healthcare provider. First they have surveyed their patient population to find out just what is most important to their patients. Second, staff have assembled a process to proactively work with patients and resolve issues or problems as they come up. Finally, and probably most importantly, staff consistently "talk up" patient relations. This begins at the top of the organization and permeates the entire medical center.

So there is something different at The Queen's Medical Center. You'll notice it when you walk in the front door. But don't for a minute think this unique environment happens by chance. This environment is a result of well-planned action.

**CHAPTER**

# Customer Service Commandos

## Holy Cross Hospital's War to Improve Patient Satisfaction

**D**riving through this older, blue collar neighborhood on Chicago's south side it was a hard to envision it as the home of "the most improved" hospital in the history of Press-Ganey's patient satisfaction survey process. Holy Cross Hospital, a 346-bed facility, is located across the street from Chicago's infamous Marquette Park. Its functional-yet-austere appearance belies its national reputation for its commitment to total patient satisfaction. And their reputation is fast becoming "legend." They were named as the "large hospital" winner of *Hospital & Health Networks* Magazine's Fourth Annual Great Comebacks contest. They have eight active "commando teams" focusing on improving customer satisfaction at almost every conceivable level in their organization. During 1994–95, more than 60 hospitals have toured or consulted with the Holy Cross "Customer Service Commandos."

## BACKGROUND OF HOSPITAL'S PATIENT SATISFACTION EFFORTS

But candidly, it came as no surprise that it hasn't always been that way. There was nothing flashy or fake about this hospital. Holy Cross is not the obvious facility of choice for patients in a highly competitive healthcare market. Fourteen languages are spoken in the emergency department—definitely a diverse patient base. Yet, walking down the hallway, it has the feeling of a trip back to your home town: familiar, comfortable, and caring. Holy Cross has achieved a "customer-focused" environment that's not dependent on the physical surroundings of the facility. Many of the pictures on the walls are of satisfied patients: customers. That's not a bad touch, and a great calling card, in any market.

However, for five years, Holy Cross languished in the lower fifth percentile of Press-Ganey's patient satisfaction index. Liz Jazwiec, RN and "leader" of the emergency department at the hospital, has a practical view about the value of patient satisfaction.

> For us, it was a matter of survival. Our cash reserves had dwindled dangerously low over a very short period back in 1991, and our patient satisfaction survey scores were in the "cellar." We desperately needed to increase our market share and recruit primary care physicians. Candidly, its pretty tough to do those things under the best conditions, and if you're not providing patients with satisfactory service, it's all but impossible. We had to do whatever was necessary to improve our patient satisfaction scores.

Holy Cross implemented a number of stopgap financial measures to "stop the bleeding" in late 1991 and early 1992, with little measurable impact on patient satisfaction levels. They moved only 9 basis points, "peaking" at the fourteenth percentile. And they were frustrated. That's when Mark Clemons, CEO, and Quint Studer, senior vice president of strategic implementation, set a goal to be in the seventy-fifth percentile within 12 months. Studer explained the logic of the seemingly impossible 600 percent improvement goal. "Our intention was to be a 'premier' healthcare organization, and somehow patient satisfaction ratings in the fiftieth percentile just didn't say 'premier,' even though that would have been a significant stretch based on where we'd been. We really couldn't settle for less than the seventy-fifth percentile."

But why the focus on patient satisfaction when Holy Cross was still struggling financially? Clemons reasoned that low patient satisfaction scores were a symptom of more serious problems within his organization. "As a hospital, if patient satisfaction is not in your strategic vision, what are you there for? If you have a patient satisfaction problem, you have a problem with the values of the organization."

## ADDRESSING PATIENT SATISFACTION WITH "SERVE"

Clemons explained that in his view the key to success in the quest for excellence was for the entire organization to gauge every action against the values the staff had adopted for the new Holy Cross Hospital: customer needs and expectations. Those values are service, excellence, respect, value, and enthusiasm (SERVE). "If an action is not actively contributing to our values, implementing a SERVE behavior, or adding value to a customer, we eliminate it," Clemons said.

As a result, organizational development is the centerpiece of Holy Cross' strategic plan. "Our employees have truly become our partners. We have an open book management style here. Our strategic plan goes out to all 1,500 'partners.' Each of the department leaders has both a yearly and 90-day work plan. If a leader is unable to improve patient satisfaction, we have to take action. Effort is no excuse for lack of results," Clemons stated.

Effecting the kind of fundamental organizational change apparent at Holy Cross required a revolutionary approach. Studer prefers the term "declaration of war." He felt denial was a real factor in their lack of success. "We didn't understand our scores, and many of our partners feared that disclosure of a problem could have a negative impact on their career. Just like any dysfunctional setting, we had to admit we had a problem before we could begin to 'heal.' Clearly, we had to change the corporate culture." He explained that the first major battle in their war to improve patient satisfaction was on "home turf."

> We looked inside and it wasn't pretty. We really didn't like who we were; what we had become. Our employee base, as well as our patient base, had become very diverse. We were treating drug addicts and trauma victims, and we didn't "like" them very much. We wanted badly to "blame" our problems on errors of our previous administration or on poor supervision. We somehow wanted to see ourselves as victims, because that would have made it easier to accept.

He paraphrased Stephen Covey. "Once we become a victim, we're no longer accountable for our own success or failure."

Studer feels this fundamental change in attitude, accepting responsibility for who they were, what they were to become, at every level of the organization, was the cornerstone of their successful turnaround. Within a very short time, he said, they started feeling good about themselves and the jobs they did. "Once we changed the culture internally, we were ready to take the war outside," he commented.

## Commando Leaders

As the battle plan unfolded, it was clear that Studer's approach was not conventional. The "commando leaders" that were to become a key part of the new Holy Cross culture were asked to become responsible—accountable—for initiatives that would cross departmental boundaries, impacting areas for which they did not have direct control or supervisory responsibility. He explained that in his mind, true leadership in healthcare is achieved through facilitating change. He stressed that the interdependency of one manager on another ensured cooperation and ultimately the success of the whole plan, rather than the individual success of one department or manager. "Traditional organization structures don't provide a great deal of incentive for departments in a large institution to cooperate with one another. That's obviously counterproductive to our value of meeting the customer's needs rather than our own and had to be eliminated," Studer explained.

"Commando leaders" have the ability to "draft" troops from any department. As a result, some "partners" are actually participating in three or four of the eight commando teams or, as Quint Studer refers to them, "platoons."

## The First Platoon: Customer Satisfaction

The first platoon deployed in the war to improve patient satisfaction at Holy Cross Hospital was charged with measuring customer satisfaction in all areas and improving satisfaction by coordinating measurement tools. Their first action was to eliminate all surveys except Press-Ganey. "We had to agree on one consistent measurement system. Departments had learned years ago that asking a question a different way could produce completely different results, so we had all kinds of surveys measuring the same thing. We were confused, the patient was confused, and we weren't improving," Studer stated.

Dan Dean, team supervisor of radiology at Holy Cross, was asked to become the "commando leader" of this initiative, and as result, has become the "guru of measurement" for many Press-Ganey participants. Liz Jazwiec, leader of the emergency department at Holy Cross, provided the accolades: "Dan can look at a Press-Ganey number and tell what you need to do to improve it. Not the obvious things; he can identify the subtle and, more importantly, effective actions that need to be taken. He's known throughout the industry and is contacted frequently by other hospitals."

Quint Studer provided an example the staff encountered with their physical therapy department. "Patient satisfaction scores for our PTs were very low and it didn't seem to make logical sense. From our observations, they were very friendly, consistently doing the things we felt were necessary to put a patient at ease. Dan helped us identify that the issue was not friendliness, but privacy. Many of the things that the staff were doing to be 'friendly' were conflicting with the patient's desire for privacy. We changed our approach, and our scores improved dramatically."

Dean also provided the hospital with a good reason to keep lengths of stay to a minimum. His research indicates that patient satisfaction scores decline significantly for patients whose length of stay exceeds five days.

Early in their efforts to improve, Dean realized that the conventional quarterly reporting of Press-Ganey was just too long to wait to determine whether a corrective action had affected a measurement successfully. He initially designed a system to provide monthly feedback and then decided that was too long. Weekly reports worked for a while, but now he is able to update his measurement database daily so that the commando teams have almost immediate feedback on customer satisfaction.

## The Second Platoon: Customer Communication

The next platoon to be deployed focused on customer communication. Once again, the hospital felt that a conventional approach probably wouldn't produce the results they needed. They weren't particularly interested in changing brochures but did generate a patient admissions booklet and map as one of their early projects. According to Studer, the group's real objective was to communicate a positive message to a patient as early during his/her stay as possible:

> For a patient, the only really credible source that our customer satisfaction levels are high is another patient. It really doesn't matter what our brochures say or promise; if another patient relates a positive experience, it is far more likely that a patient will perceive our service positively. That's where the idea for the "Who's talking" campaign came from. We have pictures of satisfied patients saying good things about the hospital posted throughout the facility. We wanted patients to begin to see our best side as soon as possible: First impressions are critical.

One of the hospital's early failures ultimately became one of its greatest success stories. Studer jokes that the payer mix at Holy Cross is "government"—including a heavy influx of trauma patients from the emergency department. Staff currently have to be prepared to speak 14 different languages—and new Arabic dialects prevalent in the area are likely to add to the challenge.

The department had a history of low patient satisfaction scores and attributed its poor performance to the inherent challenges of an inner city ED. That was before Liz Jazwiec took over as commando leader for the team. She reported:

> We were in the eighth percentile, and dragging down the performance of the rest of the hospital. Most of the change was attitude, and I give Mark Clemons and Quint Studer most of the credit for changing the corporate culture. Once we took responsibility for our own success, we found we could be "winners." Last quarter we were in the ninety-eighth percentile.

Jazwiec's approach was broad based and included improving patient communication, minimizing wait times, and redesigning the facility. But she attributes most of the success to the attitude of the "partners."

## The Third Platoon: Removing Patient Irritations

The next platoon was asked to "identify and remove patient irritations"—not an insignificant challenge. The team's initiative included addressing everything from the evaluation and improvement of parking accommodations to patient complaints about the billing and collection system. Food service, security, and the overall appearance of the facility received their attention.

But one initiative Jazwiec noted best summarized the "commando" touch, which differentiated even common types of patient satisfaction projects:

> We asked food service personnel to inquire about the patient's room temperature when they delivered meals. If the patient was concerned, the partner was instructed to go to the telephone immediately and request that the engineering department adjust the temperature. The building department handles the requests as a high priority. Patient response was phenomenal. They were surprised that they'd been asked; but when the employee took immediate action, many were astounded.

## Other Teams

Other commando teams focused on areas that had been identified through the measurement process as having a significant impact on overall customer satisfaction:

- Physician satisfaction—Interestingly, Holy Cross physicians told the commandos that the number one thing the facility could do to improve their (the doctors') satisfaction was to better meet the needs of their patients. The hospital now provides physicians with a separate report of the satisfaction levels of each one's own patients. Together, 44 focus areas have improved since the team was organized. As a result, the hospital is successfully recruiting and retaining additional medical staff—a key corporate goal.

- Adding value—This team attempts to identify "little things" that add value to the patient's experience. As a result of the group's efforts, the hospital started providing free parking to outpatients and day surgery patients. They arranged to have "guest trays" available at the discretion of a partner; if a staff member feels it's appropriate, the tray is provided, no questions asked. The group's "tactical plan" calls for dozens of similar small, but significant initiatives to differentiate the Holy Cross experience.

- Setting standards of performance—To help determine the proper "standards" of partner behavior, the team asked for input from the customer-focus groups. Using their findings, the team defined a clear set of standards for attitudes and responses to call lights; partner appearance; phone etiquette; privacy; discharge planning; patient wait times; and other key customer service measurements. By clearly communicating the standards to the staff and rewarding staff who consistently exceeded expectations, the hospital was able to pinpoint areas to redress for an immediate impact on patient satisfaction scores.

- Linking human performance to customer need— Perhaps the quickest way to show corporate commitment to customer satisfaction is to effectively tie employee performance evaluation to customer feedback. This team was able to incorporate customer, peer, leader, and self-evaluation into the appraisal process. The objective is to *develop* employees, not add another level of judgment.

The result of the comprehensive program was a record turnaround in Press-Ganey performance. Holy Cross was in the lower thirteenth percentile in September of 1993;

they had improved their performance to the ninety-seventh percentile—a jump of 84 basis points, exceeding even their own most optimistic goals.

We were obviously impressed by the program but curious about whether the focus on customer satisfaction had paid off for Holy Cross financially. The slight but detectable smirk on Quint Studer's face told us he was ready for that question:

> Our inpatient admissions were up 5 percent this year, but perhaps more importantly, outpatient admissions were up 30 percent. Our cost per discharge was down markedly, from $4,400 to $4,100. We recruited 40 new physicians last year and have opened several new clinics. We went from being "unratable" two years ago to a BBB+ rating in our most recent $25 million dollar offering. Nobody is declaring victory, but we've won our share of battles.

Studer was anxious to add a closing comment. "As in every major undertaking in my life, I've learned a lot of lessons along the way. Perhaps clearest to me is that success has nothing to do with what you're doing for yourself. It's about what you do for others."

# EPILOGUE

It's rather ironic to be saying providers of healthcare need to practice better customer service. (It's akin to saying church clergy should practice what they preach.) It also seems more than a little ironic that providers today often separate healing from compassion, communicating, friendliness, and a sincere concern for patients' emotions and feelings. Yet that's what thousands of former patients representing nearly half of the states reported during our 1995 research: There is a lack of caring and kindness by providers and a whole lot of indifference. Somewhere along the line, healing got separated from humanitarianism. Apathy replaced affability. Boorish behavior overcame benevolence and good nature.

The patients we surveyed and interviewed rated hospitals' customer service issues on average at a poor 7.7 on an index of 10, and physicians slightly better at 8.1. However, younger patients (under 35) rated their last hospital experience at a shabby 6.7 and physicians at a sorry 7.7. The younger generation is the work force. They are the ones to whom employers are listening, and they are the age group most dissatisfied with providers.

So it would seem this dispassionate indifference has created such impassioned hostility among its customers—patients—that they are rising up in a mock revolt. The managed care phenomenon has allowed for the public to rise up in mass and organize what one might call an insurrection against indifference.

And that undeniable insurrection will impact income to the providers, generally more or less of it depending how the provider reacts to the demands for better customer service. The provider who understands that will survive. The ones who do not, will not.

Patients passionately want a change in behavior by the staffs providing healthcare in this country. They justifiably want to be treated with dignity and decorum. They are not demanding the moon, just simple things like friendliness, a certain amount of compassion, and explanations of what is going on in their treatment and why. And, oh yes, patients detest waiting for hours for procedures that take minutes.

Our research reveals employers are moving swiftly toward making quality and patient satisfaction decisive issues. Managed care organizations will be their carriers of justice. And justice will be served. Customer service in the healthcare industry will become the new buzzword. Cost control is a given. How patients are treated is the new frontier.

Our findings also lead us to conclude that the vast majority of providers are not paying attention to the omens. Most don't hear the discontented masses forming outside their doors. They don't seem to sense the coming together of a disgruntled public and a willing majority of employers to create this crescendo of change.

But transform they must. Providers' penchant for putting customer service on a low priority will undergo a transformation in the next few years. The revolt has indeed begun; the providers are just a little slow to recognize the signs. But as revenue and patient volume are affected, the not-so-subtle message will echo loudly throughout the industry, and at long last the patient will certainly come first, foremost, and last.

**Dave Zimmerman**

# I N D E X

## A

Accountability, 193
Administration, 162, 163
   problems, 127–130
   walls, 158
Administrative partner, 95
Administrative staff, 84, 129–131
Admissions, 79
Adopt-a-floor program, 84
Agency for Health Care Policy and Research, 44
Ambulatory procedures, 100
Ambulatory surgery, 101
Ambulatory/outpatient surveys, 45, 46
Analysis groupings, 50
Ancillary department, 186
Angry patients, 51–64
Attentiveness, 88
Attitude adjustment, 172

## B

Behavior, 82, 83
Belief, 116
Benefit costs. *See* Healthcare
Benefit packages, 13, 46
Benefit plans, 28
Billing information, 92
Billing process, 54

Bradley Memorial Hospital, 82, 87, 98, 107–116, 133, 135, 139–142, 146, 147, 149, 150, 154, 161, 164–165
   Guest Excellence Creed, 143–145

## C

California Employees Retirement System, 3
Cap rates, 29
Care teams, 185, 186
Cash flows, 54
Cheerfulness/decor, 100
Chicago Business Group on Health, 24
Client hospitals, 83
Client service, 30
Clinic administrator, 85
Clinical quality, 32
Clinical staff, 189
Clinics, 53, 59, 60, 84, 85, 87
Collection expense, 92
Collection process, 54
Collections, 92
Commando leaders, 198–199
Commando teams, 195, 202–204
Communication, 56–58, 72–73, 78, 83, 98, 102, 123, 142, 173, 187, 205
   skills, 62–63
   techniques, 169

# S

Salary reviews, 165
Satisfaction index, 85
Self-confidence, 123, 124
Senior management, 154, 161,
     175, 187, 188
  team, 156
Senior staff, 162
Sensitivity strategy, 167
Servant attitude, 163
Servant leadership, 117–135,
     162, 164. *See also* Hospi-
     tals
Servant philosophy, 119
SERVE. *See* Service, excellence,
     respect, value, and
     enthusiasm
Service, excellence, respect,
     value, and enthusiasm
     (SERVE), 197–198
Services, 7, 63, 75
  industries, 85
  perception, 54–56
  quality, 32
  standard, 172
Service-oriented parameters, 17
SESCO employee opinion
     survey, 140
Silent paging systems, 181
Site facility, 125
Site visits, 178
Skill-based training, 172
Social agencies, 190
Socialization, 123
Spiritual conversion, 116
Staff, 185, 190
  buy-in, 99
  education, 177
  employees, 113
  friendliness, 60
  frustration, 84
  members, 187
  participation, 97
  training, 102, 103

Strategic plan, 197
Strategic planning, 193
Strategy, 14–16
Subscribers, satisfaction, 29
Summary reports, 49–50
Super department, 132–133
Survey data, 96
Survey format, 45–46
  questions, 46–47
Survey information, 20
Survey methods, 47–49
Survey process, 186
Survey programs, 95
Survey questions, 46
Survey results, 32, 56–62, 177
Surveys, 98, 199

# T

Tactical plan, 203
Task forces, 132, 138, 163, 165
Team building, 146
  skills, 98
Team members, 141
Team-building, 131
  attitude, 130
Teamwork, 94
Technicians, 77, 80, 141. *See
     also* EKG technicians
Telephone answering, 169
Telephone assessment tools, 92
Telephone interviews, 48
Telephone surveys, 48, 92, 192
Time frames, 145–147
Timing, 47–49
Total quality management
     (TQM), 90, 129, 131, 132
TQM. *See* Total quality
     management
Training program, 112
Training requirements, 172–174
Treatment plan, 78
Trending reports, 49–50
Triage, 110, 114

# ABOUT THE AUTHORS

David Zimmerman

**David Zimmerman** has had 30 years of experience in the healthcare industry, including stints at Blue Cross and the HealthCare Financial Management Association, as well as 17 years in a variety of hospital management positions. He has made his mark as both an entrepreneur and an author.

For the past ten years, as President of his own healthcare consulting group, Zimmerman & Associates in Milwaukee, Wisconsin, David Zimmerman has helped hundreds of healthcare institutions throughout the country implement proven strategies for increased profitability. He is also the author of nine diverse healthcare books,

including this present effort, *The Healthcare Customer Service Revolution,* co-authored with his wife, Peggy, and Charles Lund. One of his previous books, *Reengineer-ing Health Care,* co-authored with John J. Skalko, was one of the most popular books in the industry in 1995; another book, *Cash Is King,* won him wide critical acclaim in the industry.

A popular nationally known lecturer, Mr. Zimmerman is quoted regularly in a wide variety of newsletters and national trade magazines, including *Hospitals and Health Networks* and *Modern Healthcare,* and has been interviewed numerous times on television and radio.

**Peggy Zimmerman,** prior to her present position as Executive Vice President of Zimmerman & Associates, held a variety of positions in the public relations and human resources departments of Miller Brewing Company, Blue Shield, and the Medical Society of Milwaukee County.

She lectures, presents seminars, and is active as a volunteer

Peggy Zimmerman

Charles Lund

for private organizations such as schools, churches, nursing homes, and Children's Hospital of Milwaukee. She has also organized and led a leadership program for teenage girls. In addition to being a wife and mother, she has also found time to assist in fund-raising activities for the Wisconsin Institute for Studies and Development.

**Charles Lund,** Vice President for Zimmerman & Associates, has an extensive background in hospital receivables consulting in addition to banking and charge-card collections. His financial background includes an assignment as Assistant Vice President of the Federal Reserve Bank of Chicago, where he managed the largest

check-processing operation in the world. He has directed the turnaround of three troubled bank operations, resulting in dramatic improvements in employee productivity and reductions in operating expenses. As an officer of the Federal Reserve, he presented a number of seminars to banking professionals.

In the healthcare field, he has worked as project manager for numerous diagnostic reviews, as well as serving as the on-site facilities manager for a number of the firm's turnaround assignments. He is also a popular seminar leader and has made numerous presentations at HFMA and AGPAM meetings.

Other books of interest to you from Irwin Professional Publishing . . .

## THE FOR-PROFIT HEALTHCARE REVOLUTION
### The Growing Impact of Investor-Owned Health Systems
Sandy Lutz and E. Preston Gee
ISBN: 1-55738-650-1

## NOT WHAT THE DOCTOR ORDERED
### Reinventing Medical Care in America
Jeffrey C. Bauer
ISBN: 1-55738-620-X

## THRIVING ON REFORM
### Meeting Tomorrow's Healthcare Challenges Today
E. Preston Gee
ISBN: 1-55738-618-8

## STRATEGIC HEALTHCARE MANAGEMENT
### Applying the Lessons of Today's Top Management Experts to the Business of Managed Care
Ira Studin
ISBN: 1-55738-631-5

## HEALTHCARE MARKETING IN TRANSITION
### Practical Answers to Pressing Questions
Terrence J. Rynne
ISBN: 1-55738-635-8

*(Continued)*

**WORKING TOGETHER**

**Building Integrated Healthcare Organizations through Improved Executive/Physician Collaboration**

*Seth Allcorn*

ISBN: 1-55738-614-5

Available in fine bookstores and libraries everywhere.